María,

Daughter of Immigrants

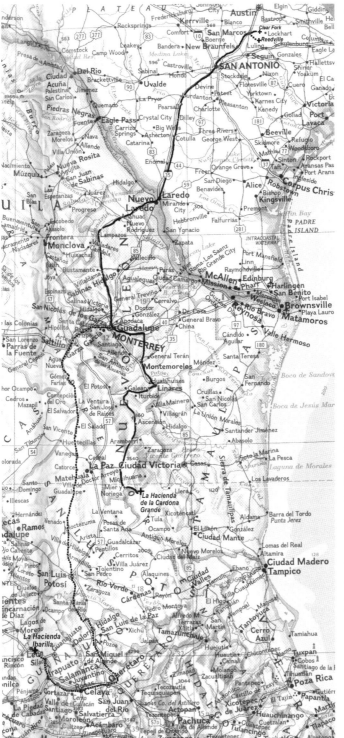

A Map of the Journeys of the Rodríguez family (from La Hacienda de Ibarilla, near León) and the Arredondo family (from La Hacienda de la Cardona Grande near Mier y Noriega), north to settle in small towns in central Texas. See Appendix (page 297) for a more detailed description of this journey.

María,
Daughter of Immigrants

María Antonietta Berriozábal

San Antonio, Texas
2012

María, Daughter of Immigrants
© 2012 by Wings Press for María Antonietta Berriozábal

Edited by Elise D. García, OP
Cover art: "Maria, Daughter of Immigrants" by Enedina Cásarez-Vásquez,
used by permission of the artist.
Cover art photographed by Cynthia Edwards.
Author photograph by Roberta Barnes.

First Edition

Print Edition ISBN: 978-1-60940-244-0
ePub ISBN: 978-1-60940-245-7
Kindle ISBN: 978-1-60940-246-4
Library PDF ISBN: 978-1-60940-247-1

Wings Press
627 E. Guenther
San Antonio, Texas 78210
Phone/fax: (210) 271-7805

On-line catalogue and ordering:
www.wingspress.com
All Wings Press titles are distributed to the trade by
Independent Publishers Group
www.ipgbook.com

Library of Congress Cataloging-in-Publication Data:

Berriozábal, María Antonietta, 1941-
  María, daughter of immigrants / María Antonietta Berriozábal. -- 1st ed.
    p. cm.
  Includes bibliographical references and index.
  ISBN 978-1-60940-244-0 (hardback : alk. paper) -- ISBN 978-1-60940-
  245-7 (epub ebook) -- ISBN 978-1-60940-246-4 (kindle ebook) -- ISBN
  978-1-60940-247-1 (library PDF ebook)
  1. Berriozábal, María Antonietta, 1941- 2. Women city council members-
  -Texas--San Antonio--Biography. 3. Mexican Americans--Texas--San Anto-
  nio--Politics and government. 4. San Antonio (Tex.)--Biography. I. Title.
  F394.S21153B473 2009
  976.4'063092--dc23
  [B]   2012027336

Dedicatoria

Dedico este libro a mi madre, Sixta, y mi padre, Apolinar,
a mis hermanos y hermanas,
a toda la familia Arredondo y la familia Rodríguez que me formaron
y especialmente a mis sobrinos y sobrinas, visobrinos y visobrinas
que son mi esperanza para el futuro.
Y con todo mi amor a mi querido Manny.

I dedicate this book to my mother, Sixta, and my father, Apolinar,
to my brothers and sisters,
and to the Rodríguez and Arredondo families who formed me
and especially to my nieces and nephews,
grand nieces and grand nephews,
who are my hope for the future.
And with all my love to my beloved Manny.

Contents

Preface

HISTORY IS A FRIEND. Twenty years ago I decided that I needed to write a book documenting what I learned during the ten years I served my hometown of San Antonio, Texas, as a member of the City Council—the first Mexican-American woman elected to do so. That was its genesis. When I started to chronicle my public life, however, it became evident that what had motivated me to enter public service, and the actions I took once in office, were shaped by the story of my family, my community, and a people. Bonds of love, faith, hard work, persistent struggle, and hope for a better future, connected me to past generations, calling for acknowledgment.

I started by going back to the time of my birth along the river bordering Mexico and the United States. Once there, I found that the book had to include the stories my parents told me as a child, stories of their past that helped to shape me. My parents were still alive when I began writing the book; I was able to hear the stories again, the history they remembered, often with revealing new details. The stories took me across the border to the country of my parents' birth, Mexico, and to the extraordinary immigrant journey that brought them to the United States during the Mexican Revolution of 1910—the year they both were born.

Writing this book has been a twenty-year journey, with numerous interruptions. It evolved in pieces: I drew material from my personal journals and archives. And I drew from reflections I wrote at night on stories my parents told me during our daytime visits, on recollections of my life, or on events happening in my city or the world.

A river of intertwined lives and historical events flowed out of all the material, taking shape as a story of seven decades lived across many kinds of borders. The book moves from controversies over politics, water, and nuclear power to faith and religion; from economics, peace, and social justice to depression and elder care; from immigration and *cultura* to spirituality and honoring and caring for *la Madre Tierra*. It is my story but also the story of a family and a community. It is the story of a city told from the underside of history, the kind of history that is not usually told in our textbooks and is now, in fact, being banned in Arizona and disparaged elsewhere in our country.

María, Daughter of Immigrants stands in direct resistance to these and other efforts to disrespect, shun, or erase the stories of a people. My hope is that the book will play a part in moving us in a new direction as a nation: One that deepens understanding and appreciation of our wonderful diversity as a people and expands the narrative of our national history so that it embraces the stories and contributions of *all* the men and women on whose shoulders we stand. I offer it as a prayer that the ties that bind us to our richly diverse past will extend as a shared blessing to future generations.

María Antonietta Berriozábal
San Antonio, Texas
2012

María,

Daughter of Immigrants

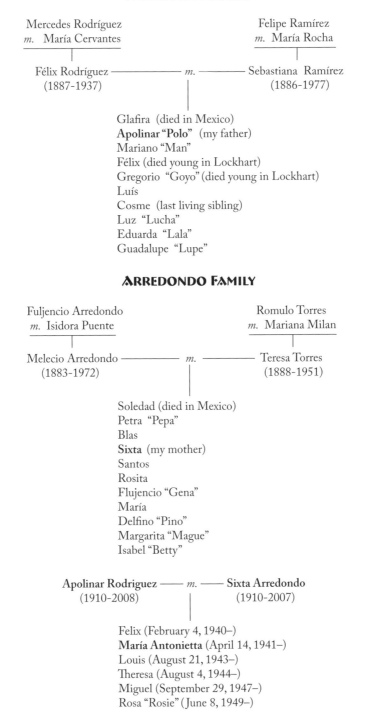

RODRÍGUEZ FAMILY

Mercedes Rodríguez
m. María Cervantes

Felipe Ramírez
m. María Rocha

Félix Rodríguez —————— *m.* ————— Sebastiana Ramírez
(1887-1937)   (1886-1977)

Glafira (died in Mexico)
Apolinar "Polo" (my father)
Mariano "Man"
Félix (died young in Lockhart)
Gregorio "Goyo" (died young in Lockhart)
Luís
Cosme (last living sibling)
Luz "Lucha"
Eduarda "Lala"
Guadalupe "Lupe"

ARREDONDO FAMILY

Fuljencio Arredondo
m. Isidora Puente

Romulo Torres
m. Mariana Milan

Melecio Arredondo ————— *m.* ———— Teresa Torres
(1883-1972)   (1888-1951)

Soledad (died in Mexico)
Petra "Pepa"
Blas
Sixta (my mother)
Santos
Rosita
Flujencio "Gena"
María
Delfino "Pino"
Margarita "Mague"
Isabel "Betty"

Apolinar Rodriguez —— *m.* —— **Sixta Arredondo**
(1910-2008)   (1910-2007)

Felix (February 4, 1940–)
María Antonietta (April 14, 1941–)
Louis (August 21, 1943–)
Theresa (August 4, 1944–)
Miguel (September 29, 1947–)
Rosa "Rosie" (June 8, 1949–)

CHAPTER 1

De Donde Empezamos

I am, by birth, *una mujer de la frontera,* a woman of the borderlands. I was born one block away from the Río Grande/Río Bravo—about as close a person can get to being born right on the U.S.-Mexico border. I experienced poverty as a child but not the dire poverty of my immigrant parents, Apolinar Rodríguez and Sixta Arredondo, who with their families left their war-torn Mexican homeland in search of a future.

One of my father's regular admonitions was that I should judge myself *"de donde empezamos"*—from where we started. *"Y empezamos de abajo,"* he said. We started at the bottom. My grandparents on both sides had come from Mexico during the Mexican Revolution of 1910. Some families escaping the revolution came as landowners, doctors, lawyers, politicians—as wealthy or middle class professionals. Like millions of other immigrants, my family came as workers, landless and poor. Papá's words, whenever I crossed a personal or professional milestone, were to remind me as I progressed that I had to consider where I had come from, those on whose shoulders I stand.

Seen through those eyes, my parent's children have traveled very far, as have the children of so many other Mexican immigrants, bringing treasures with which to build this country. I owe them this story.

Empezamos de abajo

My father, Apolinar Ramírez Rodríguez, known as "Polo" for most of his life, was born in north-central Mexico on January 8, 1910, at La Hacienda Ibarrilla on the outskirts of León, in the state of Guanajuato. He was the second child of Félix and Sebastiana Ramírez Rodríguez, but became the oldest after his parent's firstborn, a little girl named Glafira, died.

Apolinar's was a typical *campesino* family. His father Félix was a shepherd boy until he was old enough to work the fields. There was no school. As long as there was work to do alongside the adults—either in the *hacendado's* house or out in the fields—children were not children, just workers. There was no such thing as being a "teen-ager;" most people were married in their early teens. The lives of the *campesinos* were controlled by the *hacendados*. They had no rights and had to ask for everything. One time, when a child died, the father had to go to the *hacendado* to ask for money to bury the child; the *hacendado* refused.

Before they were married on April 14, 1907, Sebastiana and Félix had each found work at a textile factory. There were not many factories, so factory work was rare—and all the more so for a woman. Sebastiana was among the first women in her town to work outside the home. At age 19, she was considered a "spinster." But it was not her destiny to *vestir santos*. At the factory, Sebastiana met Félix, and they fell in love. They sat across from each other, playing footsy under the worktable.

Sebastiana and Félix, were unusual in another regard. We don't know how, but they both learned to read on their own. As an adult, Félix read the Bible to his children from beginning to end—more than once. This in an era when the Catholic Church disapproved, if not outright prevented, the reading of the Bible by the faithful! A Claretian priest had given the Latin/Spanish Bible to my grandfather. It bears the imprimatur of the founder of the Claretian order, Bishop Antonio María Claret, and is now in the possession of my brother, Felix.

Within months after Polo was born, Sebastiana and Félix left the hacienda and their home in León for a new life south, in Mexico City. "*Los dos inditos se fueron pa' la capital,*" Papá would say. The young couple, in their early twenties, settled in the famous *Barrio de Tepito*, a poor and tough working-class neighborhood known for its huge open-air market, dating back to pre-colonial times—a *barrio* with character featured in many Mexican movies.

They were there in September of 1910 when Mexico celebrated the centennial anniversary of its independence from Spain. Sebastiana stayed away from the crowds because the baby was so small, but Félix braved them to see President Porfirio Díaz ride in the parade. One month later, the president would be challenged by an armed revolt that eventually led to his exile in France. And one month after that, Félix and Sebastiana would find themselves escaping the chaos and poverty of Mexico City with their infant child, Polo. Journeying back the way they came just a few months earlier, they traveled beyond their home in Guanajuato, *pa'l norte*. They were interviewed by U. S. authorities upon reaching Laredo and granted permanent residency, crossing the U.S. border on November 6, 1910.

In the midst of the political turmoil, Félix had received word that his widowed mother, María Cervantes Rodríguez, was ill. His father, Mercedes Rodríguez, had recently died and *despues de que enviudó,* María had migrated north to the small town of Reedville, Texas. Her son Pablo had settled there two years earlier, in 1908. Her daughters, María and Concepción (Chonita), were also in Texas, living with María's husband, Aristeo Mojica. Many from Guanajuato and elsewhere in Mexico had headed north.[1] A new type of cotton had been developed that grew well in south-central Texas. Ranchland needed to be cleared and the owners of the land, largely German immigrants and their descendents, looked to Mexico for cheap labor to do the intensive farm work. Most of the first families to come were Nuevoleónses. They looked down on the poorer people coming from Guanajuato. They would call them *Silaitos* after Silao, a city near León, Guanajuato. Growing up, I knew being called a *Silaito* was not a compliment.

As it turned out, María was not sick at all. It was a ruse she used to get Félix to come north. Ruse or no ruse, María's timing was right! On November 20, 1910, exactly two weeks after Félix and Sebastiana crossed the border with their infant child, *estalló la revolución.* The revolution that would last a decade and claim up to two million lives broke out.[2]

It was not, however, the turbulent political situation in Mexico that caused María to call her son north; María simply wanted her whole family to be together. That is how Sebastiana and Félix came to escape the revolution and settle in Reedville, Texas, working on the ranch where María lived. My great-grandmother María, I was told, was *alta y flaca* and had blue eyes. I recall seeing her in a photograph. María sat in a chair, with cotton fields in the background, grabbing her knees over a long white skirt. She was lanky and fair-skinned. Her hair was white and her serious, deep-set eyes stared at you.

But María wasn't the oldest member of the family in Reedville. Her mother-in-law, my great-great grandmother, Apolonia Ochoa Cervantes, had also come to Texas. *"Andaba a gatas,"* Sebastiana would say. Apolonia was not able to walk, only crawl. She died shortly after Félix and Sebastiana arrived in Reedville. At the time, there was no cemetery where Mexicans could be buried, so her burial site was a plot of ranchland granted by the owners. When we were little and would go visit our relatives in Lockhart, my father would point to it. Unfortunately, I do not recall exactly where it is.

My family worked the fields in Reedville and, on Sundays, walked two miles to Martindale to attend the Immaculate Heart of Mary Catholic Church. It was staffed by Claretian priests, who had come from Mexico in 1908, in response to a request from a U.S. bishop for Spanish-speaking priests to serve the Mexican immigrant community.

It was one of those priests who gave my grandfather Félix the two-volume Bible.

The Mexican parishioners at Martindale were very energetic and active, and eventually the Cordi Marian Sisters joined the Claretians in the mission. When Polo was old enough, he attended the parish school in Martindale, where he was taught in Spanish by a laywoman. He also served as an altar boy at the parish church.

Within a few years, my father and his family left Reedville, and moved ten miles east to a ranch in Lockhart. It was there that Polo met my mother, his beloved Sixta. They were both twelve.

Flor de Mayo

Sixta Arredondo was born in northeastern Mexico on August 6, 1910, the fourth child in a family that fled the Mexican Revolution when it was in its furor. Sixta's parents, Melecio and Teresa Milan Torres Arredondo, also were *campesinos*.

Melecio was three years old when his father, Fulgencio Arredondo, was shot dead as he answered a knock at the door. No one knows why Fulgencio was murdered, but with his father gone, Melecio became a shepherd at a very early age. His mother, Isidora Puente, was the daughter of *hacendados*. She fell in love with this hired hand and, against the will of her family, married Fulgencio. Ostracized by her family, Isidora lost her life of privilege—and then her husband. Isidora was left with seven children and *después de que enviudó*, a man *se la llevó*—attacked and raped her. Isidora's suffering didn't end there. A few years later, two of her older sons were killed by death squads; they were still young *cuando fueron fusilados*.

Teresa's father, Romulo Torres, was a butcher from Pamplona, Spain. Sixta always remembered her maternal grandfather and her grandmother, Mariana Milan, with great tenderness. She called her *abuelita*, Mamá Miliana.

Melecio and Teresa Arredondo lived and worked at La Hacienda de la Cardona Grande in Mier y Noriega, a small town in the state of Nuevo León. By the time the revolutionary soldiers reached the hacienda in 1914, the *hacendados* had already fled the country, leaving the workers behind to care for their property.

Mamá would tell us the story of how, as a little girl of four, she peeked from behind a curtain at the hacienda and saw very well fed soldiers sleeping on the floor. The soldiers stole their food and farm animals. But the most serious concern was that they were taking young girls and raping them. Sixta's older sister, Petra, was already a young lady. Fearing for her safety, Melecio and Teresa decided to escape the imminent danger and dire scarcity in Mexico and make the journey north to the United States. Their firstborn child, Soledad, had died a few years earlier, so they left with their five surviving children—Petra, Blas, Sixta, Fulgencio (Gena), and Santos. Melecio's widowed mother, Isidora, also went with them; but Teresa left her parents behind, never to see them again. Sixta did not want to leave. She used to tell us how *se agarraba de las piernas del abuelito.* Hanging onto her grandfather Romulo's legs, *ella no se queria venir.*[3]

Before they left Mexico for good, Sixta's father, like many Mexicans, had traveled north numerous times, across the fluid border and back, for work. Mamá told us about one particular trip her father, Melecio, took, traveling across the *sierras*, over into Texas, and then north past San Antonio to San Marcos. Although Mamá never shared as many stories as Papá, this is one we would often ask her to repeat.

Mamá told us that when Welito Melecio finally got to San Marcos, after days of travel, he had to walk a long way *en el camino de fierro.* Following the railroad tracks, Melecio eventually came to a bridge where, exhausted, he decided to stop for the night. Another young man who also was traveling soon joined him, and they both slept under the bridge. In the morning, the young man lit a fire and got water from somewhere. Using a small container he was carrying, he boiled some coffee grounds and offered Melecio a cup of coffee. Welito Melecio said it was the most wonderful coffee he had ever tasted! After they finished their coffee, Melecio got up to resume his travels. He turned to thank and say goodbye to his fellow traveler, but the young man was gone. He seemed to have disappeared into thin air! In our family, it is a given that the young man was an angel sent to help my grandfather as he neared the end of his very long journey.

So when it was time for the Arredondo family to leave the hacienda at Mier y Noriega, Melecio not only knew the way, he and his family also felt the consolation of being watched over as they fled the war. Accompanied by other refugees, Melecio and Teresa and their five children rode burros through the *sierras*, making their way across the rugged terrain, one hundred miles north to Monterrey. It was in the middle of summer—July of 1915. Mamá used to tell us how she rode a burro carrying lots of *carne seca* for people to eat during the trip. There were two sacks of it, one on either side of the burro. At one point, as they made their way through the *sierra*, her burro started to slide down a steep *barranco*! A man traveling with them reached out just in time, pulling her and the burro to safety. Mamá said she

was close enough to the edge to see how far down the bottom was—
¡y estaba muy abajo!

My siblings and I were impressed. When we started learning U.S. history and how the first immigrants crossed the ocean on the Mayflower, we would say to Mamá, to her great amusement, *"Pues ustedes cruzaron la sierra en burros—el burrito suyo era su Flor de Mayo!"*—Your burro was your Mayflower!

When the Arredondos arrived in Monterrey, they got on a train that took them to Laredo. My mother remembered how a nice man sat her down next to a window on the train. He told her that she would see *muchas cosas bonitas.* Indeed, Mamá would always say, she did see beautiful things out that window. At the border, they were interviewed by U. S. authorities and granted permanent residency. They transferred to another train bound for San Marcos. When they arrived, friends picked them up in a horse-drawn wagon and took them to what would be their first U.S. home, in Clearfork, Texas, near the town where the Rodríguez family had settled.

Soon, the two families, the Arredondos and the Rodríguezes—coming four years apart, from different areas of Mexico, during the revolutionary war years—would end up living on adjoining *ranchitos* in Lockhart, Texas.

In our teen years, when my brothers and sisters and I were old enough to begin to be curious about our family history, we tried to find our roots. My older brother, Felix, got far enough back into our history to declare that our family had been nomads, hence, there was no recorded history. At least that is what he thought. From the area of Mexico where our families originated, we figured we were Chichimecas. But Chichimeca is "an umbrella term that the Spaniards used to describe most of the indigenous groups scattered through large parts of Guanajuato" and other adjoining states.[4] Even though I do not know our exact lineage, I do know that the blood that runs through my veins is that of the indigenous people of the Americas. I am a *mestiza*, carrying the DNA of Spanish colonizers and indigenous people.

¿Cuantas manos?

My maternal and paternal grandparents and their children all worked as sharecroppers on the Texas ranches. They were called *medieros*. That meant they gave the owner of the land one-half of all they harvested. After the harvest, they would *pepenar*—go back to scavenge the fields, gathering every bit of what remained. To survive, it was important for the sharecroppers to have good acreage. A critical requirement for getting good acreage was the number of *manos*—hands—the sharecroppers brought. *¿Cuantas manos?* That was the key question. Children counted as *manos* and went to work very young, perhaps as young as seven. No names were required; the peoples' labor was all that counted.

The Rodríguez and Arredondo families grew large after they settled in Texas. Polo became the oldest of nine Rodríguez children, including six more boys—Mariano (Man), Félix, Gregorio (Goyo), Luís, Cosme, and Guadalupe (Lupe)—and two girls, Luz and Eduarda (Lala). Sixta's family grew to include ten children. The Arredondos had four more girls—Rosita, María, Margarita, and Isabel (Betty)—and one boy, Delfino (Pino), who was Margarita's twin, bringing the total to seven girls and three boys. The Rodríguez family was the near reverse, with seven boys and two girls.

Alongside the harsh reality of backbreaking work and struggle was the beauty of a whole new life they were creating, bringing many customs from Mexico into contact with the new. Faith, family, community, and hard work remained at the core. There also was laughter and play. Just hearing the little songs my mother would sing around the house, I know that my parents played the kind of games that children have played for generations, like *canicas*, marbles, and the Mexican counterpart of London Bridge Is Falling Down—*La víbora de la mar.*

> *A la víbora, víbora de la mar, de la mar*
> *Por aquí pueden pasar,*
> *Los de adelante corren mucho,*
> *Los de atrás se quedarán.*
> *Tras. Tras. Tras.*

Community events like the *Diez y Seis de Septiembre*, Mexican Independence Day, were exciting times for all. There would be dances and patriotic events where speeches, music, and *declamaciones* were heard. When she got a little older, my mother belonged to *La Cruz Azul*, an organization of young women. They would proudly sing the Mexican National Anthem. My mother memorized patriotic songs and poems that she could still recite into her elder years.

Other social events centered on the church—festivals, baptisms, weddings, Holy Week, Christmas celebrations. My family created a community that mirrored what they had left behind. They brought their culture and strong communal networks where people helped one another, consoling each other in sad times and sharing in the joy of good times. As they encountered new ways, they blended them into the life they were creating on the borderlands.

A La Rorro Niño

Polo and Sixta were twelve years old when they encountered each other at one of the furrows in the fields, picking cotton. Polo planned it that way. Sixta had already attracted his attention at their one-room schoolhouse, where all the boys were on one side and the girls on the other. *"Estaba largita,"* he would say later, with a twinkle in his eye, meaning that she was thin and tall for her age. Polo calculated exactly how he would meet up with the pretty girl when they reached the same place in the fields—his big *movida en el surco*, where they would have a few minutes to talk alone. It was a love at first sight that would grow through their childhood and family friendship.

A year later, Polo and Sixta's families spent Christmas Eve together. Sebastiana had ordered a small statue of the baby Jesus from Mexico for her *acostada*, a tradition on Christmas Eve of laying the infant Jesus down to sleep in his crib. Years earlier, Sebastiana's brother-in-law, Pablo Rodríguez, had begun the *acostada* tradition in his home and the whole Rodríguez family would gather there on Christmas Eve. It was at his Tío Pablo's house that Polo first learned to sing *A La Rorro Niño*,[5] a Mexican lullaby to the baby Jesus. Over time, other families brought the tradition into their homes in the *ranchitos*, including Sebastiana and Félix.

On this first Christmas Eve with their new Baby Jesus, Sebastiana invited the Arredondo family to her *acostada*. Polo had become friends with Sixta's brother, Santos, and it was through their friendship that the whole Arredondo family was invited. Over the years the friendship between these two families flourished, embracing Félix and Melecio, Sebastiana and Teresa, and, of course, Polo and Sixta. My mother would proudly say that the Arredondo family was the only one invited to the Rodríguez *acostada*.[6]

My grandmother Sebastiana was an organizer and a very religious woman; she took seriously her orders from somewhere on high to evangelize, starting in her own home. Her *acostada* involved singing, praying the rosary, meditations between each mystery of the rosary, and many prayers at the end—each committed to memory, received probably from generations past. The liturgy culminated in singing *A La Rorro Niño* to the Baby Jesus, sometimes with everyone holding burning sparklers. The youngest child in the family would then take the Baby Jesus around for everyone to kiss, and lay him to sleep in his manger. After that, everyone feasted on homemade *tamales, champurrado,* and *buñuelos*—and enjoyed fireworks.

The *acostada* of 1923 marked the first time that Polo and Sixta, age thirteen, prayed the rosary together before the new Baby Jesus. In 2006, when that Baby Jesus was 84 years old, Polo and Sixta celebrated the *acostada* together for the last time, surrounded by children, grandchildren, and great-grandchildren. That Baby Jesus has seen us through all our lives and knows many histories; I have checked in with him each year. My mother treated that statue with sacred tenderness—her destiny was tied to it.

Seven-Minute Frosting

In Lockhart, Polo and Sixta attended the one-room Prairie View School. It went up to sixth grade and was one of the first English-language schools in Texas that Mexican children were allowed to attend. Work, however, came first. Classes for the children of sharecroppers started *after* they finished their fieldwork.

Sixta and Polo liked school and their teachers. For Sixta and her sisters, learning how to cook different food was also a treat. The teachers would invite the girls to their homes to teach them how to bake cakes, pies, and other foods. Seven-minute frosting, lemon pie, and Southern-style cornbread stuffing were treats we got to enjoy growing up, cooked by my mother from those lessons learned years before. The Mexican children were also taught traditional U.S. Christmas carols, which my mother would later sing.

At that school, my parents learned how to read and write in English. As we were growing up, my mother would recite, "This is Will. This is May. How do you do, Will? How do you do, May?" She would smile, remembering how wonderful it was to go to school. One of her greatest regrets in life was that she was taken out of school so early. She was about twelve years old. *Ya estaba muy grande.* Her hands were needed in the fields and at home. There may also have been concern about a fast-maturing girl being in a place where her parents could not watch over her. Her oldest sister, Petra (Pepita), never went to school.

Sixta's formal education ended in the third grade; Polo's ended in the sixth grade. He, too, was probably quite a bit older than the average sixth grader today. Despite their brief formal education, my parents were lifelong readers and learners. My mother loved music, singing, and poetry. My father had a thirst for knowledge and a curiosity about the world. Later in life, he opened his mind further by reading newspapers like *El Todo* and *La Prensa* and listening to world news from Mexico and Latin America over a crystal radio. Education meant the world to my parents. It was key. They would raise the bar very high for their children when it came to education. *"La educación nadie te la quita,"* they would tell us.

Making It Rendir

Perhaps it was the experience that my grandmother Teresita had working as a house servant inside the hacienda in Mexico. Or perhaps it was because there were so many girls in the Arredondo family. Maybe it was because Teresa later got sick with asthma and could no longer work in the fields, so she felt she had to work double inside the house. Whatever the reason, the Arredondo household was known for its resourcefulness, both inside the house and out in the fields. They could do more with less than almost anybody.

Teresa Arredondo knew how to stretch scarce resources and make them *rendir*. She could make one chicken *rendir* for her whole family of twelve by adding potatoes and lots of home grown vegetables, like squash, tomatoes, and onions, creating a hearty *sopa*. She could bake delicious bread and sew her children's clothes—and she taught her daughters all these skills, giving them lots of responsibility. For example, when Welita Teresita* put my mother in charge of the chickens that meant Sixta was responsible for them from beginning to end—from their laying eggs, to their hatching, to their becoming *mole!*

Sixta learned well. Years later, Mamá would know how to *rendir* a whole life for us out of the $50 per week that my father earned as a laborer.

---

* Like many families, ours occasionally uses eccentric spellings for some family names. Thus *abuelita* and *abuelito* are used throughout as we pronounced and wrote them: Welita and Welito.

Hablan puro Latín

As Sixta and Polo got older, their family connection was a key social benefit for both. Polo was a real catch in the community! He was a fine young man: hardworking, responsible, intelligent, and courteous; a good son, brother, and friend; and a man of faith! *Iba a la iglesia regularmente.* These were the qualities Mamá saw. She never said it about herself, but she knew another reason the girls were after him was because he was handsome. In fact, she would joke with him about certain *chifladas que lo seguían.*

Girls would seek him out during the well-chaperoned dances in *las plataformas*, the venues for the Mexican festivities. Sixta was a very good dancer but Polo was not. He made up for his inability to dance with the girls by going to the well where the guests would go drink water. Standing by the well, he would serve water to all the girls. Apolinar did not need to dance.

For his part, Polo saw in Sixta not only a very pretty girl, but also someone who did not pursue him as the others did. To my mother's chagrin, he would tell stories over and over again that illustrated this. *"Ay, no digas eso,"* she would say, as he told stories like this one:

> *Una día estaba tu mamá debajo de un árbol de durazno, lleno de duraznos. Agarraba uno, le daba una mordida y lo aventaba. Agarraba otro le daba una mordida y lo aventaba como que nada le importaba. Ella seguía y yo allí nomas viendola. No me hacía caso.*

Calmly standing under a peach tree, taking a bite out of one peach after another, throwing the rest away—Sixta paid Polo not the least bit of attention. As they grew older, Papá also saw in Sixta a young woman who loved learning and was a thinker. She had her own opinions and spoke them, without regard to what others thought of them. Mamá was not a woman who needed external approval! She was sure of herself. Finally, and *very* importantly, Mamá and her family were people of great faith.

Both families worshiped at St. Michael's Church in Uhland, about ten miles from Lockhart. St. Michael's was a mission of the Martindale church. The same Claretian priest who lived at Martindale would come out to the *ranchito* in Uhland, where the church was built, to say Mass. My father's uncle, Pablo, who started the *acostada* tradition in our family, was instrumental in raising money among the Mexican community to buy a little piece of land next to the church. It would be consecrated as a Catholic cemetery where the Mexican parishioners could bury their dead. Before this, there was only a German cemetery nearby. With no consecrated burial place for Mexicans, people like my great great-grandmother Apolonia were buried wherever they could get a landowner's approval.

My mother's brother, Tío Blas, learned how to play the violin and would accompany the church choir as they sang the formal Latin High Mass. When Father Ramón Sunjé organized the choir at St. Michael's, he asked for volunteers. Most of the choir members ended up being Arredondos and Rodríguezes! Members of the choir from the Rodríguez family included Polo, Cosme, Luz, Lala, and Lupe. Joining the choir from the Arredondo family were Sixta, Rosita, María, Delfino, Margarita, and Betty, along with several cousins. Welito Félix loved Sixta, his future daughter-in-law. With so many singers of the Latin Mass in her family, he would joke, *"En la casa de los Arredondos ahora hablan puro Latín."*

A favorite of both my parents was *Panis Angelicus,* the ancient "bread of angels" hymn in celebration of the Eucharist. The choir sang it at their wedding. It was a fitting choice, symbolizing the profound faith and devotion they had for receiving Holy Communion all their lives, up to their last days. Mamá and Papá would say that they never knew how beautifully the choir sang until their wedding day. It was the only time they had not sung with the choir.

Return to Mexico

Polo was nearly 22 years old when he returned with his family to Mexico in November of 1931. From the time they left Guanajuato in 1910, Félix and Sebastiana had held onto the dream of one day returning. In fact, they first started to go back in 1918. Their family and friends tried to talk them out of it, but they were insistent! They went so far as to start getting rid of things they would not be able to take back on the train. It wasn't until Sebastiana took her sizeable and precious collection of *santos* to give to the Claretian priest at Martindale, that the plan changed; the priest talked them out of it. Polo's family remained another thirteen years, and Sebastiana kept her *santos.*

By 1931, when the long-held dream was actually realized, Polo had been living in the United States for 21 years, all but the first nine months of his life. None of his eight siblings had ever been to Mexico, all having been born here. We do not know the exact reasons why Félix and Sebastiana decided to return but we do know that their oldest son,

Apolinar, played a role in affirming the decision. His parents *contaban con sus opiniones.* My father told me one day that he had asked his parents why they relied on him so heavily and gave him so much responsibility? Because you can handle it, they told him.

The Rodríguez family decided to return at a time when up to two million Mexican nationals and U.S. citizens of Mexican descent were engaged in a mass migration—and, for many, a forced deportation—to Mexico. During the Depression, when anti-immigrant and anti-Mexican sentiment was on the rise, the Hoover Administration launched a "repatriation" program. It resulted in the forced deportation of hundreds of thousands of legal residents and U.S. citizens of Mexican descent. The Mexican government responded to the repatriation by offering free transportation from the border, reducing or abolishing import tariffs on goods the repatriates were bringing back, and providing people with land.

My father and his family left voluntarily. We think my father pushed for going back to Mexico because he thought life would be better in the city. He had either read or heard reports on the radio that in Mexico men were now carrying wood in trucks, rather than on their backs—a sure sign of progress. The family also was motivated by other things they had heard, including promises of land and certain rights if they returned to Mexico. So, in November of 1931, the eleven members of the Rodríguez family—Félix and Sebastiana, with their nine children, ages 5 to 21—piled into the Model T they had been able to purchase over the years, and a truck they bought for the trip. With whatever possessions they owned and could carry, the family drove away from Lockhart towards the border, then south to Guanajuato.

It turned out to be a terrible mistake that my father would always regret.

When they finally got to Guanajuato and went to see the land that had been promised, they found it was not arable. *No se podía cosechar.* It was full of brush, needed clearing, and there was no available water. Furthermore, as Félix pointed out to his son, *"¡Mira, los hombres todavía cargan la leña en sus espaldas!"* Men were still carrying wood on their backs. They quickly gave up on the idea of working the land and went to the city to find work.

But only my father was able to get a job. He had a car and could drive, so Polo was hired by the PRI to drive one of their political candidates around. The candidate's campaign signs were attached to the car. It was very risky work. One day, the *político* he usually chauffeured came under armed attack, shots fired at his car. Luckily, my father wasn't driving that day, but when word of the shooting reached his family and they saw the bullet holes all over the campaign signs, they were terrified. Another time when Polo was driving the candidate around, he ended up unexpectedly having to spend two days in another city. Polo was a very responsible person and would do whatever needed to be done. But his family did not know why he hadn't come home and was tortured with worry, remembering the *balazos* that had earlier been shot at the *político*.

Polo's chauffeuring was the only job anyone had in the family— and it was not working. It was too dangerous *y además* the family could not make it on Polo's pay alone. Six months after leaving Texas, they made the decision to go back. The family had to sell both the car and the truck in order to make the return trip.

This Alien

When Polo first entered the United States in 1910, as an infant crossing the border with his family, the Immigration Service of the Department of Commerce and Labor issued this admission card:

Now, despite having lived in the United States for twenty-one years and being absent only the prior six months, Polo and his parents found they could not return. The laws had changed. Only those born in the United States could re-enter, which meant all of the children except Polo—and his parents, of course. On the reverse side of Polo's 1910 immigration card, a border official penned a cryptic note. Dated May 4, 1932, it reads: "This alien returned to Mex for Visa this date. Admits returned to Mex for permanent residence 11-13-31."

Félix, Sebastiana, and Polo would now need someone from this side to vouch for their character and provide assurances of a job if they were to have any chance of re-entering. With no work, little money, and no idea when they might be able to cross over, the family decided to send the three oldest U.S.-born boys over while everyone else waited at the border in Nuevo Laredo. Fortunately, they were able to stay with Félix's brother, Longino, and his wife, Simona. Years earlier, when everyone else in the family had migrated north, Longino Rodríguez went no further than Nuevo Laredo, settling in the town built across the river from the U.S. city of Laredo.

Polo's brothers, Mariano, Félix Jr., and Goyo, walked over the bridge and crossed the border into the United States. From Laredo, they took the train to San Marcos and then walked the twenty miles to Lockhart. Goyo, sixteen, was the youngest of the three. Félix had just turned 20 and Mariano was 21 years of age. When the young men finally got to Lockhart, they had to work very hard and fend for themselves. Tío Pablo helped as best he could, but the boys moved from house to house working for others for lodging and meals; they did not eat well.

Nearly two months later, on June 24, 1932, Polo and his parents were finally allowed to cross the border through the intercession of Mr. Clark, owner of the ranch where they had worked in Lockhart. Mr. Clark had written a letter saying they were good people, worked hard, and had done well, being able to purchase two vehicles. When the whole family at last got back to Lockhart, they found the three brothers were very thin and malnourished. Even before leaving Mexico, Goyo had been weakened by a fall he took while helping to push their truck over an old bridge. One of the boards on the bridge broke and Goyo fell down into the creek. *Se calló y quedó muy debil.* Now he was even weaker. In time, all three would be wracked by a deadly, wasting disease— tuberculosis.

El Tiempo de los Enfermos

The next few years would be among the most difficult and painful for Polo and the Rodríguez family. It was a time of great turmoil, illness—and death—that began sometime after they got back from Mexico. My family referred to this as *el tiempo de los enfermos*, the time of the sick. All his life, my father carried a terrible burden of pain and responsibility for what happened. It had been a big mistake to go back to Mexico, and even more grave consequences would follow—resulting, my father felt, from what had happened at the border.

Goyo, the youngest of the three brothers who crossed the border, was the first to succumb to the disease whose symptoms were weight loss, fevers, sweats, wheezing, and bloody choking coughs. Goyo was only 18 years old when he died of tuberculosis in June of 1934, two years after the family returned from Mexico. He was buried in the Uhland Cemetery that Tío Pablo had helped to establish. Many years later, Tía Lala wrote about her brother Goyo's death in a journal she kept with stories about growing up. "It was the custom to choose *padrinos* to dress the dead boy as a saint," she wrote. Goyo, she recalled, was dressed as St. Joseph.[7]

The next year, on October 23, 1935, Félix's mother, María Cervantes Rodríguez, the matriarch of the Rodríguez family, died of pneumonia at the age of 70. She too was buried in Uhland. Within two years, two more family members would be dead and buried in the growing family plot.

Both Polo's father, Félix Sr., and his brother, Félix Jr., contracted tuberculosis. Félix Jr. fell ill first. Since the disease was at an early stage, "he had a lot of chance to get well," Tía Lala wrote, and was sent for six months to a sanatorium. When Félix Sr. got sick, there wasn't the same hope. By then they knew the disease *era contagioso*, so Polo built a little hut far away from the house, close to the edge of the fields, where his father would be quarantined. Papá would say "*Y allí iba mi Mamá y nadie de los otros podía ir.*" None of the children could go see their father— only my grandmother, Sebastiana, and on occasion my father. "We had to quit school," Tía Lala wrote. "My parents were afraid we might get the disease too. Because school was far and we had to walk in the cold mornings."

People felt very bad about what was happening to the Rodríguez family. *Les tenían mucha compasión. Estaban pobres y enfermos.* But they also were afraid of a disease they did not understand but knew to be contagious. The only neighbors who came to see them were the Arredondos. Around this time, they too experienced a tragic loss. Sixta's younger brother, Gena, suffered a ruptured appendix. It was not cared for properly and he died in excruciating pain. Gena was only 19 and about to graduate from high school—an achievement that had become possible for Mamá's younger siblings. His mother, Teresita, received his diploma posthumously.

Throughout *el tiempo de los enfermos*, Teresita and her daughter, Sixta, and the whole Arredondo family supported the Rodríguezes. With great compassion and respect, the Arredondos watched young Polo's *valor* as he cared for his sick father and brothers while working to provide for the rest of the family. They also were moved by Sebastiana's unvanquished faith; no matter what came her way, that faith was never shaken.

Isolated in his *casita* with his constant coughing, Félix Sr. was dying of the dreadful disease *que te puede ahogar* in your own blood, when Polo noticed there was a problem with the new crop. Bugs were crawling all over the new green leaves, eating them. His father saw it too. If they didn't do something immediately, the bugs would eat the whole crop. That would be disastrous—no harvest, no income for the family.

Félix told his son to go over to his Tío Pablo's and borrow the machine to dispense the *veneno*. He was too sick to do it himself so Polo would need to spray the fields alone. Polo went to see his uncle. But Tío Pablo said, "I'm sorry. I can't lend it to you because I have the same problem and need the machine today. But if you come back later, you can have it when I'm done." It wasn't until that evening that Polo was able to begin the work of spraying the fields. He worked all night. In the morning, when he was finished, his body, his eyes, his clothes, everything was covered with the fine dust. As he later told me, *"Amanecí todo cubierto del veneno, m'ija. Un polvito muy chiquito en las pestañas, en la boca. Qué crees tu que me hizo eso?"*

A few years ago, on Father's Day, when my daddy was already frail, he told me another part of this story. *"Mi Papá me dijo…"* he started to say. Then he stopped, overcome with emotion. It was one of the few times I saw him cry. My mother was nearby, watching and listening. Neither of us said a word. After a few minutes, when he was composed, I asked, "What did your father say?" His father told him that he would be with him all night. His father was so sick that all he could do to help his son was to *acompañarlo* by staying awake all night. Polo knew his father could hear him when the machine passed near the hut—and that it was breaking his father's heart. It broke his heart too.

Félix was 51 years old when he died of pulmonary tuberculosis on March 17, 1937. In her journal, Tía Lala wrote, "My 12th birthday…my father was very sick. On March 17 my brother Man [Mariano] asked me, 'How do you want to spend your birthday, with father or without?' I answer—as God's will. He died that day, so on my birthday, he was dead."

It grieved Polo that his father couldn't even say a proper goodbye to his children. *"Pobrecito mi Papá,"* he would say. *"Ni podía ver sus hijos al último."* Exactly nine months later, on December 17, 1937, the Rodríguez family had to bury yet another member, Félix Jr. His time in the sanatorium did not prevent him from dying of tuberculosis. Félix Jr. was 25 years old when the ravaging disease took his life.

The devastated family next saw Mariano get tuberculosis. He was the third brother who had crossed the border ahead of everyone. By the time Mariano came down with the disease, the family knew the importance of getting early treatment and had learned about a sanatorium in Temple, Texas, that they hoped might cure him. I remember hearing this story early in my childhood. It had a profound influence on me. Praying that Mariano's life might be spared, my father drove his brother, Man, as everyone called him, 100 miles north to the sanatorium. Papá had bought Man a *piedra de hielo.* He gave him a small pick so Man could break the ice into small pieces and chew on it during the long drive. The ice was to *quebrantar la toz,* which would help prevent him from coughing up blood.

I have a picture in my mind of my father driving the Model T, his face tight with grief over the recent loss of his father and two brothers—and deep worry over his brother, Mariano. I can see Man, just a year younger than my father, sitting in the back seat, *con un pico cortando pedacitos de hielo.* When they got to Temple, my father had to find his way to the hospital and get his brother admitted. Then he had to say goodbye to Man and leave him there alone, not knowing if he would ever see him alive again. I can only imagine what went through my father's mind as he drove home by himself.

I think I was only five or six when I first heard these stories. They molded my whole life, shaping how I came to understand my father and giving me the deepest sense of compassion for him. I remember, as a child, wondering how my father could smile, laugh, and have such a calm and peaceful face after going through all that? How did he do it? What also grew deep in me, out of that painful story, was a great compassion for all other people who hurt.

Mariano recovered. But the dread disease tried to claim a fourth victim before leaving the family. Cosme, who was ten years younger than Polo, also contracted tuberculosis. Fortunately, it was caught early, and after some time in the sanatorium, Cosme, like his brother Man, recovered. The last surviving child of Félix and Sebastiana, Tío Cosme is now 92 years old.

A Wedding

What is most surprising to me is that my parents got married only a year after Welito Félix and Félix Jr. died. Welita Sebastiana did not want a big wedding, but I think my mother's family did. The Mexican custom is for the groom's family to pay for the wedding, but my maternal grandparents helped out. It was held at the Arredondo's house in Lockhart. Teresita made *gallina en principio*, a chicken stew with onions and tomatoes and herbs; Sebastiana made *mole*. The wedding took place on October 30, 1938, at St. Michael's Catholic Church in Uhland, Texas. My parents were each 28 years old.

Their wedding celebration was an amazing feast, with live music—the famous Big Papa band from San Marcos played. There was plenty of *mole*, *gallina en principio*, and all the trimmings. Big Papa stayed so late and ate so much, he got a royal case of diarrhea after the wedding!

When my siblings and I get together these days, we usually talk about our parents. Each of us had a special relationship with Mamá and Papá. Our tears and laughter come as we share what we recall of particular stories. Each of us has different recollections—and we remember different things about the story of the friendship that turned into love. Interestingly, none of us ever asked them why it took so long to marry! Perhaps it was because of the *respeto* that their private manner demanded, even without words. We do agree, however, that Mamá had many friends as a young girl and that, within the special friendship of their families, our parents developed a strong bond—a love that matured through their youth.

I wonder now, what was my mother feeling when my father left for Mexico at the age of 21? We do not know for sure, but one day my sister, Theresa, asked my father, *"Papá, ¿cómo sabía que Mamá lo iba esperar cuando se fué a Mexico de joven?"* She says he gave her a broad and somewhat sly smile—and no answer. Perhaps by then he was already very sure of her love for him. We will never know.

But two things we do know. Nine months before they married, my father sent my mother a Valentine's card. Yes, they lived on adjoining farms, but people wrote letters to each other! The mailman simply put a pencil mark over the postage. Polo penned this poem:

> Some's have one heart, but you have two
> because my heart belongs to you.

And a few months before they got married, Sixta sent Polo a lovely photo of herself with a *dedicación* on the back:

> *A mi inolvidable Apolinar, dedico este en prueba*
> *de el grande amor que te profeso,*
> *Quien te ama y es tuya, Sixta.**

My father survived my mother by eight months. During the course of those eight months, he would ask me about that photograph. He had gone blind in his last years and now that my mother was gone, he wished he could see the picture and read those words again.

After Papá died, I found a Valentine's Day card that he had written many years before, probably when they celebrated their fifteenth wedding anniversary. On it he printed:

> *Por tí tengo vida, tengo hijos y tantas cosas.*
> *Por eso en este día te digo que*
> *Hay unos que tienen un corazón*
> *pero tu tienes dos*
>
> *Porque mi corazón*
> *te pertenese.*
> *Polo .***

After all those years of marriage, Papá had written the same poem to Mamá in Spanish that he had written to her in English, before they married. However their love started and with all the ups and downs of every marriage, we, the children of Polo and Sixta, were witnesses to the most significant gift that parents can give their children—their love for each other.

After the wedding, Polo and Sixta went on a honeymoon to Monterrey, Mexico. When they returned, they settled in Sebastiana's home in Lockhart. A little over a year later, on February 4, 1940, Sixta gave birth to their first child, a son. They named him Felix.

---

* To my unforgettable Apolinar, I dedicate this [photograph] as a symbol of the love that I profess for you. The one who loves you and is yours, Sixta.

** Because of you I have life, I have children and so many things. That is why on this day I say to you, some have one heart but you have two because my heart belongs to you. Polo.

NOTES

Chapter 1: De Donde Empezamos

1. There was nothing unusual about this. For generations our Rodríguez and Arredondo families had traveled back and forth across the border created in 1848 by the *Tratado de Guadalupe Hidalgo*, which divided off a huge swath of land that had been part of Mexico and, for millennia earlier, the borderless home of the indigenous peoples of the Americas.

2. Félix and Sebastiana probably would have headed north sooner or later. Years ago, my brother Louis asked Welita Sebastiana why they came. *"Nos estábamos muriendo de hambre,"* she said. "We were starving."

3. Romulo died four years later. Mariana died around the same time.

4. John P. Schmal, *Los Antepasados Indígenas de los Guanajuatenses: A Look Into Guanajuato's Past.* (Houston Institute for Culture, 2004), see http://www. houstonculture.org/mexico/guanajuato.html (accessed September 16, 2010).

5. *A la rorro niño, a la ro señor. Que viniste al mundo solo por mi amor.* Go to sleep my baby. Go to sleep my lord. You came to this world solely for my love.

6. One member of the Arredondo family was poignantly absent that Christmas. My great-grandmother, Isidora Puente Arredondo, had died the previous year, in 1922. We do not know on whose ranchland she is buried.

7. Tía Lala (Eduarda Rodríguez) also noted in her journal, which she wrote in 1981, that the couple her parents chose to serve as Goyo's *padrinos*, Gorgonio and Emiliana Leija, eventually became her in-laws. In 1950, she married their son, Guadalupe Leija.

CHAPTER 2

Growing Up Mexican

When Polo and Sixta returned to Lockhart from their honeymoon in Monterrey, they made their home with Polo's family, the man's, as was the custom. Those days were difficult for the new bride. Sixta was so close to her mother; she was living right nearby, in the next rancho—yet so far away. The recently widowed Sebastiana had not been too keen on her eldest son's plans to marry. It had only been a year since her husband, Félix, had died and she was also still suffering the loss of her two sons. But they all made the best of it. Even though he had not regained his full strength after his bout with tuberculosis, Polo's brother, Mariano, worked hard to prepare a room for the newlyweds. Then, soon after the couple arrived, Mariano left Lockhart for the border town of Laredo.

Tía Lala notes in her journal that in March of 1939 someone from the health department came to see her brother, Mariano, offering him training for a job that would not be so physically taxing. Mariano chose fixing radios. But it meant that he would have to move to a city. The only family they had living in a city was their father's brother, Tío Longino Rodríguez and his wife, Simona, who had settled in Nuevo Laredo, on the Mexico side of the river. So Mariano went to live with his uncle, crossing the bridge every day to learn the craft of radio repair at a shop in Laredo, on the U.S. side.

My grandmother Sebastiana did not like the idea of her son, newly recovered from TB, living away from home as an *arrimado* (a "live-in") in her brother-in-law's house. She wanted to move to Laredo to take care of him. The parish priest tried to talk her out of it, saying, "Sebastiana, you're going to leave the ninety-nine sheep to go with one?" By October, the whole family had moved out of the rancho in Lockhart and into a small house they rented in Laredo, on the corner of Salinas and Zaragoza, just one block from the bridge to Mexico.

The only ones who stayed behind were Polo and Sixta because by then, as Tía Lala wrote, Sixta "was expecting." The family's departure meant that the young couple would now be by themselves. Mamá always talked warmly about those few months when they were on their own. Being alone with Papá, waiting for the baby, sewing for him, having visits with her sisters and mother. It was wonderful! Like her own mother, Sixta was a resourceful homemaker who could make things *rendir*. She made a warm home out of the humble house that the landowners provided the sharecroppers. She would describe how Papá *empapeló el cuarto* so the wind would not come in through the holes and crevices in the walls. Using his newspapers, *El Todo* and *La Prensa*, along with pages out of the Sears catalog, Polo papered the walls of the *casita*, insulating it from the cold to protect the newborn. *"Quedó calentito para cuando nació el bebito,"* Mamá would say.

But there was a major down side to the rest of the family leaving. The *"manos"* to work the land were also gone. Polo struggled to make it on his own but, eventually, the landowner told Polo he had to give up the land. Baby Felix was born on February 4, 1940, and soon after, the young couple left the *ranchitos* where they had each grown up. Polo and Sixta followed my Welita Sebastiana and the rest of the Rodríguez family to Laredo.

An Angel Held Her

I was born on April 14, 1941 in Laredo, Texas on Salinas Street at Zaragoza in a house filled with people. The daily life of residents on both sides of the border was completely intertwined, with members of the same family living on either side. Only the river separated us. Every day, my Tío Luís would walk from Laredo, Texas, to Nuevo Laredo, Tamaulipas, to work at *El Popo*, a restaurant run by my Tío Margarito, son of Tío Longino. Work was difficult to find and at times Polo also worked at the restaurant.

On the night I was born, my dear Tío Luís was sitting in the main plaza of Laredo when he saw *el doctor* Naranjo cross the plaza, headed toward our house with his doctor's satchel in hand. Tío Luís would later tell my mother that when he looked at the satchel, he joked to himself, "There goes Sixta's baby!" As it turned out, the doctor got there too late; I was already born.

As I was growing up, Mamá would tell me the story about Tío Luís. She also would tell me that on Easter Sunday, the day before I was born, she went to the movies to see *El Rancho Grande*. I was almost born *en el cine*, she would say, laughing. She would say that I was a beautiful baby because I had felt *el aire de México* when I was born.

On my 65th birthday, I decided to ask Mamá *"¿como fué el día que yo nací?"* I had never thought to ask her about the day I was born, perhaps because I had heard all those other stories. But on this day, I heard a different story, one she had never told me before.

Sixta was alone in that small house near the river when the labor pains started. The other family members were out or at work. Two women, neighbors from across the street, came over to see her. She didn't know them very well, only to say hello. When they came, it was clear to the women that Sixta was in labor—and that she was afraid.

When Sixta had given birth to Felix, just fourteen months earlier, she had been living in Lockhart, surrounded by the loving care of her mother and sisters. Sixta had been very close to her mother. When Welita Teresita was ill with asthma, it was my mother who would *velarla*. She would stay up all night at the foot of her bed. When Felix was born, it must have been such a joy for her to have her mother with her, a powerful and sacred bond being forged between mother and daughter as a grandchild was coming into life. Mamá would say that when Felix was born, Welita Teresita would sing him a popular song of the time, *Amor Chiquito*, about a young love that was newly born.

Amor chiquito,
acabado de nacer.

eres mi encanto,
eres todo mi querer.

Ven a mis brazos,
ámame con ilusión,

porque te quiero
y te doy mi corazón.

Yo solo vivo por tí,
sufro por tí...
muero por tí...

Espero me hagas felíz,
como yo a tí,

porque te quiero
y te doy todo mi amor...

When I was born Welita Teresita and Mamá's beloved sisters were miles and miles away. Mamá often talked about how much she missed them. At age 96, Mamá shared this story with me that said so painfully much about how her life had changed from Felix's birth to mine.

After the two women came over to the house, the older one told Sixta not to worry, and sent the younger woman home. The older woman told Sixta that she would hold her until the baby came. As Mamá put it, an angel held her tight while she labored to give me birth—and she did not fear anymore. *Ese angel me abrazó hasta que naciste.*

By the time I was born that evening, around 9 p.m., the family was there. Mamá said that my Welita Sebastiana picked me up *"y dijo que era la bebita mas bonita que había visto en su vida."* Saying such things was not my grandmother Sebastiana's style, so it really made an impression on my mother!

Sebastiana and Sixta, the two women at the center of my father's life, were very different from each other. As I later came to understand, this was true in part because of social differences in their upbringing. Sixta took after her mother, Teresita, and even though both Teresita and Sebastiana had come from very poor families in Mexico and ended up in the same place in the States, the kind of service they had to perform for the *amos* in Mexico created social differences between them. Teresita had been an inside servant, as had her family members, whereas Sebastiana's family had worked in the fields and she herself had earned a living outside the home in a factory. Sebastiana married at nineteen while Teresita went from child to wife at age thirteen. Temperamentally, Teresita loved tending her home, as did her daughter Sixta. Sebastiana, on the other hand, thrived in doing things outside the home and was never the baking-cookies kind of grandmother.

Having a new person come into the family so soon after the loss of a spouse and two children must also have been stressful for everyone. I recall nuanced words from my father about those times and sensed the stress they all must have felt in so many ways. Mamá would share how Papá would save money so he could buy her certain foods, like eggs, when she was pregnant with me. In the rancho they could have all the milk, cheese, eggs, and vegetables that pregnant women need. In Laredo, it was a very different story. Needless to say, this was not a happy time for Mamá.

My mother's loneliness was not the only cloud hovering over the little house on Salinas Street. When I was born, my father was packing tomatoes at 15 cents an hour. His ranch and farming skills did not transfer to the city and he could not find a good or steady job. It was similar to what happened to them in Guanajuato when the family returned to Mexico and couldn't find work that would sustain them.

There is almost a mystical quality to the memories that surface when I think of the stories from this time, living by the river/border. I came into life at a very sad time for my mother. Babies, even in the womb, absorb their mother's emotions. No wonder I am such a melancholy woman! Yet sadness, stress, and poverty were no obstacles to love. I could never have asked for more love and pride than were lavished on me by my Welita Sebastiana, my tíos and tías, and my parents. I received an abundance of love from the day I was born.

Eight months after my birth, a much larger cloud overshadowed our world, touching my family and many others like ours. On December 7, 1941, Japan attacked Pearl Harbor. The Mexican-American boys who had grown up on ranchos in the borderlands would become soldiers, traveling across the ocean as American GI's, armed for combat. *"Naciste en las llamas de la guerra,"* my mother would tell me. It took me a while to understand exactly what she meant when she would later tell me that I was born amid the flames of war. For the family, it was immediately clear. One after another, my uncles were drafted and shipped off to war.

Tío Luís was the first to go. He had been drafted into the Army a month earlier, in November 1941. He had nearly completed basic training and was scheduled to return to Laredo on furlough. Instead, after the attack on Pearl Harbor, Tío Luís was immediately shipped overseas. He did not return until 1945. Tío Mariano was next to be drafted into the Army, followed by Tío Cosme. Sebastiana's youngest child, Lupito, enlisted in the Navy. He wasn't even 18 and needed her signature. Welita Sebastiana's family was unraveling, as our future fell into the hands of forces far greater than those within our humble home.

San Antonio

I was ten months old when we left Laredo in early 1942. Even in his last days of life, my father would recall the moment he took his *dos bebitos,* still asleep in our *pijamas,* and laid us on the backseat of the Model T. Papá could not make a living in Laredo, so they decided to leave. It was not the first time. I recently learned that we had gone back to Lockhart a few months earlier for a very brief time, also because my father could not find work. We stayed with Sixta's sister, Petra, and her husband, Trinidad, and their five-year-old daughter, María Luisa, while my father helped work at the rancho. I can't imagine how it must have been for them, with two babies, no home, and no work.

This time, instead of returning to the *ranchos* of Lockhart, they chose a new home for us—in San Antonio. Again, relatives offered help. Papá's Tía María and her husband, Aristeo Mojica, welcomed them into their home. The Mojicas were most generous, even though they already had a pretty large family and full house. In addition to their nine children, María's unmarried sister, Concepción Rodríguez, lived with them. It was a crowded house, like the one in Laredo, but my parents hoped that in San Antonio Papá would find better work and we would eventually move into our own home.

Mamá would always tell me stories of how I learned to walk between two beds. One was Mamá and Papá's and the other belonged to Tío Telo and Tía Mila, as we called them. Their generosity was abundant! My parents always held very deep gratitude and love for the Mojicas. When I ran for City Council, Tía Mila, by then a widow, Tía Chonita (Concepción), and several members of the Mojica family lived in my district. Some worked in my campaigns. After I got elected, they continued to be great supporters and collaborators. Tía Mila was 100 years old when she died.

Not long after arriving, we almost left San Antonio. My father was desperate; he could not find work and announced that he and his small family would have to return to Laredo. The Mojicas wouldn't hear of it and they tried to find work for Papá. Tía Mila and Tío Telo's daughter, Lala, started going up and down the street looking for work for her cousin. She found him a job! It was in construction, digging holes at 50 cents a hole. My father went to work and eventually ended up at Kelly Field. Although he did not enter the civil service with all its benefits, he did move up from digging holes to other construction work. He would ride there every day on his bicycle.

We did not stay at the Mojica's home very long because they bought a house next door, which Polo and Sixta rented from them. We were now neighbors on Vermont Street, and that is where my brother, Louis, was born, on August 20, 1942.

Casitas y el Parquesito

By 1943, my parents had saved enough money to buy our first home. It was on Huntington Street. It had two small rooms and an outside toilet; it cost $500. One of my most beautiful childhood memories comes from our life in that little house.

Mamá would take us across the street to what she called *el parquesito*. My brothers and I would run through the vegetation that was about as tall as we were. I must have been about two, Felix was three, and Louis was one. The sky was blue and there were little white flowers that we picked and skipped over to give to Mamá. She smiled tenderly as she took the flowers in her hands. The flowers left a terrible smell on my hands, but Mamá kept her smile. She was happy and so was I. This is the first memory I have of nature, other than the flowers in the pots at Tía Mila's house. It wasn't until years later that I learned that what we called "*el parquesito*" was actually just a vacant lot! I wonder how aware Mamá was of what she was giving us—a wonderful way to experience and learn about the natural world. In our tiny house, with no grass or trees, we would never have enjoyed the outdoors as we experienced in that little "park." With those outings, Mamá was knitting a beautiful impression of the natural world into me forever, bound up with her love.

Soon we moved again, to another small house on Picoso Street, where Theresa was born on August 4, 1944. Mamá and Papá felt it was important to own a house—no matter how humble. It was a very short "shotgun" house, again with two rooms and an outside toilet. But this house had the potential for adding on other rooms and over the next ten years that we lived there, Papá did just that.

First, he built a small room in the back that included a toilet but no bathtub; we all bathed in an aluminum tub. After we had been there for some time and our family continued to grow, Papá pondered the next steps. He would come home after a hard day's work, have his supper and then go outside and sit on the ground next to a tiny peach tree that somehow always stayed small. Papá would stare at the house. I would go sit with him. I wanted to be with him as he thought about how he would add rooms to the house. He would chat with me about it. "How am I going to build extra rooms if the roof is built like that?" We discussed the challenges of the gable roof. I felt important. When he actually started the work, I helped by handing him nails, screwdrivers, and other small items. I also "helped" with the sheetrock and tape and float process. I learned not to be intimidated by "men's" work. I also learned some problem-solving skills—and, of course, I kept bonding with my father.

Papá was a handy man extraordinaire—carpentry, plumbing, electricity, painting—he could do everything needed in a home. Eventually, he added two more rooms with the help of a friend and enclosed a small front porch. That provided enough room for the whole family, when the last two children were born—Miguel on September 29, 1947, and Rosa on June 6, 1949.

Beer and Baby Shoes

Early in our days on Picoso Street we had an experience that would become one of the stories we would never forget. I was about five when Papá came home drunk one day. Friends from Lockhart had come to visit San Antonio. Papá met them and they ended up at a bar. Papá never drank, but he did on that day. He later remembered that the patrons at the bar laughed at him because he was throwing pool balls into the slots with his hands and that people laughed at him when he rode the bus home.

I have a vague memory of him coming home, acting weird. *"¡Vienes borracho!"* Mamá said. She looked very worried. When we were older, we used to call her the head of the temperance movement because she despised alcoholic beverages. On this day she had to deal with a drunken husband. She helped him to bed. We all just watched.

When Papá woke up, sober, he saw the crumpled dirty bag he had been carrying throughout the embarrassing episode. It held a little bottle of brilliantine and a little pair of baby boy shoes. He had been on an errand and bought them for Louis. Seeing that he had carried those little shoes in his condition shamed him. Except for an occasional beer at a special family gathering after we were all grown, my father never drank again.

Going to School

"Déjelos aquí. Van a estár bien." With these words, Sister Mary took Felix on one side of her and me on the other. That is how we started our school lives. I felt safe and secure next to Sister Mary. She was round, and felt soft and warm as she hugged us both. Christ the King School was just across the street from our house on Picoso. We were starting kindergarten. I wonder if Mamá looked worried; she was leaving not one but two small children at school for the first time. I was four and Felix was five. It was his year to start school, but I was sent along so he would not go alone. Felix was still suffering from the asthma that plagued him all his childhood. Mamá had always been very protective of him. Perhaps because of his frailty, all of us in one way or another protected Felix and helped him along. I vividly recall teaching him how to tie his shoelaces.

Our new lives in school did not last long. Felix's asthma made him sick and we both started missing school. At some point, our parents just took us out for the rest of the school year. When we returned the next year, in 1946, Felix and I entered kindergarten together, remaining in the same grade until we graduated from high school.

Kindergarten was all toys and a sunny room. In first grade, Sister Antonia was wonderful, but second grade was another matter. This is when I started to experience adult-sized troubles in my young life.

I was *enamorada* with Pablito, a fair-skinned boy with blond, curly hair. I can't recall if I had ever seen a blond person before; I'm sure that was what attracted me to him. At home when my mother's radio was playing *Cuando Escuches Este Vals*, I sang it to Pablito, only in my mind, of course, so no one would hear me.

> *Cuando eschuches este vals*
> *has un recuerdo de mi*
> *piensa en los besos de amor*
> *que me diste y que te dí.*
>
> *Y si alguien quisiera robar*
> *tu divino corazón*
> *diles que mi alma te dí*
> *y la tuya tengo yo.*
>
> *Como quieres angel mío*
> *que te olivde si eres mi ilusión*
> *en el cielo en la tierra en el mar*
> *estaremos juntitos los dos.*
>
> *Como quieres angel mío*
> *que te olide si eres mi ilusión*
> *si mi vida es toda tuya*
> *y tuyo es mi corazón.*

That was a big girl love! But it went nowhere. One day, for some reason I have never been able to recall, my love, Pablito, pulled me by my pigtails clear across the playground. I did not cry even though it sure did hurt to be dragged across the pavement. What hurt the most was my broken heart. It ended there. I do not remember Pablito after that day.

Making friends was hard for me. At six or seven it just meant having someone who would talk and play or just sit with me. Of course, they had to be girls. Boys could not be friends. They were mean, as I would continue to discover.

Second grade seemed to last a very long time. Sister Mary was my teacher. She was the one who had welcomed Felix and me to kindergarten, but in second grade she seemed very different. I began to see that she favored certain children, who dressed well. She was nicer to children whose parents spoke English or helped the sisters, or who were fair-skinned. It was in her class that Nenita, a Shirley Temple lookalike, with golden curls, pretty dresses, and patent leather shoes, kept assaulting me. On several occasions she took a huge mattress needle to school and stuck my arm with it.

When Mamá went to talk to Sister Mary about this violence that actually caused me to bleed, Sister did not pay much attention. She told my mother with a smile, *"Así son los niños. Voy a hablar con ella."* Whether she ever talked to Nenita or her parents, I don't know. Nenita continued her game of stabbing me whenever she could until she decided on her own to stop. But I never told my mother again. I saw how Sister Mary did not pay attention to Mamá.

That treatment did not do much for my confidence or ability to make friends. To make matters worse, I was terrible at sports and never got picked for games. I was always the last one chosen when we had to divide into teams. I really don't blame the kids for not choosing me. I was scared of the ball—whatever kind of ball it was. When I saw one coming, I ran away from it instead of catching or hitting it. That is why my friendship with Paquita was so important.

Paquita

Paquita was my classmate and at some point or another during second grade became my friend. One day during recess some mean boys locked the two of us in a shed. The boys told us that there were *cienpieses* in there and that they would *picarnos*. One of the good things about Christ the King School was that we could speak Spanish among ourselves and the nuns spoke to us in Spanish, too. I can't remember if Paquita and I spoke to each other in Spanish or English. That memory is lost, as is the memory of how I came to learn and speak English. I did not know a word of it when I entered school. You might say we were early bi-lingual education students.

I had never heard of centipedes before. We were both very frightened and kept looking around for creatures with hundreds of feet. Recess ended and we were still locked up. At some point a sister came looking for us and got us out. After being treated in this manner, Paquita and I had something very special in common and our friendship was sealed.

I felt a lot of compassion for Paquita because she did not have a coat, or at least she never wore one to school when it was cold. Instead, she just wore several sweaters. Her older brothers would pick her up after school because her mother worked. This business of her mother working outside the home made me sad. Most mothers I knew did not work outside the home. To me home meant having my mother there, especially after a bad day at school. I do not recall ever seeing Paquita's mom. Years later, when I asked my mother about Paquita, she said that I would talk about her and that when she went to get us after school, I was usually sitting with her. Our second-grade photograph at Christ the King shows me next to Paquita. I look happy.

One day towards the end of the school year, I saw Paquita spitting up blood. She was next to a tree, holding herself up against it. I ran to tell Sister. The next memory I have is of Paquita's funeral mass at Christ the King. The second graders had to process in two's through the middle aisle and then walk on either side of the coffin. We were told to look at her. I was very scared. I had never seen a dead person before nor had I ever experienced having someone I knew die.

When I got to the coffin, which was almost at my height, I looked over my shoulder and saw Paquita. She was very white, wearing the same First Communion dress she had worn earlier that year. The dress, crown, and veil were exactly like mine. I felt something fearfully huge and cold go down through my body, very deep inside. After that I did not think about Paquita for many, many years. But her memory would return, and then another friend would help me heal from this deep childhood loss.

Niña Jefita

My parents laid down some principles as we were growing up that prepared me for what I would later experience in life as racism or classism and for dealing with difficult people. These principles flowed from their faith in a merciful God who sees all people equally. It was as simple as that. When any of us felt we had been mistreated, my parents never took our complaints and let us feel sorry for ourselves. If I came home hurt because someone in school said I was ugly, my father would ask me, "*¿Y estás fea?*"

"No!" I would say.

He would then tell me that of course there are some people in this world who will say things like that and try to make others feel inferior. But that has nothing to do with who you are. As he and my mother would then always add, "*No somos menos que otra gente, pero tampoco somos mejor que nadie.*" This message, so often repeated when anyone said hurtful words to us, reminded us that we were neither inferior nor superior to anyone else—always equal in the eyes of God. That's all that mattered. As far as looks, what mattered was how I was inside. That is what I decided to concentrate on—being good.

The hurt I felt most as a child, however, could not be so easily soothed. It was when I saw my parents being ignored or treated differently from other adults. Ironically, it was our church and school, all part of our Mexican community, that gave me my first lessons in class distinctions. Oppression begets oppression I later came to understand. Suffering the effects of racism and colonization over centuries breeds an internalized oppression where we hurt our own people. Most of my hurts as a child came from another child or an adult who, like us, was Mexican.

I grew up fast. Not knowing English well, my parents had to count on my brothers and me to translate important conversations and documents for them. At a very early age I began to take on adult responsibilities, even to take care of my parents when it came to some dealing with things in the outside world. I quickly learned that my parents could not help me with certain issues at school, so I had to take care of them. And at school, I also had to take care of my brothers because one was frail from asthma and the other was younger than I.

Our parents fed, clothed, and provided us with a home of our own. They provided us with the best education they could on a laborer's salary. They imbued in us powerful values of faith, hard work, culture, and language that last a lifetime. Deep pride in these was our inheritance. They loved us deeply. Yet, as happens with poor children around the globe, they could not protect us from a world that hurts children simply because of who they are—the color of their skin, their ethnicity, or their poverty. We had to take responsibility for protecting ourselves. And I found a way to do that as a little girl through a practice I began one day. Whenever someone hurt me, I would do or say something kind to someone else. The hurt went away. It was as simple as that.

Growing up Mexican

As a child growing up, my world was Mexican. At home, and with our extended family, we spoke Spanish. We also spoke Spanish at church, stores, and even in school as we were learning English. Until I turned eleven and my older brother discovered the "Hit Parade," we listened to KCOR, Spanish radio. At night and during the winter, our imaginations would run wild listening to radio broadcasts from Mexico

City's XEW, including *La Voz de América Latina*, *Los Niños Catedráticos*, and *El Doctor IQ*—all of which had an educational focus. *Los Niños*, a quiz show for kids, featured children who were very smart and answered all the questions in beautiful Spanish. Other favorites included *Crí Crí: El Grillito Cantor*, a singing cricket whose songs always had a lesson. Some of my favorite Crí Crí songs were *La Patita* (Little Mommy Duck), who walked to the market to buy food for her little duckies and *Los Cochinitos* (Little Pigs), who had dreams lying asleep in bed. Two of the *cochinitos* had mischievous piggy dreams, but it was the smallest *cochinito* who impressed me. His dream was about helping his *pobre mamá*.

We followed soap operas with mature subjects like *El Derecho de Nacer*. That's where I first learned about pregnancy. *"Un hombre la engañó,"* they would say. The unwed Cuban heroine from a high-class home, who had been betrayed by her seducer, gave up her baby and became a nun. I thought that was pretty noble. The saintly Mamá Dolores, the black nanny, raised the baby. There were messages about sex that might have something to do with *amor*, but then maybe not. The entertainment only went so far, of course, leaving many unanswered questions. But I did not ponder them too deeply.

During the day, it was the Spanish songs and music that delighted us. My mother had the radio on all day. Sometimes she would dance Mexican waltzes with her broom—and she would sing, beautifully, all the romantic songs: *Dios Nunca Muere*, *Cuando Escuches Este Vals*, *Morir Por Tu Amor*. *Amor* was swept all over the kitchen and around the tiny rooms of our house. I too learned the words to all these songs and to this day waltzes are my favorite music.

El Barrio de Cristo Rey was a strong, mostly Mexican and Mexican-American neighborhood. We were surrounded by solid families. *Los* Garza had a garage. *Los* González had the grocery store we called Checo's, where one of the González brothers would log our purchases in a little *cartera*. On Fridays, Papá would go *cambiar el cheque* and pay the bill.

Most of the families in the neighborhood owned their homes. Christ the King Church provided stability, since most of our neighbors were also parishioners. Like my Tíos Mariano, Luís, Cosme, and Lupito, many of the Mexican-American veterans who returned from World War II went to work for local military installations. Kelly Air Force Base employed many of the primary breadwinners in our Christ the King neighborhood. Those jobs paid well and had insurance, sick leave, and paid vacations that provided economic stability, home ownership, and a road to the middle class for the *mejicano* community in San Antonio.

My father did not go into the military. Some years ago, I saw my father's Selective Service Card for the first time. It said he was 5' 9" tall and weighed 122 lbs! In 1944, he was rejected because he was "physically unfit." Actually he was deferred; if the war had lasted longer, even he would have been called to duty. Papá's work continued to be in construction, as a laborer, but we benefited from the economic stability that the civil service provided other people in our neighborhood.

We were blessed to have our tíos and tías living in our Christ the King neighborhood, as well as Welita Sebastiana. At some point after we settled in San Antonio, Welita left Laredo with her youngest children and bought a small house on Pace Alley. It was near *la casa de los muchachos*—a house where six of the adult children of my great-uncle Pablo lived; none ever married. Other relatives, like my mother's sister, Isabel, and her husband, Emilio Rodríguez, also lived only a couple of blocks away.

Christ the King Church played a central role in our lives. My father and all my uncles were *Caballeros de Cristo Rey*, the men's organization; my aunts were *Hijas de María*. Everyone was active in church, but no one as active as Welita Sebastiana. "Vee," as we called her because my brother Felix couldn't say *abuelita*, was involved in every ladies society available and was recognized and honored as a leader in the parish.

The church not only provided a place of worship and gatherings but also served as a strong center of Mexican culture. The pastor, Father Vicente Andrés, CMF, a Claretian priest from Spain, promoted Mexican culture among the neighborhood children. He was the second Claretian to minister to our family; Father Ramón Sunjé, CMF, had presided at my parent's marriage in 1938 in Uhland, Texas.

Father Vicente, whose roaring sermons spoke of sin and damnation, would rent Spanish-language movies to show in the church's back lot. Sitting on hard wooden benches, we watched movies outdoors at night, with all the popular stars of Mexico's *Cine de Oro*: Pedro Infante, Libertad Lamarque, Jorge Negrete, María Félix, Dolores del Río. The female lead was usually a beautiful Mexican woman with thick black hair and lovely dark eyes with long eyelashes. The men wore big hats, boots, and even mariachi outfits. There was always some theme of a rich girl falling in love with a poor boy, or vice versa. Some movies showed poverty and class struggles. Poor women wore *rebozos de bollita* just like my grandmothers.

So we grew up with a lot of pride in being Mexican. Later, when television came along with ads touting Clairol, exclaiming "blondes have more fun," "blondes marry younger," and "be a blonde and find out," I was offended. How dare they say that? Why was being fair touted as being better?

I never even liked it when *mejicanos* we knew said things like, *"El bebito nació tan bonito, está guerito,"* or *"Ay, está muy bonita la bebita pero está prietita,"* that showed a bias toward children with fair features. While I did have some concerns about being very thin in a culture that prized more roundness in girls—and worried about being poor—I never had a problem with being *mejicana*, just pride! Even so, I wonder about the subliminal influence of the larger culture on me when I consider that two significant memories from my early childhood involved blond children, Pablito and Paquita.

Growing up Mexican: El Bolo

Since we were not allowed to go out of our yard, church services were an opportunity not only to pray but also to have fun. We did not have a car at the time so church was a place where the entire family could easily join in the life of our community. To get there, all we had to do was walk across Picoso Street, by Checo's store, past the beautiful house of *Los* Alvarados and the priest's rectory, and there we were. But we were only allowed to go there for official activities, not just to play or mess around.

One of the official activities took place on Sunday afternoons when there were *bautismos* and the *padrinos* were going to *tirar el bolo*. Right after the baptism, when everyone came out of the church, the godparents would throw *el bolo*, a gift of coins, up in the air and the neighborhood children would scramble to pick them up. The kid who could throw herself on the ground the quickest got the most coins. I could scramble pretty well but my brothers were really good at it. After collecting *el bolo*, we would go to Checo's and buy sugary *helados* or Cool Aid mix that we would put on our palms and lick. These were totally unacceptable snacks, but my parents never knew how much *bolo* we had gotten nor how many and what kind of snacks we bought with it. The point of the *bolo* was that a baptism was a happy and significant occasion for a family, as their new baby was being welcomed into the Church. And it certainly was that for us.

Growing up Mexican: Holy Week

We learned our Catholic faith through church rituals and religious traditions that were handed down through generations in our family. Holy Week capped them all.

The week began on Palm Sunday with a procession around Christ the King Church that sometimes went around the block, with people singing and praying. As a man portraying Jesus rode by on a donkey, parishioners dressed in costumes shouted *¡Viva Cristo Rey!* Since *Cristo Rey* was the name of our parish, it seemed to give me a strong feeling of how it must have been when Jesus entered Jerusalem.

On Monday through Wednesday there was a lot of cleaning of the church and getting things ready. We were not involved but Welita Sebastiana was one of the leaders of that effort, which took a long time because the Cordi Marian Sisters and Claretian priests organized very elaborate rituals.

On Holy Thursday, the commemoration of Christ's Last Supper included Mass and the washing of the feet in remembrance of Jesus washing the feet of his apostles. Men deemed outstanding by the priest would have their feet washed by the pastor. The ritual was to remind us that we should be ready to serve others. That part of the ceremony always impressed me. Next came the blessing of the bread. I always looked forward to getting some of the *pan bendito* that was carried in huge baskets. Sometimes I would get two pieces. My mother would always take a *pan bendito* to keep all year as a blessing for our home. It was a very sacred symbol for us of Jesus, the Bread of Life. It also held the prayer that we would always have food.

After the Mass there was a procession around the inside of the church led by the main celebrant, who held the monstrance with the Blessed Sacrament. Dressed in an ornate vestment, the priest stood under a pall, a tent-like cover held up on four poles carried by acolytes. All processed together through the church, while the congregation sang *Pange Lingua,* with an altar boy walking backwards so he could hold a censer in front of the Blessed Sacrament, filling the church with the sweet smell of incense that would at times make me dizzy.

At the end of the procession, the priest climbed a ladder and put the Blessed Sacrament in a very high temporary altar. Candles ran up the walls on either side of and above the altar. As they were lit, the whole sanctuary became illuminated by candlelight. I loved it, imagining that this was how heaven would be. Each year I looked forward to that sacred time when the music stopped, the walking stopped, and everyone just knelt down to *adorar al Santísimo*—someone greater than all of us, someone who loved me.

In those years, the church stayed open all night and members of the various church organizations took turns adoring the Blessed Sacrament for an hour. Mamá and Papá alternated so one of them stayed home to care for the younger children while the other prayed. Felix, Louis, and I also prayed for a little while and then went out to play. But it was Welita Sebastiana, who stayed all night, hour after hour in prayer. She sat, head covered with a black *rebozo*, so you could not see her face. I wondered how she could stay quiet praying for so long.

Being a member of every single one of the women's organizations in the church, Welita Sebastiana had a *distintivo*, an identifying ribbon, for each one. My uncles would tease her because every hour, as it was the turn for the members of another organization to *adorar*, she would stay put and simply change her *distintivo*. There was also some drama. From time to time, I would go back into the church to pray myself. I remember seeing my grandmother suddenly get up and start singing in an incredibly loud voice, *Bendito, Bendito, Bendito Sea Dios*. At first I was surprised and then embarrassed, worried that people would make fun of her. But slowly, beginning with other women in the church—mostly elderly—people would stand up, one by one, and join her. I was impressed! Welita Sebastiana was brave; she was even the *presidenta* of some of those organizations.

On Good Friday, the main event was *Las Siete Palabras* commemorating the final words that Jesus uttered while on the cross. By then the sanctuary was covered with a purple cloth. All you could see was a statue of Our Lady draped in a black shawl, standing in front of a cross with a white cloth across it. The service lasted for three hours—from 1 p.m. to 3 p.m.—the time that Jesus died. One or more priests spoke on each of the seven words. No organ played, no songs were sung. It was very solemn. There were so many people attending the service that chairs had to be set up outside and *vocinas* were put out so people could hear. I can almost see the faces of the people in whose shadow I grew up—a good number of them relatives, the men and women of the church and our community. They made an indelible mark on my young life.

That night there was the *pésame a la virgen*. We would go offer our condolences to Mary. A cross with the body of Jesus was lying in front of a sorrowful Mary. Very sad hymns were sung *a cappella*, all having to do with asking God to forgive our sins, because Jesus had died for our sins. The women, many of whom wore black, wept quietly. Mamá was sad.

In my childhood and early youth, the Holy Saturday service was held in the morning. That was when *¡se habría la Gloria!* Until heaven opened with the Resurrection of Jesus, Mamá would not allow us to turn on the radio and we had to be subdued. On Good Friday we understood that sacrifice was in order. But we were not so sure about other times, even though Mamá tried to have everyone in the house offer up not listening to the radio. On Saturday, Mass was said and when the *Gloria* was sung, the purple cloth that had been covering the sanctuary on Good Friday was removed, revealing, as if by magic, a magnificent scene. Along with the candles that had been there on Holy Thursday, Easter lilies covered the walls around the altar all the way up to the ceiling of the sanctuary. It was a spectacular sight! Heaven had opened and there was music and joy again.

On Easter Sunday, we went to Mass and heard the Gospel story of how Jesus rose from the dead. For me it was a happy event because Mamá would find some way to sew a new dress for Theresa and me. Mamá liked pastels and the dress would be made of a remnant of organdy or dotted Swiss she bought at Solo Serve. My father would take us to visit Welita Sebastiana and our uncles and aunts. All the messages were about rebirth, just like the Spring we were starting to enjoy.

Adventures in a 25-Foot Lot

We lived on Picoso Street for about nine years, but to me it seems like a lifetime. Four, five, and then six, children living in a small house on a 25-foot lot, particularly during the summer, made for very long years. There were summer days when I longed to go out—anywhere. *Me daban ancias*. It felt oppressive. My parents would just let us outside to go to the store, church, and school. It was a good policy because there were gangs and drugs sold within blocks of our house. All we knew was that there were *marijuanos* out there and they were not good people. The farthest we would go was to Lockhart to visit our Arredondo grandparents. That was the best time of my life, but those trips were few and far between.

We had to find outlets for all our energy and, usually, we did. My brothers were very bright and creative little boys. I recall their playing with whatever materials were available in our tiny lot—water, mud, light, bugs, ants, rain, plants, trees, wood, boxes, cans. We would create plays setting up a curtain and letting our imaginations go wild. Much of our play involved laughing at (and with) each other, but we never took the teasing seriously. Digging to find China, as instructed by my brother Felix, who was the originator of the best ideas for adventure, was fun while it lasted. My mother stopped us. The hole in the middle of the yard became a huge puddle when it rained. Like other children, we enjoyed *canicas* and jump rope but the stilts Papá built for us were unique. It was amazing to see how quickly we took to walking all over the yard on our *sancos*. I identified with the *sancos* because my parents would say that we all were *sancones*, which meant we had long legs.

Growing up between two brothers made me somewhat of a tomboy, but a careless one at that. I would climb the mesquite trees and enjoy the view from up there. But I would manage to step on the mesquite thorns, which got stuck painfully in my feet. My father hung a *columpio* from a tree and swinging on it was great fun. But I managed to make it dangerous. One day, I was swinging happily, singing the popular song, *El Columpio del Amor*. Holding a long pole close to my face, I decided to jump off the swing. Somehow the pole got stuck in my mouth and cut my *paladar*. Screaming *"¡sangre, sangre!"* as I ran into the house, I gave my mother a real scare. After she took care of the cut and calmed me down, she would remind me, yet again, of my need to be more careful. *"¡Es porque no te fijas!"*

But that backyard also had a secret place where I could be quiet. On top of the old *gallinero* I could talk to God. I would touch the mesquite tree and pick the "bananas" that the tree provided, marveling at their musky taste. I would take little pieces of paper and a pencil, write special notes, and hide them in tiny holes in the tree. Even thinking about that now gives me a sense of peace. The sight from on top of the old chicken coop was beautiful.

Our home and little backyard on Picoso Street was a place where we could joke and laugh, even about the embarrassing or painful things that happened at school. I found joy and comfort in my relationships with my brothers and sisters even though we also fought at times and made life difficult for our mother with all our running around and yelling. I had a bad habit of hitting or even scratching my brothers from time to time. When they would take a doll or other toy from me, I was usually unable to hit them because they ran faster than I. But I just waited several hours or a whole day. And when they least expected it, I would jump on them to get even. I even scratched them on the face. For that my father spanked me. *"Espera que llege tu Papá,"* Mamá would say, and I knew I was in trouble. I was also very *traviesa*. One day playing, "Guess what I have hidden in this hanky?" I accidentally killed a little coo-coo bird that my mother had rescued. My brothers could not guess soon enough and when I showed them what I had hidden, the bird fell down—dead. Poor Mamá.

To this day I cannot recall an event or a time when I felt hurt or pain because of something one of my brothers did to me. Luckily, even with my scratching, they feel the same about me. I was truly blessed with the lives of my brothers and my sisters. I have sympathy for my mother, however, with a house full of children teasing, running, laughing, joking, and being very *traviesos*. She had great patience with us. But when she had had it, we saw a certain look come over her face that quieted us right down—for a while anyway, and then we would start all over again.

Visitas al Rancho

One of our favorite treats was to leave our 25-foot lot, neighborhood, and city altogether to visit Welita Teresita and Welito Melecio at *el rancho* in Lockhart. Until we could afford our own car, which wasn't until the 1960s, Papá would borrow a car from Tío Mariano and we would take what seemed like a very long country drive toward Austin. I loved to see the small hills, wildflowers, and large expanses of land that have all but disappeared along IH-35. As I gazed out the car window, I would sing, "America the Beautiful," in a low voice. The small hills rising out of such flat land were my "purple mountain majesties." These rides out into the country helped mold my sense of nature, and were unforgettably joyful.

We knew we were getting close to the rancho when we started seeing the corn, cotton, and broom fields in their various seasons. Windmills and tiny scattered houses and barns dotted the way to our Arredondo grandparents. Finally, turning off a dusty road, their small house appeared, surrounded by a garden and crepe myrtles. The *troja, cochera* and *corales* were around the other side of the house.

The smell of animals—pigs, chickens, turkeys, horses, and one or two goats—as we opened the car doors meant we were there. Then out would come Welita, wearing her apron, Welito in his blue denim work shirt buttoned all the way to the top, and Tía Mague and Tío Blas to greet us with hugs and kisses and voices pitched high with excitement. "*¿Cómo les fué en el viaje?*" started the conversation.

Very soon there would be a delicious meal with Welita and Tía Mague's superb *té*. Fresh tea leaves simmered just right produced an iced tea the likes of which I have never again tasted. Perhaps it is just being a child, drinking it with ice cut from a block of ice out of *la llelera*, sweetened with sugar, a squeeze of lemon, and served in a huge thick goblet.

Staying with our Arredondo family meant having breakfast, lunch, and dinner in fine form. There was *pan de levadura, chorizo de la mar-*

queta, and in the month of June, fresh corn boiled in a *pila*. At the Arredondo home there were quiet *pláticas* around the table, and then the men and women went their separate ways. The children, meanwhile, went out to explore the mysteries of a working farm. As soon as I could, I would run to the back of the *troja*. Standing alone next to the tall barn with the smell of harvested corn inside, I would raise my head so I could feel the wind blowing on my face, taking in the deepest breaths and feeling so very happy. I would see the fields stretching far into the horizon, merging into the sky, broken only by one or two trees. I would think of God. God was in the wind and in the open spaces. There I would pray.

Welita Teresita

I was nine years old when Tío Cosme showed up at our house on Picoso. We had no phone and he had some news. *"Te tengo una noticia de tu Mamá,"* he said to my mother. And before he could say another word, my mother started saying, *"¡Se murió! ¡Se murió mi Mamá! ¿Verdad?"* Tío Cosme nodded, and my Mamita started screaming. Screaming. She was inconsolable. She collapsed in a chair.

I was shocked—and very worried about my Mamita. We arranged to borrow Tío Man's car and rushed off to Lockhart. It was nighttime when we arrived. My Tía Mague and cousin, María Luisa, were sleeping on the floor. I wondered how they could sleep when Welita had just died.

Welita Teresita's wake was in the house. They moved all the furniture out of the living room to make room for the lavender coffin. That is all I remember about the funeral and my grandmother's death—except that my mother was never quite the same again.

Welita Teresita had suffered from heart disease and died of a heart attack. She had been sick for a while and my mother never got over the fact that she did not know—and did not get a chance to say goodbye. Her brother, Santos, on the other hand, had known and come all the way from Edinburg in southeast Texas, arriving in time to hold his mother in his arms as she died.

After Welita died, something happened to me, too. I became very fearful about my mother dying. I could not get my mother's wailing out of my mind. I now knew in my bones how it would feel to lose my mother. When Mamá got sick, I would be overcome with fear. It was not until I was well into my adult years before that dread fear left me.

Many years after that, my mother finally did get a chance to see Welita Teresita. In 2007, on the last night I spent with her, my mother suddenly roused herself from the deep sleep she had been in, calling out, "*¡Mamá! ¡Mamá!*"

I knew it would not be too much longer before she would be with her *querida madre*; Mamá died 48 hours later.

An Elephant at the Library

When I was eleven years old, my parents decided we were old enough to go downtown to the San Antonio Public Library where a large statue of an elephant rearing up on its hind legs stood, welcoming us. The first time we went, Mamá showed us the way by bus and got each of us a library card. Thereafter, we went on our own, each with twenty-five cents to cover our bus fares—and maybe even a bag of popcorn.

The Young People's Room was a marvelous place. I had the benefit of two very inquisitive and smart brothers who loved reading—a lot more than I did. As I wandered around, looking for things I liked, mainly biographies, they would find and bring me books. A key finding was the biography of the first woman Senator of the United States, Margaret Chase Smith. I read her story and it gave me an idea for what would become my mission in life—to become a secretary and use that as a stepping-stone to any other career!

I could not get enough of *The Diary of Anne Frank*. I read and re-read it several times. And all of us read *The Box Car Children*. We were in awe of the boys and girls in that story. They made do with what they had and we understood that. On the top floor of the library was the Hertzberg Circus, the oldest public circus collection in the United States, full of all kinds of circus memorabilia, which made the library experience even more exciting for us. At the San Antonio Public Library, our curiosity found a home and our tiny world expanded.

Otras Visitas

Our best outings, as we were growing up, involved visiting our extended family. Being with all our *tíos y tías*, especially after the war when my uncles were back home and still single was wonderful—full of teasing, family jokes, laughter, and conversation. I never met my paternal grandfather, Félix, nor my Uncles Félix, Gregorio, or Flujencio, who all died young. But I was blessed to grow up surrounded by my seven *tías,* Pepita, Rosita, María, Margarita, Betty, Luz, and Lala and seven *tíos,* Blas, Santos, Mariano, Luís, Delfino, Cosme, and Lupe.

One thing they all had in common was great faith and a great love and respect for what it means to be family. The varied members of these two families all grew up together as children on adjoining ranches. They were involved in the same church and shared life together in a larger community. I saw them as happy people, gifting us for the rest of our lives with their unconditional love and attention. As I grew older, I also noticed that my relatives were optimistic, an optimism that was tied to their faith. Welita Sebastiana, for example, would say, *"Con Dios, todo va salir bien. Déjenselo a Dios."* As I grew into a young woman, she would give me a huge hug and then send me on my way with a clear command. Holding her fingers tight together, Welita Sebastiana would tap me on the chest, saying, *"Vete derechito, derechito, derechito."* Pounding those directions into my chest as if to a lost traveler, I was to go straight in life and never veer off the right path. I can still feel the pressure of those fingers today.

Welita Sebastiana's house, first on Pace Alley and then on Ruíz Street, was a favorite for celebrating *el día de las madres*. On Mother's Day, we would all don *claveles rojos* to celebrate the fact that we had a mother. Wearing a white carnation meant your mother was no longer alive.

All over the Westside—outside churches, on the street, and in small stores—people sold carnations, real and paper ones, the latter often adorned with silver or gold glitter. Our carnations were always real, picked from Welita Sebastiana's yard, and eventually from our own. It was Papá's great joy to be able to celebrate this day with his mother.

I do not recall ever celebrating Mother's Day at Welita Teresita's. Mamá never said anything negative when we all went to Welita Sebastiana's, but I know it must have hurt not to ever celebrate Mother's Day with her own mother while she was alive. I remember some years going to Welita Sebastiana's house with Papá while Mamá stayed at home with my younger siblings.

For Mamá the big days to celebrate as a mother would be our graduations, first communions, and similar milestones, which were major events in our family. Mamá would make *mole* and other special dishes on these occasions. At Welita Sebastiana's house, we would have something called *pindongo* on holidays. I have never heard that word again, but that fruit salad was the highlight of summer celebrations at her house.

Una Señorita

When I was around twelve, some changes started to take place in my life. It was not so much how my body was changing. It wasn't. I felt pretty much the same, but my parents started to treat me differently. They would tell me I was becoming *una señorita*. I did not quite understand what they meant, and no one explained. But now what I said seemed to matter more. I was being very *respetada*—and soon even got my own room. Papá had added two more rooms to the house on Picoso Street and I got the smaller one. For a time I shared it with Miguel, when he was a toddler. But then I had it to myself. I loved being able to keep it clean and decorate it, especially after we got the bedroom set from my father's boss, Frank Miceli. Their hand-me-down was my treasure—an ivory-colored dresser and chest of drawers with gold trim and thick beveled glass on top, and a matching bed frame. I felt very special. It was just the right time to feel good about myself, at least at home, because at school the sixth and seventh grade boys were getting meaner than ever.

Being a *señorita* made me more reflective about life. Among other things, I knew I had to study very hard. My parents drilled into us the importance of education. They would say that when they were growing up, all they needed was a strong back in order to make it—strong enough to work in the fields. But the future, they said, would demand more from us. We would need an education. When people would tell my father that he ought to take us out of school because we were old enough to work, Papá would say to them, *"Una educacíon es importante y necesaria para su futuro."* He would say the same thing to us, adding that an education was something no one would ever be able to take away from us.

A major shift was occurring in my generation of our family. We were moving away from an agrarian to an urban way of life, as were millions of other people around the country. My parents were visionaries. They saw that this new life would demand something very different from their children and they dedicated their entire lives to providing it. With their bodies, they labored to provide us with the one thing they lacked: a formal education. They literally made themselves into stepping-stones for us to be able to move ahead, giving us their very lives.

Los Trabajos

There was an annual ritual at the Marmolejo's house on Picoso Street, across the street from ours. Every year when September rolled around, the Marmolejos would prepare to go to *el betabel*. It would take about a week to pack up for their long trip to pick beets. A huge truck with a *lona* over it would arrive, looking like a great covered wagon. For days men, women, and children would arrive, putting all kinds of equipment, clothing, and food into the truck. Everyone pitched in. I would pay special attention to the young women because they covered their hair with kerchiefs and wore pants. I had never seen women in pants! They jumped up and down off the truck just like the men, and they would sing a lot. I remember them singing *La Rielera*. It was a proper song to sing as they drove away. *"Adios, mi rielera, ya se va tu Juán."* The young girls and boys with their legs hanging from the truck would drive off, kicking up the dust on our little street.

All this excitement we watched from our home, twenty feet away. I was always sad when I saw them drive off. It seemed like such fun, I wanted to go, too. One day I asked my father why we did not go to *el betabel*. He looked at me and explained. The Marmolejos, he said, were going very far away—to work in the fields. The children had to leave school, just as he and Mamá did when they were young. He and Mamá wanted us to study hard and finish high school so that we would never have to work in the fields as they did when they were children. Papá told me that he was working for all of us and that we already had a job. He would say, *"Su trabajo es estudiar."*

Are We White or Colored?

When Papá would say, *"Vamos al centro,"* my heart would pound with excitement. I conjured up the bus ride and the walk along Houston Street, holding Papá's hand, knowing we would soon cross over the San Antonio River. I was scared of the water below. Water always frightened me. But I was willing to take the risk because leaving our small world on Picoso Street to go to *el centro* was thrilling.

Downtown was a bustling place in those days; it was the main shopping area for the entire city. Papá was very familiar with *el centro*. He had read about San Antonio regularly in *La Prensa* and *El Todo* when he lived with his family at the ranch in Lockhart, and he and his brothers would visit the city from time to time. Mamá and Papá had actually spent a night at the Continental Hotel on Commerce Street right after they married, on the way to their honeymoon in Monterrey, Mexico. On weekends, after we moved to San Antonio, Papá would go to *La Plaza del Zacate*, across from the farmer's market, to participate in the *pláticas* on happenings in town and the latest news from Mexico. Papá was an informed man—lucky for us because we grew up asking a lot of questions. Papá and Mamá always encouraged our curiosity, answering whatever questions they could and respecting our opinions.

As we hopped on the bus to head downtown, one of us would yell, *"¡Ándale, agarra el asiento!"* as another dashed to a vacant seat. We didn't stay seated long. Soon an older patron would get on the bus and Papá would give us a certain look. Felix and Louis were the first to show *respeto* for older people by giving up their seats. Then it would be my turn. But we very quickly found a way to have *respeto*—and a seat!

The back of the bus was always empty when it got to our bus stop. Westside bus lines filled with Mexicans as they headed downtown, but the back seats, behind a "Colored Only" sign, were usually empty. Our parents had told us about signs in Lockhart that said, "No Mexicans Allowed" or "No Mexicans or Dogs Allowed." And Mamá had also told me a story about a day when she and her brother Santos had gone into town with her parents. While the adults were doing their weekly shopping, the two children went into the drugstore to buy ice cream cones. Mamá and Santos sat down at the counter and waited to be served. They waited for quite a while before an *americana* finally came up to them and said, "We do not serve Mexicans." Mamá did not dwell on the story, but I could see the sadness fill her face.

So we knew those signs at the back of the bus were just plain wrong. And when we saw all those empty benches in the back, we went over and sat down. We knew nothing of civil disobedience, but in our childish way, that is what we were doing. Papá would join us. Without saying a word, Papá offered a profound lesson—just by sitting next to us with the gentlest look on his face.

We learned other things going downtown. At the S.H. Kress & Co. "five and dime" store, the water fountains had "Colored Only" and "Whites Only" signs. My siblings and I wondered out of which fountain we Mexicans should drink. Papá did not have an answer. So we drank out of both, giggling the whole time. Again, we gave no deep thought to our small acts of resistance. But I soaked in the awareness that there was no place for Mexicans like me in a world that some people divided into "Whites" and "Colored"—and that there was something very mean, and even dangerous, behind all those signs.

I also soaked in a powerful antidote to these ugly messages. I do not recall the precise words Papá used to tell us, "This is wrong," but that message came across loud and clear. Perhaps it was the way we felt his permission to express ourselves in whatever way we saw fit when it came to things like drinking out of water fountains or where we sat on the bus. It certainly came across in the theme we heard from both parents from the time we were old enough to remember: *"Todos somos hijos de Dios. No es bueno hacer menos a nadie."* We are all children of God. It is not right to treat anyone as inferior.

La Casa Grande

In 1954, when Felix and I were in the eighth grade, my parents called us together to take a vote on a very important matter. We all had seen the house on West Martin Street that Mamá and Papá were proposing to buy. It was bigger than our house on Picoso and had a beautiful backyard with grass, flowers, and trees and a large garage where my father could store all his tools. Should we buy this house? My parents wanted each of us to vote because if we bought it, we would have to go without even more. Each month we would have to pay the mortgage, they explained. I was excited and more than ready to vote yes. The motion carried, nearly unanimously. My brother Felix was the lone holdout. He probably knew better than any of us the kind of sacrifice it would mean for our parents and us.

We never could have bought the house had we not been able to sell the one we lived in on Picoso Street. A man with a heart of gold, Eleuterio Escobar, the realtor in our *barrio*, bought the house himself just to get it off my parents' hands. We cleared $2,000. Papá's boss, Frank Miceli, lent him $1,000. That meant we would have a $4,000 mortgage from the bank. Years later, when Mr. Miceli was dying of cancer, my father went to say goodbye. Mr. Miceli told my father that he forgave him any debts he owed him. Papá thanked him. What Mr. Miceli did not seem to know or remember was that we had long since repaid the $1,000 loan.

Buying that house said a lot to us and to our community. People would say, *"La familia de Polo y Sixta con tantos niños y tan pobres pudieron comprar esa casa tan grande y bonita."* How did they do it, they wondered? Well, we did it because Mamá y Papá made a commitment and everyone in the whole family, down to the youngest child, knew we would have to sacrifice and agreed to it. For years every first week of the month, Mamá would take the bus downtown to pay the $50 mortgage—my father's entire pay for the week. We called it our week of *pan y agua,* meaning we had to sacrifice even more. Mamá would often take Louis with her. When Louis got older, he would go by himself. In eleven years my parents never missed a payment. The house became ours in December of 1965. Four generations of our family have enjoyed that house and it is where my parents spent their last days in the early 2000s.

When all the furniture had been removed from the house on Picoso Street and before we left it for good, my parents gathered us in the empty house and had us kneel in prayer. Papá thanked God for all the years we had spent in that house and for all the blessings we had received. Our family, he prayed, was leaving that house intact—all of us together, healthy and full of promise. *Gracias.* I remember the emotion I felt, even as a thirteen year old, hearing this great prayer of thanksgiving.

And so we moved into our big house. By then my mother had a washing machine with a roller to wring clothes. It went into the large garage. Behind the garage, the yard was large enough for my parents to plant some fruit trees and vegetables. My mother could start enjoying the gardening she loved so much and my younger siblings had a beautiful place in which to play, especially when my father got a sturdy swing set and a very tall slide from Mr. Miceli.

We would not, however, have the entire house to ourselves. It was a duplex and a young newlywed couple lived in the side apartment. Their rent helped us make those first mortgage payments but we actually ended up with less room than we had on Picoso Street! We had to double and triple up on beds—but we made it. After the couple had their first baby, they got a place of their own and moved away. The apartment was never rented again. My father added one more room to the house and we were all well accommodated. By the time Mamá bought a more modern clothes washer and dryer, there was space for them inside. Papá also created a place of honor for all our schoolbooks, which grew as we continued our education. Three long shelves on a wall became a library. Mamá and Papá took care of our books long after we all left home.

Boys

Being born between two boys should have made me comfortable around them, but that is not my story. I was very close to my two brothers, Felix and Louis, and very protective of them. When we were little, my older brother Felix was frail. With his asthma, just breathing was a huge challenge. And Louis, of course, was younger than me. Both had been admonished not to fight by our parents, but they did not differentiate between starting a fight and defending themselves, as I eventually did. From time to time other boys would beat them up—and I remember coming to their defense, jumping on their attackers. Fortunately, my brothers were very smart and eventually their intelligence won over the brawn of the mean boys.

The incident in first grade when Pablito dragged me by my pigtails was followed by painful incidents of boys harassing and hitting my brothers. Then my memories of boys jump to the horrible sixth and seventh grades. I grew tall very fast and was very thin. It did not help that as a pre-teen the nuns at school made me cut my hair. My father was particularly unhappy about the idea but eventually he and mother succumbed to the nuns' request. Mamá took me to a neighbor who worked in a beauty shop and the woman cut my hair. Goodbye braids and hello frizzy hair. What on earth do you do with wavy hair that insists on frizzing wildly? Braids had been convenient for Mamá, who patiently washed my long hair and braided it neatly, as well as for me. For a young girl who was taller than most of the boys, very thin, and who now had a bad hair day every day, having a good body image was a struggle! Thank God I had been taught that looks weren't everything and that what counted was what I was inside and how I treated people. I worked hard on that!

My biggest test of living out this philosophy was the horrible treatment I got from some of the boys in school. They were downright abusive. They made fun of me, calling me a toothpick and *gargajo*. According to the Velázquez Dictionary, *gargajo* is "Phlegm or mucus brought up by coughing, expectorated matter, sputum." But none of us kids needed Velázquez to know what they were saying. It was humiliating and hurtful and I wanted nothing to do with boys in my middle school years.

I recently asked my brother Felix if he knew why the boys treated me that way and whether they treated other girls like that. "No, they did not treat the other girls like that," he said. "I think they saw you as different because you were tall and thin. And, you also were assertive. You defended yourself and us. You would even climb up behind a boy when he was beating one of us."

"What did you see me do when they were calling me names?" I asked.

"You just took it in stride. Like that's the way things were. No emotion."

"Felix, why didn't you do anything?"

"Well, Mamá had told me never to hit anyone. Even when they hit me, I did not run away. I stood there; I let them beat me."

That kind of harsh bullying, as we now know, can hurt children for life. At the time I felt there was no recourse except to ignore it and pretend it did not hurt. I did not allow myself to share with my parents what was happening. Neither did my siblings, who witnessed the abuse—and experienced it themselves. The support I felt at home and in my extended family was so great, I learned how to deal with it. However, I now think that much of my hesitancy with men, going so many years without being involved in relationships, came from the harm done in my tender years. It took the kindest man in the world to change things for me and I waited a long time for that.

Miracle of the Heart

In May of 1955, Felix and I graduated from the eighth grade, with great fanfare. Mamá made me a dress to match the one all the other girls at Christ the King would be wearing on graduation day. It involved several yards of chiffon over a heavy satin lining, with a string of pearl buttons running down the front. I wore high heels for the first time, and a little white hat and gloves. Felix had to wear a suit. On graduation day, we each got awards for having gone to Christ the King since kindergarten and, thanks to our seventh and eighth grade teacher, Sister Josephine, Felix received a $50 scholarship to Central Catholic High School from the Cordi Marian Sisters. Somehow, that made it possible for me to go to Providence High School. The whole family was very excited. We even had our photo taken at a studio. For my parents, it was a moment of great pride. For me, it was the beginning of an astonishing summer.

After graduation, I had started to feel bad physically. I had no appetite. Except for fried tortilla chips and grapefruit juice, nothing my mother fixed would make me want to eat. I also had a discomfort at the pit of my stomach. Worried, my parents decided to take me to a doctor. So Mamá and I hopped on a bus to the Polyclinic that a pioneer group of Mexican-American physicians had established downtown, not far from an area that would eventually be torn down by urban renewal. It included Drs. Saul Treviño, cardiologist; Ramiro Estrada, pediatrician; Joaquín González, general practitioner (and brother of the late Congressman Henry B. González); Daniel Saenz, obstetrician (who also opened the Saenz Clinic on the Westside where my two youngest siblings were delivered); and Eduardo Ximenes, general practitioner (who would one day become a member of the University of Texas Board of Regents—one of the men who would make the controversial decision to locate the new University of Texas at San Antonio at the far north edge of the city). The doctors offered excellent medical services at a reasonable cost.

It was Dr. Ximenes who examined me that day and then referred me to Dr. Treviño, the cardiologist. I began to undergo a number of tests. On the day we finally got the test results, the news was not good. The doctors told us that I had a congenital heart condition. I had a hole between the chambers of my heart and blood was flowing from one chamber to the other in ways it shouldn't. They said I would need major surgery. There was no place to do this kind of surgery in San Antonio, however, so I would have to be taken to Houston for the operation. Further testing would be needed.

I remember sitting at a restaurant with my mother on Santa Rosa Street, near the doctors' offices, after receiving this news. I was shaking inside and wanted to cry. It looked like Mamá also wanted to cry. But neither of us did. We just sat there, a very worried mother and her young daughter, choking back tears and casting wordless looks at each other. I tried to eat my *caldito* but as it hit my stomach, it felt like the soup itself was weeping.

For the next weeks that summer, Mamá and I spent a lot of time making medical visits. In addition to whatever was wrong with my heart, there was some hormone issue the doctors were also dealing with that required frequent visits to the Santa Rosa clinic. I have never known what that was about. With Mamá's time drawn away from the house to take me on the bus to see doctors, my siblings all pitched in. Even Rosie, who was about seven, did her part helping to clean the house; everyone behaved. It is hard to conjure up an image of my father at this time. He just kept on working. I can only imagine what he was thinking and feeling. I prayed a lot, asking God to make me well.

After what seemed like a long summer, undergoing more tests and constant visits to the doctors, my prayers were answered. With a big smile on his face, one of the doctors told my mother and me that further tests showed I did not have a hole in my heart, just a heart murmur. Perhaps it was because I was growing so fast; I was so tall and so thin. Incredible news! But what did it really mean? I told the doctor I was going to high school. Would I be able to run? With another great smile, he said, "Yes! You can run and play and have a lot of fun in high school!"

It was a miracle. And once I got home and was able to start thinking about a future without surgery—about going to Providence High

School and making plans—all my symptoms disappeared. My appetite returned, my stomach felt fine and, eventually, my heart murmur disappeared.

But spending a summer in fear about my future was pivotal. I would have a future life! And I decided what I would do with it.

CHAPTER 3

My Mission

At the end of that summer, at the age of fourteen, I decided I had a mission in life. My mission was to help my parents so that my brothers and sisters could finish school and then go on to college. I didn't develop the idea too deeply. I just knew, after that worrisome summer, even more about the weight of the many burdens my parents were carrying. I wanted to help them—and I formed a plan!

A couple of years earlier, in the biography I read, Senator Margaret Chase Smith said that a secretarial job could be a stepping-stone to any career. I thought that was a great idea and it became part of my plan. Later, I learned about the possibility of going to night school, an even better idea that I added to my plan. That would open the door to someday graduating from college and eventually becoming a teacher or a social worker.

I do not recall ever telling my parents about my mission or my plan for carrying it out. I was just very aware of their situation. I saw how Mamá was always working. When we were little, she washed our clothes outside in the washtub, bent over the *tallador*. She would take in the clothes of other people, who would give her one dollar to wash them. Mamá also *planchaba ajeno* to help ends meet, even when she was pregnant. She would cook meals for us that included making flour tortillas every day in a very hot kitchen. Papá had found some paint on sale to tidy things up, but the bright royal blue seemed to scream in that kitchen and made it feel even hotter. "*¡Salte de aquí, mi'ja, está muy caliente!*" she would say, as I tried to help.

I felt sorry for her. There were things Mamá needed at home and I wanted her to have them. Cups. Plates. I remember the day my baby sister, Rosie, was baptized and her *madrina* and *padrino* were coming over for a special meal of *costillas* after the ceremony. We rarely had anyone over for a meal. Mamá wanted it to be nice. "*Anda con el Señor Elizondo y compreme dos tasas.*" El Señor Elizondo's store was a block further than Checo's and he had housewares. "*Mamá quiere unas tasas 'pa café,*" I said as I held the money ready to turn it over. "*No tengo,*" was el Señor Elizondo's response. "*Pero sí tengo estas,*" he said as he showed me some small glass custard cups. My heart sank. I could not imagine drinking coffee out of those tiny things. I do not recall if my mother sent me back to get them. I just remember how very sad and embarrassed I felt walking back home. I was around eight.

I also felt sorry for my father. He would come home after a day's work all sweaty, dirty, and his hands were full of calluses. I knew that he would be careful not to get close to people on the bus because he felt they might be offended.

Growing up, seeing these things year after year, I just wanted to help. Also, as the years went by, I saw how smart my siblings were and how hard they worked to get good grades. All five were very good students, and they never pushed my parents to get them things that other children had, like toy cars or dolls or new clothes. As our bodies grew taller our shirts, pants, and dresses could never quite keep up with our long limbs.

If we ever did compare what someone else had with what we did not have or what someone else did that we did not do, Mamá or Papá would say, *"Eso no quiere decir que ustedes deben de tenerlo o hacerlo tambien."* Other people's rules and possessions did not apply to us. Furthermore, as we were often reminded, *"La comida y la educacíon son primero."* Food and education came first. And for my parents, education meant parochial school. As Mamá and Papá would say, *"Fe en Dios es lo más importante. Es para toda la vida."* They also felt that is where we would receive the best education.

But six children going to eight years of elementary school and four years of high school was expensive no matter how low parochial school tuition was in those years. Not only did we have to pay monthly tuition and purchase uniforms and particular kinds of shoes, there were also the requirements for First Communion, Confirmation, and special school events like plays and graduations. And all this on my father's $50 per week salary as a laborer.

Mamá, however, was a miracle manager. She knew how to make food *rendir* and made do with whatever she had. She would sew for us, mending our clothes nicely. *"Pobres pero limpios,"* she would say. And she taught me how to sew on her Singer pedal sewing machine. That way I could help out. I started sewing non-school clothes for my little sister Rosie and me when I was about twelve.

We knew very well what we did not have. But after each reminder of the family priorities—food and education—we would all agree that they were good ones.

This is how my mission in life started to take shape. But before I could do anything for anyone else, I had to get through high school. I was fourteen—and on my way!

Words That Matter

Starting high school meant, first of all, taking in the smells of my brand new uniform. I wore a navy blue jockey cap, skirt and weskit, with a white blouse and navy blue and white oxford saddle shoes. My brother Felix wore khaki pants and shirt with a black tie. Carrying our books, very proud in our new school uniforms, the two of us walked to the public bus stop two and half blocks away. We would now be leaving our familiar *barrio*, crossing town to attend our new schools. Central Catholic High School was over a hundred years old, established by Marianist brothers and priests as a college prep school for boys. Providence High School had been founded four years earlier by the Sisters of the Congregation of Divine Providence. They were right across the street from each other. Aided by the Cordi Marian sisters' $50 scholarship for Felix that was used for fees, our parents paid $10 monthly tuition for Felix and $7.50 a month for me.

At Providence, I entered a life that up to then had been present only in schoolbooks and the public library. With its ivory colored walls, library, shiny floors, and wide windows looking out onto lovely trees, the school provided a great environment in which to study and learn. My fellow students all looked beautiful in their uniforms and were very smart, I thought. No one acted out like in grade school. Then again, most of those who had acted out were boys and this was an all-girls school.

When Felix and I rode the bus to school, we not only traveled across the city but from one culture to another—from our Spanish-speaking world of brown people to an English-speaking world of mostly white people. I do not recall being intimidated by the different environment. I made the daily transition from my house to the school and back quite comfortably. There were major differences in how people lived and behaved, which I noticed. But I reminded myself that my parents had sent me to the sisters to listen and to learn. Mamá and Papá would say that they could not teach me what I would learn in school. But by the time I went to high school, my parents had already poured into me the greatest teachings in life—their values. Those anchored me as I adjusted to a radically new environment.

Something else anchored me, as well. The very first week of school, my homeroom teacher, Sister Miriam Fidelis, asked a question during our homeroom period. My hand shot up and she called on me. I had the correct answer. As I was leaving the classroom, Sister Fidelis stopped me and said it was good for me to have raised my hand. She complimented me on my answer. "Keep on doing it," she said. "Class participation will be part of your grade." These simple words of encouragement in a strange new world had a powerful impact on me, setting me on the right path at Providence. Over the many years that have unfolded since then, I have shared this story with the sisters of the Congregation of Divine Providence. I have shared it with adults who work with young people. I have had the opportunity to thank Sister Fidelis for them on several occasions. Those simple words, which stayed with me all these years, helped me remain conscious all my life of the power that teachers, older friends, and mentors have on young people. Sister Fidelis's affirmation provided powerful motivation for my self-expression. My first journey out of *mi barrio* started in a grand manner! I had something to say and I would say it.

El Rancho Grande in English

I chose to enter the commercial track at high school because it would prepare me for my mission, *i.e.,* getting a job right out of high school. But I made a point of absorbing every detail of the new world that Providence opened up for me. Fresh as if it happened yesterday is the scene of a talent show held very early in my first semester. On stage I see a group of girls in flowing, pastel-colored gowns with long pointed hats singing, "Someday my prince will come." One girl sang a solo, "They wouldn't believe me…that from this great big world, you've chosen me!" Wow! I had never heard those songs before. Quietly, I noticed every detail. And one thing that really drew my attention was how girls were showing leadership in putting on that show and performing. I loved it.

The Cordi Marian sisters at Christ the King School had provided me with a very strong foundation in the core subjects, so I did very well in high school, especially in English. I was a queen of diagramming sentences and rolling out those parts of speech. I enjoyed composition classes and History came naturally. My greatest challenges were typing and shorthand—key commercial classes! I am not very well coordinated and that was a problem because I needed these skills to carry out my mission after high school. As it turned out, by graduation I could type 95 words per minute (wpm) and even received a pin for taking shorthand at 120 wpm. Although these were not the highest scores anyone achieved in the class, they were good enough to help me be job-ready. I had to keep my eyes on the prize even as I had fun in my other classes.

Music classes were a special delight. Who would have thought you could sing *El Rancho Grande*—that old familiar song from the Mexican movies we watched in the back lot of our church—in English? With great gusto, I joined my classmates in belting out, "I like to roam and wander..." The first time I heard Chopin's "Polonaise in A Flat," my heart felt like it could not contain it. I felt the same when I heard Franz Liszt's "Lebensraum." Some of the classical music was familiar. I had heard it on Spanish radio, but now I was learning the names of the compositions and composers. I was discovering that there were other ways to sing, "I love you," besides the way Jorge Negrete, Pedro Infante, Toña la Negra, and Libertad Lamarque did. Or besides the way the Hit Parade Songs did. With classical music, the soaring sounds said it all.

In the commercial track, biology was the only science class I took; it was astonishing. Every single word that Sister Eutropia uttered stayed in my mind exactly as she spoke it. I never had to study. It was as if my brain were taking pictures of the lessons. They were completely clear, as if in front of me, during the exams. I wanted to tell Sister how much I was learning, how it felt as if she were writing her knowledge directly into my brain, but I could not find the words. I remember the sheer awe when I first looked into a microscope and saw the pistil of a rose. It was tiny. It was beautiful. It was life, as I had never observed it. Of course, I went home and shared all this with my mother. She especially enjoyed hearing my biology stories because she, too, was a lover of nature. I imagine she also was just plain happy to know that I found such joy in learning.

At lunchtime and during other breaks, I hung around with the few other Mexican-American girls at Providence. Mary Helen Alvarado and Mary Tavares had graduated with me from Christ the King and there were a handful of other Mexican-Americans from Catholic schools on the Westside. The majority of the students, however, were *americanas*. On no-uniform days and special events, most girls, including Mexican Americans, wore the teenage fashions of the day—plaid pleated skirts, twin sweater sets with fur at the neck, full felt skirts with poodles on them. I did not have that kind of clothing, but that was not new. There had been girls with pretty clothing at Christ the King, too. Providence was just another place to be different that way, and that was all right with me.

Spelling the Civil Rights Movement

In May of 1955, the year I started at Providence High School, the United States Supreme Court handed down its final decision in *Brown vs. Board of Education*, ordering that desegregation occur with "all deliberate speed." In San Antonio, Archbishop Robert E. Lucey had already integrated the Catholic schools. Although Providence was still mostly Anglo, there were some Mexican-American girls there when I arrived and, during my four years, a few African-American girls also enrolled.

That December, Rosa Parks stood her ground by remaining in her seat at the front of the bus. I knew what those terrible signs at the back of the bus were like—and the courage it took for her to ignore them. She became one of my heroes and a life-long muse.

Throughout my high school years, the struggles in the south for civil rights were part of our daily news. After we got our first television set in the mid-1950s, we tuned into the *Today Show* with Dave Garaway every morning as we got ready for school. In the evening, we watched the national newscasts. It was in front of that TV that we experienced the shock of the beatings, water hosing, and violence inflicted on black people as they pursued their civil rights. Martin Luther King was our leader too.

In 1956 our whole family watched the National Democratic Convention when John F. Kennedy was nominated for vice-president. It was the first time we heard of this young Catholic politician. To the youngest child, we were all impressed and excited. It also was the first time we had seen a national political convention. Within just four years, my brothers and I would be involved in Democratic Party precinct politics, working the polls for our favorite candidates even though we could not vote. John F. Kennedy's election would be one of our first successes!

In September of 1957, during my junior year, the confrontation between Governor Orval Faubus of Arkansas and President Dwight D. Eisenhower received major television coverage. The president federalized the Arkansas National Guard to protect nine black students who simply wanted to receive their public education at Little Rock High School, in accordance with the new *Brown vs. Board* landmark legislation. I watched in amazement and could not get enough information about what was happening to these young men and women who looked a lot like me.

But at school, civil rights and issues of race or class were never discussed. Nor were they ever discussed at church! We heard the Gospel message and Jesus' command that we love one another, but it was never related to the racial unrest around us. An exception was Archbishop Lucey, who acted to desegregate Catholic schools and spoke publicly about the issues of our time. He also supported the union movement for which we were grateful because my father was part of the laborer's union for part of his working life.

The closest we came to touching on these issues at Providence was during a spelling test that Sister Patrick gave us around the time President Eisenhower sent the U.S. troops to Little Rock High School. Pacing up and down the aisles, with a book in hand and her habit swishing as she passed by, Sister Patrick pursed her lips to enunciate carefully the words we were to spell: "Se-gre-ga-tion." "In-te-gra-tion." "De-se-gre-ga-tion." She may even have stated the definitions of each word. I knew they were powerful words! But we did not talk about them. We just spelled them.

A Minus Turned Into a Plus

Early in my freshman year, we were told that a class period once a month would be devoted to attending a club meeting. We could join the Future Homemakers of America, the Future Teachers of America, the Thespian Club, or a number of other clubs. It was the Marian Choristers that really attracted me because I love to sing. It did not take me long to find out, however, that I would need to pay dues to belong to these clubs—and that for the Marian Choristers I also would need to buy a choir gown and attend many choir events. I could never ask my parents to do any of this. There was no money and we did not have a car to chauffeur me to numerous events.

I told one of the sisters that I could not join any of the clubs because they all had dues and other expenses that my family could not meet. Were there any free clubs I could join? "Of course," the sister said, telling me about the Confraternity of Christian Doctrine (CCD) and the Sodality of Our Lady. I was already doing CCD work in my church, teaching children catechism. I did not see any sense in repeating those works of mercy at school, but the Sodality was new to me, so I joined.

Besides giving me plenty of opportunities to "Pray To Jesus Through Mary," which was our motto, I got to meet students that later became the school's leaders. Because club functions were the only times, other than in class, where most Mexican-American and Anglo girls interacted, I was able to engage with white students in ways I never would have otherwise. I observed their behavior—how they spoke, how they organized events. When I went back to Providence in 1984 for my

25th reunion, I remembered the names of most of the women. Had I not been a public figure in elected office by then, few of my former classmates would have known me. They told me I was very quiet in school. I told them I was observing and learning.

The Sodality offered the opportunity to meet individually with the group's moderators, Sister Mary Michael and Sister Liberta. I also met with the school Chaplain, Father Moore. That had never happened before. Having an adult, particularly a teacher or a priest, to talk to about my life and my spirituality was significant. Confession didn't count; it was about sin and seemed punitive. Now I was able to discuss other things about my spiritual life, typically my "spiritual exercises," *i.e.,* daily mass, praying the rosary, and mental prayer. Sodality was about living a good life and I liked the challenge, even though many of the duties, like attending daily mass, were logistically difficult and "mental prayer" I never quite got. But I gave myself points for at least trying.

The nuns and priest were kind and patient with me. I could also talk about things that were important to me like my family and my plans for what I would do after I graduated. It was in some of these sessions that I was asked by the sisters to consider becoming a nun. For me, the convent was out of the question—but I did pray about it. What if I was wrong and would be miserable all my life because I did not follow my calling? I pondered the question for a long time. At a retreat while I was still in high school, a girl asked how one could be sure of one's vocation in life. The priest gave her a long answer, some of it having to do with prayer, but what struck me were the words, "Your vocation is doing what you like to do." That did it for me. What I loved was being with people and for some reason I thought convents were not people places. In addition, I already had a mission in life. I never thought about the convent again.

Religion classes were equalizers. God was God whether in the *barrio* or at school. Being a Catholic was the same whether I was at Christ the King or Providence. When it came to that intangible place within us that makes us all children of God, I felt I was like everyone else. Not better. Not lesser. I took my religion classes very seriously. After all, that was the reason my parents were sacrificing to send us to Catholic schools. Mamá and Papá always told us that those were the most important classes.

At Providence I learned more about the history and traditions of the Catholic Church. I saw its beauty but also began to see its warts, which later in life would become painful. At the time, what really captured my heart were the social justice teachings the church found at the heart of the message of Jesus. It was not enough just to go to church.

The teachings on how we treat others had to be incarnated in our own lives. In church and grade school I had already fallen in love with the idea that every person is born with "human dignity" and, as such, merits respect and good treatment. In my child's mind, that brought to mind poor people like us. We all possessed human dignity.

Consecrated to Mary

One of the highlights of my first year at Providence was the consecration to Mary that each Sodalist made upon joining the organization. The event took place at Our Lady of Grace Church three miles north of downtown. For me it was fortuitous that my Tío Luís had given me a navy blue linen suit with a white collar for my fifteenth birthday. For the special event, I wore the suit as well as my white hat and veil, gloves, and high heels from eighth-grade graduation. Feeling very special in this blue suit, I was ready for my entrance into the Sodality. My parents and some of my siblings took two buses from our home to get to the church. It was a big event for my family. There, at the age of fifteen, in front of my family, teachers, and fellow Sodalists, I made my Act of Consecration to the Immaculate Heart of Mary.

> *O Mary, My Queen and My Mother,*
> *I consecrate to you this day all of myself.*
> *And to show my devotion to you*
> *I consecrate to you my eyes, my ears,*
>   *my heart, my mouth and my whole being without reserve.*
> *Wherefore, O Loving Mother, since I am your own*
>   *defend me as your property and protection.*
> *Amen.*

I knew exactly what I was doing. Mary would always be with me. Throughout my life these words of prayer still come to me and a wisp of a memory stirs my heart as I recall my pride that day at Our Lady of Grace, and the pride of my parents.

As I approached my senior year, it was at the meetings with the Sodality moderators that sisters began to encourage me to go to college. "You would do well," Sister would say. "But I do not have the money for college," I would answer, adding that after graduation, I planned to go to work. "The sisters can help you get a scholarship to Our Lady of the Lake College." I would not be shaken off my long-planned course of action. I vividly recall asking rather emphatically, "Would you also give me money so I can help my family?" That was something they could not do. I was satisfied I could put an end to that discussion.

Through the Sodality of Our Lady, I was provided with tools and support to develop my own spiritual anchor. The time, care, and attention I was given gave me confidence. I felt cared for, respected, and loved. I have always been grateful to all the Providence High School sisters, but my deepest gratitude goes to the ones who guided me through the Sodality. Providence was good.

There was just one big hole in my education. Despite the major role that Mexicans and Mexican-Americans had played in shaping our Southwestern history and culture—and certainly that of San Antonio and Texas—my own culture and language were never a subject of study.

Knowing Everything

In May of 1959, I graduated from high school in an amazing ceremony at the Municipal Auditorium in downtown San Antonio. I had just turned 18 in April. I felt very wise and had a marvelous clarity about my life. "Now I know everything I need to know," I thought. Graduating from high school was a major milestone in my life and I felt a huge sense of accomplishment. I made myself a white broadcloth sleeveless dress, with a short cotton eyelet top for my graduation. By then, I was an expert at making those *surcidas* skirts with plenty of material and little cap sleeves for the top.

Felix graduated from Central Catholic that same May. We had both done well. We had our pictures taken in the back yard, with our diplomas. One of the photos pictures Felix and me presenting our diplomas to our parents, in gratitude. We had done it! We completed high school. Now Felix would focus on getting to college and I on finding a job and eventually starting my night school classes at San Antonio College. I was ready to begin carrying out my mission.

CHAPTER 4

At Work in the World

My first foray into the world of work took me to places I had never seen in my city. From my uncles, who after the war had gone on to work at one of the five military bases in San Antonio, I knew that civil servants, unlike my father, were paid well and had insurance benefits, sick pay, and vacations. I learned that if I passed the Civil Service Exam and qualified for a clerk's job, I would earn $3,600 a year as an entry-level GS4 clerk. I could not even imagine that much money and all we could do with it! But after going for several interviews to military installations throughout the city, challenged by trying to find bus routes that would get me there, a kind military officer opened my eyes.

It happened on my fifth interview. Despite the logistical nightmare of getting there by bus, I arrived at Wilford Hall Medical Center at Lackland Air Force Base minutes early, dressed in my usual interview attire—a rose-colored dress I had made with wide bouffant skirt, sleeves that exploded on my arms, and the very high heels that were stylish in 1959. If hired, I would work for an Air Force officer, who was both a physician and medical administrator. The officer had a welcoming face when he asked me to sit down. After a quick review of my application papers, he looked at me gravely and said, "You know, Miss Rodríguez, you are not going to get this job. You made an excellent grade on your exam and your skills are very good, but you do not have any experience."

My heart sank, as he continued, "How many interviews have you had?"

"Four," I replied. "Well," he said, "the reason you have been called to interviews is because you did so well on your exam and Civil Service requires that three persons be interviewed for each vacancy. You are being included in those three, but you will not be hired."

I did not know what to say. He spoke again. "Go downtown and get yourself a job. Work for a year and then come back to Civil Service." I was devastated, recalling what a hard time I had getting to each of those interviews. The immediate image that came to mind was of the fallen socks. Walking between barracks a few weeks earlier, on my way to an interview at another air force base, I accidentally knocked down a clothesline where soldiers had hung their socks. The soldiers at the windows laughed and yelled at me as I trotted away in my high heel shoes and rose bouffant dress, leaving in my wake a clothesline of socks on the ground. It had all been for naught.

But I took the officer's advice. And here is where friends in high places came in handy. My mother had a *comadre* whose daughter worked at S.H. Kress & Co. on Houston Street. "*Hija, porque no vas hablar con Chelo en el Kres. A ver si te dice como puedes trabajar allí.*" I followed Mamá's advice and went to the five-and-dime store to find Chelo and ask her how I could get a job at Kress. Chelo told me how to apply and then put in a good word for me. A few days later, I got a call that I had a job. I was thrilled!

On the Job

I was not given much training, just shown how the cash register works. But my first job was easy enough. I was assigned greeting cards and belts, items that were on the aisle as people walked into the store. I made myself an official greeter. "Good morning. Welcome. May I help you?" I smiled, gracefully pointing to the greeting cards and belts. Some people would only grunt or walk past me quickly, but others stopped for help or just to talk. I think they were lonely. My best customers were older ladies and those who could not read the small print or could not read English. I would spend quality time helping them search for just the right card. My first take-home pay at the end of a week was $28.10. I used part of the money to buy material to sew some dresses and a few other things I needed for work, giving the rest of the money to Mamá.

My first job only lasted two weeks. It ended on the day Sister Mary Tecla, CDP, who had taught me shorthand and typing, and Sister Rose Annelle, CDP, another business teacher at Providence High School, came into the store. As soon as they saw me, they hurried over. "What are you doing here?" Sister Tecla demanded in a loud whisper. "This is not what we trained you for." Before I had time to answer, she pulled out a business card from somewhere inside her habit and said, "Here. These are two attorneys who like to hire girls we train at Providence. Call them and make an appointment. They need a secretary."

The attorneys' office was in the beautiful Milam Building, a landmark high rise in downtown San Antonio. The real estate attorney who interviewed me was nice enough, though somewhat stiff. I was given the job, I'm sure, only because of the recommendation of the sisters. I only lasted a couple of months. Real estate transactions required filling out multiple forms with carbon copies. I did not know how to work with carbon paper and each error meant having to start all over again, wasting another set of expensive forms. The attorneys were losing patience—and money. One would stand behind me as I typed and that made me even more nervous and prone to errors.

Furthermore, the people who worked in the Milam Building acted as if they had been there since it was built in 1929—cold, unhappy, and unfriendly. It was only a matter of time before the attorneys and I had a parting of the ways, a mutually agreed upon separation. Arriving at home one Friday evening, I announced that I had quit my job. There were no questions asked. This tiny episode, however, would return almost fifty years later as a grateful memory to share with my father.

Mi Cirineo: A Last Conversation With Papá

My father died on February 27, 2008. He lived eight months longer than my mother, and he missed her terribly. By then Papá was completely blind. But he remained engaged, participating in the daily Mass on television, listening to news on a Catholic radio station, and continuing to be interested in the lives of his very large and growing family. During those eight months, Sundays were the days when we tended to have long conversations, after I prepared his breakfast and lunch.

One Sunday his mind wandered to the past, as it tended to do. *"Hija, y cuando andabas buscando trabajo ¿cómo fué que no pudiste trabajar con el gobierno?"* Daddy's mind went back to when I was looking for work in the civil service. That was all I needed—an opening to tell him a long story. So I started to describe my first days of looking for work, embellishing the story with every tiny detail I could conjure; after all, we had the whole afternoon in which to talk. When I got to the part about my experience as a legal secretary at the Milam Building, I described it down to the last piece of carbon paper. As always, Papá listened very attentively to my every word. His blindness could not hide his delight in hearing my stories.

I told him how I walked into my boss's office one Friday and announced, with great authority, "Things are not working out. I hereby give you two weeks notice and then I will resign from this job."

"You do not need two weeks," my boss replied. "You can leave today."

Papá and I laughed at this with great gusto. Then I told him that the reason I felt free to quit that job was because of the words he spoke to me when I first went to work: *"Si un día a mi hija no le gusta un trabajo o no la tratan bien que se venga a su casa. ¡Su papá la puede mantener!"* He told me never to put up with any job I didn't like or where they didn't treat me properly; he would take care of me.

My father was quiet, thought a bit, and then said. *"Qué bueno que me dijiste eso, hija. Yo creía que quizas yo era el que te empujaba que trabajaras tanto."*

I was surprised at this. I gather my father had worried all these years that he had somehow pushed me to be his *Cirineo*. That is what he called me, *Mi Cirineo*, his Simon of Cyrene, the one who had helped Jesus carry his cross. I could see his relief and joy to know that I had not felt pushed to give up so much of what it means to be a child and young woman. My parents never asked me for anything more than they were giving. I did not know that my father would die ten days later; but not before we said these words that needed to be spoken.

Typing Too Fast

Christmas was approaching and I needed a new job. I went to the Texas Employment Commission, took a typing and shorthand test and told them I would work anywhere. As usual, my test scores were tops and I was referred to The Salvation Army. They were looking for seasonal employees to address envelopes at $1 per hour for their Christmas fundraising campaign.

I was hired along with four other young women who seemed to have a lot of street smarts. Each day, with my speedy typing, I was happily banging out about 500 envelopes on a manual typewriter. One afternoon, my four co-workers came into the little room where I was working and closed the door behind them. "You type too fast," one of them told me flatly. "We get paid by the hour and at the rate you're going, we won't have work for much longer." I didn't know what to say. But even before I could find words to respond, another ordered, "So stop typing so fast!" They left as abruptly as they entered.

I was shocked—but also intimidated. What if they shunned me? Or, worse, beat me up after work? Then I got angry. Here I've worked so hard to learn how to type fast and now they want me not to do it! I refused, continuing to do my work in the same manner—fast.

When we finished typing the 25,000 envelopes a couple of weeks before Christmas, the commanding officer, Captain Ralph Morrel, called us together. Presenting each of us with a Christmas ham, he said, "I want to thank all of you for the fine work you did. The work is over and now you can leave. Except you," he added, looking at me. "You stay."

After the others left he brought in his wife, Donna, and told me I had done such good work that he wanted me to stay until after Christmas. My work would now be to complete application forms for families that were going to get food and toys for their children. I was delighted, especially because my work would involve helping poor people.

The Morrels continued to be impressed with my hard work. After Christmas, they offered me a full time job. I would serve as Captain Morrel's secretary.

I was again delighted to get a job offer. But this time, I also was a bit worried. The Salvation Army was a Protestant organization. In those years, Catholics were not allowed to attend Protestant churches and the Catholic Church was very closed to non-Catholic institutions. Before I accepted the job at The Salvation Army I decided I had better go see one of our priests to ask if the Church would allow it.

"No!" the priest said. "If you take that job, you will slander yourself."

As I walked home, I kept going over those words. How could my working with people who were serving the poor while earning money to help my family be sinful or wrong? It just didn't make sense. So without telling anyone about the priest's advice, I simply ignored it, following my heart. In early January of 1960 I started my first full-time job, earning $40 per week. I was working in a brand-new building which my father had helped to construct. Years later I realized that I had nearly doubled my family's weekly income.

Mamá's Daily Blessings

After looking forward for so many years to the day when I would finally go to work, my memories of this time are of a happy and active household. As we were growing up, each of my siblings started to go his or her own way, even though we lived together well into our twenties, and for a couple of us into our thirties. Mamá was our core companion, the anchor who monitored all our comings and goings.

She and Papá were the first to rise because he went to work very early. I could hear their hushed tones, saying a lot in few words, as people do who have been married for a long time. I do not recall Mamá and Papá ever raising their voice to each other, much less arguing. When I heard Mamá say, "*Que Dios te bendiga*," I knew Papá was walking out the door with his *lonchera* packed. Soon after, a series of "*Dios te bendiga*" would ensue, signaling the moment each of my siblings was leaving for school.

On those weekdays, I would be the last one to leave the house at about 8:15 a.m. All ready for another workday, I would walk into the kitchen.

"¡Buenos días, Mamá!"

"¡Buenos días! Como amanesió mi'ja? ¡Mira qué bonito día!"

Most mornings Mamá would give me her expert weather prognostication. "Llévate un saco porque para cuando salgas del trabajo va estar frío." Mamá could read the clouds better than any weatherperson on television. I learned I had better take a coat when she said it was going to be cold no matter how warm it felt, or I would be sorry when that Northern wind blew in later in the day.

That little kitchen was a special place for Mamá and me. After I started working, we were able to get extra things—pots, pans, utensils, Melmac plates with matching cups, pretty things that made Mamá's *cocina* really work for her as she continued to feed a large family. When I walked into that warm space, Mamá would have my breakfast ready. A cup of coffee, an egg with real *picoso* hot sauce, and a flour tortilla—that was my meal almost every day. There I was, full of *huevos rancheros* and thin as a noodle. Mamá would sit down with me. She looked so peaceful and happy. We would chat about the little things in her upcoming day or mine.

"Hija, sabes que ya parece que se va venir un buen frío y tengo que mover y tapar las matas."

"Mamá, no mueva las matas sola, están muy pesadas."

"Ay hija ustedes ni saben todo lo que hago todo el día," and then she would laugh.

Mamá was the one who kept the house running as each of us ventured off to work or to school. She was chef, gardener, manager, and budget officer who knew how to stretch a few dollars far enough to sustain eight people. She was also our chief counselor and healer. My daily checking in with her went on day after day, year after year, until I left home when I married at age 34. In Mamá's kitchen, her faithful listening and cheering on were the nourishment that gave me the strength and courage to fly very high in my ambitions to do well. I could share my stories with her; she loved to hear them.

"Bueno, Mamá, ya me voy."

"Que Dios te bendiga, mi'ja. Cuídate." A quick kiss and then I was off, crossing the street to get catch the Martin Street bus for downtown. Mamá stood at the door until the bus came. Years later, Mamá would tell me how much she enjoyed our morning visits, seeing me come into the kitchen all dressed up for the day. "Te arreglabas tan bien, con tu cabello tan negro y te veías tan bonita," she said, remarking on how good I looked. I asked her why she never told me I was *bonita* back then. Mamá said, "*Pa' que no te chiflaras.*"

Mamá did not want me to get big headed. Modesty was a critical virtue in a woman.

Advice for a Young Woman

My parents sent me away to the world of work equipped with simple and direct advice. No preaching—just a few directions that made sense to them from their own lived experience.

From my mother came words to guide the proper behavior of *una jóven* who had to work with men. "*Ser modesta y dáte a respetar,*" she would say. To be modest had many meanings. Mamá would tell me that a woman could be covered up to her neck, to her ankles and wrists, and still be immodest. I wondered how that could be. I thought it was funny! But I did not argue. I had to be responsible for myself. Another piece of advice had to do with men's behavior. "A man will start telling a girl an innocent joke and she will laugh," Mamá would say. "The next time he will tell her a salacious joke and the girl will laugh again. The jokes will keep getting worse," she warned. "Eventually, the man will start touching her hand and the girl can never know where that will end." The advice? "Never laugh at a man's joke, no matter how innocent!" Although it sounded silly, I realized I was entering another world when I went to work. It was a man's world—and I would be on my own.

My father's advice was the same as it had been since we were very little. "Give your employer a good day's work," he would say. "If you do not do your job, it is like stealing money from your employer's pocket." For my father this meant staying busy, no matter what. "If you ever finish your tasks and have nothing to do, pick up a broom or a rag and start sweeping or cleaning. There is always something that needs cleaning. Never sit without doing anything." He had definite ideas about attendance, advising me always to get to work a half hour before starting time. "That way you can prepare your work space, sharpen pencils, tidy up a bit, and prepare yourself for the day." These were definitely the values Papá carried to his own work each day of his life.

As I started my work life, it was the message beneath these words that held power for me. It had to do with living an honorable life and with being cared for deeply. Whatever the real meaning of the words, they made me feel safe.

Soup, Soap, and Salvation

Armed with Mamá's warnings about men, I was surrounded by them at my first full-time job with The Salvation Army. Nearly all were homeless, coming to our Welfare Center for food and overnight shelter. Known as "snowbirds," these homeless men tended to travel around the country, spending winter months in San Antonio. The snowbird world was a world of white men. Some became part of the revolving staff at the Welfare Center, working temporarily as cooks, registrars, or in other odd jobs. Unlike most of the homeless men who only stayed one night, these snowbirds would sign up for a longer length of time; a few actually spent several years with us. On payday I would prepare a little envelope with $7.50 in cash for each one. That was their only pay because, as Captain Morrel would say, if they got any more they would just buy beer with it. The Salvation Army's motto was "Soup, Soap, and Salvation."

These men became my friends and our staff their family. Besides myself there was another woman office worker, a couple who were the lodge keepers, and my boss and his wife. Some of the men, like "California" and "Montana," were big and burly. Mr. Williams, with no first name, was small and had curly red hair. All had secret lives. Once in a while, one would allow some personal disclosure. Our cook had been a chef at the Waldorf Astoria in New York; one of the snowbirds was a lawyer and another a craftsman who had made wooden music organs. Mr. Moore was the gentlemanly registrar. For the time they were with us, these men were my teachers. I would talk to them about what we were doing in the office and about our special programs. They liked to hear about my family. The men lived in their own world and although they came from all over the place, many knew each other because they rode the same railway cars from one end of the country to the other. Mr. Moore had a card file. When a man showed up for food or shelter, Mr. Moore would usually know if he were in his card file.

Most of the men were surprised when I called them "Mister." They joked about it, but really liked it. I loved hearing stories about their lives, whenever they were willing to share, although they were usually tragically sad. Most of the men were victims of alcoholism. They had lost careers and families and then began wandering the country. Although they had very little money, at Christmas, Easter, my birthday, and especially on Valentine's Day, I became the queen of cards, flowers, and presents. One time they all chipped in and bought me a cowgirl hat and boots for what would be my first trip to the rodeo with my boss, his wife, and children. These rough and tough men who traveled in rail cars, slept in the streets, and went without food for days, seemed genuinely happy to treat me as if I were their own daughter. They protected me.

Inevitably, each would eventually leave. Often after holidays, I would return to find one of them gone. Captain Morrel would tell me that "Mr. X" was probably drunk someplace; he would set out to look for him. It usually happened around Thanksgiving, Christmas, or New Year's. The Captain said it was the time they missed their real families the most, and could not take it. After a drinking binge, they would feel so embarrassed they wouldn't come back. I ached for them, missing each one who left.

My best chum at work was California, a very tall strong man and a veteran. One day he got very sick and was taken to a military hospital. As soon as I found out, I gathered a bouquet of yellow mums and sent them to him with one of the other men. They told me he really liked them, but the next day, California died. Around the same time, Mr. Williams, who had hung around the Welfare Center for several years, got terribly sick. When the men were laying him down in the back of a station wagon to take him to the hospital, he was vomiting blood. It was all over him. He looked at me as they took him away and died soon after, a horrible death from cirrhosis of the liver.

I shed many tears over these men, who showed me a tragic side of life to which I had never been exposed. But they also showed me great care. Soon after being elected City Councilwoman, I faced the issue of growing homelessness in San Antonio, especially in the downtown areas. By then, homelessness was not just an issue for me; the homeless had a face.

The Vague Apprehension

During my six years at the Salvation Army, I came to know a few other people who were wonderful work friends and mentors. Matilda, a Salvationist, was the friendly social worker. She shared her love of poetry and music with me and would ask me questions about my life and family. I could ask her things I would never ask my mother about being a woman when women's roles were changing so much. She moved out of town after a year, but we remain friends to this day.

Another Salvationist was a frail, thin woman in her late sixties whose job was to collect money at local bars on Friday and Saturday nights. Of course, we never used the word "bar." Mrs. Harris simply collected along "the route." On Mondays she would arrive with bags of money, mostly coins that I would count and prepare for the Captain to deposit at the bank. The best routes were on the Westside where her donors were mostly Mexican. Passing around her fundraising tambourine, Mrs. Harris would collect a little something from practically everyone—the bar owners, bartenders, waitresses, and patrons. They called her Grandma. In exchange, she would give them a smile and offer to pray for them.

Experiences with some other people at The Salvation Army were difficult. They came up in the context of my being, for the first time in my life, pretty much alone in a white world where racism was an ever-present undercurrent, just under the surface, if not bubbling up outright.

In her autobiography, Pauli Murray, one of my heroes, described so well the feelings it evokes. "More often race was the atmosphere one breathed from day to day, the pervasive irritant, the chronic allergy, the vague apprehension which made one uncomfortable and jumpy."[1]

The vague apprehension sharpened acutely with The Salvation Army's intake worker who arrived after Matilda left. This white woman was the individual who dealt with all the people, mostly brown women and children and some black, who came to us with their myriad needs, from food and shelter to medicine and clothing. I would always have a sinking feeling of embarrassment and powerlessness when I would hear her arguing with or yelling at clients. Often she would come to my door and ask me things like, "Why do Latin people ask, '*Who me*?' when I ask them a question and they are the only ones in the room?" Or, "Why do Latin women have babies when they are not married?"

I was stunned by her questions and hurt by the grimaces she would make, as if talking about disgusting people. She was much older than I and I did not know how to respond. Eventually, I shared the incidents with my boss and he would talk to her. She quit her behavior for a while but then would start again. At some point, she started asking me to help her translate for the Spanish-speaking clients. By using words other than those she spoke I could spare at least some of the clients her disdain. But why was she treating me like an exception?

Captain Morrel and his wife, Donna, tried to insulate me from the outright racist attitudes that would rise from time to time. So did their successors, Captain Rolan and Mrs. Doris Chambless. When someone at the dining table would start talking about an African-American or a Mexican, they would change the conversation. I noticed and appreciated that, but I also started to see more deeply into the unfairness and injustice of these attitudes and the way they were institutionalized. I saw how people of color and marginalized communities were provided services but also put in a category of "other." We served them but they were not part of us.

I was treated like an exception. I was the young Mexican-American woman who was not like the other Mexicans or Mexican Americans. I was a good Christian, from a good and hard working family. I was *different*. That was the message I got, and it was what made me feel so uncomfortable. I did appreciate being treated kindly, but I was not different from anyone else in my community. It hurt when I saw the condescension in behaviors toward people who looked like my mother or father, or who were poor. I was part of my community, and proud of it. Treating me one way and my people another was not right.

On a few occasions, there was nothing subtle about the atmosphere of race we breathed. The women from our office had a routine of going to Joske's for a special lunch at the elegant Camellia Room on Fridays. That weekly outing was very special for me. One Friday in 1961, we stood in line behind a roped-off area, waiting to be seated. When our turn came, the hostess moved the rope aside to let our party into the dining room. Mrs. Morrel and Matilda were in line ahead of me as the hostess gestured for them to pass through. As soon as she saw me, however, she put the rope back in place, blocking me from walking into the dining room.

My heart sank and my face flushed with embarrassment. I saw the shocked faces of my fellow workers. Mrs. Morrel told the hostess, "Let her in. She is with us." The hostess looked at me and then removed the rope. My stomach was in knots. But I followed my co-workers to our table and we sat down to lunch.

It was not until after I got home and had time to think about it that I had a chance to take in what had happened. Then, my embarrassment grew. But this time it was over the fact that I actually walked into that dining room instead of walking out. I knew that African Americans were working to integrate San Antonio's restaurants at that time. Now, just because some white people spoke up for me, I was let in. I felt I had crossed a picket line. To this day that action shames me. Not long after this incident all the lunch counters and restaurants in San Antonio were desegregated; but I did nothing to help the cause when I had the chance. I made up my mind that I would never make that kind of mistake again. I had to live my values in every part of my life.

Cruelty

Eventually, Mrs. Harris also left The Salvation Army, as did the Morrels and their successors, the Chamblesses, who also were very kind employers and great mentors. The officer who came after Captain

Chambless, however, was very different. As soon as he arrived, he started taking responsibilities away from me, giving them to a woman he had brought with him. I got the clear message that I would have to look for work elsewhere, and I did, finding another job very soon. I gave him two-weeks' notice.

One morning soon after I had turned in my letter of resignation, he called me into his office. The entire staff was there, standing in a circle. With a hateful face that I will never forget, he accused me of telling stories about him. He said I had accused him of having an affair. When I heard those words—total untruths—my mind blurred and I went into some kind of shock. Through the blur, I heard a threat that he was going to sue me and take me to court. In one second, as if in a dream, I saw what "sue" and "court" could do to my family. I was unable to speak. My co-workers all just stood silent. Terror gripped me, my legs went weak. Slowly I slipped to the floor and as I did, a wail of fear came out of me.

I do not know how long I was on the floor or much of what happened after that. I just remember that the officer's wife, a kind woman who had not been in the room, eventually picked me up and helped me into my office where I continued crying. By then the office had emptied of others. The cruel officer's wife was my angel that day. When I finally was sufficiently composed, I left the office. Still stunned and deeply distraught, I knew I could not go home right away. Instead of going to my bus stop, I walked to West Commerce Street, walked under the expressway, and then kept walking. I walked and walked until I reached St. Joseph's Church downtown. This was not something I could share right away with my family. It was too painful. There was only one place where I could shed all the tears I had and leave behind my pain—with Mary at the Christmas crèche set up in the sanctuary.

After I got home, I told my family that I had to leave work quickly because they had not been nice to me. That evening my father and one of my brothers took me back to the office to pick up my things. I never again returned to that place where for six years I had been so happy. It had become like my second home. I made a promise to myself after leaving The Salvation Army: I would never again give everything to a job the way I did with that job. And I learned a painful lesson—doing well is no guarantee that you will be treated well.

Four days later, on December 26, 1966, I started my next job—at Hemisfair '68.

Behind the Scenes 1

During these early years of my work life, the nation was undergoing great political foment and unrest. But neither my workplace nor my evening classes at school were places where I could engage in discussions about current events, particularly those involving politics. My political views, however, continued to be shaped behind the scenes of my daily employment, at home and in my neighborhood.

My brothers continued to bring home books from the library and would share what they learned in school. Some of the most interesting books I read in those years shed light on the history we were living, especially on issues of racism. In *Malcolm X* and Eldridge Cleaver's *Soul On Ice*, I read from black men themselves about the conditions people faced in our country. I was fascinated by *Black Like Me*, where John Howard Griffin tells the story of how he, a white man, traveled the South disguised (painted!) as a black man, encountering the ugliness and danger of racism. Of course, we also avidly followed the unfolding civil rights movement and other current events on television. Martin Luther King continued to be our leader.

My first foray into political activism was in response to an invitation from my brother Louis to attend a demonstration in front of the Majestic Theater in 1961. At the time, African Americans had to enter through a "Colored" door in the back of the theater and sit in the highest balcony in the back. A group of college students from St. Mary's University organized a stand-in, led by Lionel Castillo. As described in a history journal, "twenty-five white or Hispanic students paired with black would attempt to buy tickets at the main entrance. When the blacks were refused admittance into the theater, the pair would move to the end of the line and start the process again."[2] I only attended one of these stand-ins but several were held throughout the year. Eventually, the Majestic Theater was desegregated and other theaters in San Antonio followed.

In the early 1960s, our entire family became supporters of Cesar Chávez in his efforts to secure better working conditions for farm workers—something we all understood. We followed his United Farm Workers movement and stood in solidarity with him and the farm workers. When he called for a boycott of grapes we joined; our family did not eat grapes for many years.[3]

The feminist movement was also stirring at this time but I was not taken by gender issues, at least not as they were being played out in the mainstream media. I was intrigued by all the fuss around Betty Friedan's

The Feminine Mystique. She wrote of the feminine mystique that had women stuck in unhappy marriages, about reproductive restrictions and motherhood. It was difficult for me to identify with those issues; my reality seemed so different. I was nowhere close to being a married woman, much less a mother. I did not even have a boyfriend. My focus was on being a breadwinner for a family living in poverty and on pursuing a higher education—the first woman in my family to do so.

Bringing money into the home had brought with it authority, which I shared with my parents as I helped to make family decisions. Even though I was living at home, I never felt my life restricted or impeded in any way. Had I thought more profoundly about the issues Friedan was raising, I would have seen that it was I, a young woman, who was out working to help the family. I would also have seen that sexism and misogyny were around me and had been present in the lives of my foremothers.

But I did not go there. The messengers at the time were not speaking to my experience. The women I related to and whose lives inspired me and gave me strength were my grandmothers, aunts, neighbors, women at church, and my own mother. It was as if what was being written on women's issues did not include the bravery and the struggles of these women simply to put food on the table and raise children against incredible odds. These women were part of a strong community that they nurtured and led. They struggled for their families and communities. My point of reference for achieving womanhood was being a strong woman. As my mother would say, "*Ya eres una mujer hecha y derecha,*" meaning I was already a woman with strong values and character.

Nonetheless, I did consider myself a feminist as I defined it. I was a woman who was creating her own path, had her own mission in life, was proud of who she was, and worked hard to fulfill her dreams. I was proud to be walking a path that women in my family had not been able to walk before. I was actually moving to liberate not only myself from poverty but also my entire family.

I would have to wait a while to gain a more in-depth analysis of the women's liberation movement and how it affected Mexican-American women. I would have to wait until I met other women like myself, who would join to found the Mexican American Business and Professional Women's Club of San Antonio. And for my birth as a Chicana feminist, I would have to wait until the fortuitous day after I was already married and a full-time student, when I read Martha Cotera's *The Chicana Feminist.* Martha would provide new ideas on how to look at my life. She would affirm my new self-identification as a Chicana.

Behind the Scenes II

The first time I learned about politics with a small "p" was when I was thirteen at Christ the King School. One of the Cordi Marian sisters gathered a group of girls and invited us to join the *Juventud Cordi Mariana* (JCM), a group dedicated to good works. One day one of the sisters announced, "We are having a meeting to plan going over to a poor *barrio* to teach the children catechism." I wondered what a neighborhood poorer than ours would look like. And I was intrigued by the idea of going to a "meeting;" I had never been to one before.

When the meeting was over and we went to teach the children, I recall feeling very happy about the whole project. I thought how wonderful it was to have a "meeting," to plan with others and then do something good together. That was politics with a small "p"—and my first membership in an organization. My aunts and father were a bit disappointed that I had not joined the *Hijas de María*, which was the church organization that the women in my family had belonged to when they were young. But my mother was happy with my choice. I did not like the *Hijas* because I thought they were too pious; they only got together to pray. I wanted more action, and the JCM provided that for me.

Now, as a working woman who also attended school at night, I made time to engage in my neighborhood and in issues involving our Mexican-American community. Most of my efforts involved our church, whose leadership had changed in 1969 when some socially conscious diocesan priests were assigned to Christ the King. These young priests were animated by the pronouncements of the Second Vatican Council, with its new view of church as "the people of God" and its outlook of engagement in the world. These priests were not afraid of change, encouraging young people to get involved and participate.

Our liturgies came alive and the music we used was modern. We took responsibility for parish decisions as we created the mandated parish council. My pastor, Father Lawrence Matula, encouraged me to run for president of the newly formed council. He even wrote me a letter, telling me I had leadership skills that I should apply. No one had ever told me that and I took his words to heart. But I was not brave enough to run for president of the parish council as he had urged me; I ran for vice-president and won.[4] When the invitation went out for women to become lectors, I became the first woman to read Scripture in the sanctuary of Christ the King Church. It was actually the first time I stood before a microphone and spoke.

The Vatican Council had directed the Catholic Church to open its windows and move with the signs of the times. Father Matula and Father Richard Kramer not only opened windows, but also doors, making our church buildings available for all kinds of community meetings. It was in that church hall, under the auspices of the Catholic Archdiocese Office of Mexican American Affairs, that I attended my first leadership-training course given by Father Edmundo Rodríguez, SJ. Father Rodríguez led us through an analysis of the Vatican II documents. I recall being moved when I read that Christians needed to be everywhere in the world—in education, business, health, and government. In those words I heard "political involvement" receive a blessing. I saw it as a way to promote the social justice teachings of my church.

Among the meetings I attended at our church hall were some sponsored by the Community Action Program (CAP)—a federally sponsored initiative spawned by President Lyndon Baines Johnson's War on Poverty. Its purpose was to help provide input at the grassroots level on strategies to address poverty.[5] This was a time when policymakers were seeking to provide poor people with a "hand up" rather than a "handout." It required grassroots action, participation, and initiative.[6]

Determined to make a difference, I seized the opportunities being offered, becoming part of the group of local citizens who created our own bottoms-up local community action corporation under the federal CAP initiative. I did not choose to serve on the board of the corporation but had input into its mission and the selection of board members from our neighborhood; we were to hold one-third of the seats. That organization would go on for years, helping many people on the Westside until the federal government, under future presidents, eliminated the program.

Although there has been much debate over the success of the War on Poverty—it certainly did not eliminate poverty—the effort offered some important opportunities. Through the CAP effort, my neighbors and I realized that we had a rightful place at the table along with elected officials and others in making decisions that would affect our future. We developed leadership skills, gained confidence, and learned valuable lessons about community organizing and how government works. I learned more about the wisdom held by our people and also, painfully, about the depth of poverty in my community. Most importantly, I came to understand the critical necessity of citizen participation in government.

Two Worlds at HemisFair '68

When I realized that my work at The Salvation Army was not on a sure footing, I again went to the Texas Employment Commission to apply for work. I took a typing and shorthand test and passed with flying colors. They sent me to the HemisFair '68 offices to interview for a job where I would serve as the sole secretary for the legal department. HemisFair '68 was a major public-private venture built on nearly 100 acres in San Antonio's southeast downtown. The first designated "world's fair" in the U.S. southwest, HemisFair '68 hosted pavilions sponsored by more than thirty nations during the six months it was open, from April to October of 1968. A central feature of the Fair was the construction of the 750-foot-tall Tower of the Americas.

My extensive experience at The Salvation Army and a recommendation from one of its board members landed me a final interview with John A. Daniels, the General Counsel for HemisFair '68, who would make the decision. I was very honest and explained why I had left my previous job. I have no idea what I put in my application because the only question Mr. Daniels asked me was, "How on earth did your father send all of you to Catholic schools on a laborer's job?" Mr. Daniels was a Catholic himself. He then announced, "Although you have never been a legal secretary, we think you can do the work. You are hired." I later learned that there had been twenty-seven applicants for the job.

Mr. Daniels accepted my request to advance my starting day. A tough and efficient guy of few words, Mr. Daniels was a good family man and a kind employer. There were many young people working at Hemisfair '68 and it was an exciting place to be employed. I was trained in the most up-to-date office technology available.

In the executive offices where I worked, I again found myself to be the only Latina and person of color. I did not make close friends. The vague discomfort I had experienced at The Salvation Army was ever present. By then, however, I figured that anywhere I went I would face discrimination, whether blatant or subtle. It was something I would just have to live with.

The Fair actually comprised two tiers of workers and actors. One was the hundreds of young workers who did the hands-on work building the projects or working in places like the mailroom; the others were the heavies who made the decisions and led the departments.

My father was among those who did the hands-on work, helping to construct the tower. He would drive us to work everyday. As we drove straight out Martin Street and then onto Nueva, we could see the

HemisFair tower rising higher each day. It was exciting for both of us. On the way, we would talk about what was happening at work. I was very busy and loved my work; Papá was proud of his. After dropping me off at my office, he would go to work on the site.

I would arrive very early, before the other people who worked inside—the heavies, the fair officials, and department heads. The only other person at the executive offices at that time was the president of HemisFair, Jim Gaines. We would chat as he prepared his broth and I fixed a cup of coffee. I arrived full of energy; he seemed very tired and worried all the time.

Counterculture from a Window

HemisFair '68 was an environment charged with people who held great power and influence. Mr. Daniels had key political friends who were tied to the Good Government League (GGL) that had held political sway in our city government for decades. I would often accompany Mr. Daniels to meetings with these influential individuals, taking notes. The power they leveraged was impressive. Sometimes after a quiet luncheon where I had heard certain names mentioned and decisions made, I would read a story in the newspaper later that showed those decisions had become public policy.

In those years Texas was a one party state. Democratic. I soon learned the differences between the conservatives and the liberals of the party. There were even interesting spats that played out in the news media. A few men had decided we would have a world's fair and governments would be involved and it happened. What occurred to me was that if politics could be used to create a world's fair, politics could also be used to improve my community. My job then was to remain focused and continue my education so that one day I could put to use what I was learning.

At HemisFair '68 I learned something else about powerful men. When I was alone in the office one day, one of the city's well-known and influential businessmen came behind my desk and accosted me. I was shocked. He was someone who visited often and I thought he was a respectful man. I quickly managed to get out of his grip and ran out of the office. It says a lot about the times and my own consciousness at age 27 that I never said anything to anyone about this. *I* was embarrassed! The man never tried anything like that again—and in all my years of work no one ever disrespected or harassed me in that manner again. But it was a learning experience. And the day I came across a book about women's rights in the workplace, I bought it. I made it my business to learn what I could so that I could protect myself and be of help to other women. It was not until then that I realized what sexual harassment was—it was not simply a personal matter.

There were other changes occurring around me that reflected the major social changes underway in our country. From the window behind my desk I could see the young staff of the Design & Architecture Department walking in and out of their offices. "Hippies," some of the executives called them. A few of the young women had long hair and wore bandanas, long colorful skirts, paisley blouses, sandals without hose, and no makeup. The young men sported colorful pants and shirts, sandals, and several had really long hair. That was as close as I came to the countercultural revolution of the 1960s! The only influence they had on me was to inspire a more adventuresome "look." I started wearing pants to work—and even to church! Polyester pantsuits, at that.

Despite the highly charged political atmosphere at HemisFair, I was stunned to find it was "business as usual" when I walked in after Martin Luther King was assassinated on April 4 and Robert F. Kennedy on June 5 of 1968. The tragedies had been the subject of all our conversations at home and in my neighborhood. We were devastated. At work, however, it was as if nothing unusual had happened. Perhaps some people felt as I did. I do not know; no one talked about the deaths. When Bobby was murdered, I thought for sure we would postpone the opening of the Fair. But the grand opening was held as scheduled, on June 6, 1968.

It was another example of the major disconnect I continued to feel between what I experienced at home and in my neighborhood and my life at work.

Big "P" Political Realities

During the couple of years I was on the job at HemisFair, I met many politicians—the Governor of Texas, a U.S. Senator, Congressmen, and local officials. I was very happy when I had a chance to meet my own Congressman, Rep. Henry B. González, author of the Hemisfair '68 legislation. My family and I admired him very much. I also met business people from all over the world, as well as some heads of state and well-known entertainers.

The HemisFair legal office was a "one-girl" shop—me—so I got to do everything from transcribing and typing documents to making copies of all contracts for federal and state governments, exhibitors, concessionaires, and foreign governments that would participate in the Fair. This was the first position I held that affirmed and required me to use my knowledge of Spanish. The Spanish I learned at home served me well in my dealings with dignitaries and business people from Mexico and Latin America. I eventually decided to take some formal Spanish language and writing courses offered by a branch of the Universidad Nacional Autónoma de Méjico (UNAM), which was established on the grounds after the Fair closed. I also took such courses at Our Lady of the Lake University (OLLU).

An incredibly organized and tidy executive, Mr. Daniels pushed me as I had never been pushed before. He would assign tasks that were difficult and totally unfamiliar to me. I would hesitate but always thought, "If Mr. Daniels thinks I can do it, I probably can." I would meet the challenges each time.

In the end, HemisFair '68 showed me how political power can cut both ways. It can make you friends but also enemies.

Before HemisFair '68 ended, Mr. Daniels resigned as General Counsel because of political differences among the Fair leaders. He did not tell me this directly but I knew; so when he told me he was leaving, I responded that I would leave, too. In his dry and candid style, he said: "That's silly. I have a job to go to. You don't." To which I replied, "I don't care. If they can get along without you, they can get along without me, too." It was a matter of loyalty.

Soon after, Mr. Daniels offered me a job as secretary for the Democratic Party of Bexar County, where he served as chairman. That was my official entry into big "P" politics. I helped him open and staff San Antonio's 1968 campaign office for Democratic presidential candidate Hubert H. Humphrey. I was steeped in politics and loved it. The work was a piece of cake compared to my responsibilities at HemisFair '68. I met more elected officials and learned even more about party politics. Some of it, deeply distressing.

The year 1968 had been devastating. Political assassinations, riots, anti-Vietnam War protests. Violence erupted at the 1968 Democratic Convention. I had opened our headquarters so that volunteers could watch the coverage from Chicago where the Democratic Convention was being held. Then I had to close it because we were getting threatening calls. People were calling to say how horrible the party was being to the young people in Chicago. I understood; in my heart I too was cheering for the young people.

After we lost that presidential election to Richard Nixon, Mr. Daniels offered me a permanent job in the Democratic Party office. I worked there briefly for him and for the next chairman, but I had lost interest in big "P" politics. I resigned again without having another job. But destiny would eventually take me back to politics.

An Important Phone Call

I again went to the Texas Employment Commission and took another typing and shorthand test. I did even better than previously and was referred to Local 1517 of the American Federation of Government Employees, which represented Kelly Air Force Base. It just so happened that Fernando Rodríguez, my fellow parishioner at Christ the King, was its president. He hired me as secretary of the Local and I soon immersed myself in civil service labor issues and the workings of a labor union. I liked it, even though it took me two long bus rides to get to the Kelly area.

After only a few months of working at the union, I received a call from County Judge Blair Reeves, offering me a job as his executive secretary at the Bexar County Courthouse. Judge Reeves was a good friend of Mr. Daniels and had met me at HemisFair; he liked my work. I decided to talk it over with Mr. Rodríguez. If I accepted I would not only be leaving a job I had only started months earlier, but I had another worry.

Judge Reeves had been elected in 1966 after a very controversial campaign against the incumbent, a liberal county judge named Charlie Grace. The Reeves campaign had used a scare tactic with racist undertones that came to be known as the "Black Hand Campaign." The implication was that liberal forces were taking over the courthouse. Charlie Grace had been very popular with our Mexican-American community and we had been offended by the campaign. Judge Reeves won the election with the support of the Good Government League and San Antonio Mayor Walter W. McAllister. The GGL had held a tight grip over San Antonio's politics and government since 1954, with an at-large form of elections that left out the minority community.

Mr. Rodríguez was a wise man and trusted advisor. He told me that Judge Reeves was a good man, open and fair. By then Reeves had been in office for three years and Mr. Rodríguez respected him. "Accept the position," Mr. Rodríguez advised. "It will open doors for you and you will find ways to use the position to help your community. You and I will continue working for our community together." I took the job.

María Cervantes Rodríguez, a widow, imagined life could be better for her children. She insisted my grandparents and father be with her in Texas as the 1910 Mexican Revolution was about to start. (Place and date of photograph unknown.)

Sebastiana Ramírez Rodríguez, my paternal grandmother, with son Mariano. (Photo: July 1914)

Félix Cervantes Rodríguez, my paternal grandfather. He died from tuberculosis in March 1937 at the age of 51. (Photo: mid-1930's)

Rodríguez Family. *Left to right, top row:* Gregorio (Goyo), Félix, Apolinar (Polo), Mariano (Man) and Luís. *Front row:* Cosme, Grandfather Félix, Luz, Grandmother Sebastiana holding Baby Eduarda (Lala). (Photo: 1925)

Left to right: Rodríguez uncles Luís, Gregorio, Mariano, Félix and my father, Apolinar. (Photo: July 25 1920)

6   7

Left: Uncle Gregorio Rodríguez was first to die of tuberculosis in 1934. He was only 18 years old. *Right:* Uncle Félix Rodríguez succumbed to tuberculosis in December 1937 at the age of 25. (Photos 1930's)

8

Melecio Puente Arredondo and Teresa Milan Torres, my maternal grandparents. (Photo 1950's)

Above: Sixta Torres Arredondo, my mother, in her own hand-sewn dress. On the rancho, in Lockhart, Texas. Photo: (Photo: circa 1928)

Below: Papá stayed in touch with news of the day even at the secluded Lockhart rancho. (Photo: mid-1930's)

Sixta and Aunt Rosita showing off the fashions of the day on bridge in Lockhart, Texas farm road. (Photo: mid-1930's)

Great-grandmother María's eyes are deep set as she stares at you through the picture. Here with her children. *Left to right, standing:* Asunción (Chonita), Grandfather Félix, son-in-law Aristeo Mojica and María Mojica. Seated are Grandmother Sebastiana and Great grandmother María. (Photo: early 1930's)

Above: Teresa, my maternal grandmother, worked in the fields until she got very sick with heart disease. She loved to work inside her home, cooking and baking. (Photo: mid-1950's)

Above right: Papa's inscription behind this photo: *"En prueba de mí cariño dedico este a mí querida, Sixta."* (Photo: October 30, 1937.) They would be married exactly a year later. *Above left:* Memorable words are also on the back of this photo: *"A mí inolvidable Apolinar dedico este en pueba de el grande amor que te profeso, quien te ama y es tuya. Sixta."* (Photo: March 12, 1938.) *At left:* Apolinar and Sixta in a studio photograph taken a few days after their wedding on October 30, 1938, at St. Michael's Church in Uhland, Texas. The couple celebrated with family and friends at the rancho in Lockhart.

With my big brother
Felix. Laredo, Texas.
(Photo: November
1941)

After living with extended family for a while after we arrived from Laredo, we moved to Vermont Street. Louis was born there. (Photo: 1942)

Mamá made me a purple velveteen dress from a little *retazo* for a formal studio photograph of Felix and me as we welcomed Baby Louis. This photo was sent to Uncle Luís when he was deployed in WWII. (Photo: Reyes Studio, San Antonio, Texas, 1943)

Above: At Welita Sebastiana's house on Pace Alley just blocks from our house. *Left to right:* Papá, Sebastiana, Mamá. *Front:* Felix, Louis (on chair) and me. (Photo: 1944)

The war ended. My aunts fixed my hair in 1940's style and we captured the joyous moment. Our uncles would be coming home! (Photo: August 1945)

Felix and I celebrate our First Communion at Welita Sebastiana's house. (Photo: Mother's Day, 1948)

Me, Felix, Mamá with Theresa, Papá with Miguel, and Louis. (Photo: 1946)

In front of Christ the King Church on our 8th grade graduation day. *Far right:* Felix. *Middle, back row:* Me. (Photo: May 1955)

A magnificent day. I could now go to work, having graduated from Providence High School. *Class photo above courtesy of Providence High School archives.* (Photo: Spring 1959) *At right:* Felix graduated from Central Catholic. (Photo: May 1959)

Below: Mamá and Papá celebrate their 25th wedding anniversary, October 1963. *Left to right:* Rosie, Theresa, Me, Mamá, Papá, Felix, Louis and Miguel.

As administrative assistant to the Bexar County Judge. (Photo: early 1970's)

29

Our first steps together as Manuel and María Antonietta Berriozábal.
(Photo: August 9, 1975)

Creativity at the Courthouse

Arriving at the Bexar County Courthouse in June of 1969, I felt like I had gone back in time. The work was neither challenging nor stimulating. But with Judge Reeves's encouragement I began to create a new role for the County Judge's office and a new job for myself.

Judge Reeves insisted that I use my knowledge of the community to create ways to help people. He was very affirming, telling me that because of my community and church work, I had influence in the larger community. I should use that influence in the office. "With influence one should help the public," he would say.

Whether it was the constituents who would come in for waivers for marriage licenses, or liquor licenses, or ex-parte birth certificates (birth certificates where no father's name appears on the document), I enjoyed relating to the public. I listened to people's problems and found ways to take care of their issues. I was able to provide services that had never been delivered through that office before. I did things like help families locate relatives who had been sent to jail in a system so inaccessible that their relative actually got lost in the antiquated paper-only system. There were people who needed social services or food or who had problems with employment or were roaming the streets homeless—all these got my serious attention.

Judge Reeves used his resources to adapt or change policies, making our office more constituent friendly, particularly when it came to language and culture. Over time, word got out. We had many more people coming to avail themselves of the services and I had a much more satisfying job. One of the most wonderful things that occurred was that my brother, Louis, passed the bar exam and was hired by the district attorney's office. By 1971, Polo and Sixta had two children working at the courthouse. They were rightly proud.

When I first arrived in Commissioners Court I was again the only Latina; I also was much younger than the other workers. Opal Fling, the administrative assistant who had worked there for thirty years, and David García, the probate assistant, were very helpful and supportive but there were others who posed challenges. My "office" was a fish bowl set up in the middle of the public area. I could hear everything when staff and others in the courthouse gathered to talk—even what was said in individual offices near my work area, if it was loud enough. While most people were respectful, some of the comments I overheard reflected the ever-present, underlying racism that seemed to permeate every institution. There were times when someone would call out a racist joke and people laughed. I pretended not to hear, saying nothing while I just kept working. I sometimes wondered if they even knew what they were saying because it was so blatant and accepted. It made it even harder for me that everyone was so much older than I; how could I call them on it?

One day when Judge Reeves was driving me home because of bad weather, I told him that I was going to quit. "There are people in the office who make racist remarks about Mexicans and African Americans," I said. He quickly responded, "If you ever want to quit because you are going to get married, or go to college full time, or you just do not like me or the job, I will accept your resignation, but not for this. What you do, María," he advised, "is continue to do your job well, helping people. Use my name and the resources of my office as much as you can to find ways to help more. That is the way you respond. Stay and learn and do all you can." I followed his advice.

That secretarial job would eventually develop into the major position that exists today in county government. It was during my watch that the duties started to evolve. During those years, the federal government was creating major programs to be managed at the local level in an effort to shift greater control to local and state governments.[7] However, it was cities not counties that were the recipients. Eventually, county government was made eligible too. On occasion I would open the Judge's mail and announce, "Hey, here is a way that the county can get a lot of money. All we have to do is fill out this form." His response was always the same, "But who is going to do it?" To which I would respond, "I will." His big approving smile was all the nod I needed to go after the funds.

At the time there was no infrastructure at the Courthouse to help me fill out those application forms. I found ways, however, seeking the help of people and offices outside of county government, such as Al Notzon of the Alamo Area Council of Governments. His staff would get me the statistics we needed and I would do the rest. These were among the first steps taken in establishing new ways that county government could help its constituents. In doing this work, I gained experience that went far beyond the job of an executive secretary. After a couple of years, when Opal Fling retired, Judge Reeves promoted me to serve as his administrative assistant, a position I held until I left the job in June of 1975.

Gaps

In addition to encountering racism at the County courthouse, I also came face to face with sexism in the form of the disparity in wages between men and women. I had been responsible for bringing the County Judge's office up to modern times. I had created new ways that the office could serve the public. I had done the research, submitted applications, and worked through the logistics of setting up offices to manage new federally funded programs. Yet even though I attained the title of administrative assistant to the highest elected county official, my salary did not match my new responsibilities.

I asked Judge Reeves several times for a raise. He seems to have tried, but he would say that he could not do it because the Commissioners would not support more funds for me when their secretaries could not get the same treatment. I never even thought to apply for the director positions of the new offices I was helping to set up, such as employment and training. I now see that I could have been very competitive with the men who actually got the positions. The proverbial glass ceiling was well in place when it came to my courthouse position; Judge Reeves could not or would not break it. Still, I think he was the best employer he could be under the circumstances. He was a good man in the midst of an archaic system trying to join the modern world.

By the time I left the County Judge's office, I left behind a very different office. Judge Reeves hired Ed Day to manage federal grants and programs. He had already hired two young women to help with the secretarial duties and casework—a Latina and an African American. Over the years, people's behavior in our offices became more accepting of the diversity of our city, perhaps because we were seeing so many new faces in our office due to the services we had added. The times were changing too. I left with a whole education on inter-governmental relationships and human relationships, as well as two thoughts about Judge Reeves.

Judge Reeves's motto on elected public service has always stayed with me. I took it to heart when I became an elected official: "Never love your job so much that you are afraid to lose it," he would often say. The other thought concerns Judge Reeve himself. Fighting as a Marine during a battle at Okinawa in World War II, Blair Reeves suffered a spinal wound that rendered him a paraplegic. He suffered terrible pain all his life, yet he never let it affect his work. Judge Reeves and I became good friends; our friendship continued until his death in 1999, at the age of 74.

Standing with Chicanas/os

One of life's great ironies for me at this time was that while I was working inside the bowels of an entrenched political system, learning about the different strands of the Democratic Party and the ins and outs of Commissioners Court, young Chicanas and Chicanos—"militants," they were called—were working outside, creating a new party called La Raza Unida that was to change Texas politics forever. They were also creating a movement that would also impact my life forever. While I definitely was being influenced on the inside by what I did not see—*i.e.,* very few people of color—it was what was happening on the outside that moved my heart and incited my political passions.

El movimiento Chicano had caught fire in my own Westside community and beyond. Demanding self-determination, the Chicano Movement was challenging the system that had clung to power in San Antonio since the 1950s—the Good Government League system that supported the very officials with whom I worked. The GGL had created an at-large system of elections that ran contrary to one-person-one vote. By the late 1960s, my brothers and I had become active in our precinct politics. But no matter how hard we worked in our neighborhood for candidates of our choice, such as those fielded by the Chicano Movement, we could never win under this at-large GGL system. The exception was the election of Peter "Pete" Torres, who ran as an independent and for the first time cracked the GGL. "Torres, a young lawyer [who] had been politically involved with the Bexar County Courthouse Coalition" served from 1967 to 1971 when he was defeated.[8]

There were times when I wished I could be with the activists, demonstrating and rallying for the rights of Mexican Americans. Instead, there I was in my polyester pantsuits working in a bastion of the GGL system, helping to support my family. At work I shared with Judge Reeves what I was doing or thinking and we would have interesting discussions. We agreed to disagree, whether it was about these local issues or U.S. involvement in the war in Vietnam, which he favored and I opposed.

I knew a few of the young Chicanas/os agitating for political change and would later meet many others. I was solidly in their camp, proud of them and grateful for what they were doing for our community. One decision I made was to identify myself as a Chicana. My parents and some of the elders in my community did not like the term. It reminded them of language that was derogatory towards Mexicans. Eventually they would understand. But for me at the time, it was a way of settling the discomfort I had always felt about not being totally Mexican or totally American. It also was a way to identify with those who were making history outside the system—remarkable people like Rosie Castro, Gloria Cabrera, Fernando Piñon, Bertha Pérez, José Angel Gutiérrez, Irma Mireles, Willie Benavides, Jo Ann and Gil Murillo, Bambi Cárdenas, Choco and Danny Meza, Mario Compeán, Willie Velásquez, and Juan Patlán. Even if the name did not reflect it, there were many Chicana leaders within the *movimiento*. Their contributions were major, but they have never received proper credit for their prophetic work.

Thanks to these and other courageous Chicanas/os, it became possible for someone like me one day to get elected to public office. Their courage and determination would be a marker for me years later when I served on City Council. I tried to do my work in a manner that reflected and honored their sacrifice.

One hot day in July of 1970 I found a small, symbolic way to stand with the Movement. As I stepped out of the Courthouse during the lunch hour, I saw a crowd of people demonstrating outside the San Antonio Savings and Loan Association. They were demonstrating against Mayor Walter McAllister, who owned the savings and loan. The mayor had recently appeared on national television, on the NBC Huntley-Brinkley Report, and made some very insulting remarks about Mexican Americans. Responding to a question about civil disobedience by Mexican Americans in California, the mayor said, "They're very fine people. They're home loving. They love beauty. They love flowers. They love music. They love dancing. Perhaps they're not quite as, uh, let's say as ambitiously motivated as the Anglos are to get ahead financially, but they manage to get a lot out of life."[9]

When my family and I heard those comments, we were furious. Now here right in front of me was a group of Chicanas/os demonstrating in front of the mayor's savings and loan, chanting, "Mayor McAllister is a racist!" I crossed the street and stood with them during my lunch hour. The leaders encouraged those of us who had accounts there to close them. As it turned out, Mamá and I each had a small savings account there. A few days later, Mamá and I went to the savings and loan and told the teller to give us our money back. We told her that we were closing our accounts because of the actions of Mayor McAllister and that we were in support of the students. The action made me feel a little closer to the movement.

Inside the Court, I had the good fortune of meeting one of the Chicano heroes of the day—Albert Peña, Jr., the first Chicano Commissioner elected to the Bexar County Commissioners Court. His presence was another exception to the GGL rule. Commissioner Peña was a passionate advocate for Chicanas/os and a lone vote against policies he deemed unfavorable to poor and working class people. From him I learned the power of a "no" vote: It's the power to say that not everyone in the city agrees with a particular direction the majority might be taking. When Commissioner Peña voted "no," he explained why, giving expression to the views of not only his own constituents but also those of people like me who were not in his precinct.

I was surprised when I first met him. I had only seen Albert Peña on television and he always seemed angry. In real life, he was always calm, a gentle person who spoke in a low voice. That was another good lesson for me. A person's image can be distorted by selective coverage, especially when that person is rocking the boat.

Behind the Scenes III

In 1973, the Archdiocese of San Antonio became associated with a young Chicano leader named Ernest "Ernie" Cortez. He was conducting a study of our Westside neighborhoods in order to identify the issues that concerned us. Father Lawrence Matula was asked to recommend church leaders for Ernie to interview and I received a visit from him. We talked for a long time; Ernie asked many questions about my neighborhood that I was delighted to answer. I told him about all the problems we had. Ernie was not clear at the time about what would happen with the information he was gathering, but I was excited at the prospect that something might emerge that could help our communities, which were in such great need.

At some point the following year, talk started in our church about a new organization, called Communities Organized for Public Service (COPS), coming to Christ the King to seek our engagement. Emerging from the work of Ernie Cortez, COPS had already started to take root in other Westside parishes, with parishioners being trained in community activism to help make our city government more responsive to the needs of the people in our neighborhoods. We would have to vote affirmatively if Christ the King were to be part of this new community-organizing group. But there were a number of people, particularly among our elders, who did not want any part of it—including my Welita Sebastiana.

Father Matula encouraged me to talk to my grandmother and ask her for help. We needed her vote and, further, we needed her to persuade others who followed her advice to vote in favor of COPS. I set about lobbying my grandmother to see if she would support bringing COPS into our parish.

"*Oiga, Vee,*" I said, using our family nickname for her, "*queremos votar que la organización COPS entre a Cristo Rey. ¿Puede Ud. votar para que se haga eso?*"

She was deadset against it. "*Yo pienso que la iglesia no se debe meter en la política y eso es política.*" A church should not be involved in politics.

"*Pero si ingresamos a COPS podemos ayudar a mucha gente.*" We could help a lot of people if we brought in COPS, I argued. We spent some time talking about the matter. At the end, she said, "*Bueno, voy a ayudarte. Lo voy hacer por ustedes, los jóvenes. Ustedes son los que van a seguir depues de que nosotros ya no estemos. Dios los bendiga.*"

Welita Sebastiana decided to support COPS for the sake of us young people. She not only voted in favor of digging into our church coffers to pay the dues required of participating churches but also persuaded the other church elders to do likewise. Our parish became a COPS 'local'. My father and a couple of my siblings joined COPS as active members. Although eager to be part of this new grassroots organizing effort, I ended up having to watch it unfold from a distance. The organization was interested in grooming leaders from the community. I was turned down. I did not qualify because I was already "known" in politics due to my work with Judge Blair Reeves. COPS wanted to groom individuals who were not in any way known in political circles. I was permitted to attend the meetings, however, and thus able to learn what the others were learning.

The more I got involved in politics at the grassroots level and took advantage of opportunities for leadership, the more I learned just how much we were missing in our barrios. The more I was exposed to information in my leadership training and in school the more I understood inequality. As a child I had a keen awareness of scarcity. I witnessed the sacrifices my mother made to keep a home going. I saw how much my father had to work for measly wages. As I traveled across my city and observed the newer areas under development, the more I would see the disparities between the neighborhoods where I was raised—where my family and friends still lived—and the newer areas of town. In barrios all over our city, Mexicans and Mexican Americans worked hard; yet, poverty was the rule, not the exception, in our communities. These conditions were not new but somehow we had to change them.

Through my involvement with COPS, I soon began to be engaged in two critical issues that would impact our city for decades—water and nuclear power.

Father Albert Benavides, a COPS leader and young diocesan priest I greatly admired and respected, began to educate our community on water issues. We learned that developers and other business interests promoting growth on the Northside, supported by our elected officials, wanted to build a surface water reservoir, a man-made lake, on the Southside of the city. The officials warned that we were running out of water. Father Benavides and COPS opposed building a costly reservoir, arguing that instead we should protect the Edwards Aquifer, a vast natural resource and pristine source of water that lay underground. We needed to plan urban development and insist that developers pay their own way instead of having all ratepayers foot the bill for water infrastructure that would benefit new areas of growth. He had become an expert in our community on water and I followed the debate closely. The answer on whether or not we needed this reservoir, for me, became an emphatic, No!

Another major citywide debate focused on whether to invest in two new nuclear reactors in Bay City, Texas. Our local government leaders told us that these would provide cheap energy once the plant was built. The problem was that we would have to pay for the construction of the plant up front, and there was no cap on how much we would spend. Furthermore, there were no plans on how the radioactive nuclear waste would be handled and stored. As with the water issue, once I became informed, my response to whether we should build these two nuclear reactors was also an emphatic, No!

As my eyes were opening to the systemic issues confronting my city, I became more aware of the need for fundamental change—and of my desire to be part of the solution.

Reliving Good Times

These years as a young workingwoman were joyful ones. I enjoyed my work, whether it was at The Salvation Army, the union at Kelly Air Force Base, HemisFair '68, the Democratic Party, or the Office of the County Judge. These were carefree and happy years when I was able to help my parents support a family, pay off the mortgage on our house, and even modernize parts of it. Although I did not drive and always rode the bus, I went in halves with my father to buy our family the first new car we ever had—a Chevrolet Nova. Papá loved it and he and Mamá enjoyed it for many years until he decided he was too old to drive. I was responsible for all my expenses, opened my own checking account, secured credit cards, and established a very good credit rating. I had proven that I could support myself and felt very independent and in charge of my life.

When I hear the music of the 1960s and early 1970s, or see photographs of teenagers dancing the latest tunes or television images of the sixties generation, I see it all as a backdrop to what I was doing in those years. I was an observer of those times lived by other young people while I focused on work, night school, my volunteer work, and family life.

During those years our house was full of music and conversation among young people excited about the future and working hard towards it. Spanish and English would go back and forth on the radio, television, and the records my brothers would buy for all of us to enjoy. The music ran the gamut from Broadway musicals like *South Pacific* and *Oklahoma* to Mexican rancheras and waltzes blaring on Mamá's KCOR radio station. Like many families of the era, we watched "The Perry Como Show," "The Hit Parade," the "Ed Sullivan Show," and Mitch Miller's "Sing Along With Mitch" on television.

My favorite songs were those filled with drama—hopeless love and much longing. I felt the words deep in my young heart and would say to myself as I listened to Eydie Gormé y Trio Los Panchos, "One day, I will know how that feels."

No es falta de cariño.
Te quiero con el alma.
Te juro que te adoro
Y en nombre de ese amor
Y por tu bien
Te digo adios.

In spite of the drama, I was a very happy young woman—and so was our home. We had every reason to be joyful. We were all healthy and we were taking a huge step—through the concerted effort of all eight of us—to move our family out of poverty. We had made the leap out of our family's impoverished agrarian past into urban poverty, and now we were creating the possibility of a better future for all of us.

Felix attended San Antonio College and then earned his bachelor's degree from St. Mary's University. Louis graduated from Holy Cross High School with honors and went on to St. Mary's University for undergraduate studies and then to earn a degree in law. Miguel graduated from St. John's Seminary and then enrolled in St. Mary's University where he too earned a law degree after his bachelor's. Both Theresa and Rosie graduated from Providence High School and then went on to earn degrees in education from Our Lady of the Lake College. Theresa later earned one of the first master's degrees in Bi-Lingual Bi-Cultural Education at UTSA under the tutelage of legendary educator and author Tomás Rivera. Through work-study jobs, grants, loans, and odd jobs, my brothers and sisters paid for their own schooling and personal expenses.

For our parents, the special ritual of having a daughter or son present them with yet another diploma—from high school, college, or law school—was a dream come true. Our lives would not be as difficult as theirs. The jury was out on what each of us would do with what we had attained, but our parents had given us everything we needed to make a better future possible. It was a deep source of pride for me that we all moved forward together, leaving no one behind.

By 1971, when Rosie, the youngest, had graduated from college and shortly thereafter got married, my other siblings were also working and helping with family finances. That was important because two years earlier, in 1969, we had all urged Papá to retire. My father had suffered an accident on the job at the site where he worked before HemisFair. A steel beam hit him on the head. I still have the hard hat that saved his life; it's indented where the beam hit.

Papá was taken to Methodist Hospital and was there for a week to ten days. At first, the top of his head and eyes went purple, then black. After that, as each day passed, the bruising lowered, first to his nose, then mouth, then throat, until it disappeared. After he was released, his company, Lyda & Lott, and their doctor gave us a form to sign that said Papá was okay. Not knowing any better, he signed it. He never was the same, suffering from dizzy spells that would come unexpectedly.

When Lyda & Lott transferred him to work at HemisFair, my heart would leap every time our office got a call that there was a construction accident. Whenever there was an accident, the first office to get a call was HemisFair's legal department, where I worked. Mr. Daniels would deal with it. I knew Papá was out there up on catwalks, experiencing sudden dizzy spells. That's when I started thinking, "I don't want my father to work anymore." We all urged him to stop and he finally agreed. It was too dangerous for him to keep working, but at age 59, he was not yet old enough to receive Social Security. So we all pitched in to help make ends meet.

I continued working fulltime and attending evening classes at San Antonio College, waiting until there was more financial stability at home. But I had begun to think in a more serious manner about my future. Over the prior years I had thought about marriage from time to time, wondering if I would ever meet a man I wanted to marry. Now the question seemed real. I was not getting any younger! After pondering it, I recall reaching a moment when I concluded, "It's not going to happen." I remember next pondering whether I was ready to live a life without children. I reckoned I could; after all, I had already helped raise a family. And so, feeling no great internal pressure to be a mother, I just kept going on with my life.

NOTES

Chapter 4: At Work in the World

1. Pauli Murray, *The Autobiography of a Black Activist, Feminist, Lawyer, Priest and Poet*. Memphis: The University of Tennessee Press (1987), 36.

2. Robert A. Goldberg, "Racial Changes on the Southern Periphery: The Case of San Antonio, Texas, 1960-1965" in *The Journal of Southern History*, 49 (August 1983): 349-374.

3. Many years later when I was an elected official my family and I got to meet Chávez when he visited our church. I joined him in planning one of the boycotts in San Antonio through an invitation of Archbishop Patrick Flores.

4. A parishioner named Fernando Rodríguez was elected president. Years later, when I went to apply for work at the American Federation of Government Employees, Fernando was the president of that union, becoming my boss for a brief period of time.

5. According to presidential historian Kent B. Germany, the War on Poverty "begun officially in 1964, was an ambitious governmental effort to address the problem of persistent poverty in the United States. Over the next decade, the federal government—in conjunction with state and local governments, non-profit organizations, and grassroots groups—created a new institutional base for antipoverty and civil rights action and, in the process, highlighted growing racial and ideological tensions in American politics and society." See http://www.faculty.virginia.edu/sixties/readings/War%20on%20Poverty%20entry%20Poverty%20Encyclopedia.pdf (accessed April 27, 2011).

6. *Ibid.*

7. Some of these programs included the General Revenue Sharing Program created in 1971 where the federal government would return money to localities; the Comprehensive Employment and Training Act (CETA) enacted in 1973 to provide employment for low-income and long-term unemployed people; and the Law Enforcement Assistance Administration (LEAA), established in 1968 to provide money for a variety of crime and law enforcement initiatives.

8. See Rudolfo Rosales, *The Illusion of Inclusion: The Untold Political Story of San Antonio* (Austin: University of Texas Press, 2000), 90.

8. Randy Ontiveros, "No Golden Age: Television News and The Chicano Civil Rights Movement," *American Quarterly*, Volume 62, Number 4 (Johns Hopkins University Press: December 2010), 897-923, citing NBC News, July 6, 1970.

CHAPTER 5

A Time for Everything

It was 1972 and the first day of spring. I was 30 years old, about to turn 31. A year earlier, Rosie had graduated from Our Lady of the Lake College. The baby of the family was now married and teaching. All my other siblings had also completed their college educations and were busy pursuing careers. Together, as a family, we had reached a major milestone. My parents were rightly proud—and so was I. The mission that I, at age fourteen, thought would take a lifetime to accomplish was over!

I was thinking about the rest of my life as I went home that evening in March after an ordinary day at the County Courthouse. Mamá had prepared *mole* because our pastor was coming over for dinner. Father Matula had invited my older brother, Felix, and me to attend an archdiocesan meeting that night as representatives of Christ the King Church.

Father Matula had opened the doors of our parish like never before and made it possible for young people like me to develop leadership skills. Having Felix and me represent Christ the King at this meeting was an example of the way he raised up young people as leaders. The meeting had been called by then Bishop Patrick Flores. Vocations to the priesthood were waning, and he wanted to hear from the faithful in local parishes about what ought to be done with some of the empty buildings at Assumption Seminary. The Bishop wanted the buildings to be of service to the Mexican-American community.

I dressed for the meeting, donning the most practical rage of the day, a polyester pantsuit. Practical and washable, it was a working girl's dream. I even recall the color. Aquamarine. After enjoying the delicious *mole* dinner, we headed out for the meeting. But by the time Father Matula, Felix, and I arrived at the grounds of the seminary and found the room, the meeting had already started. We were late!

I was led to an empty seat right in the middle of the room. As I sat down, a distinguished looking man in the seat in front of me turned around. He had a beard and was wearing a green suit, olive green. As he caught sight of me, a startled look came over his face. He stared at me for what seemed like a very long and awkward time. I have a clear picture of it in my mind. That startled look was frozen on his face and behind him, on the wall, was a clock. It seemed to sit on his head, declaring the time: 7:05 p.m. That was the exact moment, on March 20, 1972—the first day of spring—when a new chapter of my life began.

The man with the clock over his head was Manuel P. Berriozábal, a professor of mathematics at the University of New Orleans. He was in town during his spring break to see about obtaining a position on the faculty of the new University of Texas at San Antonio. Manuel was staying at the rectory of Our Lady of Guadalupe Church, deep in the heart of our Westside.

The pastor of the church, Father Edmundo Rodríguez, was Manuel's friend—and mine too. Edmundo had taught the first leadership development class I ever attended. That amazing class provided me with a theological framework for the social justice work in which I was already involved in my community. That is where I first heard about liberation theology, the grounding of faith in peace and social justice and a preferential option for the poor. Edmundo had invited Manuel to the meeting at the seminary with the promise that they would have dinner afterwards.

As the meeting proceeded, we broke into small groups according to numbers. Within each group a person volunteered to lead the discussion and another to take notes. Although drawing a different number, Manuel somehow found his way to the group I volunteered to lead. He arrived just as we were beginning the process of getting to know each other. As leader, I really pushed the process. "Manuel, tell me about yourself?" (He was single.) "Manuel, tell me about your family." "Manuel, what are your thoughts on the needs of our Mejicano community?"

When the meeting ended, Manuel came over to me and said, "Do you think we could go somewhere and continue this interesting discussion?"

"I can't," I said. "I have to work tomorrow."

"Can we have dinner tomorrow after work?"

"No, I have night school."

"Well," he said, "Do you think we could have lunch before I leave town?" By this point I knew he was just visiting. "I could pick you up at home," he offered. I certainly didn't want him to pick me up at home, where I would face a million questions! "Okay. Why don't you pick me up at work?" As I leaned over to write my name on a piece of paper, with the address where he would come pick me up, I wrote "*Miss ...* María Antonietta Rodríguez." I wanted to be sure he knew I was a "Miss" and not a "Mrs." At the end of the meeting, plans were in place for lunch a day or two later.

But the night was not over yet! As I was getting ready to go home, a strange woman came up to me. "Here is my home address," she announced, handing me a piece of paper. "I am having a meeting this Sunday. I am organizing Mexican-American women and we need young ladies like you. So come," she said. Then she turned around and left, as abruptly as she came.

The woman was Luz Escamilla—an extraordinary Latina who would become an exceptional mentor. That Sunday, my sister Theresa and I attended her meeting—the first of many thereafter. Eventually, I joined Luz and a couple of dozen other women in organizing the Mexican American Business and Professional Women's Club, a group that would launch my activism on behalf of Latinas.

That night in March of 1972, my destiny was revealed. Its key strands were all woven together—in the new spirit of liberation theology that was infusing my church and connecting faith to social justice, in the activism of Latina women ready to forge a new future for *mujeres* and our Mexican-American community, in the recognition of my leadership potential … and in that startled face.

The very next day, a quick call to Edmundo was a must! "Who is that man you brought with you last night?" I asked. "Ahhhhhhhhhh!" Edmundo said. Then a big-belly laugh, "Ha! Ha! Ha!" And then another, "Ahhhhhhhhhhh!" All of which gave away his matchmaking approval before he said a word. Edmundo told me he had met Manuel in New Orleans. He was a leader in that archdiocese, doing work with Latinas and Latinos.

Manuel stayed in town for several more days, at the rectory, of course—always trying to save money! We went out for lunch and then had a few other chances to visit. Manuel got to meet my mother and was even bit by our dog, Sancho Panza. By the time he left for New Orleans, I knew this was the man I would marry. In time, I would learn that the same idea was born in him during these days.

The poet Amado Nervo reminds us, "*Si plantas rosales, cosecharás siempre rosas.*" My mission was over. Now it was time to gather roses.

"When You Educate A Woman, You Educate A Family"

Meeting Luz Escamilla on the same evening I met my future husband, Manuel, and right when I was seriously starting to think about my own future, was providential.

Luz symbolized a new type of woman in my life—a woman who worked in an office. The Mexican women I had known since childhood were homemakers or fieldworkers, or the saleswomen at department and grocery stores. Tía Lucha was the only woman in my family who did something else, working in a clothing factory.

Luz Escamilla had risen to a mid-level position at Kelly Air Force Base—a rare feat at that time for a Mexican-American woman. Impeccably coiffed and always dressed in a most professional manner, Luz had a powerful presence and intellect. She was a walking library of issues relating to equal employment, affirmative action, and the discrimination experienced by Mexican Americans, particularly Mexican-American women, in the workforce. When I met her, Luz was at a place in her life when she could have just enjoyed the benefits of her hard work. Instead, she chose to take the struggle for Mexican-American women outside the confines of a military base.

Over the years of rising through the ranks of civil service at Kelly, Luz had learned the importance of formal structures for mutual support. Although there was a long tradition of business and professional women's clubs in San Antonio, the membership tended to be white and older and was not very welcoming of women of color. Luz saw the need for an organization of, by, and for Mexican-American women and she set about doing the research and the legwork to organize one.

Recognizing the value of connecting with a long-established national organization, Luz worked to found the new organization as an affiliate of the National Federation of Business and Professional Women's Clubs (NFBPW). She obtained a charter from the Texas chapter of the organization. BPW's purpose nationally was to eliminate sex discrimination in employment, promote equal pay, and support a comprehensive equal rights amendment. At the state level, BPW similarly worked to expand opportunities and achieve equity for women.

The proposed Mexican American Business and Professional Women's Club (MABPW) incorporated the goals of the national and Texas organizations, while adding two more: elevating the status of the Mexican-American woman in society and teaching parliamentary procedure. The first goal would be accomplished by educating ourselves on critical issues facing Mexican-American women and their families and then creating strategies and public venues to promote what we were doing. A major focus would be on working to improve how Mejicanas were portrayed in our local media. As for parliamentary procedure, Luz had learned that it was a valuable tool to master, particularly when one was in the minority.

By the time I met Luz that spring night at the archdiocesan meeting and went to her house as commanded, she and other women had already done most of the groundwork to create this new organization.

Three months later, on June 21, 1972, twenty-nine Mexican-American women, including my sister, Theresa, and me, joined Luz Escamilla in obtaining the charter to establish the Mexican American Business and Professional Women's Club.[1]

It was the first such group to be chartered in Texas. Luz had to overcome strong objections on the part of the National Federation leadership; they did not want to approve the name "Mexican American" in our charter. There were no BPW clubs with "ethnic" names. I recall how moved I was when I learned after the fact that Luz had wept when she went before the Texas Federation to present our application. Luz was not an emotional person. She gave her heart to this cause and fought for us.

At one of the meetings of the newly formed group, Luz appointed me Chair of the Public Relations Committee—without even asking. "I have never done anything like that," I objected. "How will I do it?" Her totally unsympathetic reply was, "Go to the library and check out books on public relations. You will learn."

Luz pushed me in ways that were infuriating. Nothing I did was ever good enough. I would get so angry at her criticism that I would promise myself to do better the next time and really show her. I took on more and more work while all the while, of course, I was developing new skills—and great patience! I witnessed the dynamism, energy, boldness, creativity, and courage of Luz Escamilla. She was strong, forceful and blunt—a tough-love mentor with no patience for mediocrity, hidden agendas, or incompetence. The larger than life presence of Luz Escamilla and her uncompromising insistence that I could do whatever I was assigned had a powerful impact on me in those years.

In October of 1972, we had our Installation of Officers. It was a formal evening-gown affair held in the ballroom of the Hilton Palacio Del Río Hotel, the first such event I ever attended in my life. I had never even been to a high school prom. But that night, I was not so much concerned about how I looked in evening attire as I was about whether the media would show up to cover the event! As Chair of the Public Relations Committee, the responsibility rested entirely on my shoulders. As it turned out, we had a full court press! I had done my part to get out the media—writing press releases, hand-delivering them, making follow up calls to news directors, and the like. It did not hurt that we also had our own stars and friends in the media to help us, including Veronica Salazar of the *San Antonio Express-News*, Martha Tijerina of KWEX TV, and Yolanda Ríos Rangel of WOAI TV. Later, María Elena Torralva, another media personality, would join us. These were all our Latina pioneers in the news media.

MABPW provided a safe space for its members to meet and exchange ideas. Our membership included a wide range of women—some community leaders; a few civil servants, including a handful like Luz who had achieved mid-level positions; some entrepreneurs; teachers; an attorney; and a few in the media, including popular personalities in the Mexican-American community. Among the members were also several secretaries like me.

Luz's motto was: "*Cuando se educa un hombre, se educa un individuo. Cuando se educa una mujer se educa una familia.*" Educating men is about educating individuals; educating women means educating families. Thus MABPW was not just about the professional advancement of women. We wanted better lives and upward mobility not only for ourselves but also for our community. We got our parents, siblings, spouses, children, and friends involved in our many activities.

Our events in those first years focused on a wide range of topics, including bilingual/bicultural education, careers and raising children, the political process, college preparation and entrance exams, money management, and civic participation. We also engaged in activities like fundraising for student scholarships and providing financial assistance to high school girls at risk of dropping out of school. And we worked for passage in Texas of the Equal Rights Amendment! All this we did as a fledgling non-profit with no office and no staff, operating on volunteer help from women working full time jobs. One of MABPW's most significant contributions to Mexican-American women in San Antonio was to provide a structured space and place for ongoing mentoring. The more experienced women mentored the younger ones, and we all mentored each other.

For me, the most exciting and innovative activity we planned was the "First Consultation on Spanish Speaking Women in Employment," held in March 1974. I had never heard of a consultation. It was Luz's idea to invite top employers in the city, such as the City of San Antonio, the Texas Education Agency, Kelly and Randolph Air Force Bases, USAA, Bell Telephone Company, and others. We organized panels with top officials from each organization or their heads of personnel. They were to respond to the question: What is the status of Mexican-American women in your agency or government unit? The answer: Not good.

We invited two special guests from Washington, D.C.: Vicent Barraba, Director of the U.S. Census, and Carmen Maymi, Director of the Women's Bureau of the U.S. Department of Labor. The event was hugely successful. We made many friends in key positions throughout the city, received extensive news coverage—quite a feat for a new organization—and the experience MABPW members obtained was invaluable. By virtue of our activities, we were changing the way Meji-canas were portrayed in the media at the same time that we were able to win commitments from many employers to create a better climate for Mexican-American women in their work places. There were still immense needs among our women and our commitment was for the long haul.

Our leader in this life-changing effort, Luz Escamilla, is now living in a nursing facility. Her husband Paul died recently. Luz suffers from Alzheimer's disease. She cannot walk and does not recognize people. I believe that gratitude and love go beyond human understanding. Each time I visit her, as I prepare to leave, I look into her eyes when I go say goodbye. I tell her I love her and thank her for being my mentor. At some level, I know she understands.

The Man in the Green Suit

In seeking to obtain a position on the faculty at the new University of Texas at San Antonio, Manuel was hoping to return to his birthplace and also to realize a dream of being part of a university in a largely Mexican-American community. Manuel was born in San Antonio on July 12, 1931, in the midst of the Great Depression. While he was still a baby, his parents moved to Independence, Missouri where his maternal grandparents lived. His father, Manuel, a Mexican of Basque descent came to the United States from Zacatecas, Mexico, at the age of 17. His mother, Emma Louise Wand, was the daughter of German immigrants. Manuel was very close to his maternal grandparents—Matilda Ulrich and Phillip Wand—in whose home he and his parents lived when they first moved to Independence, where they remained until he was eight. His younger sister, Dolores, was born in Independence; she still lives in Missouri, as do his two nieces and their families.

Manuel's maternal grandparents spoke German, so he was exposed to the German language at an early age, even though his parents spoke to him in English. His grandfather Phillip was a sausage maker in Kansas City. Manuel never met his paternal grandfather, Venancio Berriozábal; his paternal grandmother, Dolores Escarzaga, died when he was very young, so he never learned Spanish as a child. His German grandmother Matilda also died when he was young. They were still living with his grandparents and Manuel remembers the sadness he felt, as a boy of five, mourning her loss. His grandfather Phillip eventually was remarried, to a woman named Nettie.

Manuel's love of learning started early, as did his passion for mathematics. At age nine, he took his first job, stacking cans in the neighborhood grocery story. He has never stopped working, continuing to teach even now at the age of 80. During the Second World War, as a young teenager, Manuel collected scrap metal for the war effort, using some of the earnings to gain admission to the movies down the street. Heeding the church's instruction that children should be sent to Catholic schools whenever possible, Manuel's parents sent him and his sister Dolores to St. Ann's Catholic School in Independence, Missouri, run by the Religious Sisters of Mercy. He loved school and his teachers, crediting Sister Mary James, RSM, with preparing him, through her special tutoring, for a scholarship to De La Salle Military Academy in Kansas City, Missouri.

At De La Salle, the Christian Brothers continued to provide him with an excellent education. A very disciplined student, Manuel was the valedictorian of his high school graduating class. With the support of his family and earnings from his part-time employment, Manuel enrolled in Rockhurst University in Kansas City. At Rockhurst, the Jesuits not only continued to provide an intellectual environment that matched Manuel's love of learning but also when he completed his college work in 1952, they encouraged him to pursue a master's degree in mathematics at the University of Notre Dame. His primary mathematics professor at Rockhurst, Father William C. Doyle, was instrumental to his going to Notre Dame. After one year of study at Notre Dame, Manuel was drafted and served in the U.S. Army until 1955. Thereupon, he resumed graduate studies at Notre Dame and was awarded a Master of Science Degree in Mathematics in 1956.

At Notre Dame, he was encouraged to pursue a doctorate by one of his mathematics professors, Dr. Wladimir Seidel. From 1957 to 1959, Manuel was a mathematics instructor at Loyola (now Loyola-Marymount) University in Los Angeles. During this time he resumed doctoral studies in mathematics at the University of California at Los Angeles (UCLA) and served as a mathematics instructor at UCLA Extension from 1959 to 1961. In 1961 he was awarded his doctorate in mathematics and then served as a lecturer in mathematics from 1961 to 1962. From 1962 to 1966, he served as an assistant professor of mathematics at Tulane University in New Orleans. When I met him, he was teaching at the University of New Orleans where he served as an Associate Professor and Professor of Mathematics since 1966.

What I saw in this man from the very beginning was a gentle and wise person who was very sure of himself and felt no need to compete with others. Although our childhood stories were very different, we had shared values centered on people not possessions. Manuel's deep commitment to his profession and devotion to his students impressed me then and now. Manuel's teachers were his most powerful role models, mentors, and friends. He remained in touch with Dr. Arnold Ross, a professor at Notre Dame and Ohio State University, until he died at the age of 96. Arnold was a great influence on my husband as he developed and conducted the San Antonio and Texas Prefreshman Engineering Programs. Manuel's teaching and students became his children—and ours.

Courtship and Marriage

Not long after I met Manuel and he returned to Louisiana, he called to invite me to come to New Orleans over Easter to go sailing. I was scandalized!

"I don't visit men," I said emphatically.

"Oh. Okay," he said. And thus commenced a long distance courtship, conducted mostly through the mail. I now know how unusual this was for Manuel. He is not a writer. The envelopes he used were yellow, probably unused for years. I would write about my family and what I was doing at work. He would write about school and his new political activities at his local precinct. The letters came and went every couple of weeks and he would call from time to time.

That summer, during his vacation, Manuel came back to San Antonio for a visit, returning again in December over the Christmas break. Manuel came to our home and my family got to know him. We were becoming friends but there was no talk of anything permanent. The plan was that Manuel would move to San Antonio to teach at UTSA and then, once he was here, we would have a chance to get to know each other better.

By the following Easter, my friends Yolie and David said, "Why don't you go visit that guy?" I obviously had been talking quite a bit about this math professor. "I can't go by myself!" I said. They offered to go with me. And so, properly chaperoned, I went to visit Manuel. He put me up in a fancy hotel, the New Orleans Dauphine. One evening, he told all of us to "dress fancy." He was taking us out to dinner. Dress fancy we did and he took us to the Pontchartrain Hotel for the most fantastic buffet I had ever seen in my life. He wined and dined us. "Man," I said to myself, "this is a big spender." I was not quite sure what to think of that. Of course, it turned out to be a dead-wrong conclusion.

This kind of spending was totally out of character for Manuel, who has always lived simply and well below his means.

It was a beautiful trip. But then more time passed, more letters, more calls. UTSA seemed to be in no hurry to offer Manuel a position on the faculty—even though he would be the first Mexican-American in the mathematics department. I did not want to move to New Orleans. Manuel did not want to move to San Antonio without a job. We were at an impasse, and things started to get a little gnarly.

As the third Easter of our long-distance courtship rolled around, Manuel came for another visit. We were still at an impasse, neither going forward nor breaking up. It was unseasonably cold that Easter Sunday in 1975 when we attended the famous mariachi Mass at St. Patrick's Church in San Antonio. Manuel was surprised and delighted to hear Beethoven's Ode to Joy, one of his favorite pieces of music, sung in Spanish by a mariachi choir as *El Himno de la Alegría*. A wedding program had been left behind in the pew where we sat and when I casually picked it up, a powerful excerpt of words struck me. Adapted from Naomi's vow to her mother-in-law, Ruth, in Scripture, the excerpt read, "Wherever you go I will go. Wherever you live. I will live. Your people will be my people, and our love will be the gift of our lives."

After Mass, as we walked hand in hand out of the church, surrounded by joyful people, the mariachis started belting *"Las Mañanitas."* It felt like a *serenata* just for us. By the time we got to our car, we had set the date for our wedding—August 9, 1975—just a few months away.

Sadly, Manuel's beloved grandfather, Phillip Wand, died the week before we married. It was the only sad note in an otherwise joyful and beautiful wedding ceremony at Christ the King Church. Members of each of our families comprised our wedding party and served as witnesses as we pledged our love to each other. In addition to the traditional Catholic wedding rituals and blessings for husband and wife, we added a blessing at the end that was given by my first boss and friend, Major Ralph Morrel. His prayer was that God join our lives not only for each other's joy but also in service to God's people. Surrounded by the love and good wishes of our beloved family and friends, we started our life together and to unfold what has become my life's most precious gift—Manny's love.

Living Short in the Big Easy

After enjoying a wonderful honeymoon in Puerto Vallarta and Guadalajara, I moved with Manny to New Orleans, joining the community that he had been a part for nearly fifteen years. It was fun to learn more about Manny through the company he kept and activities he engaged in. He had a full and rich life in New Orleans with a core group of great friends in whose homes he was treated like a brother or favorite uncle. Some had traveled with their children by train to come to our wedding in San Antonio. They were all curious about this woman that their long-time bachelor friend had finally chosen to marry.

I was welcomed by his fellow parishioners at Our Lady of the Rosary Church and by activists at the Alliance for Good Government, a clean government group in which Manny was involved. Manny sang in the Mariachi Choir of Santa Teresa de Avila Church and in the New Orleans Concert Choir. There was also a large contingent of mathematics professors from the faculties of various colleges and universities in New Orleans who met often in social settings.

A wonderful treat was going to dinner with Manny's older colleagues, especially Dr. Anton Heyn, a Dutch botanist, and his wife, Frances Forbes Heyn, a writer and former librarian. It was a lesson in southern grace and hospitality. Their house had the smell of a library. There were books in every nook, sharing space with gorgeous china and art on elegant pieces of antique furniture. After enjoying pre-dinner conversation and appetizers with tiny crocheted napkins on our laps, Frances would say to me, "Now please help me set the table. We will put the books and papers on the floor."

As the guys continued their math talk, we would proceed to clear the table and gently place the books on the floor where they joined piles of others. "We will use the pottery today," she announced, bringing in plates and bowls from her southern pottery collection followed by the loveliest cobalt blue glasses and goblets.

"Now come, Manny," Anton would announce. "Let us enjoy Frances' famous seafood gumbo." That was scrumptious gumbo for sure, but the best part of the evening was always the conversations we engaged in. They ranged from university politics to gumbo recipes to immigrating from Holland to growing up Mexican in San Antonio's Westside.

The whole ritual took several hours. When the final drink was downed and we said our goodbyes, I would leave thinking that someday my Manny and I would be like that. We would live in an old house crowded with books and have many stories to share with young people.

As soon as I settled in, I became active in the local LULAC chapter and the SER organization on whose board Manny served. But the top priority of our young marriage was for me to complete my college education. For the first time, I enrolled in college as a full-time student. As I was filling out the forms to apply to the University of New Orleans, I remember being stumped by a question about my major. Part-time college applications had never asked about a major. I asked Manny what he thought I should elect as my major. "What do you like studying?" he responded. "Politics!" I replied immediately, answering my own question. My declared major became political science.

Nine months later, our new life as a married couple in New Orleans came to an end when Manny was offered a faculty position at UTSA. Late that summer we moved to San Antonio and in the fall of 1976, Manny began to teach as a fully tenured professor and I to study as a full-time undergraduate student. Manny brought with him years of experience not only in teaching and research but also the trajectory he had started in New Orleans of addressing the educational needs of minority students. His goal was to help students, particularly minorities, to acquire the rigorous study skills needed to be successful in pursuing math and science studies once they reached college. It was a trajectory that would eventually earn him national recognition and give tens of thousands of students an opportunity to excel.

The Undergraduate

In 1976 there were very few non-traditional students in my classes at UTSA; most of my classmates were young people fresh out of high school. But it did not take long for me to find my little niche in undergraduate circles. I took precise notes in shorthand and then typed them, a practice that proved very valuable to my fellow study-group chums!

Life as a full-time college student in my early thirties was an incredible luxury, appreciated in the way that only someone older could. Not knowing how to drive, I would accompany Manny to UTSA in the mornings and return home with him in the evenings, delighting in our time together. I would spend my days in class, studying at the library, or engaged in student activities. I became involved in the Movimiento Estudiantil Chicano de Aztlán (MECHA) and served as the community reporter for the student newspaper.

My political science courses, particularly those with Dr. Richard Gambitta, a young professor who had just joined the faculty, were most gratifying. It takes a rare person to tailor classes to young people just out of high school and at the same time provide intellectual challenges to non-traditional students like me. I had a treasure trove of experiences to build on and Dr. Gambitta gave me opportunities to go beyond what I would have learned as a traditional student. I had learned a lot about politics in my work place; in my political science classes at UTSA, I learned to apply critical analysis to my life experiences. I gained a scholarly context for the civil and human rights to which I was very committed.

At one point, Dr. Gambitta suggested that I do an independent study on Mexican-American women responsive to the question, "Why are there no Mexican-American women in elected office in San Antonio?"

I created the methodology and selected 20 of the most influential Mexican-American women in San Antonio as my subjects. I included them on my list because others deemed them to be political leaders even though they themselves, for the most part, did not. My paper was titled "Chicana Women in Bexar County: An Insight into Their Political Participation." I learned how far we needed to move as Chicanas/Latinas to recognize the value of the political capital we possessed.

We were not only absent in local elected offices; Chicanas were generally absent on the faculty of UTSA. There were no classes I could select offered by Latina faculty members. That had also been true when I was enrolled in night classes over the years. I did find ways of collaborating with the few Latinas on the UTSA faculty, including Drs. Ellen Riojas Clark and María Luisa Urdaneta, and sought their expertise in my community work. But I regret that absence in my education.

Another significant teacher for me was Dr. Ann Fears Crawford, a political scientist, prolific writer, and pioneer in the feminist movement. She was a fun-loving woman who taught by her presence. She exuded confidence. In one of her courses, she gave us the assignment of developing an election campaign for a fictional woman. I seized the opportunity to focus on Chicanas in politics. My fictional candidate was a Mexican-American woman running for the San Antonio City Council! I developed her message, wrote her campaign platform, and designed the logistics of her campaign. A few years later, when I took on the role of that fictional character and won a seat on the City Council, one of my congratulatory letters came from Ann Fears Crawford. She died in 1999.

During my last year at UTSA, I had an internship in the office of Councilman Henry G. Cisneros, who represented us in Council District 1. I engaged in casework, enjoying it thoroughly. It never occurred to me that I would ever be on the City Council, much less within three years. With the guidance and encouragement I received from Professors Crawford and Gambitta I could have continued my education in social research. Instead, without my realizing it at the time, my path in politics was already being paved.

On May 29, 1979, twenty years after I graduated from high school, I crossed the stage to receive my college diploma to the cheers of my parents, siblings, and extended family, with yet another young generation present. The most moving memory I have of that day was actually related to me after the grand event. As my name was called and I walked across the stage, Dr. Manuel P. Berriozábal, Professor of Mathematics, in full academic regalia rose and stood in silence, paying me the greatest tribute of the day.

The year 1979 was a great one for both Manny and me. That spring I graduated from UTSA, finally earning my long-sought college degree. That summer Manny conducted his first Pre-Freshman Engineering Program (PREP) at the University. Forty-four students, ages 16 to 19, enrolled in his rigorous math enrichment program—a program that would grow by leaps and bounds in the ensuing years.

A Count that Counts

As the 1970s came to an end and a new decade was about to begin, the country geared up for the constitutionally mandated decennial census count that would determine high-stakes issues like the number of representatives a state could send to Congress, formulas for state appropriations of federally funded programs, and a host of other demographics-related outcomes. Word was out that the Census Bureau was looking for locals who would be charged with the count. Equipped with my new degree in political science, fifteen years of work experience, and established leadership in my local community, I thought the position of District Director for the San Antonio Central Census Office would be a perfect match for me.

The position required recommendations from city leaders. I sought and obtained them from Congressman Henry B. González and William C. Velásquez, Founder and Executive Director of the Southwest Voter Registration and Education Project (SWVREP). This was a coup because it was well known in those years that the two had some serious political differences. Congressman González was a long time Democratic Party leader while Willie Velásquez was one of the new leaders who had surfaced through the Chicano Movement. I had worked with both men, collaborating over the years with Rep. González's office beginning with my work at Hemisfair '68, and working with Willie

Velásquez on voter registration and community issues.

I secured the appointment and was scheduled to begin work at the start of the New Year. Instead, on December 31, 1979, as I was thinking about our plans for that evening's New Year's celebrations, I got a call from a truck driver, saying he was downtown and ready to deliver the materials for the San Antonio Census office. He said he needed help unloading. I immediately called my brothers and friends. When Manny and I got there, I was stunned to see a *huge rig*! The driver said he had six hours and after that he was leaving, whether the truck was totally unloaded or not. We quickly ran out to find some men to hire for the day and then proceeded to unload desks, tables, chairs, file cabinets, and acres and acres of census forms and boxes of other materials. We made it, just in time.

I started going to Dallas to participate in the extensive training program offered to all district office managers. One of the great challenges of every decennial count, we learned, is ensuring that all individuals who live in large urban centers like San Antonio are counted. People of color and poor people who tend to live in these areas are particularly difficult to count. The charge was to hire people from within these enumeration districts as census takers as they would know and be known to their neighbors, engendering trust. We were warned, however, that we would find it problematic to find people within these areas to work for the Census Bureau—and that there would be a major turnover of workers.

As I soon discovered, San Antonio was more than ready for the task. With the community competency and personal commitment that our citizens possessed, we overcame the difficult issues about which we were warned, hiring the workers we needed with minimal turnover. The big problem we had was with the Census Bureau itself—with the officials in Dallas responsible for the Texas count. These were career employees, part of the bureaucracy that worked in between the decennial census years.

It was only a few months into our census-counting process in 1980 when we discovered that the one-size-fits-all methodology I was receiving from our regional office in Dallas was creating problems in our city. The scheduled steps and timeframes that we district managers were given for each step of the census process did not work in our communities of color. More time was needed to gain trust and cooperation from people reluctant to provide information about themselves to the government. Given the challenges, we actually were doing quite well. But towards the end of the time period for the house-to-house calls designated by the Dallas office, we had not yet been able to get to all the neighborhoods in communities of color.

The crew leaders we had hired, very responsible leaders in the communities in which they were working, voiced deep concerns to me that time was running out and there were still areas that needed to be covered. Their results to date were proving that they were able to obtain cooperation from hard-to-reach populations by approaching the effort with respect and sensitivity. But this required time. I voiced our concerns to the officials in Dallas, but they fell on deaf ears. More time meant more money to retain workers and keep offices open. After pressing the issue yet again, I was shocked when my Dallas supervisor asked me, "María, are you more loyal to the community or to the Census Bureau?" He insisted that I back off.

I didn't. I kept pushing. Instead of shifting the timetable so we could complete the census work, my bosses in Dallas ended up stripping me of my authority as director. I would now have to answer to the census liaison, one of the permanent bureaucrats who would comply with the demands of the Dallas office. Our office would close before we had done everything we could to ensure an accurate count. My staff was so devoted to the work that some employees even volunteered to work pro bono until we finished. But the bureaucrats in Dallas would not allow anyone to work for free.

Although I felt devastated by the actions of the census officials and totally embarrassed before my staff in San Antonio, I refused to give up. So much was at stake. I began to reach out to stakeholders who were interested in an accurate count.

I had a ready list of individuals and groups to reach out to in both the private and public sectors, including government, business, community, and church organizations. Our efforts had the strong backing of the Archdiocese of San Antonio, the Mexican American Legal Defense and Educational Fund, Southwest Voter Registration and Education Project, as well as local elected officials and many community organizations. I had met Vincent Barraba, then-Director of the U.S. Census Bureau, when he was our special guest at a MAPBW event and had befriended Leo Estrada, one of the top demographers for the Census Bureau and an expert in the demographics of the U.S. Latina/o population. I contacted them as well.

The pressure was so effective that I was reinstated in my position and we were given more time to do our work. The regional director of the Census Bureau in Dallas was transferred to another state. I do not know exactly why this action was taken but the net result was that I was told we would get what was needed to complete our work. In the year following the 1980 census, a number of lawsuits were filed in other large cities alleging undercounts of minorities. San Antonio, in contrast, received a commendation from the U.S. Census Bureau for having one of the best-run census efforts in the nation.

During this brief census-taking time, from December 1979 to October 1980, I learned a great deal, including some bitter lessons about how government can function (or fail to function), subverting the Constitution and the rights of the people. But the power of a committed citizenry and the impact of putting one's core values on the line were also underscored for me. I knew I could trust my own judgment and that of my community.

On one of the last days before we closed our office, I sat with a Census official and shared some of my bitter disappointments in government. I pointed to the census map of San Antonio that had been posted on the wall behind my desk for the duration of the census, with every neighborhood highlighted. I was not exactly sure what I would do next, I said, but I would not waste my knowledge—all that I had learned about our city and from the experience. Whatever I did next, I said, in words that were clearly more of a promise to myself than anything else, it would be for the benefit of my community, a community I had seen disrespected and discounted by our government.

I had no idea then that just two months later my promise would take the form of an announcement. On December 27, 1980, in front of my parents' house in the heart of San Antonio's Westside, I announced my campaign to run for City Council, representing District 1.

NOTES
Chapter 5: A Time for Everything

1. The other charter members of the MABPW were Bertha Cardwell, Arcadia López, Anna María T. Leal, Mary Espíritu, Santos M. Dávila, Delia C. Arzola, Rachel O. Soliz, Eugenia Ybarra, Rebecca C. García, Elida C. Cárdenas, Alicia Gonzales, Dolores E. Valdez, Mary Jessie González, María Antonietta Cárdenas, Francisca M. Montemayor, Pauline C. Martínez, Martha Tijerina, Irma M. Lozano, Yolanda Ríos Rangel, Jean H. Ortiz, Mary A. Garza, Diana Armijo, Yolanda de León, Rebecca de León, Julie Marquez, and Luz Elena Day.

CHAPTER 6

Running for Office

Family and friends had festooned the front yard of my parents' home with brightly decorated tables, baskets brimming with *pan dulce,* and coffee for all on that lovely sunny day at the end of December 1980 when I announced my candidacy for City Council. My young nieces and nephews waved hastily printed red-on-white signs created by Rubén Munguía, declaring, "María Antonietta Rodríguez Berriozábal for District 1." Father Larry Matula and Captain Rolan Chambless offered prayers. A host of friends, neighbors, and supporters were there—Luz Escamilla, Fernando Rodríguez, Doris Chambless, Mike Casey, among others—bringing to mind my years of involvement in the community.

Under my mother's blooming crepe myrtle, flanked by my husband, parents, siblings, and three generations of family members, I stood before a bevy of radio and television microphones and cameras and spoke my intentions in running for office. Among other things, I addressed the need to have a trained and educated workforce that could meet the needs of prospective employers and of the "right of an individual to a decent home." The next day's paper quoted me as saying:

> San Antonio, I believe, is on the threshold of great things, but only if we can truly value what we have, if we know what it is that we need to fulfill the lives of our citizens and if we can be creative and clever enough to know how to satisfy these needs in spite of shrinking federal funds.[1]

My friend and newly recruited campaign manager, John Alvarado, was also quoted, saying we would have an "eyeball-to-eyeball" campaign. That announcement made clear that ours would be a grassroots-driven effort from beginning to end, supported by the people whose issues and concerns I intended to bring to the table. As I wrote in one of my first fundraising letters:

> To improve the quality of life in District 1, we must address the need for equitable distribution of municipal services, adequate police protection, revitalization of our older neighborhoods, and economic development of our downtown area. Priorities must be

set and a balance must be struck to insure this development is in harmony with the development of new areas of our city.

This understanding of my District's needs and my commitment to act on them would pose huge challenges throughout my decade on City Council. But on this bright December day, my thoughts turned to the long journey that had brought me to this moment. Standing at that podium, announcing my political campaign, it was clear how far I had traveled from the life my parents and grandparents lived at the start of the 20th century. It was equally clear to me, however, that many others, particularly in our Mejicano community, were still struggling to meet basic needs and make dreams come true for their families. I now had an incredible opportunity to respond to my parents' constant admonition to help one's neighbor, "*ayudar al projimo*," but in a more systemic way. And at this point in my life, I had a pretty good idea of the kind of help my neighbors needed.

Analysis on the Bus

For twenty years, from 1955 to 1975, I rode the bus in San Antonio—first going to school, then to work. During those years, the view through the window gave me more than a classroom education on the changing urban landscape and socio-political pressures impinging on our neighborhoods.

The bus route I took each day ran in front of our house on West Martin Street. During the 1950s and early 1960s, the neighborhoods I traversed were humble but stable. Most houses were small, well-kept wooden structures with attractive front yards where some mamá or abuela's green thumb was evident in the brightly colored roses, crepe myrtles, and bougainvillea. Once we crossed Zarzamora Street, the size of some of the houses increased, some even grand looking. One house, in particular, captured my imagination. It was large and white with a front porch and bay window. I could make out the lace curtains hanging on the interior as my bus rode by. In the front yard a sign advertised, "Margarita Rocha, *profesora de piano*." I imagined a very *educada* and *muy propia* Mexican woman living in that beautiful house, teaching little ones piano lessons. That image inspired me each day as we drove by the house. A couple of blocks over the railroad tracks there was an industrial area with Scobey Moving & Storage, the Carpenter Paper Company, and Pro Plus Mills, whose huge silo-like structure hovered over the trains that blocked traffic, unexpectedly making you late for school or work every once in a while.

As we got closer to downtown, but before we reached the Robert B. Green Hospital, the county hospital that served low-income people and was always bustling with activity, we passed through a multi-ethnic area with thriving small businesses, featuring colorful storefronts. One I remember in particular was the Pizzini store, which sold fancy olive oils, cheeses, and other Italian delicacies. Nearby, St. George's Maronite Church and St. Anthony de Paola Catholic Church stood guard right before we made the turn into downtown. Surrounding these churches were Italian and Lebanese neighborhoods that, together with our Mexican-American barrios on the Westside, provided a strong market for downtown department stores.

When I was in school, and later when I worked at The Salvation Army, I got off the bus on Houston Street and St. Mary's, in front of the Hertzberg Jewelry clock, and walked east, past the Majestic Theater. Busy storefronts and people-filled streets greeted me as I caught my transfer bus at Walgreens Drug Store on Navarro Street. Downtown San Antonio was thriving; it was everyone's downtown in those days.

Admittedly, all was not perfect on the Westside—nowhere near! Substandard housing and horrible streets abounded beyond Martin Street and families in poverty were the rule, not the exception. This daily bus ride, however, reflected the stability that was still present in the working middle class families, providing a human scaffolding that held everybody else up.

As the years passed, I began to see changes while traveling that route; some were gradual, others seemed to appear overnight. Urban Renewal, whose purpose was "to remove urban blight" and "deliver a decent home and suitable living environment to every American,"[2] was changing our neighborhoods. When the razing started a few blocks away from West Martin Street as we neared downtown, I saw how the stability of all the surrounding neighborhoods was threatened. Some of my friends who lived close to Immaculate Heart of Mary Catholic Church had to leave their homes; others left businesses. Pizzini's was among other stores that closed shop and left; so did the Maronite Church. Saint Anthony's lost its congregation. In time, that kind of erosion would also impact our stable Christ the King barrio.

In accordance with eminent domain's requirement that a public need be met for destroying public property, something should have been created on the carcasses of those barrios. But for years they remained barren.[3] Mexican barrios were destroyed and it was painful to see that no value was given to the sense of community that was eliminated. Destroyed were *tienditas, yerberias,* small mom-and-pop stores, entertainment venues and, most of all, that sense of community that helps poor people get through life's challenges because in tightly knit neighborhoods, neighbors help neighbors.

Over the years, I saw from the bus the enormous stress placed on neighborhoods near those that were eliminated by urban renewal. I saw the impact on San Antonio's downtown as the large surrounding market of people dwindled. White flight from other areas of the inner city and the advent of shopping malls further drained population from the city's center. Eventually, when I saw Margarita Rocha's house vacated and the piano-teacher sign go down, it was a powerful symbol to me of the deterioration that had taken root. The house that had so inspired me had become one of many abandoned houses dotting our neighborhoods with weedy yards and faded paint, giving them that old-wood look.

This was the view from the bus. But other changes, not so evident to a young girl, had also been taking place in my city while I was riding the bus. Starting as early as 1951, when I was still in grade school, our city government began to change. That year a reform-minded group of men got rid of the former political-machine city government. They wanted San Antonio to take its place as a Sunbelt City with a good economy. The goal was laudable enough but the impact on our barrios definitely not. By 1955, the group had a name: the "Good Government League." It would control city politics for the next two decades.

The board of directors of the Good Government League (GGL) constituted "the economic and social elite of San Antonio."[4] A new city charter was created that maintained power in the hands of a few—those with money. There would be nine councilpersons elected at-large and a city manager, hired by the entire council, would run the city. There would be no strong mayor position. The charter allowed for a stipend of $20 per meeting for council members and $50 for the mayor. This, of course, meant that a majority of the people in our economically poor city would not be able to run for City Council.[5] These changes to the city charter enabled the reformers to pursue what they saw as the primary function of city government, "growth and economic expansion."[6] Thus, it was "not a quirk of the market" that the particular growth and expansion that occurred was one "where the east, west, and south sides of San Antonio were left out."[7] It was intentional policy.

While we achieved some progress in eliminating the overt political machine of the past through the GGL, we exchanged it for another, subtler, machine. In the ensuing years, the GGL would field its own City Council ticket and win all the elections. A critical feature of the new city charter was that elections would be "non-partisan." This was a significant provision because by 1955, the Mexican-American community was gaining some power in the Democratic Party. But if city elections were non-partisan, the Mexican-American community would not benefit from that political party power.

The GGL's priorities of growth and expansion meant that scant, if any, attention was given to the social issues that plagued the Mexican-American community. The focus on economic growth was not on economic growth for all; the people behind the GGL were about *new* growth, not investment in the central city or other areas where minorities tended to live. Much of the growth of the period was through annexation, a government tool used for expansion. Investment was then focused on these newly annexed areas rather than on the housing needs or decaying infrastructure of our downtown neighborhoods. GGL council candidates were white, with one or two Mexican Americans and one African American as a token gesture for minorities in the city. The GGL's minority candidates, for the most part, worked for the status quo and most lived on the city's affluent Northside.

But during these years, a generation of children grew up who would become beacons of change for our community. They came of age witnessing the effects of the closed political system and began to act, creatively addressing issues that had been unaddressed for decades. Top among them was self-determination, inclusion in decision-making, social reform, civil rights, and provision of public services to minority communities. Chicana/o youth started to go after not only the GGL but also the Democratic Party, demanding change. The Chicana/o youth did not see the benefit to our communities of a growth-and-expansion agenda, whether promoted by the GGL-run city government or the Democratic Party, that did not take into account how our minority and low income communities were faring. Simply put, it was wrong for our community not to be represented in our local government where decisions impacting our future and welfare were being made.

In 1969, a group of young Chicanas and Chicanos organized the Committee for Barrio Betterment (CBB), fielding candidates for City Council from our precincts. My neighbors, family, and I strongly supported Mario Compean, Dario Chapa, and Candelario Alejo for City Council that year. For the first time, we saw a new kind of competition—brown vs. brown—in a few political races, as CBB-sponsored Chicanos ran against Mexican-American insiders sponsored by the GGL. Our Westside precincts voted overwhelmingly for the CBB candidates, but with the at-large system of voting, the votes from the Northside—GGL votes—won each time.

The CBB tried again in 1971. This time, in another "first," two Chicanas ran—Rosie Castro, a brilliant young activist (now mother of San Antonio Mayor Julián Castro and State Representative Joaquín Castro) and attorney Gloria Cabrera. Willie Benavides also ran for a council seat and Mario Compean ran again. Although each of these candidates lost their races, they gave powerful expression to the nascent Chicano Movement they had created—a movement that would eventually change Texas politics. Thanks to their efforts and the grassroots pressure that the Movement brought to bear, the GGL and the big-business establishment behind it saw the writing on the wall. After years of "tumultuous transition,"[8] and through invocation of the Voting Rights Act of 1965, the GGL's control over local government through the at-large system was brought to an end. In 1977, we began to elect our City Council members by district.

This victory, defeating the political system that had dominated San Antonio for years and oppressed minorities and poor and working class people, came on the heels of an unprecedented flourishing of political engagement by young Chicanas/os and others in the Mexican-American community. Finding ways to work around the oppression of our local and state political institutions, a generation of young people birthed a host of new institutions that were to make a mark not only in San Antonio and Texas but nationally. The 1960s and 1970s saw a litany of activism born out of our community that has few parallels.

The courageous struggle, creativity, and dedication of hundreds of individuals in the Chicana/o and Mexican-American community of San Antonio created a critical mass of activism and wisdom that educated and raised consciousness in our community, fomented pride, and forced doors to open doors that others, like myself, would later enter. Neither my victory in 1981 nor that of Henry Cisneros, who was elected mayor of San Antonio that year, would have been possible without it.

The extraordinary years of struggle and their impact were not lost on me. If I was going to run for elected office, it could be for no purpose other than to carry forward that legacy of dedication to the community through my service on the Council, representing District 1.

A Litany of Activism

The 1960s and 1970s saw a litany of activism that has few historical parallels. More than three dozen organizations were given birth by our community, including:

Liberal Bexar County Democratic Coalition—1959

Political Association of Spanish Speaking Organizations (PASSO)—1961

San Antonio Literacy Council—1965

San Antonio Neighborhood Youth Association (SANYO)—1965

Mexican American Nationalist Organization (MANO)—1966

Barrios Unidos—late 1960s

Mexican American Unity Council (MAUC)—1967

Mexican American Youth Organization (MAYO)—1967

La Universidad de los Barrios (LUD) through MAUC and MAYO—1967

United Farmworkers Union-Texas Group—1967

Mexican American Legal Defense and Educational Fund (MALDEF)—1968

VISTA Minority Mobilization Program (VISTA MMP) through MAYO—1968

Committee for Barrio Betterment (CBB)—1969

Padres Asociados para Derechos, Religiosos, Educativos y Sociales (PADRES)—1969

Texas Institute for Educational Development (TIED)—1969

La Raza Unida Party—1970

Bexar County Chicana Political Coalition—1970s

Chicana Welfare Rights Organization—1970s

Bexar County Democratic Women—1971

Bilingual/Bi-Cultural Coalition on Mass Media (BBC)—1971

Democratic National Committee's Chicano Democratic Caucus—1971

Las Hermanas—1971

American Federation of State, County and Municipal Employees (AFSME)—1972

Mexican American Business & Professional Women's Club (MABPW)—1972

Mexican American Cultural Center (MACC)—1972

AVANCE Parenting Program—1973

El Centro del Barrio (dba CentroMed)—1973

Intercultural Development Research Association (IDRA)—1973

Communities Organized for Public Service (COPS)—1974

MALDEF Chicana Rights Project—1974

Southwest Voter Registration and Education Fund (SWVREP)—1974

Mexican American Democrats (MAD)—1976

Centro Cultural Aztlán—1977

Mexican American Neighborhood Civic Organization (MANCO)—late 1970s

Performance Arts Nucleus—1978

The Advocates Social Services—1978

United Public Employees Union (UPEU)—1978

PAN Consortium—1980

Guadalupe Cultural Arts Center—1980

The Lay of the Land in District 1

The district I sought to represent lies in the heart of San Antonio. The San Antonio River meanders through its historic downtown buildings and neighborhoods, including areas settled by Spanish colonists and missionaries and—for millennia before that—native peoples. It remains home to the diverse neighborhoods that have long surrounded the downtown area, notwithstanding urban renewal. On the west side of the district laid neighborhoods like Our Lady of Guadalupe, a cradle of the Mexican and Mexican-American community. At the time, to the east, long time African-American neighborhoods were dotted with congregations of strong churches. South was the historic King William neighborhood, built by German immigrants. And on the northern fringes of District 1, our own Beacon Hill neighborhood, typical of others in transition, continued to work to keep itself alive.[9]

These downtown neighborhoods—the face of San Antonio—held a vital history, character, and strength that deserved to be protected despite the decline caused by urban renewal, white flight, and suburbanization. While there were a few affluent people in these neighborhoods, most were low-income or middle-class working families, in addition to some very vulnerable populations. At the time I ran for office, a census tract showed that within the city the poorest children under the age of five and the poorest elderly over 65 lived in my district's Westside.

At age 39, I understood the needs of the inner city not only intellectually but also viscerally. My family and I had lived them. I had devoted my young adult years to working with neighbors and friends in a variety of institutions and organizations to address issues of education, literacy, community development, political engagement, employment, affirmative action, immigration, leadership development and the empowerment of women and our Mexican-American community. I had seen the serious challenges but also the extraordinary courage and hope of a strong community, working to solve their problems.

The GGL politics that resulted in years of disinvestment in our downtown neighborhoods were clearly evident in the sub-standard housing and vacant structures in District 1. Flooding was still as horrendous as our family had experienced when rains made our little backyard on Picoso Street seem like a lake and my mother had to carry Felix across the street to school. Residential zoning was at risk in neighborhoods like Beacon Hill, Tobin Hill, Government Hill, and others that still held stately structures. These "neighborhoods in transition" were in danger of demolition by neglect, arson, and lack of public services. The distinction between "old" and "historic," where one is disposable and the other preserved, can be very subjective. Chronic disinvestment in our inner city was also evident in District 1's poor education and literacy levels, community development, and services for the elderly, children, and families.

Despite these challenging conditions, there was also cause for hope. As noted earlier, a new era of civic engagement had dawned in our city. Not only was there a burgeoning of political and civil rights activism but, at the neighborhood level, pressing needs provided an impetus for citizens to organize and speak out. In this, District 1 was a leader. It had been an incubator for the creation of voluntary neighborhood associations. While they were not yet recognized for the political potential they held, they were gaining strength in older areas of the city.

Among the first such groups to be organized were King William, Lavaca, River Road, Arsenal, Alta Vista, Monte Vista, Tobin Hill, Beacon Hill, and Government Hill. The residents in these areas banned together beginning in the late 1960s to maintain the value of the houses whose sturdy construction and pleasing architecture added character to the older areas of the city. After returning to San Antonio in 1976 and purchasing our home in Beacon Hill in 1978, only a few minutes' drive away from my parents' home, Manny and I were one of four couples that organized our neighborhood association in 1978. The late Liz Davies took the lead in the organizing. She became a valued mentor to me not only on neighborhood issues but also on water policy.

In District 1, Communities Organized for Public Service (COPS) had gained a foothold in Catholic parishes, providing another lever for grassroots organizing. I had already worked with COPS leaders at a number of parishes, including Our Lady of Guadalupe, San Juan de Los Lagos, Sacred Heart, St. Henry's, St. Agnes, and Christ the King, which together represented a large portion of District 1. By the early 1980s, COPS had a reputation for challenging big developers whose quest for growth necessitated large infusions of public funds to pay for infrastructure, such as water main extensions, to new areas of the city to the detriment of older areas. The group engaged in Saul Alinsky-styled tactics to hold elected officials accountable, working to ensure that monies appropriated for infrastructure on the west and south sides of town, such as drainage projects, were indeed spent there and not reallocated to other areas of the city.

At the time I announced my candidacy for District 1, COPS was challenging two major proposed projects involving millions of dollars in public investments for the South Texas Nuclear Power Project and the so-called "Applewhite" surface water reservoir. I had longstanding connections with COPS. One of my last memories of my grandmother, Sebastiana, is seeing her walk slowly up the stairs behind City Hall to support her local COPS organization at Christ the King. Wanting to know the issue they were concerned about, I asked her, "*¿Qué discuten?*" She answered, "*No se, hija, pero les vengo ayudar hacer bulto.*" My grandmother did not know the issue but she was there to help, if only by adding one more body in solidarity. That was the kind of loyalty COPS commanded.

Such was the lay of the land in District 1 as I made my campaign announcement. I had been integrally involved in the evolution of my community's movement toward self-determination. It was a key value I wanted to help sustain as I promised strong advocacy in City Hall to help maintain public services and improve the quality of life in District 1. But this determination to bring my advocacy directly into the halls of city government by winning a seat at the Council table was not something that grew in me spontaneously. Like everyone else in my district, when Henry Cisneros announced he would be stepping down to run for mayor, I was eagerly looking around for who might next represent us.

Why Not You, María?

When my job with the Census Bureau was completed I wanted to slow down for a while. I hoped to finish fixing up our house—a task postponed because of my college studies and work at the Census. We had bought a home in the Beacon Hill neighborhood, about four miles north of downtown, as part of our commitment to the inner city. It was a stately house, but like many in neighborhoods surrounding the downtown area, it was old and rundown and in need of a lot of repairs. Also, Manny and I very much wanted a family of our own. Marrying at the age I did, I had decided that when children came, we would live on one salary and I would devote myself fulltime to raising them—a decision Manny fully supported.

For the short term, however, I would volunteer full time to help my City Councilman Henry Cisneros in his campaign to run for mayor. I was very supportive of his candidacy. Cisneros was the most qualified, having already served on City Council for almost six years. If elected, he would be the first Latino to serve as mayor of San Antonio in contemporary times. I wanted to help create that hopeful history in any way I could. In the meantime, people were engaged in lots of speculation on who would fill the vacancy created by Cisneros. Some Latinas felt it was time for a Mexican-American woman to be elected to City Council. I joined a small group of Latinas, including Sylvia Rodríguez, Rosie Castro, Choco Meza, and others in an effort to identify a candidate. As I started to ask potential candidates about taking the leap, however, the response was always the same: "No."

There was a wide range of reasons why the women said no. Some were just not interested in public office; others felt they did not have the qualifications. A few said their husbands would not support them or allow them to do so, and others had children they needed to care for. A huge impediment was that the position paid only $20 a week; family budgets could not take the financial stress the position would impose. There also were those who felt that San Antonio was not ready to elect a Mexican-American woman.

To my surprise, after saying no, some of the women would then turn the question around and ask, "Why not you, María?" They would say things like, "You have the qualifications. You spent all those years working in government and political offices. You already know what it's like in there." But an idea like that had not entered my mind. It was not what a young girl growing up on the Westside of San Antonio aspired to in those years, for sure not me! In time, however, as more people started talking to me about the district race, negating whatever excuses I offered, I began to think about it. When word got around to people in my old and new neighborhoods that I was thinking about it, I started hearing not only words of encouragement and excitement but also, more importantly, offers of help.

All of this brought back memories of my first visit to Washington, D.C. in 1969 when Congressman Henry B. González had offered me a job in his Washington office. As he gave us a tour of the Congressional chamber, I felt a powerful desire to sit in Congress someday. But it was a fleeting thought that immediately left me! I also remembered a local news story that had appeared almost ten years before. It read that I, along with six other Mexican-American women, was being considered as "a possible successor to the late Mayor Pro Tem Gilbert Garza." Ironically, this was a GGL selection—a very far-fetched idea at the time.[10]

I began to give the possibility serious consideration, discussing it with my husband. One day as Manny and I were yet again on the topic and I continued to find all kinds of excuses for not running, he said, "I think you are afraid of losing." Manny is a man of very few words; those gave me pause and insight. I thought about them carefully and finally concluded, "No way am I afraid!" The comment, however, pushed me over the edge. Although I did not tell him at the time because that would have made it official in my mind, I had decided there really was no reason *not* to run—and many reasons to do it. As I pondered the positions I had held, my work experience and involvement in my community over many years, and my education, I felt I had the qualifications needed to carry out the responsibilities of the office. I was confident I could represent the people of my district because I understood the issues. It had always been my desire to serve my neighbors—and I had found ways to do it through every position I held, from secretarial to administrative. How much more would I be able to do to serve the people I loved through elected office and public policy development?

Men, Money, and Women

I decided to meet with several men whose opinion I respected to let them know I was considering a race for District 1 and to solicit their advice. These were political science professors at local universities, including a couple of former college professors, whom I considered friends. Although they were individuals who often served as advisors to political candidates and politicians, it soon became evident that they were not used to having a woman—a Latina!—approach them about a quest for elected office. The meetings did not go well.

After my last such visit, I was feeling quite deflated. As always, the professor was kind, offering brotherly advice, but all he talked about were the challenges I would face. I knew there would be challenges! What I yearned to hear were a few positive words—a suggestion, an offer of help, or a simple affirmation to "go for it!" notwithstanding the challenges.

As I rode the bus home along Cincinnati Avenue, pondering this last conversation, I started to think that the lackluster responses I had received not only from him but also from the other professors were signs that I should not run. I recalled what one professor told me about needing at least $10,000 to run a credible campaign. I could raise $5,000 through fundraising events and small donations, he said, but the rest had to come from big donors. "Who on earth were these big donors?" I asked myself. "And why would any of them give me money?"

By the time I got off the bus, I had made the decision that I could not and would not run. I neither had the resources I needed nor any way to get them. It was a perfectly valid and legitimate excuse. I felt relieved.

After I arrived home, I picked up the mail and found a letter from my dear friend, Irma Martínez, a dedicated schoolteacher I had met twelve years earlier when we were taking evening business courses at Our Lady of the Lake College. As I opened the envelope and pulled out its contents, I was stunned to find not only a note but also a check. It was a $100 campaign contribution—no small amount in 1980. Irma's note said she was sending the check with her best wishes for my campaign and an offer to do anything she could to get me elected.

What an omen. I had just made the decision not to run because there was no way I could raise the money and I come home to find an unsolicited check for $100 from a schoolteacher who kept her politics pretty close to her heart. All I could think was that if a schoolteacher could dig into her pocket and send me $100, how could I say, no, I am not going to run?

The generosity of one woman coupled with her loving message made up for all the negativity of the men I had consulted. In time, there would be many generous offers of support from other men, especially those from Christ the King Church and neighborhood associations, and, of course, from many other women. But Irma's spontaneous gift that day spurred me on to launch the campaign that sunny morning of December 27, 1980.

Patio Andaluz

My sister-in-law, Dolores, helped me set up my campaign head-quarters in our home. As soon as I had enough money, Dolores and her small children, Miguel and Cristina, walked with me, up and down popular streets on the Westside, to help find a more suitable location. After much searching, we heard about an empty storefront in the Patio Andaluz building at the corner of Colorado and West Commerce, two very prominent streets deep in the Westside.

It was an historic site. The structure was originally built as a union hall in 1927 and until the 1980s, the Patio Andaluz had been a popular dance hall for the Mexican and Mexican-American communities. Now, except for a couple of small businesses on the ground floor, the place was vacant and in dire need of repair. We got a good deal for a small space with street access through the front and back. But it was an even better deal for the owner. He got a tenant who fixed up the place, such that it is occupied to this day.

Family and friends volunteered to help clean it, with my father taking the lion's share of the responsibility. I did not realize until many years later how much my political involvement pleased him. Whether he was cleaning the office or providing an analysis of my work, Papá cheered me on throughout my political career. At the campaign head-quarters, my father built sturdy dividing walls and repaired whatever needed repairing. He volunteered to be the maintenance person, taking out garbage, keeping the bathroom and office clean, and serving as the go-to handy man for whatever was needed. Papá was also a "fly on the wall," observing and analyzing everything he saw. From time to time, he would share his opinion with me. Since some people did not know he was my father, he could hear things no one else heard. Every candidate needs that kind of sleuth!

I recruited my first group of volunteers by sending invitations to people on every list I could find, from our wedding and Christmas lists to people in organizations to which I belonged, to former work col-leagues, fellow parishioners and people involved in neighborhood asso-ciations. I came up with about 500 names and we sent a letter to each, informing them of my decision to run and why, and inviting them to a planning meeting at La Sociedad de la Union Hall on West Com-merce Street. Fifty people—mostly relatives, friends, and a few new people others had brought—showed up. From that group we secured volunteers for the different committees. My grade school friend, Mary Helen Alvarado, had obtained fancy multiple-copy volunteer forms from her boss Phil Hardberger, a young attorney who had run an un-successful state senate race and had hundreds of these left over. Do-lores typed the names, addresses, and phone numbers of each person, noting how we thought he or she might help. With this novice team of volunteers, we set to work.

Low Profiles in Politics

"Volunteers" was the operative word of our campaign. We had no funds to pay a soul, not even a campaign manager, so I had no hope of bringing on board anyone with campaign experience. John Alvarado be-came part of my team when I learned that he, a fellow parishioner from Christ the King, had just retired from Kelly Air Force Base. I had gone to school with his children and decided to ask him to be my campaign manager. Mr. Alvarado told me that he had never run a campaign. I told him I hadn't either so we would learn together. John Alvarado was kind enough to accept. He was highly respected and had been active in the community and in grassroots politics for many years.

"We need to go visit some Mexican-American powerbrokers," Mr. Alvarado suggested early on. "You need their support and their money." I agreed. And since I knew some of these gentlemen, I told Mr. Alvarado that I would meet with them and ask for help. I prepared myself for these meetings, coming up with well-thought-out reasons for running for office and talking points on my key issues. We began to make some visits, with me laying out my well-prepared opening statement. Then came what always turned out to be the first question: "Who is supporting you?"

I eagerly rattled off the names of people I knew who were supporting me. "Well, Emilia and Frank Ramos, Fernando and Oralia Rodríguez, Joe and Minnie Maldonado..."

"Who else?" the powerbroker interrupted.

"Rosie and Richard Guerra, the *entire* family of Anastacio Juárez, Ana Álvarez, Liz Davies, Mike Casey..."

"Yes, María. But who *well-known* is supporting you?"

That's when I understood that I would not be running anything approaching a conventional campaign. All these wonderful people—people from the neighborhood of my youth, fellow community workers, voters, new friends—didn't count when it came to big "P" politics. My supporters were not people who won endorsements from powerbrokers who did not even live in our district.

We would have to reach out to new voters—the very people who needed my attention. It was their vote I would seek, one by one. These were the people in whose midst I had lived most of my life on Picoso and West Martin Streets. The people from my church and the Latinas with whom I had been collaborating. The activists in the fledgling neighborhood association movement, the small business owners downtown, and so many others. With that idea and approach, we slowly began to attract support from a large number of people, many now deceased, who were very committed to my candidacy but had no political experience.

Florencio Hernández, a childhood friend and a CPA became my campaign treasurer. A retired Army colonel, E.J. García, called very early in the campaign to say, "My wife and I would like to meet with you about your campaign."

"Great," I said. "When?"

"As soon as possible," he responded, "and bring your resume."

I met the colonel and his wife, Lupe, for lunch. They asked me a lot of questions about my platform. I felt like I was applying for a job—and I was! The next day, I got a call from the colonel. "María, Lupe and I decided that I will help you. I will volunteer in your headquarters five days a week from 9 to 5, but I will be off weekends. I will do whatever you want me to do. We like what you stand for." At this point we still had no headquarters, but he joined Dolores in working out of our house. After we set up our office at the Patio Andaluz, he continued to be an outstanding volunteer, winning the respect of everyone with whom he came in contact. He was a solid force in my campaign office for the duration.

One day I received a visit at our home from Choco and Danny Meza, who were very experienced campaign workers, having been part of La Raza Unida Party as college students. I had gotten to know Choco after she joined MABPW. We were talking about how my campaign was going when Danny asked, "Have you done your precinct targeting?"

My answer—"What is that?"—made clear we were doing no such thing! An integral campaign tool, precinct targeting is about analyzing which precincts should be given priority. Danny offered to be my precinct captain and Choco volunteered to serve as my campaign coordinator. Sylvia and Gene Rodríguez also started to help. I had met Sylvia when she was secretary to State Senator Joe J. Bernal and I was working at Hemisfair. Gene, a longtime friend working with UTSA at the time, had asked me to help him with a special community project on unemployment when I was about to graduate from UTSA.

My MABPW friend and mentor, Luz Escamilla, volunteered to be my finance chair. "We will create budgets for every event and all who help will have to prepare reports of every penny we raise," she said, taking charge immediately. With her brand of tough leadership, Luz led a group of friends and volunteers in organizing home fundraisers, a theater performance, a birthday celebration for me, food-plate sales, and other activities where tickets were *al alcance de todos*. In other words, the price of admission was low! The most expensive event was $30 per person. The few donations we received over $100 were from friends. MABPW members were generous; two dug into their savings to contribute $500 each to the campaign.

Our first big fundraising event, held even before I announced, was at a nightclub called Mad Michael's. At the Christmas event we charged $7.50 per person and Mateo Camargo's band played. Mateo was a popular radio personality at KCOR Spanish radio. I had met him when I worked at the Courthouse. He had always been very helpful to me when I needed publicity for some special cause or needy person. We bought inexpensive radio announcements for the fund-raiser. With venue, music, food, and everything else donated, we raised $1,500 with 200 persons in attendance. It was a very successful event where I gave one of my first speeches. My favorite memory was of my father dancing with me, he was so happy! I had never even seen my father dance before. Actually, I also rarely danced. But that day, truly happy, we both danced.

Long on Name, Short on Funds

I had been told that people with long names do not win elections, but what could I do? I had changed my name to "Berriozábal" after I married. I knew people would recognize me by my picture, so our signs included my picture and my name—all of it—*María Antonietta Rodríguez Berriozábal.* José Soria, a young man who had been my fellow student at UTSA, became my sign coordinator, getting them posted in yards of supporters around the district. A crew of people made the silk-screened signs under the direction of Danny Meza. Even Danny's father, Joe Meza, helped us hang all those wet signs from strings that my father had hung in our storeroom. Papá searched high and low through neighborhood grocery stores for large cardboard boxes that we would cut up and use as backing for those first homemade red and white signs.

Our first campaign mailer was similarly bare bones—a black and white flyer on cheap paper with a picture of me in front of City Hall. It listed my qualifications and priorities for the district. Later, I went to a neighborhood photography studio and had a more formal campaign photo taken.

Although we still had very little money, the combination of growing numbers of people who were very committed to my candidacy but had little or no political experience plus a few very experienced workers added up to a great team. We had a strong community-based, grassroots campaign where people contributed their talent and many also gave of their modest treasure. In her meticulously kept handwritten ledger, Mary Helen Alvarado kept track of every donation, most well under $100. To this day, I smile looking at the properly receipted checks or money orders for $1 or $2, each faithfully accounted for in the ledger. We began simply, trusting in democracy and exercising it in its most authentic form by working hard, going door to door, concentrating on what we needed to do to get votes. I gave little thought to who was running against me. I had no idea the cards were stacked against me as an outsider, although with time I would discover this. For now I was just sure I was going to win because of the kinds of things that would happen as I went block walking in my district.

One warm, sunny day, for example, I knocked on the door of a couple who, according to our county elections office rolls, were consistent voters. These are the most sought-after voters as they are people who have voted in the past several elections and are most likely to show up again at the polls on Election Day. A man met me at the door. With my optimistic smile, expecting the favorable response I had been receiving in that precinct, I said, "My name is María Antonietta Rodríguez Berriozábal. I was raised in this neighborhood and I am running for City Council District 1…."

Before I could utter another word, much less ask for his vote, the man cut me off. "*¡No! Vamos a votar por Peeler.*"

Just as the man was telling me they were going to vote for Al Peeler, a woman stuck her head out of the kitchen door behind him with a little child standing next to her. She gave me a big smile, motioning "yes" with her head and giving me a big thumbs-up! This story would repeat itself throughout my walks. Women made up their own minds, with many supporting me despite the fact that their husbands were supporting my male opponents. My candidacy gave many Latinas who had never participated actively in a political campaign a new opportunity to do so. I think we all felt the excitement of potentially making history.

People Who Left Their Mark

Profound feelings of gratitude and joy filled my heart during those days as I witnessed the generous commitment of so many people to the campaign. I often thought, "This is how it feels to fall in love with a whole community of people." The campaign atmosphere was that of a large family working together, learning as we went. These individuals, most now long deceased, have stayed in my mind over the years. They represent the best in a government of the people.

- **Bernice Alvarado,** a widow, was an octogenarian who had raised thirteen children, including one who died in World War II. During the campaign, Mrs. Alvarado sent entire Lenten meals to our campaign headquarters with her daughter Mary Helen. We had no money to feed workers so these meals were a wonderful gift of nutrition and support.

- **Magdalena Tijerina,** another widow and mother of pioneering Spanish-television personality Martha Tijerina, went house to house on my behalf. A very elegant elderly woman, Mrs. Tijerina even sported the bright red T-shirt with my name splashed on it as she sought votes.

- **Teofila Arellano,** an elder parishioner at Christ the King, was the wife of a neighborhood politician and mother of several sons who also were active in politics but she had never gotten involved in politics. Mrs. Arellano went house to house for me, asking for votes, and was ever proud when her candidate defeated the one her husband and sons chose!

- **Patricio Lombrano,** a friend from Christ the King, and **Robert "Papa Bear" Edwards** led the campaign efforts in the gay community, introducing me to many people I would never have met. Later, Papa Bear educated me on the disaster of the HIV/AIDS epidemic when it hit San Antonio; I helped him as he founded the San Antonio AIDS Foundation.

- **Hap Veltman,** a downtown property owner and inner city entrepreneur, was a strong supporter. He had a huge campaign poster in his "Big Country" nightspot on the river and promoted me in areas of the district where I was not known.

- **Fay Sinkin,** founder of the Aquifer Protection Association, wrote a $50 check when I asked for her support. She was not in the district but her endorsement was important. Fay became a friend and mentor, especially on water issues.

- **Mateo Camargo,** popular KCOR Radio personality, sent out 3,000 postcards to friends, stretching what he could do as a media personality. He and his wife Belia had a huge constituency because of their years in Mexican theater and the *Carpas* (tent shows) in the 1930s in San Antonio.

- **Mitchell Battros,** owner of Mad Michael's nightclub, contributed the biggest donation by far—$1,000—all based on Mateo Camargo's recommendation.

- **Frank and Emilia Ramos,** Christ the King Church members and parents of many children they succeeded in putting through college, had seen me grow up. They gave me their total support during the campaign and then throughout my years in office.

- **Liz Davies,** conservationist, environmentalist, and neighborhood leader, was especially helpful with neighborhood associations and on water issues.

- **Mary Esther Bernal,** educator and wife of former State Senator Joe J. Bernal, supported me, adding to my credibility as she was highly respected in political circles.

- **Julia Ross** and **Janie Adamé,** residents and leaders in Alazán Apache Courts, got the other residents to the polls and were justifiably proud that we won that public housing complex for our campaign. While some candidates tended to overlook public housing projects, we worked those in our district. They were drawn to our campaign by their concern over the quality of life for their children.

- **Fernando Rodríguez,** my former boss at the AFGE union, supported me. A very formal man, I remember hearing him yell at the top of his lungs on election day from behind the distance markers at the largest polling site, "*¡Voten por la primer Latina para el Concilio!*" The most powerful message being that he and a bunch of other older Mejicano guys were excited about a Latina running for office.

- **My entire family,** Manny, my parents and siblings and their spouses, aunts and uncles and cousins—all who were able—pitched in, providing invaluable support. Respecting the voter was a high value for me and one way I wanted to show this was by having at least one family member at each of the twenty polling places on Election Day. We had enough family members to do this and, according to reports, we did very well in the respect arena—with one notable exception. **Tía Luz Rodríguez Zertuche,** who was not a shy soul, had to defend me when someone took my election-day "push" card and tore it up in front of her. She was not going to stay quiet while someone disrespected her *consentida* niece—and told them off! Other than this, the day was peaceful and people commented on the many workers I had in their brightly colored red T-shirts.

District 1 Candidates Face Off

I ran against three Mexican-American men in my campaign to represent District 1. From the start, Alfonso "Al" Peeler, a police lieutenant with twenty-four years of service in the San Antonio Police Department, was seen as the frontrunner and likely successor to Cisneros. The other two candidates—Frank "Pancho" Monreal, a long-time community leader who had run and lost six years earlier, and José M. Aguilar, an individual who had been active in political campaigns and was running for office for the first time—ran low-key campaigns that garnered very little attention.

Peeler and I shared similar platforms and concerns about issues relating to streets, drainage, libraries, public transportation, and economic development in our district. We both realized that tough decisions were coming up, with shrinking federal dollars in the new Reagan Administration, and we each made the case as to why we were the ones who would make the right choices on how to spend money. Notwithstanding these similarities, there were a few issues that clearly distinguished us among the electorate.

Gender was the most obvious! Although sexism was not a dominant issue in the race, it clearly was a factor. "While her campaign is populated by women volunteers, she is having to fight a latent group of voters who would prefer to be represented by a man," the *San Antonio Light* reported on March 15, 1981.

Another difference was in how we characterized our campaigns. Peeler was very upfront about promoting himself as a protégé of Cisneros. "I'm hanging onto his coattails and I'm going to win that way," he was quoted as saying.[11] I ran on my own record and issue commitments.

A third difference was one I brought forward. It centered on the issue we had struggled for decades to win—self-determination! Peeler had been living in north San Antonio for the previous seventeen years, moving back to District 1 prior to announcing his campaign. This was a huge issue for me, given how hard our Mexican-American community had worked for single-member districts. That we would again have someone representing us in City Hall who hadn't been a resident of our district would be a huge step backward. I talked about self-determination and our ability to govern ourselves from within the district. "For seventeen years, Mr. Peeler surveyed the happenings in District 1 from atop his home in Inspiration Hills," I was quoted as saying. "His journey back to District 1 was prompted by political aspirations," I charged, contrasting my own history as a lifelong resident of the district.[12]

Finally, there were two major issues on which we differed. Peeler supported both the South Texas Nuclear Project and the Applewhite surface water reservoir—two multi-million-dollar projects that were strongly backed by the business community. I, on the other hand, opposed both. Although these critical issues barely surfaced in the primary, they would become defining issues during my time in office.

One issue that did garner quite a bit of attention was public safety and the role of the police. This was in part because Al Peeler was a police officer and former president of the Police Officers Association, but also because the inner city needed adequate police protection and was instead often victimized by police violence. The problem rose to the forefront during the campaign when a police officer killed Hector Santoscoy, a young undocumented immigrant from Piedras Negras, Mexico. The policeman killed him while Santoscoy was hiding under a house. The Westside Chicano community organized protests and I joined them in a protest march. Politically, a candidate out protesting police action was a risky act. But I was seeking a seat at the table where the issue of police violence against the very people it is sworn to protect needed to be addressed. There was no way I would sit this one out.

After four months of vigorous campaigning, we took the city by surprise on Election Day. There would be a runoff election in District 1! The ballots cast on April 4, 1981, showed Al Peeler leading with 44% of the vote and me coming in a close second with 42% of the vote. Trailing were Monreal at 10% and Aguilar at 4%. Peeler carried eleven precinct boxes; I carried nine.

Our victory took those who had thought I was just a nice lady running her little grassroots campaign by surprise. I had been underestimated. That would not be the case in the runoff. The campaign would get tougher, but we had gotten tougher, too.

The Runoff

During the primary, I garnered strong support from the neighborhood associations and community groups within the district. Al Peeler had the endorsement of most of the unions, the police and fire associations, and important government officials. As the *Express-News* reported, "Among luminaries supporting Peeler were 4ᵗʰ Court of Appeals Associate Justice Rudy Esquivel, state Senator Bob Vale, state Reps. Joe Hernandez and Paul Elizondo, former state senator Joe J. Bernal, San Antonio School District Board Chairman William Elizondo, San Antonio College District Board Chairman George Ozuna and former City Councilmen Claude Black and Pete Torres."[13]

Some of this support, however, worked against Peeler. On April 15, 1981, the *San Antonio Express-News* endorsed me, albeit in a backhanded way. The editorial assailed Al Peeler's campaign for using school district personnel at the urging of School Board Chairman William Elizondo and Pete Torres, a school board attorney. "The Elizondo team, which has already raised taxes sharply now has cuts in federal aid and has plenty of problems of its own. We advise voters to send the school leaders back to those problems and rebuff their involvement in the city election by supporting María Berriozabál."

The following day, the weekly *Westside Sun*, an arm of the *Express-News*, also endorsed me. It was a full-hearted endorsement. Noting my "outstanding qualifications," the editorial cited my work on the census and with Judge Blair Reeves, my internship with Henry Cisneros, my academic background, and my many community involvements as reasons for supporting my candidacy.

But there also were hints of some significant opposition coalescing against my candidacy.

The bigger story in the election that put Al Peeler and me into a runoff was the historic victory that brought a Mexican American, Henry Cisneros, into the mayor's office in San Antonio. Now that the mayoral campaign and all the other district races were over, there was a greater focus of attention on the runoff in District 1. In what would foreshadow the pivotal opposition I would face as an elected leader, a story in the *Express-News* revealed some behind-the-scenes efforts to prevent me from winning. "Word is out that the business community, becoming uncomfortable with District 1 runoff candidate María Berriozabál's stand on surface water and the nuclear plant, had Shipley approached to see if he would handle her opponent's campaign. He declined, opting instead for an earned rest from the rigors the campaigns."[14] George

Shipley had been the top campaign consultant to Henry Cisneros in his victorious mayoral campaign.

Hitting Below the Belt
Makes the Gut Stronger and Skin Thicker

During the runoff, Peeler challenged my record at the Census. He charged me with being "an incompetent administrator," saying our office had "undercounted the population by thousands." [15]

I had no idea where Peeler got this claim; he had nothing to back it up. I countered that San Antonio had a very successful census operation and that while other cities with large numbers of minorities had lawsuits filed against the Census Bureau for undercounts, none were filed in San Antonio. In fact, we had worked closely with the Mexican American Legal Defense and Educational Fund (MALDEF), the entity filing those lawsuits in other cities! It was precisely because we had taken the time to go after the hard-to-count, largely minority, populations in the inner city that the regional bureau tried to close down our office. I had objected and worked hard, with community support, to finish the critical job. The "incompetence" charge never gained traction in the press; no one picked it up.

Although I had not thought that much about gender politics before I launched my campaign, gender issues did present themselves, particularly in the runoff. When I tried to get Al Peeler to engage in a debate with me, for example, he refused. "In my culture," he said, "a gentleman does not debate a lady."

"I am asking him for a debate, not a dual," I responded. He never debated me.

Another issue that cut close to gender appeared in an ad that his campaign ran in the *Westside Sun*. The ad compared Al Peeler's record and qualifications with those of "the Opponent"—*i.e.*, me. In one section, the ad described him as "a family man" who "knows how to deal with youth related problems." About his opponent, the ad stated, "She has no children. Can she deal with youth related problems?"

The ad backfired. My supporters, especially those who had known me most of my life, were hurt and angry. Typical was Emilia Ramos, who approached me with tears in her eyes, "*¿Como se les ocurre decir eso de ti porque no tienes hijos?*" And then, "*No saben como tu me ayudaste con mis hijos en la iglesia. Hasta les enseñaste catecismo?*" Mrs. Ramos was outraged that I would be so judged because I had no children. She reminded me how I had taught her children catechism and worked with youth at the church.

The ad turned out to be a galvanizing force for Mrs. Ramos and other Mexican-American women who had known me since childhood. "*¡Pues nosotros te vamos ayudar más!*" Mrs. Ramos pronounced. Other women likewise committed to redouble their efforts. Both Frank and Emilia Ramos (now deceased) not only worked harder in that first campaign but continued their staunch support for the duration of my ten years in office, becoming valued neighborhood leaders and very good friends.

Reading the ad today, I can see how far women have traveled in politics during the past thirty years. But I must admit that as thick as my skin had started to grow during that campaign, this was one charge that cut through. Not having children was not our choice. "Man proposes and God disposes," the proverb goes. Fortunately, there was little time then for me to waste on hurt feelings over a fact of life. We had a campaign to complete. With Manny's ever-present support and the help of hundreds of San Antonians, we were about to make history.

A Winner!

On April 18, 1981, when all the votes were cast and counted, I was named the victor, elected to City Council with 55% of the vote, becoming the first Mexican-American woman to win the office. I was proud, grateful, elated—and four days past my fortieth birthday. We achieved this victory against a strong political establishment using the same grassroots effort we had used throughout the primary. How our campaign was conducted, going house to house to seek votes, spoke to me of how I would serve. The same hope, enthusiasm, energy, hard work, and spirit that were exhibited by a whole group of committed workers were what I would try to embody in my public service. I made important commitments that I intended to keep, and the first of these was never to forget who owned the seat I would occupy at City Hall—the people of District 1.

Very soon after the election, Norma Rodríguez, the first Latina City Clerk of San Antonio, conducted my swearing in at a private ceremony at the City Council Chambers. Manny was by my side, as were my parents; they could not have been more proud. Also present in the chamber were other family members, including my young nieces and nephews, and a few friends and supporters.

The formal swearing-in ceremony took place on May 2, 1981, at a public event at the Centro de Artes of El Mercado in downtown

San Antonio. I was sworn in again, along with Mayor Cisneros and my fellow Councilors: Joe Webb (District 2), Helen Dutmer (District 3), Frank Wing (District 4), Bernardo Eureste (District 5), Bob Thompson (District 6), Joe Alderete (District 7), Gene Canavan (District 8), Van Henry Archer (District 9), and Jimmy Hasslocher (District 10). Hasslocher and I were the only two new members of that Council; the others had been re-elected to serve another two-year term in office.

I felt deeply humbled on the day of our formal swearing-in. During the campaign, I had visited some luxurious homes in the few affluent areas of my district. But most of my time was spent knocking on doors in some of the poorest neighborhoods of our city. I would meet an elderly person living alone or young families with little children, all living in tiny houses on streets where curbs and sidewalks were non-existent and where mounds of uncollected trash seemed a permanent fixture. Vacant houses and weedy lots adjoined the tiny houses so you could never quite tell where the private property began or ended.

Yet, close to the house, I would often see a "María Antonietta Rodriguez Berriozabál for District 1" sign and then meet friendly people inside. Sometimes they were *ancianitas* who would invite me in to show me my campaign picture. It would be on the altar next to images of their family, John F. Kennedy, Henry B. González, Our Lady of Guadalupe, and the Sacred Heart of Jesus. Some would ask if they could give me a *bendición*. Of course, I said. I would leave with feelings of deep gratitude and affirmation, but also thinking, "I must do something about these conditions." I thought that if our city could improve the quality of life in the poorest neighborhoods and help the most vulnerable, everyone's life would improve! But I was in for a disquieting surprise. Maintaining the status quo is a mighty force in government.

NOTES

Chapter 6: Running for Office

1. *San Antonio Light* (December 28, 1980).

2. See "A History of Urban Renewal in San Antonio" by Meghan McCarthy at http://soa.utexas.edu/crp/planningforum/downloads/pf13-14_sa_urban_renewal.pdf [accessed August 26, 2011].

3. *Ibid.* McCarthy writes: "Citizens did not expect urban renewal to displace low-income families. Nonetheless, urban renewal became the tool by which city governments could wipe out slums and blighted areas and replace those areas with whatever the city saw fit, usually commercial development since it improved the economy of the city.... In urban renewal project areas across the nation, the alternative housing for those displaced never materialized."

4. See Rudy Rosales, *The Illusion of Inclusion: The Untold Political Story of San Antonio.* (Austin: University of Texas Press, 2000), 49.

5. Rosales writes, "As a consequence, 65 percent of all candidates, including many Chicano candidates, came from the more affluent north side of San Antonio. They were 'in short, representatives of the social prominent and the economically powerful'" (p. 49), citing David R. Johnson, John Booth, Richard Harris, *The Politics of San Antonio: Community, Progress, and Power* (Lincoln: University of Nebraska Press, 1983), 49.

6. *Ibid.*, 105.

7. *Ibid.*

8. *Ibid.*, 81.

9. Redistricting has since caused District 1 to move north, excluding deep Westside and Eastside areas; King William and Beacon Hill remain in the district.

10. "7 Mexican-American Women In Running for Council Seat," *San Antonio Express-News* (November 19, 1972), 4.

11. *San Antonio Express-News* (March 15, 1981).

12. *San Antonio Light* (March 19, 1981).

13. *San Antonio Express-News* (April 15, 1981).

14. *San Antonio Express-News* (April 12, 1981).

15. *San Antonio Express-News* (April 18, 1981).

CHAPTER 7

Public Life

I carried hundreds of people in my heart on May 7, 1981, the day I walked into City Hall and first occupied the Council seat for District 1. With me were my immigrant grandparents and parents, my aunts, uncles, teachers, and all the people who had shaped my life from my earliest days. With me also were those who helped me win the seat and voted for me, as well as all the constituents who had not supported me. My husband, neighbors, and longtime friends, many of whom would now also be my constituents, were also there. The dais was crowded! I felt profoundly joyful and grateful, but now it was imperative that I do a good job. I was a "first"—I had to give it my all.

I spent the morning hours in my new office. Around noon, I crossed the street to have lunch at Luby's Cafeteria, returning in time for our 1 p.m. Council meeting. As I walked in, I noticed that my fellow Council members were all coming out of one room; a couple had toothpicks in their mouths. Curious, I asked a staff person, "Where are the Council members coming from?" Surprised, she said, "The Council eats together in the conference room prior to each meeting. Didn't anyone tell you?"

I am sure no one planned my exclusion. For me, however, it became a prophetic symbol of my outsider status. To be in a system and yet out of it would be the story of my decade on the San Antonio City Council.

Tracks Are Laid

Joining the City Council in May of 1981 was like jumping onto a fast moving train. It stopped neither for Jimmy Hasslocher, the other new Councilman, nor me. Before the month was over, two of our city's most fundamental and controversial issues—water and energy—were on our agenda. The water issue centered on the proposed construction of a surface water reservoir, dubbed the Applewhite Reservoir. The energy issue focused on the South Texas Nuclear Project (STNP). Both issues had been the source of debate in our city for several years—Applewhite since 1979 and the nuclear power project since 1973. I knew enough about each of these issues through my grassroots activities to oppose them.

In time, I grew to understand that these macro issues go not only to the heart of concerns about *la Madre Tierra* but also to the heart of who holds political and economic power in our city. They would become defining issues in my political life, even as I dedicated most of my time and energy to addressing the critical micro issues facing my district—poor housing, run-down streets, improper drainage, safety, and so on. There is no life without water, and without energy a city ceases to function. I understood this on a practical level. But it would take time for me to connect the dots and see how the politics behind the macro issues impacted the politics of the micro issues—and the forces driving each.

Within my first three Council meetings, the Applewhite Reservoir and the nuclear issue were on the docket and debated for hours. I listened carefully to my colleagues. They held strong opinions and the debate was impressive. Councilwoman Helen Dutmer was the most informed on water. I learned much from this politically astute woman, who had been active in civic and political affairs long before her election to City Council. Protection of the Edwards Aquifer was a priority for her. Being the oldest member of our Council, she carried the distinction with great aplomb. She was staunchly against Applewhite, although not against surface water per se.

A consummate liberal, Councilman Bernardo Eureste was the member with whom I felt most closely aligned politically. Our neighboring districts had much of the same needs. Bernardo was passionate and faithful in his representation of his entirely Westside district. It was home to the poorest real estate in the city but also the treasured history of the Mexican and Mexican-American community. Councilman Eureste was against surface water from any source.

Our new Mayor Henry Cisneros, on the other hand, was strongly in support of the Applewhite Reservoir, arguing that this surface water lake was needed because of our population growth and as part of our efforts "to attract industry."[1]

At our meeting on May 14, 1981, Mayor Cisneros pressed for approval of bond revenue money that included $4 million for the City Water Board (CWB) to start purchasing land for the Applewhite Reservoir. I cast my first "no" vote against Applewhite that day. The questions I asked the general manager of the City Water Board reflected my concerns about the problems we were neglecting as we pursued this surface water issue—the many broken pipes in my district, a complaint I heard constantly while block walking through the neighborhoods. With two Council members absent, the votes for Applewhite could not be mustered that day.[2]

The following week, the issue was back on the agenda. This time all members of the Council were present. The general manager of the CWB informed us that in the future one reservoir would not be adequate; "a number of reservoirs" would be needed "to take care of the needs of San Antonio."[3] That day the march towards construction of Applewhite moved forward, but in a subtle way. After some debate, the City Council, including me, voted to put $4 million in escrow in a "capital fund."[4] But surface water was not specified; the Council was leaving its options open. Before any final decision was made on use of these funds, public hearings would be held. The Applewhite issue was put aside. It would resurface with heated debate over my tenure but no action would be taken until July 1988.

That same day, May 21, 1981, at my third City Council meeting, the Council cast a vote on a rate increase proposed by the City Public Service Board (CPSB). Although the STNP was not addressed as the reason for the rate hike, many San Antonio residents and several of us on the City Council tied it to the nuclear project and its huge cost overruns. San Antonio's participation in the STNP dated back to 1973, when the GGL-led City Council approved our participation in the project with one lone vote against.[5] Located near Bay City, Texas, on the Gulf of Mexico, about 200 miles east of San Antonio, the STNP was to consist of two nuclear reactors that would provide 1,100 megawatts each of nuclear fuel to be shared among the owner cities, including Houston and Corpus Christi.[6]

The Resolution authorizing our city's participation in the STNP stated that there would be "fuel shortages for both domestic and industrial purposes," that the mode of energy production would be "safe and efficient," and that our participation was necessary "in order that San Antonio may be assured of safe and adequate electric power after 1980."[7]

From its founding in 1974, COPS had raised numerous issues about the nuclear project, including concerns related to construction problems and runaway spending, urging that a cap on spending be placed. Other community groups and individuals had also expressed deep concerns. Among the most vocal and tenacious were Lanny Sinkin, co-founder and co-director of Citizens Concerned About Nuclear Energy; Carol Ryan with Mothers and Others Organizing for Survival; the Sierra Club; and activist Godfrey Connally. They too were concerned about the hazy cost projections, as well as the issue of nuclear waste storage and nuclear safety in general, urging investment in renewable energy, especially solar. After the Three Mile Island accident in March of 1979, safety concerns sharpened in San Antonio as they did across the country.

Over the years, the nuclear project had been ladened with complaints about construction. There were work stoppages due to workers' issues with fines levied against the owners. Despite rising costs and concerns about safety, six votes could never be mustered on City Council to secure a cap on costs or sell the city's percentage of the project. The nuclear plant's construction took its course; by the time it was completed in 1989, the STNP cost $5.5 billion—500% more than its original projection—and was seven years late.[8]

When I took office in 1981, Unit 1 of the nuclear plant was supposed to have been ready. It was not; Unit 2 was experiencing similar delays. At my third Council meeting, with many of the above issues clearly evident, I was in a minority of Council members who cast a "no" vote on the utility rate hike.[9]

Soon after we cast these "no" votes against the surface water project and the utility rate hike, as spending on the nuclear reactors went unchecked, a powerful community leader pulled me aside to share an insight. City Council was free to do a lot, he said. But I had to know that the *utilities belonged to the establishment.*

It was a prophetic observation. I came to understand it very well. But we need to go back in time to comprehend the context. When these two major utility issues were proposed and initially approved in the 1970s, San Antonio politics were in transition. The Good Government League was losing power; the business establishment wanted to be sure that key steps concerning water and energy were taken to ensure that new development continued, regardless of how city politics changed in response to the new Chicano Movement and demands for district-based elections.

By the time my tenure on City Council began, these two projects were like train tracks that had been laid, dictating the path that the train would have to follow. It was a path that had been created without the open participation and inclusion of the citizenry even though it concerned such critical issues. To understand the water issue going forward, it is necessary to visit the past.

Behind the Scenes: ¡Agua Es Vida!

From San Antonio's founding at the banks of the San Antonio River, which springs from the Edwards Aquifer, water has been at the heart of the city's history. It has also been one of our most contentious political issues in recent decades, as San Antonio has grown into one of the nation's largest metropolitan areas.

In 1975, we residents of San Antonio became aware as never before of the incredible gift we have in our sole source of water, the Edwards Aquifer. The awareness emerged through the threat posed to the aquifer by the proposed construction of a large shopping mall over its recharge zone and the organized efforts against the mall.

Approximately 180 miles long and anywhere from five to forty miles wide, the Edwards Aquifer "is one of the largest and most important karst aquifer systems in the United States."[10] It serves as the primary water source for the City of San Antonio and surrounding communities. Formed over millions of years by limestone deposits ("karst"), the Edwards Aquifer has several distinct features. These include an artesian zone located directly under our city where millions of acre-feet of water are stored in honeycombed, water-bearing limestone, trapped under impermeable rock; and a recharge zone north of the city where "highly faulted and fractured limestones outcrop at the land surface, allowing large quantities of rainwater to flow into the Aquifer."[11] Because of its porous karst nature, the Edwards Aquifer is particularly vulnerable to surface pollution as toxins flow through thin soil cover, dropping into sinkholes and caves.[12] It is both incredibly vast *and* fragile. Protecting the recharge zone means protecting the aquifer.

In 1975, Barshop-Kaplan Industries proposed to build a 1.5-million-square-foot mall on a 129-acre tract of land over a sensitive area of the Edwards Aquifer Recharge Zone, at the southeast corner of IH-281 and what soon after became the city's outer beltway, Loop1604.

The proposed mall was the subject of heated debate, centering on the great risk such a massive development would have on the aquifer against its potential to attract luxury department stores, like Neiman Marcus, and new jobs. In a 5-4 vote, the GGL-dominated City Council approved the development. A new City Councilman, who had only been in office a few months, was among the minority who voted against it. After the vote, District 1 Councilman Henry Cisneros made an impassioned statement, reflecting the views of many people in his district and the city about the development's rationale:

> I think there's a few words that have to be said about that because that's the rationale that's used all the time to get anything through no matter what its merits are, that it means attracting jobs and so forth. And my point is that some of these kinds of things do virtually nothing for the people in this town who need the jobs, work for the areas in this town that are hit worst by unemployment, for the

areas of this town where the economic development needs to proceed, except to assure the continued patterns of development that deteriorate some of the older areas of the City and the downtown will continue and in my view it is wrong to use that rationale.[13]

It was at this time that I met Fay Sinkin, who had founded the Aquifer Protection Association, as well as Liz Davies, then-president of the League of Women Voters. These two powerful women became my mentors on water issues. I also learned much about water policy from two COPS leaders, President Andy Sarabia and the Reverend Albert Benavides. Father Benavides analyzed water issues from a social justice perspective, using his platform in the church to educate our community.

These individuals and many others played an active role in fighting the mall's construction. The debate it generated in our city began our public education about the awesome source of our water and the critical need to protect it. In many ways, it was and has continued to be a debate over whether the Edwards Aquifer is a precious gift to be shared by all or a "utility" belonging, as I was told, to the establishment. Politically, water policy—and, specifically, development over the Edwards Aquifer recharge zone—would soon become a wedge issue that could make or break a political candidate in San Antonio, as I learned firsthand.

Although the rezoning was approved, that particular mall was never built. But the door, once opened to rezoning, led to the massive and intense development over the entire area we see today on top of some of the most sensitive recharge features of the Edwards Aquifer.

A few years later, in July 1979, the City Council passed a Resolution to purchase thousands of acres of land on San Antonio's Southside, on Applewhite Road, where a surface water reservoir would be built.[14] The purported purpose for developing the man-made lake was to have a secondary source of water to supplement the Edwards Aquifer in times of drought.

The project, known as the Applewhite Reservoir, was supported by land developers, real estate interests, construction and engineering firms, and many other interests behind the scenes in the penumbra, represented by chambers of commerce and other informal, but powerful, "business elite" groups. They urged that the man-made lake be built, arguing that a Sunbelt city like San Antonio needed surface water if it were to grow, develop, and attract new industry. They showed projections that our population would grow and that we could not just depend on the Edwards Aquifer to meet the needs of business, industry, and a growing population.

Proponents of the Applewhite Reservoir pointed out that the springs downstream in San Marcos and New Braunfels were fed by the aquifer. These needed a constant flow both because of the economic needs there, as well as the requirements of the federal Endangered Species Act, which protects seven endangered and one threatened aquatic species.[15] In times of drought, the springs could run dry, threatening those species. In those times, water from the Applewhite Reservoir could be pumped to supplement the aquifer, they argued.

On its face, the plan was preposterous. We would be supplementing a gift of nature that held an estimated 200 *million* acre-feet of water with 48,000 acre-feet of water from a man-made lake. Built clear across town and at a lower elevation, it would be the first body of water to evaporate in times of droughts. Never mind concerns about the quality of the water that would be collected not only from upstream creeks but also plain runoff from our streets and drainage. Never mind the estimated $180 million it would cost to construct the lake and the complex pipes that would pump the water 1,000 feet uphill from its site on the southern end of town to our city's northern boundaries. Never mind the concerns over flooding thousands of acres of land that held significant archaeological and cultural sites pertaining to the history of our city or its devastating impact on the natural habitat and wildlife.

We who opposed the project thought our water policy should be based on sound scientific information. If we committed ourselves to protecting the Edwards Aquifer, it would provide water for generations to come, especially if we maximized capture by building recharge dams to collect water that flowed downstream in torrents, wreaking havoc on our city's drainage systems and ruining our downtown streets. We argued for effective water reuse policies and placed a major emphasis on developing an ethic of conservation with ensuing practices.

In addition, it would be working class and poor people who would end up paying disproportionately for this project for years to come through their water bills. In my view, developing something as essential to our future as a good and effective water policy had to come about through community consensus.

Why had the big business interests, developers, chambers of commerce, etc., of the city united behind a plan to "solve" San Antonio's potential water problem by building this man-made lake? A number of people, myself included, subscribed to the theory that the real intent behind building what amounted to the equivalent of a cup of water to supplement an Olympic-size swimming pool was to render mute a law that stood in the way of uncontrolled and subsidized development. Known as the "González Amendment" for its sponsor—Congressman Henry B. González—it prohibited, under the Safe Water Drinking Act of 1974, any federal assistance for projects that might contaminate an aquifer or its recharge zone, posing a significant hazard to public health, if that aquifer were "the sole or principal drinking-water source for that area." [16]

Once there was another source of water, the Edwards Aquifer would lose its sole source status and development could occur unhindered. Supporters of the Applewhite project took exception to this theory. As evidence, they pointed to the Congressman's urging that San Antonio hurry with securing another source of water so as not to depend entirely on the aquifer. I was never persuaded; our theory was the only argument that made sense.

Sitting on the Dais

When I took my place on the dais in May of 1981, all of the Council members, except Jimmy Hasslocher and me, had already worked with each other for at least two terms. Theirs was the first City Council that had been elected through the new single-member district system.[17] Meetings were long. Debate had increased. The local media called it divisive; yet, this was the healthy result of a representative democracy that had finally arrived. The members of that part-time City Council worked hard during these years of great transition for our city. It was an exciting political atmosphere. I relished it.

Fresh in my thoughts during my first months in office were the issues that arose during my campaign. My mind was full of the needs I saw and heard about in the neighborhoods, as I walked house to house. Bad housing conditions, crumbling streets, flooding, no sidewalks, and the myriad other needs in a poor and older area of a big city. As I traveled downtown every day, the need for urban revitalization was clear and undeniable. It was an urgent priority for me.

I worked hard to keep up with all the reading and research needed for Council meetings. People had been waiting for the "fulltime Councilwoman," so phone calls were plentiful from people needing a variety of things. My calendar was full of events. There was much to learn and it was all on-the-job training, but I loved the challenge.

Uppermost in my mind were my promised goals of openness and inclusion. The history of the Chicano Movement and its quest for self-determination were never far from my thoughts. I was very conscious of this as I worked diligently, casting my votes as my conscience and the needs of my district dictated. About a year into my service, reality struck.

Short End of the Stick

A City Hall reporter pulled me aside one day. "Councilwoman, as a reporter I must maintain my distance from you, but I must tell you this. People are talking. You are coming up on the short end of the stick on votes too many times. If that continues, you are going to have a difficult time getting reelected."

The reporter's words troubled me. It was true—I had been losing some votes on matters pertaining to my district, including a couple of big ones. Wasn't that just part of the political process? However, the reporter's words led me to think about the votes I had cast and what I might have done to be a better advocate for my community. I decided to examine my work over the previous year to see what conclusions I could draw from my actions and those of my fellow Council members. I focused in particular on two important issues, one involving the downtown area and the other, our city neighborhoods.

The downtown issue involved the Rand Building, an historic structure owned by a local bank whose owners had deep roots in the community. In an effort to bring people back downtown, a plan had been proposed to tear down the building and construct a parking garage on the site. Pressing City Council for demolition of the building were major downtown business owners who saw parking as a necessity in revitalizing downtown, even if an historic structure had to be sacrificed. While I too was interested in revitalization of the downtown and agreed with the need for parking, I opposed tearing down the historic building as the means to address that need.[18] Further, as a long time bus rider and advocate of public transportation, I saw improvement of public transit downtown and good pedestrian amenities as another preferred option.

With my urban planning studies still fresh in my mind, I knew it was the character of our downtown that made our city unique— and San Antonio's historic structures were what gave our city its character, its uniqueness. We had already lost too many in recent years. Our city, as I discovered, had no real process in place to determine which buildings were historic; we depended on the private efforts of the San Antonio Conservation Society to protect our history.[19] When the "public" is absent in public policy, private interests and politics take over. That troubled me.

In the end, as I analyzed this big vote I lost, I concluded that the differences between me and those on the "long end of the stick" were about how to achieve our city's revitalization—they were ideological differences.

The other issue I revisited involved proposed zoning changes in the neighborhoods that surrounded downtown in my district. I consistently voted "no" whenever a proposal came before City Council that would move a residence from residential to business zoning. Converting a residence into a beauty or tire shop, a bail bond business or a convenience store, might seem like a worthy idea. But I knew from experience that removing residential zoning from a neighborhood eroded its viability. As I had learned over the years of living in the district and riding the bus, housing was at the core of investment or disinvestment. Good housing stock and strong neighborhoods mean a stable population and sound tax base—the tax base used to fund our public schools.

My votes against those kinds of zoning changes took those factors into consideration and were, in essence, votes in favor of keeping our neighborhoods strong. Some of my colleagues did not share my views on residential-to-business zoning changes; they voted against me even when it involved proposed changes in my own district. Zoning was not a priority issue even for residents in most of my neighborhoods. As I came to realize, people simply did not have the information they needed to be engaged. Zoning was a key issue that would continue to surface, critically affecting the quality of life in our community, but much public education was needed for people to understand its significance. In zoning decisions, ideological differences also were at the root.

Our city had no plan for neighborhood protection or revitalization. As in the case of downtown historic preservation, decisions were made on a case-by-case basis with no overarching vision for the city, much less one for protecting inner-city neighborhoods. Whether an issue involved demolition of an historic structure downtown or removal of residential uses in a neighborhood, I felt we needed to have sound and transparent policies for vetting the question with much more public dialogue. Instead, the issues came down to a yes or no vote on demolishing this building or rezoning that neighborhood.

Absent dialogue and debate to develop plans for the development and revitalization of the city's downtown and neighborhoods so that decisions could be uniformly applied, we were left with a barter system. To get the votes I needed for issues affecting my district, I had to bargain for them. That was a totally alien way for me to make decisions. An additional challenge was the fact that my district encompassed the heart of downtown where issues were more visible and difficult. Complicating matters further, the former Councilman for District 1 was still in Council chambers, occupying the mayor's seat. As mayor, Henry Cisneros continued to weigh in on these issues. Neither of us spoke to the other about these matters outside Council chambers. Had we talked, perhaps things might have been easier.[20]

Rather naively, until the kind reporter spoke, I had not even thought that I could or should be part of whatever negotiations and behind-the-scenes discussions occur within any political body. All my exchanges with fellow Council members took place in public, at the official Council meetings. The pattern I had set for myself, as a new Council member, was to listen to my constituents, do my own research, and then cast my vote. Looking back, I see that I was pretty much paving my own way on how I would serve; it did not fit the norm. That always poses a challenge within group dynamics and there are usually negative sanctions—sometimes blatant, but more often subtle—for veering away from established group behaviors.

With the distance of time, I also now see the reality of my being the first and only Latina on the City Council as an added factor, impacting the interpersonal—and, consequently, political—dynamics. A Latina with definite opinions working with a group of Latinos and others holding the same rank was a new path in the still largely man's world of politics. I did not think about these dynamics at the time. I had to do a good job. No excuses.

But as I thought about my coming up on the "short end of the stick" and what I could do to change that reality, I found that in addition to holding profoundly different ideological views on key recurring issues that came before City Council, I faced another intractable issue that was at odds with my commitment to address the needs of my inner-city constituents: the clash between those needs and the path for economic development and growth that had been established years before any of us got to City Council, going back to the GGL years. Lurking behind every decision we made was the goal to grow and expand—and this meant always and everywhere privileging the *Northside*.

My first memory of this movement went back to the 1960s, when I was part of an inner-city community lobbying effort to prevent our public hospital, the Robert B. Green Hospital on West Martin Street, from being moved miles away from the people it was created to serve. In the early 1960s, the University of Texas (UT) Board of Regents was authorized to establish a medical school in San Antonio. The authorizing legislation required that the teaching hospital for training the medical students be a public institution. Inner-city community leaders urged that the medical school be located near the Robert B. Green Hospital in the large vacant site that had been cleared by urban renewal. Instead, with the blessing of GGL city officials and the business community, county officials created a hospital taxing-district to build a new public hospital and medical center in the then-rural northwest edge of the city where no development existed.

In 1968, the new medical school and Bexar County Teaching Hospital (now University Hospital) were dedicated. As soon as the new public hospital opened, the Robert B. Green Hospital, which had been built in 1916 to serve indigent patients, began to lose critical services like maternity care.[21] The city's full-service public hospital was now bus rides away from the people it was built to serve—and a new growth generator was created that would lead to massive commercial and residential development surrounding the medical complex.

That same year, 1968, the UT Board of Regents decided, after years of lobbying by the Chicana/o community, to build a four-year public university in San Antonio. The growing number of inner city and Southside minority students in our city had created the need for the public institution. The Board of Regents, appointed by the Governor of Texas, had the responsibility of identifying the school's location. Once again, inner-city communities urged that it be located on the still-vacant urban renewal site at the west boundary of downtown close to the Robert B. Green Hospital. Other sites were suggested as well, in the inner city and on the Southside.

Again, with the blessings of local elected officials and the big-business community, the Board of Regents chose to locate the new university far beyond the neighborhoods of the underserved students it was established to serve. The University of Texas at San Antonio was located fifteen miles northwest of downtown San Antonio, in an undeveloped area at the edge of the Texas Hill Country. It was dubbed "Boerne U."—given its proximity to the small Hill Country town.[22] It too would become a growth generator, driving massive commercial and residential development out to and beyond the institution and over the Edwards Aquifer.

These major publicly funded complexes, sited far beyond the inner city, created a path dependency that was difficult, if not impossible, to change. In path dependence, as urban historian Martin Melosi notes, "major constraints" are placed on present alternatives because of past choices.[23] The decisions to construct these major public institutions in distant undeveloped areas resulted, predictably, in leap-frog growth and urban sprawl.[24] We had to invest in constructing new streets and drainage and in extending public utilities and other city services. New utility transmission systems and water infrastructure to support booming new neighborhoods are services everyone pays for in their tax dollars, along with the cost of building the initial growth-generating institutions. This growth path was set with no analysis of its long-term implications—who benefited, who paid. How would the goal of growth and expansion affect our city's families, particularly the most vulnerable among them?

This kind of single-minded decisionmaking is what the Chicana/o activists had sought to change in the struggle to end the GGL system of government and create a new one where diverse voices would sit at the table, representing the views of our city's residents. Elected on the coattails of that movement, I was carrying an agenda of empowerment and inclusion, of fighting for the provision of services to areas of the city and communities that had been left behind by the growth and expansion agenda. Meeting these needs required major structural change and a new direction in governance that would be as energetic about investing in the inner city and our people's human needs as in Northside development.

By the time I got to City Council in 1981, even though a democratically elected Council was in place, the priorities of how the city should grow had not changed. I had a definite vision for my district and our city, but it was way beyond getting six votes to advance.

I drew some key conclusions from my analysis of being "at the short end of the stick." First, given my values, political beliefs, campaign commitments, and the needs of my constituents, there was no way I could or would change the way I was voting. Second, given our city's path dependence on growth and expansion—and the powerful forces behind it—it was highly unlikely that my voice for an alternative vision would carry the day. I would remain at the short end.

Out of this conclusion came a conscious decision as to how—win or lose—I would do my work. My service would be anchored in the people. I would work hard to keep my constituents informed, educated, and engaged in the issues that impacted them. I would always have a constituency with me on any given issue for which I had to advocate. This is the path I would forge in my public service. This would be my response to the reporter's admonition.

My Response

The needs of my district were not theoretical. They could not be more concrete, as my constituents continuously made clear:

- "There are vacant houses, no sidewalks, weedy vacant lots in my neighborhood and they are a real danger to children passing to and from school. You must do something!" So spoke Mary Salazar, whose neighborhood on the southern side of the district was a de facto cul de sac, due to the construction of an expressway. Ambulances and police had a hard time finding her neighborhood on emergencies.

- *"Ratas, señora, hay muchas ratas. El otro día una se callo del* light fixture *en la mesa!"* There were so many rats at the Alazán Apache Courts on the Westside that one fell on the table through a broken light fixture. *"Dormimos con la luz prendida porque han mordido la oreja de mi bebito."* We sleep with the lights on because they bit my baby's ear. So spoke the mothers living in the public housing.

- "María, do you know that a very large number of houses adjacent to the church have been bought by some business interest? They will be demolished." So spoke Monsignor Martin Wangler, pastor of Our Lady of Sorrows Church in Tobin Hill, on the northern boundary of my district. He made an emergency visit to my office after learning that a major developer had started eliminating dozens of homes for high-rise structures. Neither my constituents nor I knew a thing about it.

- "María, there is a disease growing in San Antonio and other parts of the country that will bring the nation to its knees." So spoke "Papa Bear," aka Robert Edwards, who with these words introduced me to a disease so lethal its only prognosis, in the early 1980s, was death. It was Robert who later founded the San Antonio AIDS Foundation.

These were the kinds of calls that would come into my office on a daily basis.[25] This day-to-day reality lived by my constituents was the backdrop against which I made decisions as I joined the other Council members at chamber each week. While majority votes were being cast to siphon public resources for mega development projects on the Northside, I responded by continuing to vote "no" *and* by using my office as a vehicle for informing and organizing my constituents—and providing them access to their government. I redoubled my efforts at listening to the voices of people like Mrs. Salazar on Baylor Street, the moms in public housing, Monsignor Wangler in Tobin Hill, and Papa Bear worried about a dreaded disease.

On these and other issues, I would work with organized groups in the neighborhoods and downtown—and where they were non-existent, I would organize them. In following this path I would accomplish the goal I had set out in my first campaign, to empower people and to do my work in a transparent manner. If it were a zoning case, a street project, or any other issue, my job would be to do outreach and educate the community and provide access to government. They would be the ones to push for their issue, coming to City Hall to hold the entire Council, including me, accountable.

Many years prior to serving on the Council, I had been inspired by the words, "And when the work was done, the people said, we did it ourselves." This concept of being a "servant leader" doesn't quite fit into the world of politics where successful leadership is measured by the visibility of the leader in any victory. I was an elected official, after all, not an organizer whose job it is to stay in the background! There was a risk in staying in the background instead of leading the pack. But that was what I chose to do in one neighborhood issue after another, one zoning vote after another, one street project after another.

Contrary to the reporter's prediction, I was re-elected to a second term in 1983 without opposition—the only Councilperson to have none that year. I would serve ten years, running unopposed each time except for 1987 when two men ran against me. I won with 75% of the vote.

In time, I saw a few successes, as City Council adopted good policies to help people help themselves. In June of 1983, for example, the Council adopted an ordinance creating a Neighborhood Planning Process that would provide "some voice [for residents] in the development of their own neighborhood." [26] The process called for the participation of businesses and other institutions in the neighborhoods, as well. The push for this ordinance came from leaders of District 1 neighborhoods who understood at firsthand the need for such a process, especially in neighborhoods in transition. I was proud to make the motion for its passage. Another involved the adoption of an extensive inventory of Historic Sites and Structures. It brought together diverse interests and public participation in identifying the sites, which helps in future efforts to protect them.

A key success that illustrated the type of leadership I chose to engage involved creating neighborhood associations where none existed in District 1. I worked closely with small merchants in El Mercado/Market Square, Alamo Plaza, La Villita, and in the surrounding neighborhoods to provide a vehicle for their voices to be heard. From these emerged the first Downtown Residents Association and the first Downtown Owners Association where I worked with Ben Brewer, its first and current Executive Director.

Throughout the years, I used my office as a venue for organizing all types of constituencies, whether in my district or not. Topics around which we organized were affordable housing, downtown housing, small businesses, homelessness, children and families, water, immigration, leadership development, family violence, concerns of the elderly, upward mobility, employment, civil rights, and issues of Latinas and their families. Community leaders emerged through each of these efforts. Long after I left office, they have continued to carry the issues forward themselves.

Here are three stories illustrative of the people I was privileged to represent.

1. They Are My Constituents, Too

During my first campaign, as I was block walking, I met a woman who would become my friend and a great blessing in my life. I asked for her vote. "Yes, María, we have heard of you and our family will vote for you," she responded immediately. But then added, "We cannot help you with money but if you come on next Thursday we will pray for you at a Mass."

Laura Sánchez and her husband Marcos led *Proyecto Hospitalidad*. They had been using their home as a quiet place of ministry for refugees from Central America who arrived in San Antonio, fleeing from horrible civil wars in their countries. When I arrived for the Mass, I was deeply moved by the chapel that Laura and her family had created in their backyard. It was made of wood and looked like a little chapel I had once seen in a far away village in Mexico. Inside were women, men, and children—the refugees, sitting on low benches. The priest wore a colorful stole with indigenous symbols. A rustic wooden crucifix hung behind a wooden box that acted as the altar. We sang old Spanish hymns I had sung as a child. Afterwards, we shared a meal and there was plenty of singing and guitar playing.

Manny joined me at that first Mass in Laura's backyard. In the ensuing years, that little church would become a very special part of our lives, and for the entire decade I was on City Council, I collaborated with *Proyecto Hospitalidad*.

Laura welcomed refugees into her home and helped them prepare their papers for migration to Canada. She sheltered women who had fled with their young sons to prevent them from being captured by the military and forcibly inscripted into their wars. She cared for men who lost limbs after falling off a train. She provided sanctuary to people who were fleeing for their lives. Through her eyes and the generosity of her heart, I saw the suffering of people whose families were maimed by war and wounded by separation. I understood the horrors of what was happening in Central America not from our country's news sources but from people who, without being able to vote, were my constituents too.

I was able to use my bully pulpit on issues of immigration and in direct response to abuses by authorities. One day, the Immigration and Naturalization Service (INS, now ICE) dared to pursue a refugee into a place of worship, entering the courtyard of San Fernando Cathedral. Laura and I joined Archbishop Patrick Flores; the rector, Father Virgilio Elizondo; and Father Balty Janacek in a press conference taking exception to the violation of the church's space.

On another occasion, I got involved when San Antonio police officers called immigration officials to help them arrest a group of people gathered at the Patio Andaluz on West Commerce Street. The INS came and took a busload of the people across the border to Nuevo Laredo, where they dropped them off. Some of the individuals did not have their papers, but not all. The day after the arrests, I got a call from the father of one of the men who had been taken. "Mrs. Berriozábal, my son was hauled off and dumped in [Nuevo] Laredo and he is a citizen!"

Through my efforts in response to this situation, I learned that our city had a policy that our Police Department would not get involved in immigration arrests. It had been formalized when Henry Cisneros represented District 1. Our local police should not have been involved as they were. After this incident, the City Council recommitted the city to that policy, which exists to this day.[27]

Growing up poor created an affinity in me for communities that are poor—and in the case of immigrants, communities so poor they do not even have a country.

During my time in office, I had the opportunity to meet Father Gustavo Gutiérrez, foremost proponent of the theology of liberation that shaped my faith life as a young woman. At a presentation at the Mexican American Cultural Center in San Antonio, he stood before a blackboard, drawing hills and mountains, some short and some very tall. Then, with a stroke of his chalk, he drew a line straight across the middle, showing how the tops of the tall mountains would be cut off so there could be room for the small hills to grow. Jesus came to "even out the mountains," he said. Those who had more would lose and those who had less would gain.

I recall asking myself as I looked at the drawing, why would those who gain from the status quo work to create an even playing field? That "preferential option for the poor" was always going to have a hard time in politics.

Another muse for my advocacy on behalf of poor communities was El Salvador's Archbishop Oscar Romero, who was beloved by the immigrants I met. His influence grew even greater after his assassination while saying Mass in March 1980. It was felt in our country, too. In Laura's house, I would see his photograph each time I visited. He inspired all who walked in.

Work with the powerless yields few successes in politics. Some of my friends would tease me about my involvement with immigrants, "María, these people cannot even vote!" That was true. However, in the neighborhoods of our cities where undocumented people live, we see women and men contributing to the life of our communities. Justice is involved. It has no borders.

2. Houses Mean Neighborhoods

When Monsignor Wangler surprised me with the news that a developer was buying dozens of houses behind his church, I was understated in my response. "No, Monsignor, I did not know that. When did you find out? Who is buying them?" He seemed uncomfortable as he replied. "Well, I was told sometime ago but I was asked not to talk about it."

An elderly priest, Monsignor Wangler had been the pastor of Our Lady of Sorrows Church in the Tobin Hill neighborhood for decades. He had known for months. But now he was seeing the pain in people who were being pressured to sell but did not want to leave. He was also considering the impact on the church of having so many people move away from the area.

I listened patiently, but inside I was bristling. How could all this be happening in my district and I not know about it? This kind of thing could be occuring in other areas of my district, endangering neighborhoods. When housing in an urban area decays or is arbitrarily demolished, the risk for the entire community is great.

Tobin Hill was a good example of a neighborhood in transition, feeling the impact of change. During the flight to the suburbs and decline of downtown, Tobin Hill was one more inner city neighborhood that suffered the stresses of disinvestment. The families that moved in after others fled, however, helped keep the character of the area alive and make it a good place to live. Even 100 years after the neighborhood was built, its housing stock, built durably, remained solid with a variety of housing types. There were many large, architecturally unique, and beautiful wood homes. Its residents ranged from a few very wealthy citizens living in houses owned by their families for generations to young professionals. But most residents were working class families, living in modest but well-built homes. That was the case around Our Lady of Sorrows, where most of the residents were Hispanic. The church provided cohesion and Tobin Hill had a strong neighborhood association where residents were working hard to reverse the trend of decline.

Soon after receiving the distressing news from Monsignor Wangler, I met with the developer. The proposed development was huge. The company intended to raze nearly fifty houses in order to build a twin office high-rise with "multi-use and retail development." The high-rise would occupy the area around the church, bounded by three neighborhood streets and IH-281, in a key area midway between the San Antonio International Airport and downtown. It was an ideal location for business development, but what would this development do to the character of the residential neighborhood? The proposed project was one block from the Monte Vista historic district.

I told the developer that I would share the news with my constituents but I doubted they would be supportive of the project. Having worked with constituents in Tobin Hill, Monte Vista, and surrounding neighborhoods, I anticipated their negative response. They were working too hard to maintain what they had to risk the impact of a development like this. I told him that I could not support the project, as it would put the residential character of an entire area at risk.

The developer had already invested a lot of money in the project and acquired a good chunk of land. Although he still had to come before City Council for zoning changes that would allow the business uses and variances on building height restrictions he was proposing, I had no doubt he would find the six votes needed. These huge projects usually involved a lot more than a single district and most developers, like this one, had a lot of political clout. It would be impossible to defeat without significant outside pressure.

When I met with area residents and filled them in on the proposed project, they were very upset that it was being done quietly and without notice. They, too, saw the project as intrusive and incompatible with a residential neighborhood. We proceeded to study the issue and then organize, engaging the support not only of the Tobin Hill Neighborhood Association and Our Lady of Sorrows Church, but other neighborhood organizations as well, including Monte Vista, Alta Vista, Beacon Hill, and even the King William Historic Association though it was clear across the downtown. In addition, the fledgling Coalition of Neighborhood Associations, its leadership issuing from District 1, and the San Antonio Conservation Society also joined the effort.

San Antonio residents beyond Tobin Hill felt the project was an attack on inner-city neighborhoods and a threat to historic preservation efforts. The lack of inclusion of the impacted neighborhoods in any discussion of the matter was totally unacceptable. A committee composed of representatives of the various organizations was formed, meeting weekly at Our Lady of Sorrows Church. It included Monsignor Wangler, Cecilia Moreno, Bruce Cox, Barbara Witte Howell, Larry DiMartino, Linda Comeaux, Al Notzon, and José Villarreal, among others.

My public opposition within City Hall combined with mounting public pressure from outside organizing efforts persuaded the developer to agree to a period of negotiations with neighborhood leaders. The goal was to create a compromise that would lessen the intensity of the uses and make the project less intrusive. The development would not be as high and dense, and a buffer of new housing would be part of the reconfigured plan. This still meant houses in good to excellent condition would be demolished. Nonetheless, the consensus-building process within the neighborhood committee and with the developer went well. It took time, however, and in the end other forces intervened. An economic downturn prevented the project from moving ahead. The developer was left with acres of land and no use for it.

A positive move on the part of the developer that mitigated some of the harm done was that they deeded 1.2 acres to the adjacent neighborhoods to create the Kings Court Housing Corporation. A nonprofit entity, a requirement of its establishment was that some of the neighborhood committee members would serve as directors of the board. The Kings Court Housing Corporation called for construction of 32 housing units for the elderly behind Our Lady of Sorrows Church. That housing remains to this day. Only seven of the original houses on the block are still standing. Three other structures hold small offices; another building housed a grocery store opened by a chain, but it closed after several years. It was recently purchased by Trinity Baptist Church to house their Tri-Point Center, a multi-purpose community venue with church functions, a café, and a branch of the YMCA.

The Kings Court Housing Corporation has maintained viability with its 32 housing units for the elderly. Vacant land still remains along the expressway and next to Our Lady of Sorrows Church, where good homes ones stood. No high-rise structure has been built west of IH-281, however. For now, a strong inner-city neighborhood is still standing.

3. ¡Las Mujeres Valientes!

After my re-election in 1983, I decided to follow up on a plan I had been mulling over for several years. I had long felt that investing in Latinas and their families was an investment that would reap benefits for the whole city. Latinas were and remain the largest single group of people in San Antonio. It was clear to me that how Latinas fared in the future would determine how our city would fare.

Although Latinas in San Antonio faced numerous challenges, they also had incredible resources that could be shared with one another. Whether it was an education, personal time and treasure, a particular expertise, leadership abilities, or a track record of giving back to the community, Latinas had much to offer.

I decided to use my position and forum in our city's leadership to bring together Hispanic women from all walks of life. I wanted to create an opportunity for Latina women of all socio-economic backgrounds to come together, meet each other, and form networks that could be mutually beneficial. My plan was simple: we would organize a conference.

In mid-1983, I started the planning process with a committee of 117 (!) Latinas, each of whom responded to an invitation I issued. The theme that emerged for the conference was *Hispanas Unidas: The Force of San Antonio*. We designed an exciting weekend program of, by, and for Hispanas, providing transportation, childcare, and delicious meals. With the support of other friends, MABPW President Barbie Hernández, and I raised enough private funds so that no woman who desired to attend was prevented from doing so.

Over the weekend of March 23-25, 1984, the campus of Our Lady of the Lake University (OLLU) was filled with over 1,000 women of all ages and from all parts of San Antonio and neighboring communities. The campus was made available to us through the generosity of the Sisters of Divine Providence under the leadership of Superior General Jane Ann Slater, CDP; OLLU President Elizabeth Ann Sueltenfuss, CDP; and Sister María Carolina Flores, CDP, Director of the OLLU Center for Women in Church and Society.

The Hispanas Unidas conference was a true celebration of Hispanic women. The women who led the event formed a roster of who's who in leadership in San Antonio. In addition to local leaders, we also invited Latina luminaries from other parts of the country. Among them were Martha Cotera, Chicana activist and author; Dr. Alicia Valladolid Cuarón, author and entrepreneur; and Senator Polly Baca of Colorado, one of only two Latina State Senators in the country. These women had inspired me and I wanted them to inspire women in my community.

With the help of hundreds of volunteers, the event was successful beyond our expectations. Pride in our roots, confidence in our abilities, enthusiasm, and a deep appreciation of our own power and agency were the outcomes. A powerful energy was unleashed that was felt years after. Stories about Hispanic women ran in both of San Antonio's daily newspapers before, during, and after the event.

As a result, we decided to hold another conference in 1986. By this time we had incorporated "Hispanas Unidas" as a nonprofit organization, with a founding board that included Mary Helen Alvarado, Luz Elena Day, Sister María Carolina Flores, Lupe Ochoa, Sylvia Rodríguez, and myself, as founding president. Every other year, for the next ten years, we continued to sponsor an Hispanas Unidas conference. Like the first event, each conference was entirely planned and led by volunteers.

It was through Hispanas Unidas that I got to meet the legendary Emma Tenayuca, a woman who struggled for justice for workers and the oppressed in the 1930s when she was still a very young woman. At our 1986 Hispanas Unidas Conference she graced us with her presence as we honored her as a Tejana heroine. When she died in 1999, her family asked me to lead the rosary at her wake.

In 1996, I decided to step down from the board. Janie Barrera and Elise García had agreed to join the board and help re-shape the mission of Hispanas Unidas based on the response of Latinas to a needs survey. A year earlier, with a grant from the SBC Foundation, Hispanas Unidas had completed a study on Latinas in San Antonio. A major finding was the serious problem of teen pregnancy among Latina girls. In response, the board of Hispanas Unidas, chaired by Dr. Antonia Castañeda, sought funding to hire Susana López, Esq., the organization's first Executive Director. Susana worked with Dr. Josie Méndez Negrete to develop a culturally sensitive after-school curriculum for girls ages 8 to 14.

In 2000, Hispanas Unidas launched its *Escuelitas* Program," supported by a grant from the Kronkowsky Foundation. Its purpose was to strengthen the personal, academic, and leadership skills of the girls and help them expand their vision of the future through a mentoring and distinguished guest speakers program led by Latina leaders in the community, many of whom had participated in the bi-annual conferences. Named after the *escuelitas* that Mexican women set up in their homes upon arriving in the United States at the turn of the twentieth century, the *Escuelitas* Program continues to this day under the leadership of Adela Flores, Executive Director, and her board of directors.

For an entire decade, from 1981 to 1991, I was able to put my platform as an elected official at City Hall in the service of Latinas and their families. One of the most difficult issues to advocate for in City Hall is providing assistance to families, especially children. In Dr. Gloria Rodríguez, founder of the AVANCE parenting program, and Rebecca Barrera, owner of a childcare center (Niños Unlimited, Inc.), children found powerful advocates. They were two of my strongest collaborators on issues of children and families. We worked together to organize women to advocate for their issues.

I also did everything I could to promote equal employment and upward mobility of Hispanics. There is no better economic development program than to give people a chance to obtain a good-paying job with the possibility of advancement. We were just beginning to see what might approximate fair representation on City Council (at least among men of color!), given the majority minority population of San Antonio. But City Hall employees did not reflect our population—much less in management.

Because of my interest in the issue, Mayor Cisneros appointed me Chair of the City Council's Equal Employment Opportunity Committee. With the help of Norma Cantú, Esq., of the MALDEF Chicana Rights Project, I spent long hours conducting a study and analysis of the city's employment of Hispanic women. The findings were bleak. Most Latinas employed by the city held the lowest clerical positions or jobs in maintenance. Those who fared better on the pay scale were stuck for decades in paraprofessional positions while new management staff was brought in from outside the city's employment. There were few Hispanic women in supervisory positions and none as department heads. Only City Clerk Norma Rodríguez led a department, and her position was supervised by the City Council not the city manager.

During my term in office, I made it my business to disseminate information about every board and commission position that opened so Latinas could apply. I took advantage of my power to appoint a large number of women—a majority of my appointments were Mexican-

American women—to city boards and commissions. After several years, we began to see progress in the upward mobility of Latinas—as well as Latinos.

Finally, I took great pride in networking with and extending the use of my office to valiant women who were founding and/or leading organizations in our community that were empowering people and enriching all our lives. We would be immeasurably poorer today were it not for these women, who provided great though largely unsung leadership in our city in so many key areas, as follows:

Arts: Enedina Cásarez-Vásquez, *Ene-Art*

Childcare: Rebecca Barrera, *Niños Unlimited, Inc.*

Children: Blanche Russ, *Parent Child Incorporated*

Communications: Gloria Parra, *Communication Workers of America*

Education: Drs. Bambi Cárdenas, Ellen Riojas Clark, Arcadia López, Berta Pérez, and María Luisa Urdaeta; Leticia Rodríguez, Helen Austin

Elders: Alicia Martínez, *Prospect Hill*

Family Violence Prevention: Patricia Castillo, Jane Shafer, *The PEACE Initiative*

HIV/AIDS in Women: Selina Catalá, Yolanda Escobar

Homelessness/Transitional Housing for Women and Children: Sisters Dorothy Ettling, CCVI, Neomi Hayes, CCVI, Cindy Stacey, CCVI, and Yolanda Tarango, CCVI, *Visitation House Ministries*

Inner-City Family Support: Patti Radle, *Inner City Development*

Leadership Development/Mentoring: Barbie Hernández, *MABPW*; Adela Flores, *MALDEF* Leadership Program.

Legal Issues/Equal Employment: Norma Cantú, Mary Esther Escobedo, Helen Monica Vásquez

Literacy: Margarita Huantes, Mary Cantú, Dr. Arcadia López

Media: Martha Tijerina, María Elena Torralva, Berta Salazar, Belia Camargo, Verónica Salazar, Yolanda RíosRangel

Municipal Employees: Linda Chávez Thompson, *American Federation of State and Municipal Employees*; Rosa Rosales, Angie García, María Valenzuela, *United Public Employees Union*

Non-Traditional Women Students: Dr. Lina Silva, *San Antonio College Center for Women*

Parenting: Dr. Gloria Rodríguez, *AVANCE*

Public Housing Outreach/Lincoln Courts: Rosie Castro, Susan Klein, Elisa Vásquez, United Methodist women

Small Business/Economic Development: Herlinda Cortez Dimas, Carmen García, Gloria Hernández, Gloria Iruegas Mackay, Gloria Martínez, Elva Quijano, María Lourdes Ramírez, Leticia Van de Putte, Santos Viera, Gloria Zamora

Socially Conscious Investments: Sister Susan Mika, OSB, *Socially Responsible Investment Coalition*

Social Justice/Cultura: Graciela Sánchez, Gloria Ramírez, *Esperanza Peace and Justice Center*

Teens with Challenges: Sister Mary Boniface, *Healy Murphy School*

Women/Family Empowerment: Petra Mata, Viola Cásarez, compañeras, *Fuerza Unida;* Choco Meza, YWCA

Women's Networking: Jane Shafer, Sister María Carolina Flores, CDP, *Our Lady of the Lake University Center for Women in Church and Society*; Ginger Purdy, *Network Power Texas*

Workforce Development: Nancy López, *Women's Employment Network*

Over the years, it was not uncommon for our City Council conference room and my office to be full of women organizing, networking, and using their creativity and energy to empower our community. Our Latina community—*mujeres fuertes y valientes*—took full advantage of this.

Actions That Define Us

Towards the end of my Council tenure, among the hundreds of votes I had cast in ten years, there were three that came to define my public service—three votes by which I was judged as a leader of my city. They dealt with water, sports, and tourism. What did these three issues have in common? The powerful interests that promoted them and an ideology about what constitutes a "big-league" city. Looking back, I think it is appropriate that my service should be judged by these three votes, given what they and I stand for.

1. Applewhite Reservoir

The Applewhite Reservoir project returned for a vote in 1988. Not much public discussion had been held on the project since it surfaced at my first Council meetings at the start of the decade. In 1987, Mayor Cisneros appointed a Council committee to examine the water issue in our city and present a long-range plan. Neither Councilwoman Helen Dutmer nor I, both known opponents of the Applewhite Reservoir, were on the committee. On July 7, 1988, Mayor Cisneros announced that the committee's work was complete and that it had prepared a 25-year "Regional Water Resources Plan" for San Antonio. The plan included the recommendation that the Applewhite Reservoir be constructed.

On that day, a schedule was created for the Council's consideration and action on the report.[28] It called for an "informal briefing" for Council members three days later, on Sunday, July 10, 1988. At the insistence of Council members who opposed the reservoir, a public hearing was added to the schedule, to be held the following day, Monday, July 11, 1988. The Council would have a work session and follow-up briefing three days later, on July 14, 1988, during our regularly scheduled Council meeting. A vote on the Applewhite recommendation would take place a week later, on July 21, 1988. Finally, the Council would vote on the entire water plan on July 28, 1988.

In sum, the City Council and people of San Antonio were given two weeks to consider the plan's most controversial recommendation, the Applewhite Reservoir, and three weeks to consider the entire 25-year proposal regarding our city's future water use. The rail-roading of this critical issue was a deep concern that I voiced on the day of the important Applewhite vote.

The public hearing, held at the Convention Center, attracted a very large audience. The vast majority of those who spoke were against the Applewhite Reservoir. Of all the public hearings I participated in as a Council member, none was as impressive as this one. Opposing construction of the Applewhite Reservoir were strong community and environmental groups, as well as many individuals speaking on their own behalf.

Supporting it were the various Chambers of Commerce, builders and developers, large environmental firms, construction companies, and big business interests. The pro and con positions were articulated as before. Many, myself included, continued to believe that construction of the Applewhite Reservoir was being advocated in order to clear the way for more development over the Edwards Aquifer. With another source of water available, we would no longer have the federal protections surrounding the Edwards Aquifer as a "sole source" for our area. Although we could never prove that this was the reason why so many powerful interests were supporting such an ill-conceived project, the reality is that growth and water are two sides of the same coin, especially in a Sunbelt city like San Antonio.

By the early 1980s, there was a new consciousness in our city about caring for our water, thanks to the work over the years of citizens like Kirk and Carol Patterson, Fay Sinkin, Liz Davies and others who shared their extensive knowledge of water hydrology and water policy with many of us. Starting with the ill-fated shopping mall proposal back in the mid-1970s, concern had been growing among San Antonians about the amount of development that was occurring over the recharge zone of the Edwards Aquifer, along with a greater appreciation of the gift of nature we have in our Edwards Aquifer. Nonetheless, during the decade I was in office, despite the warnings of environmental groups, community organizations, and even city staff at times, zoning changes for more intensive uses over the recharge zone appeared regularly on our Council agenda. They generally passed, facilitating further development and the construction of acres and acres of impervious cover that prevented the aquifer from replenishing itself with rainwater.

I was very consistent in voting "no" each time such a zoning change was proposed. My objection became routine. It did not change the result, of course, but it was an act of resistance I took on behalf of countless people who understood that this kind of uncontrolled development posed a great risk to our aquifer and the quality of our water. In my view we were recklessly endangering future generations, even if the effects of our actions were not felt immediately. To this day, no effective study has ever been done of the cumulative effects of such development over the Edwards Aquifer.

Although the vast majority of people who showed up for the public hearing on July 11 spoke against the project, the David vs. Goliath power dynamics were alive and well in our city. Notwithstanding the strong public opposition, on July 21, 1988, by a vote of 8 to 3, the City Council voted to construct the Applewhite Reservoir. Councilwoman Dutmer, Councilman Walter Martínez and I were the "no" votes.[29]

Councilwoman Dutmer and I gave it our all that day. Helen and I were political opposites. She was socially conservative, representing a district with a large number of Anglo voters, but we both understood water and the urgent need to protect it. We spoke extensively that day, as did Councilman Martínez, who had succeeded Bernardo Eureste in 1985. We knew the votes were not there to defeat the measure. But public service has other dimensions, particularly on an issue as critical as water and the way a decision is made. Sometimes the power in elected office lies simply in providing facts and explaining what is at stake, whether it changes a vote or not.

The three of us who opposed the Applewhite project spoke to all the reasons for voting "no," beginning with the lack of transparency in the planning process and ramming things through. We then turned to the issues at stake in the proposal to build Applewhite and other features of the plan: the dirty water that would infiltrate the aquifer, not using augmentation and recharge dams upstream, the escalating expense, the eradication of thousands of historic treasures, no money for mitigation of natural habitat, the threat of opening the door wide open to further development over the Edwards Aquifer, and all the holes we saw in the long-range plan. We did not put a philosophical or ideological statement on the table. It was all facts.

As I view the video of that Council meeting now, years later, what I see is that we laid down a foundation of facts. We built the public record so that people could get their information and proceed as they saw fit. The last words on the videotape of that meeting that I have kept all these years were spoken by Mayor Cisneros, who said, "We've taken a major step in our water future and the future of San Antonio generally." But it is Councilwoman Dutmer who has the last prophetic words. "James Hasslocher," she states, "this is only the kick ball. The game still has to be played."[30]

The controversial vote sparked deep resentment. A decision was rendered on a major public issue affecting all area residents, with hardly any public discussion or input. The discontent was organized into a petition drive, calling for a referendum on the issue. Eventually, enough signatures were gathered to put a measure on the ballot, calling on the city to stop construction of the Applewhite Reservoir. It coincided with the City Council and mayoral election of May 1991.

Agua es vida. Water is life. I knew this from the time when, as a child, I first tasted the delicious cold water that my Tío Blas pulled out of the well for me at my grandparent's *ranchito* in Lockhart, Texas. We drank it from an aluminum dipper. *¡Y el agua estaba muy frrria!* Cold and pure. Years later, sitting in Council chambers, when I would hear about pollution of our water or water scarcity, my mind always went back to that pure and delicious *agua de la noria.* That was my frame of mind. What were we doing to the water I had tasted as a child? My response was visceral. We had to protect the people's precious water.

2. Alamodome

For several years, Mayor Cisneros and other political and business allies had a vision to build a football stadium in San Antonio in the hopes that it would attract a National Football League (NFL) team to the city. It was part of a vision that was typically articulated as making "sleepy" San Antonio a "big-league" city or "putting San Antonio on the map." It was a vision that, in my view, always seemed to involve building things that benefited developers and big business, with low-paying service jobs to sustain them. Striving for greater educational achievement or a higher standard of living or better neighborhoods for our people never seemed to be part of that "big league" vision. It was, however, my vision for our city.

The idea of the stadium was not popular among the citizenry because it required public funding. But the mayor and his allies, being politically savvy, figured out a way to do it. They proposed using the taxing authority of the city's transportation system, VIA Metropolitan Transit, to levy a transportation sales tax. A one-half cent transportation sales tax over five years would pay for the estimated $150 million cost of building the stadium. The transportation system, of course, had no authority to raise taxes for a football stadium; the stadium would be part of a "terminal complex."

On August 11, 1988, just two weeks after the Applewhite Reservoir vote, Mayor Cisneros brought the issue before City Council, first distributing an *Atlanta Constitution* newspaper article about Atlanta's efforts to build a stadium and its purported benefits to citizens. Council members in favor of the idea spoke to the advantage of a stadium to the city, noting that with the proposed tax to fund its construction, there would be no longterm debt incurred. An amendment was proposed that would direct the stadium's first profits to "street maintenance and infrastructure."[31] Councilwoman Helen Dutmer, an opponent of the stadium, countered that "based on other stadium experiences there would not be any profits to share in the end."[32]

A Council majority directed the city staff to negotiate with VIA for the development of a multi-purpose domed facility. I voted against it.[33] State law allowed the issue to move forward through VIA. Mayor Cisneros was able to get authorizing legislation from the State Legislature for a domed stadium to be built, but the law required a vote of the people. An election was held in January 1989 on a measure "to increase the VIA sales and use tax for construction of a stadium or terminal complex including a regional economic development facility." The so-called "economic development facility," which would be attached to a bus terminal station, was actually the proposed domed stadium. After its construction, the city would be responsible for its management.

I actively campaigned against the ballot measure, urging a "no" vote. I opposed the stadium for several reasons. First, a sales tax is regressive, penalizing low-income people more than anyone else. Second, VIA taxes should be used to support our city's public transportation—not for other purposes, like building a football stadium. Third, there were no assurances that if we built a stadium an NFL team would come. Fourth, the site that had been chosen for the stadium, which required 57 acres,[34] was on the eastern boundary of downtown where old neighborhoods would be at risk with such major development. It was a largely African-American area of town with a significant history that would be impacted negatively.

The sales pitch made to voters during the campaign was that the domed stadium would be a "cash cow." The chairman of San Antonio's Greater Chamber of Commerce at the time was Bill Thornton.[35] He and I participated in a radio debate where I argued my position against a publicly funded stadium. After the debate, as we said goodbye, Thornton told me not to worry, that a lot of money would be made and it could be used for the needs of "your people."

Mayor Cisneros put much of his political capital into this ballot measure. In the fall of 1988, he had announced that he would not be running for re-election when his term was up in the spring of 1989. But he won this last big issue of his tenure: By a vote of 53% to 47%, the people supported construction of the stadium. According to news reports at the time, the result caused the mayor to reconsider re-election.[36] Ultimately, however, he re-affirmed his decision to step down from office.

Four years and approximately $186 million later, the "Alamodome" stadium opened on May 15, 1993.[37] No NFL team, however, was in the picture at the opening ceremonies—or has been since.

As the Alamodome was under construction and none of the hoped-for NFL teams it was built for seemed interested in coming, we started having discussions about alternative uses for the massive stadium. I'll never forget a presentation given to the Council one day by city staff, showing how the San Antonio Spurs, our city's basketball team since 1973, could use the football stadium. Since a basketball court would not require the entire football field, a curtain would be installed in the middle of the structure to accommodate the new use, the staff explained. A few of my colleagues expressed support for such a creative solution. Wondering how this would work, I asked what material would be used for the curtain. "Cloth," was the reply. I remember sitting there wondering if there was something wrong with me. How could using half a football field, divided by a cloth curtain—with utilities running throughout the stadium and the other half remaining unused—be seen as a good idea? Moments like these made me wonder how much longer I could keep doing this work.

When the Alamodome opened in 1993, the Spurs moved there from the HemisFair Arena, where they had been playing. The arena was eventually torn down to allow for expansion of the city's convention center. It was just a matter of time before the Alamodome football stadium was found to be unsuitable for basketball. In 2002, Bexar County voters approved the increase of hotel and car rental taxes to pay for another stadium—for basketball. Known as the AT&T Center, it is now the home of the Spurs.

As for the National Football League, in the summer of 2011, a $50,000 study commissioned by the City of San Antonio and Bexar County found that our city did not have the assets necessary for an NFL or Major League Baseball team. We do not have enough Fortune 500 companies, our media market is too small, and our median household income is too low.[38]

In the meantime, the city of San Antonio has continued managing and spending public funds to care for and upgrade the multi-purpose Alamodome. The complex continues to be used for assorted functions, including musical concerts, some football games and college sports, and practice games of the Dallas Cowboys. It has definitely *not* been a cash cow.

3. Fiesta Texas

When, in the late 1960s, the county hospital was moved to a rural area miles north of downtown as part of the new medical school, followed in the 1970s by the decision to locate UTSA fifteen miles north of downtown, the direction for San Antonio's growth was set. Determined by elected officials using public funds, these major economic generators laid the tracks for the city's future growth—with all signs pointing north, over the Edwards Aquifer Recharge Zone. In 1990, yet another government decision was made to drive additional development north, across Loop 1604, with another major economic generator and another public decision to build over our sole source of drinking water.

One of the city's major employer's, USAA, partnered with Opryland USA, to build a theme park that would come to be known as "Fiesta Texas." They controlled a large piece of land at the northwest corner of IH-10 and Loop 1604 and requested the creation of a Reinvestment Zone from the city, with tax abatements, for the entire 618 acres.

I was not against tax abatements per se. Three had come before City Council, since they were allowed under state law, and I had voted for two of them. But in this case, I felt the price we were paying in tax subsidies for the new development was just too high. First, we would once again be incentivizing development over the Edwards Aquifer Recharge Zone. The proposed project would be an economic generator attracting even more development in an area that should be protected from dense development. Second, the vast majority of theme park jobs were seasonal with low wages. Providing tax incentives to create these kinds of jobs was not something I could support.

Yet another troubling part of the tax abatement proposal was that it would be granted for all 618 acres of land even though only 200 acres would be allocated for the theme park. The remaining 418 acres would also be granted the ten-year tax abatement, regardless of the land's future use. The developers would not need to go back before City Council to obtain approval of the project; the tax abatement would automatically apply.

On top of everything else, the proposal was coming to us at a terrible time. We were in an economic downturn, facing growing lack of confidence in City Hall, and we had just imposed a 12% property tax increase to help make ends meet. Anti-tax groups had launched a campaign for a "rollback" election that was scheduled to take place the following month. If successful, the tax increase would be rolled back to 8%. The Council's vote on the tax abatement was scheduled for January 11, 1990; the tax rollback election for February 4, 1990. It was not a good time to be voting for tax abatements.

The rest of the Council and Mayor Lila Cockrell, who succeeded Cisneros as mayor in May of 1989, were in strong support of the tax abatement for the theme park. They argued it was a win-win situation because we would eventually receive higher taxes from the theme park than we had been receiving from land that used to be a quarry. They also argued that saying no to the USAA/Opryland partnership would send a bad message to the business community at a time when we wanted to attract new businesses to our city. The San Antonio business establishment echoed these views, strongly supporting the project.

On one of the days leading up to the City Council vote on granting the tax abatement, I participated with other Council Members and business people in a press conference urging San Antonians to vote against the tax rollback. After the press conference, Bill Thornton, of the Greater Chamber of Commerce, approached me. He said that I should vote for the Opryland tax abatement. "I am not going to vote for it," I responded. He said my vote was needed because "the Hispanic culture would be featured in the park and the people at Opryland wanted all the Hispanic councilmembers to vote for it."

I told him that a majority of the Council members were going to vote for it, but that I was not. His demeanor changed abruptly. "If you don't vote for it we are going to wrap that vote like an albatross around your neck and you will never get elected to anything in this city," he threatened.

At the time, I did not dwell on the remark. On the day I cast my vote against the tax abatement, I alluded to it—but I did not explain who said it or how it transpired. Now, with so many years behind me, I think I should have stated plainly in open session what Bill Thornton said. The audacity of threatening an elected official who was voting her conscience was a clear sign of the arrogance of power of an elite few who wield inordinate control over public policy decisions in our city. One year later, I was able to connect the dots in understanding how this power dynamic works in a way that I never could have had I not run for mayor—and come so close to winning.

The decision to cross Loop 1604 and encourage more intense development over the Edwards Aquifer recharge zone was monumental; its impact is clearly evident today. There may not have been much we could do if the project were being funded entirely with private monies. But here was another case involving development where our elected leaders had a choice, yet there was no discussion of what constitutes good economic development and growth. We never stopped to consider who benefits and who loses. Or what the impact of this project would be on older neighborhoods like those I represented—or, even less, the impact it would have on future generations.

The defining vote to grant USAA and Opryland the tax abatements passed by 10 to 1. Mine was the lone "no" vote.[39] Six Flags Fiesta Texas opened in March of 1992. The surrounding area over the recharge zone is now dense with commercial and residential development.

A Time for Decisions

In September of 1988, Henry Cisneros made the surprising announcement that he would not run for a fifth term as mayor. As the realization emerged that the mayoral election in 1989 would be wide open, constituents and others from throughout the city began urging me to run.

I gave serious consideration to the possibility, going through a discernment process with my family and friends. But in the end, I decided against it. My heart was just not in undertaking such a race at that time. I felt that representing the people of District 1 remained the best way I could serve my city, and I still had work to do.

On November 23, 1988, I held a press conference to announce that I would not run for mayor. I seized the moment to speak of the priorities I had advocated during my years in office:

- Equity in the distribution of basic city services throughout the community as the city grows.

- Creation of housing opportunities for all of our citizens.

- Expansion of educational opportunities and job training because it is the only way our economy will truly prosper in the long run.

- Investment in our children; the fact that we have many children at risk in our city is simply unacceptable and puts our future and theirs in jeopardy.

- Promoting the understanding that fighting crime includes not only spending money on police officers, equipment, and facilities but also investing in programs and services that will enable our young people to avoid involvement in criminal activity.

- Responsible growth, which benefits *all* sides of the city.

- Protecting our precious water supply.

- Balanced growth—we cannot simply grow away from the older areas of the city, leaving them to deteriorate while we reach ever further outward.

Today, as I look at the yellowing paper on which these words are written, I see how consistent these concerns are with those I articulated when I first ran for City Council. Eight years in office had confirmed for me the magnitude of the problems we faced. The issues were not isolated to a single council district, but citywide. I did not feel called to run for mayor at that time but after due diligence, I decided to ask my constituents for a fifth term—and was reelected, unopposed.

During my last two years in office, my constituents and I continued our work with the never-ending challenges of being in the heart of a growing city that was not quite coming to terms with the realities of its growth. I had organized my district well. While we had lost some major battles to save housing, we had prevented the destruction of other housing in vital inner-city arteries. We were successful in maintaining historic structures that were now providing vitality and business opportunities for some neighborhoods. I had led in the creation of a Housing Trust Fund, which would provide housing and revitalization opportunities in the future. District 1 had established itself as a leader in the neighborhood association movement, and there was much civic engagement generally throughout the district.

I had taken transparency in government to heart. I did my research, engaged my constituents or other experts, and made it my business to explain to the public the reasons for my votes, especially when I was in the minority. I wanted my constituents to understand that these votes reflected my philosophy of growth and what constituted economic development.

By the fall of 1990, I had decided that I would not run for another Council term. I had reached a point where I felt I had done all I could for my district as a Councilwoman. I had a vision for my city, but it could not be realized as a single Council member. I did not yet know what I would do next with my life. The decision to step down from office stood alone.

In time, I would decide what my next step would be. My departure from City Council could be a quiet or a rousing one. I would opt for the latter.

NOTES
Chapter 7: Public Life

1. See City Council minutes, May 14, 1981, pp. 17-19, quoting Mayor Cisneros. "…[S]ince 1970 we have grown by almost 21% of the size of our City. …[W]e're making a stronger effort than were being made in 1970 because the sun belt movement is faster today than it was in 1970 because we're trying to attract industry and we were not in 1970. The only thing I know is that the safest way to proceed is to start developing a surface water supply, not only for San Antonio but for the development of South Texas as well."

2. Voting aye were Cisneros, Wing, Thompson, Canavan, and Hasslocher. Voting nay were Dutmer, Eureste, Alderete, and Berriozábal. Webb and Archer were absent. See City Council Minutes, May 14, 1981.

3. See testimony of Robert Van Dyke, CWB General Manager, City Council Minutes, May 21, 1981.

4. See City Council minutes, May 21, 1981.

5. Councilman Claude Black, an ordained minister, voted against the Resolution indicating: "I long ago gave up the idea that religious leadership was infallible. I have also given up on the idea that there are no options. I believe that we are caught up in a kind of economic movement that speaks to us as if there were no options. I think, therefore, I find myself committed to the idea that I could not give my endorsement to this." Voting aye were Mayor Lila Cockrell, Alfred Becker, Glenn Beckman, Glenn Lacy, Cliff Morton, José San Martín and Leo Mendoza. Absent was Alvin Padilla. See City Council minutes, June 28, 1973.

6. City Council minutes, June 28, 1973.

7. *Ibid.*

8. http://www.nukefreetexas.org/downloads/STP 8 years_late.pdf (accessed July 6, 2011).

9. The others voting against the rate hike were Councilmen Alderete, Eureste, and Webb. See City Council Minutes, May 21, 1981.

10. http://www.edwardsaquifer.org (accessed June 28, 2011).

11. http://www.edwardsaquifer.net/intro.html (accessed July 11, 2011).

12. http://www.aquiferalliance.org (accessed July 6, 2011).

13. City Council minutes, October 16, 1975.

14. City Council minutes, July 19, 1979.

15. http://www.edwardsaquifer.net/species.html (accessed December 19, 2011).

16. http://www.celebratingtexas.com/tr/idr9/21.pdf (accesed July 6, 2011).

17. With the exception of Bob Thompson's defeat of Rudy Ortiz in 1979 in District 6.

18. I had actually worked in a part of the Rand Building in 1968, when the Democratic Party headquarters was housed there.

19. Through the graces of the San Antonio Conservation Society, the building was not demolished; a privately funded parking garage was eventually built next door.

20. Henry Cisneros and I grew up in neighboring barrios. He was raised in the Sacred Heart parish next to my Christ the King neighborhood. Like me, he was educated in Catholic schools, all the way through high school. Six years younger than I, Henry was elected to the City Council around the time I got married and moved to New Orleans. My family and I strongly supported him as our District 1 Councilman. When Manny and I moved back from New Orleans in 1976, Henry was teaching at UTSA while serving on the Council. We had a very good relationship with him. During my political science studies at UTSA, I did an internship in Henry's office, mostly doing casework for him. I learned a lot. He pretty much left me alone in the office with his younger sister, who was only 16; I had a great time.

    When I was elected to City Council, our relationship became strictly political. As I would find out over the years, we did not agree on some rather significant issues during our time of service together, between 1981 and 1989. In fact, as history (and this narrative) records, I vehemently disagreed with him on some of the major issues he supported. But the differences were not personal; Henry and I had ideological differences on how to move our city forward. He saw economic development in the traditional sense of promoting new growth with the support of the business community. I saw economic development through the lens of strong consideration of environmental sustainability, inclusion of our city's older areas, and an emphasis on investing in human capital. It was very much of a minority position on the City Council, which made for a very difficult and lonely road to forge on that dais.

    Henry deserves full credit for raising San Antonio's national visibility. He also brought great pride to our Mexican-American community and city when he was elected mayor. Although our differences were political, not personal, there was a certain dynamic about our relationship that I under-stood at the time and that has since become clear—the role of gender.

In an interview José Angel Gutiérrez conducted in July 1996, Rosie Castro talked about how men do not support women. As an example, Rosie quoted Henry as stating about me, "I love her like a sister, but, you know, she has never been pro-business. And I am not sure that, she, her, you know, her leadership skills are developed to the point where...." And at that point Rosie got upset and did not complete the sentence (see http://library.uta.edu/tejanovoices/xml/CMAS_123.xml, accessed December 19, 2011). Our leadership styles were very different. Our understanding of leadership was different. Gender and sexism were the big elephants in the room. Were we an anomaly? I do not think so. Is this something that needs to be ad-dressed? Definitely. How Latina elected officials and Latino elected officials are going to work with each other for the betterment of our community in the future is critical to how our community will move forward.

Henry and I never talked about our work all those years. Our relation-ship was cordial and respectful, as has been captured in public. In retrospect, I think we might have made a major contribution to our community had we worked more closely together in areas where we shared common ground—issues relating to children, women, housing, inner-city development, and human services. I carry regret in my heart about that. Why did it not hap-pen? I think we each could do some soul searching to answer that question.

21. Today, as overcrowding continues at the northside's University Hospital, there is a multi-million-dollar renovation and construction effort at the origi-nal site. It has been named the Robert B. Green Campus for many years.

22. In 1995, after years of community pressure, the UTSA Downtown Cam-pus was located in the old Urban Renewal Site. Both Manny and I lobbied vigorously and consistently for a downtown campus.

23. "'Choices made in the first generation eliminate some alternatives (yet to be discovered) that will be available...in the second generation.' Or, put an-other way, there are major constraints on present alternatives because of past choices." Martin Melosi, *The Sanitary City: Urban Infrastructure from Colonial Times to the Present* (Baltimore: Johns Hopkins University Press, 1999), 10, citing Louis P. Cain. I am grateful to Dr. Marisol Cortez for introducing me to the concept of path dependency.

24. Leapfrog development is also referred to as urban sprawl as the devel-opment of lands in a manner requiring the extension of public facilities. In addition the services are extended on the periphery of an existing urbanized area where such extension is not provided for in the existing plans of the local governing body. *Foster v. Anable*, 199 Ariz. 489 (Ariz. Ct. App. 2001).

25. At the time, City Councilmembers had a half-time secretary (Tina

Blanco was my secretary) and an administrative assistant (Julia Hoyt) shared by all ten of us. Four years into my service, we were allocated a small discretionary fund that we could use to hire staff. I hired one assistant, Susan E. Klein, who worked with me during my last six years in office. Over my ten-year tenure, I also engaged the services of thirty interns, recruited from local colleges and universities, who helped me with research and casework, one semester at a time.

26. City Council minutes, June 2, 1983.

27. In the 2011 Texas Legislative Session, an effort to pass legislation that would have mandated local police to enforce immigration laws was defeated.

28. City Council minutes, July 7, 1988.

29. City Council minutes, July 21, 1988.

30. Videotape of City Council meeting, July 21, 1988.

31. City Council minutes, August 11, 1988.

32. *Ibid.*

33. *Ibid.* My recollection is that Councilwoman Helen Dutmer and Councilman Walter Martínez also voted against it; the minutes, however, show all three of us as absent.

34. *Ibid.*

35. William E. "Bill" Thornton was elected mayor of San Antonio in 1995 and served a single two-year term.

36. "Pleased that voters have approved building a new, domed stadium, Mayor Henry G. Cisneros said he may run for re-election, although he earlier said he would leave politics because of personal problems." See Associated Press, "San Antonio's Mayor May Run Again, After All," in Los Angeles Times, January 24, 1989.

37. http://www.alamodome.com/default.asp?alamodome=27 (accessed December 18, 2011).

38. *San Antonio Express-News*, July 29, 2011.

39. City Council minutes, January 11, 1990.

CHAPTER 8

María for Mayor

When I decided to throw my hat into the race for mayor of San Antonio, I felt both comfortable and excited. I thought it was a great opportunity and worthy challenge. I had already made the decision to leave office after nearly ten years of service. I could either leave quietly or with a bang. I decided to go out with a bang, using the mayoral race as a vehicle for bringing forward my vision for the city and the issues I had worked on for years. It would be a great challenge, I knew, and that's what I decided to call my campaign—"The Magnificent Challenge."

On a very sunny and warm fall day, October 27, 1990, I announced my candidacy from the backyard of our home in Beacon Hill. My supporters had built a large wooden platform with railings and a tall wooden podium, decorated in red, white, and blue. People held black-on-white posters with the theme, "For All of Us Who Believe." Manny introduced me with great joy as my parents, siblings, nieces and nephews, and other relatives surrounded me. About 500 people packed around the platform, with mariachi music blaring and great enthusiasm filling the air. It had the same community feeling and grassroots aura that had been present in all my years of District 1 work, this time with friends, old and new, gathered from all around the city.

My campaign team was already in place. I had asked people to help me who were longtime friends, knew my trajectory in politics, and were making important contributions to the community: Laura Calderón, campaign manager; Frank Herrera, finance chairman; Mary Helen Alvarado, campaign treasurer and office manager; Daniel Meza, precinct chairman; Dean Barbara Bader Aldave, ethics advisor; Susan E. Klein, administrative assistant; Richard Gambitta (Gambitta & Associates), research and polling; Rosie Castro, campaign advisor; Lionel Sosa (Sosa, Bromley, Aguilar & Associates), advertising; and Juan Solís, general assistance. Luz Escamilla once again took over the reins of grassroots fundraising. Other individuals on my campaign leadership team included Carlos Guerra, Dr. Louis Agnese, Renee Watson, Mrs. Elvira Cisneros, José Villarreal, Helen Austin, Dr. Cervando Martínez, and Darlene Murnin.

Our goal was to raise money in small amounts, as we had always done. People talked about having to raise $400,000 or more to run a competitive mayoral race. I had confidence we could do it although when I think of this daunting task today, I am amazed that we even dared. By the end of the campaign, we actually raised more than that amount.

When I asked media guru Lionel Sosa if he would help me with advertising, he asked me to meet with his partners, Al Aguilar and Ernest Bromley. I was excited to answer their question, "Why are you running?" The words just flowed as I spoke about the issues I had championed at City Hall, the way I had done my work, the community activities I had been involved in since my youth, and the vision I had of a city government that is fair, open, consistent, and inclusive.

I spoke too of my vision of marrying economic development with investment in human capital.[1] For me that meant investing in people's lives, especially in the very young, so that they could obtain good educations and be trained to contribute back to their community. I had the example of my own family where my parents had invested in their six children's education and a family was taken out of poverty. I was witnessing what my husband was doing with his PREP students. He was changing lives. We could do that as a city.

In San Antonio, we had students who were not graduating from high school; high levels of illiteracy, juvenile crime, under-employment, and low-wage jobs; and high poverty rates. Our city's population was growing and it was diverse. That was an untapped treasure! The potential of our people was our city's greatest asset. Having a well-trained and educated workforce was not only good for our people but an imperative to the entire city's well being. We could use our incentive programs as leverage to attract good industries, seeking jobs with good wages. Everyone in our city should benefit from our development policies, not just a few.

On that point, I would not shy away from the votes for which I was being criticized—saying "no" to Applewhite, Alamodome, and Fiesta Texas. I was running on those "no" votes and what they meant in terms of the link I thought we should make between human capital investment and economic development, as much as on other issues I supported. From the start, however, the way my focus on investing in human capital was covered made it sound like it was just about increasing social services. It was not. The day after my announcement, the *San Antonio Light* reported:

> Berriozábal's challenge in the next six months is to articulate what differentiates her from Cockrell and Wolff. Although she puts a

heavy emphasis on social services, she also has opposed the Apple-white Reservoir and the domed stadium projects."[2]

Out of the conversation with Lionel Sosa and his colleagues came the values and vision we would articulate in our campaign—and from which we never wavered.

After agreeing to help with the campaign, Frank Herrera and Lionel Sosa offered to loan me $115,000 so that I could get started on the advertising and publicity efforts. They both felt I was a good candidate with an important message and good organization. Frank's loan would be for $50,000 and Lionel's for $65,000. When I hesitated to accept, Frank, whom I had met when he was a young man, said in a tone more like a brother than a financial advisor, "If someone has enough confidence in you to offer that, you take it." I did. With that support, we were able to start our advertising campaign before any of the other candidates. Those early funds encouraged others to start donating. We sent out the message that this was a serious campaign.

The day after my announcement, an ad appeared in both major newspapers, focused on the values of our campaign and asking those who believed in them to join us.

For All Of Us Who Believe…

- That the power of many is stronger than the influence of a few.
- That business and government together are stronger than business or government alone.
- That education is stronger than poverty.
- That families and neighborhoods are stronger than crime, drugs or gangs.
- That faith is stronger than fear.

Sosa & Associates created some beautiful television ads in English and Spanish. We were able to run some but did not have enough money to do justice to all of them. We did no negative campaigning.

"Too Hispanic"

Early in our campaign Sosa & Associates conducted focus groups to identify my positives and negatives. There were no surprises. Some people disagreed with some of my votes, and that was good to know. But there was one point—one of the findings—that intrigued me. It is something that is rarely discussed openly because it is, of course, racist.

"María, some people think you are too Hispanic."

For a lifetime I had worn my *cultura* with pride. I had never tried to fit into any mold that some in society might demand as the price of admission or for advancement. I certainly was not going to change that now. My parents' admonishment was as fresh as ever in my mind: We were neither less than nor more than anyone else. My response to the "too Hispanic" comment was to continue being who I was—María Antonietta Berriozábal, or better yet, just María—with great pride. Shortly thereafter, bright blue and white posters started going up all over the city, with small yard signs or huge billboards declaring, simply, "MARIA FOR MAYOR."

About a month before Election Day, some two thousand people joined me at a fundraising event as I celebrated my fiftieth birthday at a county park. It was a joyous occasion with mariachis and a huge sheet cake festooned with the words, "María for Mayor," in blue and white frosting. The campaign was, indeed, magnificent in its level of energy and enthusiasm. I could go for fifteen hours a day or more, including block walking, and never tire; the people energized me. Supporters wrote poems, songs, and even a *corrido*. Children made banners. Volunteers worked hard, raising funds and block walking. Lila Aguirre was my volunteer driver and we would belt out wonderful *rancheras* in the car, as we drove between events. Manny accompanied me to evening and weekend events. He enjoyed it too.

Applewhite for Mayor?

A key issue that came up at every campaign stop, whether it was a small venue where I was the only candidate present or a mayoral forum with all the candidates on stage, was the Applewhite Reservoir project. Applewhite foes had gathered enough petitions to put the issue on the ballot. In addition to voting for mayor and city councilors, San Antonio voters faced an issue referendum that would force City Council to abandon the Applewhite Reservoir, if it garnered a majority of "yes" votes.

Eleven names were on the ballot for the mayoral race but only six of us attended the candidate forums: Van Henry Archer, a former councilman; Lila Cockrell, the incumbent mayor; Jimmy Hasslocher, a five-term councilman; Kay Turner, a business woman and leader of the anti-Applewhite campaign; Nelson Wolff, a two-term councilman; and me, a five-term councilwoman.

I was the only City Council incumbent in the race who opposed the Applewhite Reservoir and had voted against it. I spent a lot of time explaining my vote. Many people had not been well informed about the project and I found myself gaining a lot of support for my position and for a "yes" vote on the ballot issue to abandon Applewhite. There was another controversial issue on the ballot, calling for strict term limits on City Council.

As individual candidates were raising money for their campaigns, the referendum on Applewhite was also generating large sums of campaign money, mostly from pro-Applewhite business supporters, who mounted a major media effort urging voters to vote "no" on the referendum. A week before the election, a news story reported, "The Water Now! Committee raised $425,756 in the last three weeks, bringing its fund-raising total to $574,694 for its effort to save the Applewhite reservoir."[3] Grassroots opponents of the Applewhite project, in contrast, ended up raising around $5,000.

The city's two daily newspapers, the *San Antonio Light* and the *San Antonio Express-News*, both editorialized against the two referenda issues, urging "no" votes on abandoning Applewhite and on passing strict term limits for City Council. The *San Antonio Light* endorsed Nelson Wolff and the *Express-News* endorsed the incumbent, Mayor Lila Cockrell.

In its endorsement of Wolff, the *San Antonio Light* added a long commentary on the mayoral race. In it, the editors complimented my work on City Council but said they were "uncomfortable" with my opposition to growth issues, citing my votes against the Alamodome, Applewhite, and certain tax abatements. The editorial added, "Berriozábal brings new energy and new emphasis to the campaign. She has served her district well for 10 years, built a solid following and gained political influence beyond the city. Her platform of investment in human capital deserves city attention."[4] The editorial then went on to say, "She often stood alone on issues, unable to influence council members to her positions."

The editorial cited Councilman Wolff's business background as cause for the endorsement, noting that as a leader of Target 90, the city's strategic planning project, Wolff had "reached out to all segments of the community."[5] The editorial also noted that Wolff had been a visible Council member, representing his district well.

On May 4, 1991, the people spoke. To everyone's surprise, a Latina—María Antonietta Berriozábal, daughter of Apolinar and Sixta Rodríguez, Mexican immigrants from San Antonio's Westside—led the field of eleven candidates with 30.95% of the vote. The results put me in a run-off election against businessman Nelson Wolff, who came in second with 26.15%. Wolff was followed by Lila Cockrell with 20.68%; Van Henry Archer with 16.11%; Kay Turner with 3.85%;

Jimmy Hasslocher with 1.64%; and the remaining five with less than 1% each.[6]

It was an historic step and a wonderful affirmation of the ten-year record on which I had run. The victory was sweet. I shared it that evening with hundreds of volunteers who had poured their hearts into the campaign, at an events hall that had been part of the old Frost Bros., a luxury department store that had anchored a thriving downtown for many years until it closed. At one point that night I remembered the "Frost Bros." logo emblazoned onto the second-hand black velveteen shoes with crystal stars that my father had gotten for me from his boss Frank Miceli, when I was twelve. I will never forget the look on my parents' faces, captured in a photograph taken of them that evening as they sat on the stage, gazing out over the noisy crowded hall. What had occurred that day had not sunk in; their faces looked dazed and amazed.

Against the odds, the people of San Antonio also voted that day, 51% to 49%, to abandon the Applewhite Reservoir surface water project that their Mayor and City Council had supported. And in yet another strong message to City Hall, reflecting a lack of trust in their government, the voters also adopted some of the strictest term limits in the country for mayor and city council members. This was not a position I supported—strict term limits can be counterproductive—but I understood the frustration expressed in that vote.

On Monday, May 6, 1991, *The New York Times International* carried a short story headlined, "2 Council Members Defeat San Antonio Mayor." Not much else was said, but my father, an historian at heart, always savored the importance of that moment. Not one to hand out big smiles, he would give me a huge one that made his cheeks crinkle as he would remind me that I was mayor of San Antonio for two weeks! That's when he also would remind me of how far we had traveled from where we had started. He was so very proud *¡qué ganamos!* That we won—emphasis on the "we."

Now we had a runoff election before us. It would be a new campaign where the monied powerful would consolidate against us. We did not blink. We went right on as before—delighted to be in the arena.

Powers That Be

Immediately after Election Day, I announced that I would support the vote of the people to abandon Applewhite. In fact, I proposed to City Council that we issue an ordinance to make the vote formal. On

May 9, 1991, Nelson Wolff also declared that he would abide by the wishes of the people to abandon Applewhite.[7] With those declarations, Applewhite ceased to be an issue for voters in the mayoral campaign; its impact would still be felt in our campaign, negatively. Through research data, I later found out that with Applewhite off the table as an issue, I would lose some voters—Anglos—to Wolff.

Our runoff campaign was not much different from the primary. We kept it positive, focusing on getting votes. But in the runoff, we experienced two eye openers.

The first occurred at a candidates' session sponsored by COPS/ Metro Alliance, intended to hold Councilman Wolff and me accountable. As usual, the group had gathered a huge crowd. At this gathering, Father Rosendo Urrabazo, the Catholic-clergy leader of the group, stepped up to the microphone. I had known him from Christ the King Church, where I had taught his siblings catechism. "Mrs. Berriozábal," he asked, "if as a Councilwoman you could not gather the votes for your issues, what makes you think you can get them as mayor?"

It was the only moment in the campaign when my answer did not reflect my thoughts. My brain got stuck, fixated on the white collar in front of me. I do not recall what I said in response; my instinct was to spare the priest and my supporters in the crowd embarrassment. But I clearly recall what I was thinking: "I did not get the votes because it was the people's agenda—and *yours*—that I was carrying!" That day, an idea that had been inchoate in me for some time crystalized. There were people in the church that had taught me about social justice who were more political than I could ever be.

The other eye opener came from the other end of the spectrum. I always knew there was "an establishment" in our city. I had felt their power and subtle presence over the years and encountered their lobbyists at City Hall. I would see some of these powerful men at public events I attended as a Council member, but I had never been lobbied by any of them personally. As I told a newspaper reporter once, "I had never had an audience with them."

When Councilman Wolff and I got into the run off, all the polls showed we were tied. The election was up in the air. Key business leaders, who had supported Lila Cockrell in the mayoral race, were now in a quandary. In the primary, the race between Mayor Cockrell and Councilman Wolff had gotten pretty heated, with Wolff leveling criticisms against some of Cockrell's big business supporters.[8] These same individuals were leery of me. But Wolff and I were now the only choices available in the mayoral run off. I had never had any big business leaders among my supporters—and doubted I ever would. But one day a call came into my office. General William McDermott, the chairman of USAA and, in the opinion of many, the most respected and influential businessman in our city, wanted to meet with me. A meeting was scheduled for May 13, 1991, at a downtown office building. It would include other business leaders as well.

On the appointed day, I arrived accompanied by a friend I had asked to go with me. In addition to General McDermott, the other men attending the meeting were Bill Greehey, chairman of Valero Energy Corp.; Cliff Morton, a big developer; Jim Dublin, a partner in the Dublin-McCarter & Associates public relations agency; and Bob Coleman, chairman of the San Antonio Sports Foundation. General McDermott and Bill Greehey had been "among the staunchest supporters" of the Applewhite project, as well as supporters of Mrs. Cockrell.[9] "Valero and USAA donated much of the half-million dollars spent on the unsuccessful campaign to continue Applewhite construction."[10]

The meeting opened with the usual first question asked of any candidate, "Why are you running?" I had the distinct impression these business leaders really did not know what they were going to do in terms of the mayoral endorsement. I repeated what I had shared hundreds of times and at many venues, including my ideas on human capital investment. We then spent time talking about education. We all agreed on the necessity to have an educated and well-trained workforce. I told them that, as mayor, the duly elected representative of the public, I would work with them to bring together two important groups—the public sector and the private sector. I shared my views about how a good and stable government that is fair and inclusive is an asset for business. I said I would work for that.

The talk then turned to the defeat of the Applewhite Reservoir. The men in that room were clearly not happy with the election results. The unequivocal message they delivered was that the next administration at City Hall had to see to it that the Applewhite Reservoir got built. My response was instantaneous: "The people have spoken. I will support the people." That comment ended the discussion.

The meeting continued for a few more minutes on other issues. Then, as if truly puzzled, General McDermott asked me, "Why *are* you doing this?" It was not the same question asked at the beginning of the meeting. The tone was very different; it elicited a different response from me. I said, simply, that I wanted to serve people and that I loved public service. It was what I wanted to do with my life. Looking at me straight in the eye, General McDermott said in a very calm voice, "You are doing the right thing for the right reasons. At the end that will serve you well." With that statement, the hour and a half meeting came to an end. It was the first and last time I ever met with members of San Antonio's "establishment."

The next morning, a story appeared in the newspaper headlined, "Berriozábal huddles with Cockrell pals."[11] I was quoted as saying we had a "candid dialogue." Bob Coleman, chairman of the San Antonio Sports Foundation, said each business leader "would make up his own mind" and that they hoped to have a similar meeting soon with Nelson Wolff. According to the paper, "Wolff characterized the meeting as an attempt by the group's members to hold onto power, and perhaps 'cut a deal' with Berriozábal."[12]

On May 17, Councilman Wolff met with General McDermott. and his friends. On May 18, General McDermott issued a statement to the media strongly endorsing Nelson Wolff for mayor. According to the *San Antonio Light*, McDermott found that "Wolff was more in tune with San Antonio's need for a united economic development effort, aggressive building on existing economic strengths, and improvement of the city's infrastructure."[13] McDermott said, "Nelson Wolff's track record is consistent with these goals," the paper reported.[14]

The Passion Does Not Die

On May 26, after the polls closed on Election Day, my family and I watched the results on television in my hotel room at the El Tropicano Hotel, on the banks of the San Antonio River, where we planned to host the post-election party with friends and supporters. I had my back to the television set when I suddenly saw the expression change on the faces of Manny and my father. In that instant, my heart sank. "I lost," I thought. Just as instantly, another thought crossed my mind. "No way is this a loss." Minutes later Richard Gambitta, who had been keeping up with the results, called to give me the details, saying it was time to go down and talk to my supporters.

In an instant, my role had changed. It was now my job to thank people and to mark and celebrate the historic nature of what we had just accomplished. I first took time to express my profound gratitude to Manny and the rest of my family. They had worked so very hard not only in the mayoral race but also in lending me their support and unconditional love all the years I had been in office, especially my dear husband. As I was expressing these thoughts, my teenage niece, Rebecca, a recent high school graduate on her way to Rice University, spoke up. Looking at me from her perch on the floor, she said in a loving voice,

"Thank you, Aunt Mary, for what you have done. The young people in our family will never forget this."

Her words confirmed what I had begun to feel. The impact of the day would hit me differently later, but now it was time to celebrate!

Hand in hand with Manny, followed by my parents and siblings with their families and my campaign team, we walked into the hall. There were over 1,000 people packed into the Coronado Ballroom of El Tropicano, raising "María for Mayor" signs. Starting with "Stars and Stripes Forever," Luz Escamilla had made sure that the music would soar as we entered the election night victory party. The one-man band then blared, *La Rielera,* the old tune I had heard as a child when our neighbors would leave to pick beets each summer. In the raw video taken that night by my uncle, Jesse Zertuche, I see a woman who looks radiant and happy as a winner, as she steps forward to greet her supporters.

My first words to the crowd were to tell them a story about something that had happened very early that morning, significant to this moment and this campaign. At the polls, I had met two elderly and very proud voters on the Westside. They were people who had actually known my parents in Lockhart, Texas!

"What a wonderful moment in history it is that these 87-year-old former sharecroppers, raised like my parents in the fields of Lockhart, Texas, could on this day vote for a Mexican-American woman for mayor of their city." With pride, I paid tribute to my ancestors, reminding everyone "that we stand on the shoulders of those who came before us—on the shoulders of those who opened doors for us." I asked young people to take the opportunities that were now available and "walk into those doors." I also reminded my supporters that we had participated in a significant moment of change, that much more change was needed, and to remember, "systemic change takes time." We had introduced the concept of investing in human capital in our city and we had to continue working to make it real. I asked my supporters to stay involved, particularly the young people.

I extended my best wishes to the new mayor, asking everyone to support him. I spoke of justice and gratitude. The meaning of our campaign would not go away, I said. "That passion does not die."

The Days After

As happens after elections, there was a lot of Monday-morning quarterbacking in the news after the election. It included analysis of why I had not won; I did not have enough Hispanics voting for me, or I had mostly Hispanics voting for me, or perhaps just not enough Anglos. Political columnist Rick Casey, a few months later, stated flatly why I had lost the election. I was defeated, he wrote, because during a decade on the City Council "she had failed to do what Cisneros had done in six years on the City Council—convince a majority of the public that she had a vision for the city and the ability to achieve that vision."[15]

Clearly, I failed to win a majority of the votes that election day. But Casey's conclusions overlook the deeper dynamics at work. The vision I proposed for our city did not involve a modest shift in direction; it called for radical change. The vision was about having city policies extend economic development to include the development of our people, their education and wellbeing. It was about being a city that made a priority of working to eliminate poverty and raise the standard of living for all our people, reducing the number of poor children in our land of plenty. It was about including more people in the city's progress, creating opportunities for all. Each of these and other proposals in our human capital platform meant moving in a new direction, one in which economic development decisions at City Hall would be driven by the interests of all our citizens not just those of the powerful few.

In the run off, all the forces in our city fighting to preserve the status quo were arrayed against my campaign. Even so, we won 47% of the vote. In retrospect, I find that pretty remarkable.

Last Day

A memory I have cherished all these years is of the day, May 29, 1991, when I ended my decade of elected public service. At the end of my last day of Council meetings, my family, friends, and many supporters arrived at Council chambers to be with me. A number of people took to the podium to express words of appreciation for my service. Then something unusual happened. When Dr. Gloria Rodríguez of AVANCE took the microphone, she said, "María, we came to escort you out of the chambers. Join us!" Signaling for me to follow behind her, she started a procession out of the Council chambers, with the mothers and children who accompanied her, followed by dozens of people who had joined me for that last meeting.

After a decade of wonderful work, I left City Hall walking hand in hand with Manny and escorted by family, friends, and collaborators.

Mariachis led the way as we all processed to the Spanish Governor's Palace for a lovely party. Greeting us there were Jesús Zambrano and the Christ the King Choir, along with many other friends. My formal participation in the political system ended just as it had started—with and among the people I served.

NOTES

Chapter 8: María for Mayor

1. The idea of human capital began to be widely investigated by economists in the 1960s. It is the stock of education, training, experience, healthcare and even attitudes that allows a person to be more productive. "Economists regard expenditures on education, training, medical care, and so on as investments in human capital. They are called human capital because people cannot be separated from their knowledge, skills, health, or values in the way they can be separated from their financial and physical assets." See "Human Capital" in *The Concise Encyclopedia of Economics* at http://www.econlib.org/library/Enc/HumanCapital.html (accessed August 20, 2011).

2. *San Antonio Light*, October 28, 1990.

3. *San Antonio Express-News*, April 28,1991.

4. *San Antonio Light*, April 14, 1991.

5. *Ibid.*

6. *Ibid.*, May 5, 1991.

7. *San Antonio Express-News*, May 9, 1991.

8. *San Antonio Express-News*, May 11, 1991.

9. *Ibid.*

10. *Ibid.*

11. *San Antonio Light*, May 14, 1991.

12. *Ibid.*

13. *Ibid.*, May 18, 1991.

14. *Ibid.*

15. Rick Casey, *San Antonio Light*, July 11, 1991.

30

Above: At the Mexican American Business and Professional Women's Club (MABPW) Consultation on Spanish Speaking Women and Employment with Carmen Maymi, Director of the U.S. Women's Bureau and her daughter. (Photo: March 1974)

Below: Graduation day at UTSA, May 29, 1979. Mamá, Me, Manuel, Papá with nieces, Angela, Rebecca, Cristina, nephew Miguel, and niece Anna Laura.

I chose my parents home on W. Martin Street to announce my candidacy for City Council District 1. *Left to right:* Papá, John Alvarado, Me, Manuel, Judge Irene Canales de Jansen, Luz Escamilla and Connie Reyes. (Photo: December 1980)

"The best way to meet the voter is in their homes." Blockwalking in first campaign. (Photo: 1981)

Sitting at the dias. "The seat belongs to the people of District 1." (Photo: 1981)

Promoting San Antonio with guests. (Photo: mid-1980's)

Above: As a Councilwoman and as President of Hispanic Elected Officials of National League of Cities (HELO/NLC), reading a City Proclamation. With renowned author Isabel Allende, I opened the first San Antonio Inter-American Book Fair. (Photo: November 1987)

Below: Speaking during a rally on immigration justice at the State Capitol in Austin. (Photo: 1987)

Manny and I are joined by my family at my campaign headquarters during my only City Council re-election campaign with opposition. *Left to right, back row:* Brother Felix, Manny and brother-in-law John Almaguer. *Second row:* Sister-in-law Veronica, niece Rebecca, me, sister Rosie, niece Angela, sister Theresa, sister-in-law Leonor. *Seated:* Papá and Mamá, hugging brother Louis. *On floor:* Niece Anna Laura, baby nephew Felix, nieces Lupita and Julie, and nephew Beto. (Photo: Spring, 1987)

I join Manny ("Dr. B") at the podium for one more joyous PREP Closing Day Assembly. Dr. Darwin Peek, PREP Associate Director (far right), cheers the PREP scholars. (Photo: Summer 1987)

Above: Welcoming my supporters at the opening of the MARIA FOR MAYOR campaign headquarters. (Photo: 1991) *Below:* After my final City Council meeting, constituents, family and friends invited me to leave City Hall with them. Manny and I led the procession to a farewell reception with the community at Spanish Governor's Palace. (Photo: May 1991)

Above: It was my students at the John F. Kennedy School of Government's Institute of Politics at Harvard University who first inspired me to write my memoir. (Photo: Fall 1991)

Below: After Harvard, I was back in the arena. Here with Conexion Latina San Antonio participants. The program was sponsored by National Hispana Leadership Institute (NHLI) through Hispanas Unidas. (Photo: 1993)

PREP graduation day. "Dr. B." with students *(left to right)* Danielle Tarango-Gonzalez and Emily Tarango-Chavez. (Photo: 1996)

With fellow members of Executive Committee to OAS Interamerican Commission on Women. (Photo: 1996)

Papá and Mamá join Manny and me as we celebrate my birthday and Easter Sunday, April 3, 1994.

47

Presenting a U.S. statement at a Plenary Session as Co-chair of the U.S. Delegation to Mar del Plata, Argentina, Prepatory Meeting of the Fourth World Conference on Women (Photo: September 1994)

Above: During U.N. Fourth World Conference on Women, I reached out to and organized rural women from the U. S., among whom were many from the Rural Development Leadership Network. Here we meet with our delegation. (Photo: August 1995)

Below: As the U. S. Representative to the OAS Interamerican Commission on Women I hosted a luncheon for delegates from Latin America and the Caribbean. Special guest was U. S. Ambassador to UN Human Rights Commission, the Honorable Geraldine Ferraro. (Photo: August 1995)

Above: Making history again! Opening of María Antonietta Berrizozábal Congressional Campaign Headquarters. (Photo: 1998)

Below: "We got into a runoff!" *Left to right:* Olga Kauffman, Mary Helen Alvarado, Kevin Lopez and Tomás Larralde. (Photo: 1999)

Above: Enjoying a sweet visit with Papá and Mamá while they were still living independently. Mamá was showing off her flowers. (Photo: 2000)

Below: I was already involved in the "caregiving days" for my parents when duty called again and I joined community members in an effort to stop construction of a Professional Golfers Association (PGA) Village over our Edwards Aquifer. (Photo: March 2002)

Above: A "photo-op" at a quiet celebration of Mamá and Papá's 65th wedding anniversary. (Photo: October 30, 2003)

Below: "Las Calles No Se Callan—The Streets Will Not Be Silenced." Press conference in front of the U.S. Courthouse prior to the appeal of free speech lawsuit to the Fifth Circuit Court. *Left to Right:* Rhett Smith, Jessica O. Guerrero, Enrique Sanchez, Rosalyn Warren, Brenda Davis, Justis Langford, Isable Sanchez, me, Mariana Ornelas, Michelle Myers, John Stanford, Gloria Ramirez, Larry Skwarczynski, Amy Kastley, and an unidentified woman. *Holding banner:* Marisa Gonzalez, Fabiola Torralba. (Photo: October 23, 2009; courtesy of Esperanza Peace & Justice Center)

"I tell her I love her and thank her for being my mentor. I know, at some level, she understands." With Luz Escamilla on her 60th Wedding Anniversary. (Photo: January 1, 2010, by F. Tessa Escamilla Bartels)

57

Above: *"Mujeres: La Fuerza de La Lucha* – Women: Leading the Struggle." International Women's Day March and Rally. *Left to right:* Graciela Sánchez, Petra Mata, Elizabeth "Betita" Martinez (in wheelchair), Cecilia O. Guerrero, Dr. Antonia Castañeda, me, Isabel Sanchez, Inés Estrada Valez, Aurora Olguin, and an unidentified woman. (Photo 2010, by Marí Hernández)

Below: Speaking at a press conference of interfaith leaders gathering in Washington, D.C. to lobby the Senate for passage of the Dream Act. Regretfully, the legislation did not pass. The work continues. (Photo:December 15, 2010)

58

"¡Gracias por la vida!" We celebrate our 35th wedding anniversary at the St. Catherine Chapel of Adrian Dominican Sisters in Adrian, Michigan. (Photo: August 9, 2010)

CHAPTER 9

Making Soul

A saying I heard often while growing up whenever something bad happened was, *No hay mal que por bien no venga.* My grandmother Sebastiana had another variation of this *dicho* about how every bad experience brings some good. I can hear her now, the words rolling slowly off her tongue, with an almost musical intonation, in response to some truly unfortunate situation: *"No hay mal que dure cien años ni enfermo que los padesca."* Nothing bad lasts for one hundred years and no sick person will suffer that length of time.

Loosely translated, these sayings communicated, "Yes, there's pain. But there's more to that in life, so get on with it." Although some might interpret these sayings as expressing resignation or even passivity, for the women in my family they meant quite the opposite. These *dichos* were a courageous response to the difficult realities in life over which they had no control. They prayed; they sought sustenance from other women; they took care of their sick and buried their dead and went on with their lives. There was no stopping to "heal." The healing came as they continued caring for their families.

So when difficult things presented themselves in my life, I just carried on. It was what the women in my family did; it's what I did. I was now facing such a moment. For the first time in my life, I had suffered a defeat—a major and very public loss that stopped me dead in my tracks. My days at City Hall, which had consumed all my time and energy, also were suddenly over. The future seemed unclear and uncertain—unlike any other time in my life.

In the past, when facing painful challenges, I had always followed in the footsteps of my foremothers. But this time was different. Somewhere from within me came a force that would not allow me to go on. Instead, it insisted that I go *in*. Although it did not feel like it at the time, that force was a magnanimous grace.

Entering the Emptiness

All my life I had been about reaching some goal—getting through school, making good grades, helping my family get ahead, graduating from high school and then college, campaigning to get elected and re-elected, doing a good job for those I was elected to serve. Now, instead of continuing to go up in life, I was to go *in*.

An insight from the Tao Te Ching, a Chinese book of wisdom I had read some years earlier, returned, offering me guidance during this time:

> We put thirty spokes together and call it a wheel;
> But it is on the space where there is nothing that
>   the usefulness of the wheel depends.
> We turn clay to make a vessel;
> But it is on the space where there is nothing that
>   the usefulness of the vessel depends.
> We pierce doors and windows to make a house;
> And it is on these spaces where there is nothing
>   that the usefulness of the house depends.
> Therefore just as we take advantage of what is, we
>   should recognize the usefulness of what is not.[1]

This idea of recognizing the value of "what is not" had served me well when, so often, I found myself walking into public spaces where "what is not" was the presence of women like me. As I filled a place where the voices of *mujeres* had not been heard, I often felt the attempts at marginalizing or, worse, rendering me invisible. My response was never ambivalent. I had to be there and speak my truth. I was taking others with me—women who had never been represented in that space before. So I made useful what was not there, simply by being fully present as myself, as who I am.

Now I had reached a new phase in my life where the empty space was in front of me. Although my public image and circle of friends and acquaintances had expanded significantly over the years, I felt very much alone at this time. I was facing major changes at every turn. Publicly, I was challenged by the persistent question, "María, what is next for you?" Privately, I had entered what at first felt like an "empty nest" period.

The huge endeavor of public service that was mine, and which Manny wholeheartedly supported, was gone. It had been a big piece of our life together and I felt like a parent whose last child has left home. As a woman without children of my own, I had taken hundreds of children and many others into my heart, as I advocated for their lives. Manny also felt the loss. But he had a major responsibility that consumed his energies—he was about to start his twelfth year of PREP in June of 1991. Over the years, the rigorous summer enrichment program in mathematics, which his detractors thought would never work, had become a huge success, expanding in San Antonio and then throughout the state. Through "TexPREP," Manny exported the program to major cities in Texas. That meant he now had programs in some ten sites throughout the state to coordinate and visit each summer, in addition to the six sites he directed in San Antonio. Summer was his busiest time. With my work in City Council during the previous decade, we had created a rhythm for our summers. Now we had to find our place again, a new rhythm.

My relationship with my parents was also undergoing change. Once they saw that I no longer had Council work consuming my energies, they wanted to see more of me, enjoy more of our special time together, sharing stories, laughter, and remembering. They were getting older. I knew I would soon face a big responsibility in discerning their care as they diminished—a thoughtful reflection time every son and daughter owes a parent. But something inside me shouted, "No, there is no room for that now!" I wanted to run away.

In my public life, even before elected office, I had been a connector of people. As a Councilwoman, I had an opportunity to create even more connections among individuals, groups, and institutions. Now, even as I realized that these connections would never end because I intended to be in this community for the rest of my life, I knew I had to create a new way to do this simply as a citizen, a neighbor, and a friend. I knew this when I made the decision not to run for re-election as a Councilwoman, and was comfortable with the shift. What made it painful, however, was the loss of the mayoral race.

I had given myself fully to the race in the same way that I had poured my heart and soul into my Council work. The race was not just a political exercise to see if I could gain higher office. It was one more step in my work for justice and lifelong charge to *ayudar al projimo*—help my neighbor. My campaign motto—"The power of many is stronger than the influence of a few"—was a profoundly personal conviction as well as the vision of thousands of people who had put their trust in me. It hurt deeply that I had not been able to realize that goal. And while my supporters acknowledged that it was their loss too, I felt it much more personally.

Painfully, there was one more thing. Over the decade of my public service, I had felt the responsibility to go against the tide, being deliberate and unapologetic about it, in support of what I felt was for the common good of my community. I had been open to taking the hits by speaking out publicly—and often alone—against major issues supported by my colleagues in City Hall and our city's powerful business elite.

Eventually, no matter how strong one's core, standing on the frontlines takes a toll on a person's body, mind, and spirit. The time had come for me to stop and tend to that.

So this time, instead of pushing myself to just carry on, I decided to enter the emptiness—to reflect and simply *be*. Surprisingly, as if by sacred guidance, an opportunity came knocking that helped me begin this inner journey. It would be a most unusual and multipronged gift.

Changing Seasons at Harvard

In the summer of 1991, a young friend called me. "Do you know there is a fellowship program at Harvard? I think they would like to have you participate." He had already spoken to the people at the Institute of Politics at the John F. Kennedy School of Government of Harvard University, and I was encouraged to apply. Manny was very encouraging and supportive. He said it was an opportunity of a lifetime and the time was right for me to seize it.

A major attraction was that the semester-long Fellows Program is designed for rejuvenation, providing Fellows a time for reassessment and personal enrichment. Fellows lead a Study Group during the semester to share their public service experiences with students. The Fellows are encouraged to participate in Institute-sponsored activities throughout the semester. They are asked to audit a class outside their area of expertise, and to attend seminars, lectures, and cultural events. I thought about it, made a quick trip to Harvard for an informal interview, and was accepted to the 1991 Fall Fellows Group. After a memorable bon voyage party, I was off to New England.

The Study Group I created was titled, "Women, Minorities and Public Policy: A New American Agenda." Because the school wanted the students to have information about my mayoral campaign, I took videos, tapes, campaign materials, and all the newspaper clippings published by the two San Antonio newspapers during my mayoral race.

I had an amazing group of students who already had accomplished much in their young lives. Their backgrounds were varied. Some were the first in their families to attend college; others children of highly educated parents. A couple hailed from other countries.

We discussed politics, our responsibility to the common good, and our individual manner of defining personal success. A major question for them was how do you hang onto yourself when the political winds— or any winds in life for that matter—blow the other way? Recently, I received a note from a former student who is now a very successful attorney representing a major national medical organization. She wrote:

> The impact of your class as well as my one-on-one conversations with you were critical in my development and my growth as a person. For me, you were one of those critical navigators who helped me scale some mountain passes where we carried a message that was not always welcome about fairness, opportunity, and justice. You reinforced at that critical time in my growth that standing for principle was essential and that you often have to pay a price for principles, but you should not waver or back away. You never tried to force us into a mold. You let me be…me. You told me not to change, not to conform, and that I should trust myself. Advice that cleared any doubts I may have had at the time and advice I have carried around with me for over twenty years.

From the letters and visits I have had over the years, a great value of the Study Group for the students seems to have been my affirming their diverse cultural heritages and individual identities. For me, a great value came in the way their questions drove me into deeper reflection.

Because my public service was a large part of the class, we discussed what it is like to actually serve in an elected position. No question was ever out of line and they asked plenty of them. Their questions made me verbalize why I had taken certain stands, even though I knew I would not be on the winning side. What was *really* behind those stands? How did you feel when you lost those issues—*really* feel? How do you feel about losing your mayoral race? I had to look at myself honestly as I answered their questions. Young people know when someone is not being forthright.

After a semester of prodding questions, responses, and listening, I came to see my failed campaign differently. Through the eyes of the students, it was an historic race. People no longer had to *imagine* how it would be if a Latina ran for mayor in a major U.S. city; it had been done. Furthermore, it was a Latina whose campaign agenda ran counter to the establishment of San Antonio—and she nearly won. The students valued those facts, in and of themselves, despite the electoral loss.

It was during these months at Harvard, witnessing the benefit to young people of simply sharing my story, when I decided to write a book about my experience as a public servant. Years would pass before I could actually sit down and write it, but these young people full of hope and wisdom planted the seed of the idea in my mind and my heart.

When I was not teaching, I took full advantage of being at Harvard University. Among other things, I audited a theology class at Harvard Divinity School taught by Dr. Bernadette Brooten that provided a gender analysis of the New Testament. Her class was especially exciting because of the diversity of religious traditions represented in the student body. I also joined a meditation class in the basement of a building that looked like something from the last century (which, of course, it was).

This was the first time in my whole life that I had lived alone. With no television and only a small transistor radio and tape player, I had plenty of time for reflection—and there was plenty to reflect on. It also was the first time in years that I could walk out my door and not be recognized wherever I went. I enjoyed the anonymity.

Early in the semester, one of my students, Charlene Galarneau, came to my apartment with a stack of books. "I think you will enjoy these from my women's studies classes at the Divinity School," she said. At the top of the stack was *Making Face, Making Soul—Haciendo Caras,* an anthology of writings by women of color from all over the world, edited by the prophetic Chicana writer, Gloria Anzaldúa. I began to read it that very day, captivated by the word "healing" in her opening lines. "This book aims to make accessible to others our struggle with all our identities, our linkage-making strategies and our healing of broken limbs."[2]

Soon after, in another work by Anzaldúa, I read:

> The new *mestiza* copes by developing a tolerance for contradictions, a tolerance for ambiguity. She learns to be an Indian in Mexican culture, to be Mexican from an Anglo point of view. She learns to juggle cultures. She has a plural personality, she operates in a pluralistic mode—nothing is thrust out, the good the bad and the ugly, nothing rejected, nothing abandoned. Not only does she sustain contradictions, she turns the ambivalence into something else.[3]

Gloria Anzaldúa's words sounded so familiar; I felt like I had known her all my life. While she was writing these words, I was walking into the public arena. We were living very different lives, yet her words were like a balm, affirming my Mexican-indigenous self. Fresh in my mind was my experience in the political arena where male authority reigns, where the words of women of color are dismissed, and where being a proud brown woman speaking truth to power was seen as dangerous—something to be marginalized and discouraged lest others be inspired to exercise their own agency, threatening the status quo. Her words were a great blessing and a reminder of how much my soul needed rest.

There was one more unexpected blessing—a huge red Maple tree outside my office window at Harvard. It had taken me a full half-century of my life to experience a New England fall. Accompanying me through it each day was this magnificent red Maple. When I arrived, it was a lush rich green. As the days cooled, it did its magic. Slowly changing before my eyes, the green leaves became deep red, almost purple. As I prepared to leave Cambridge in mid-December, most of the leaves had fallen off the tree; a few yellowish ones remained, now dusted white with the first snow of the season. The tree offered me a daily reflection on change and served as a reminder that there was, indeed, a time for everything. Now it was time to go back home and complete the major transition that was unfolding in my life.

The Dark Night

Returning from New England, I felt I had a new and clean slate on which to begin to compose the rest of my life. My time away from home and the presence of the young, inquisitive minds in my class provided me with the grace of openness. But that openness, I soon realized, came with a price. It surfaced a flood of hidden pains and memories.

Our minds can be wonderful friends. They are able to file pain away for another day, or maybe forever. For years, my mind spared me from painful things I had experienced as a child that could have been debilitating; I simply would not dwell on them. Perhaps it was feeling so loved at home and being taught by example to be strong. My father was a model of stoic strength, anchored by deep faith. My mother's tender presence concealed a tough-as-nails interior. They both protected their children as much as they could, but many things were beyond their power.

I now began to see and feel things, often in their raw and naked reality, I had never delved into before. Like the bottom of a clear stream, once I started poking around, all kinds of fragments started to break loose, muddying the waters. Lost memories flooded my brain, flowing down into my heart where I found myself overwhelmed by profound feelings of hurt and anger. There seemed to be no end to what I would find. It was like peeling an onion with one layer uncovering another and then another.

The first layer was what someone described years ago as "the burden of knowing." It was the burden of knowing the social inequities, injustices, abuses, and violence we see all around us—and then forever carrying the weight of obligation that accompanies that knowing. If we are to live on Earth with integrity as people of faith and justice, we simply have no other choice but to take up the struggle for change. And there is a price. Even though we may not realize it, our bodies carry that weight. The task can be overwhelming to both body and spirit, but we don't back off.

Because I was given entry into a world that most people do not see at first hand, I was able to observe, analyze, and dissect human-made structures that abuse, misuse, co-opt, deceive, corrupt, manipulate, and in many other ways violate the rights of people. I saw how greed and the exercise of power led to violations of *la Madre Tierra* herself—depleting her soils, spilling toxins in her waters, polluting her air, all with impunity.

As I took time to sit with these realities in a new introspective light, I felt as if I were struggling against a merciless troll that would not go away. He had his hand on my forehead and try as I may, I could never swing my arms far enough to reach and knock him down. I swung and swung into the air. He smiled. He always won. I could not touch him.

A deeper layer revealed the pain of struggles with racism, sexism, and misogyny. My dear friend and Chicana historian Antonia Castañeda often reminds me that women use their bodies as instruments to defend against and resist powerful forces in society that aim to hurt our people. It is amazing but also tragic that we are able to do that—put our bodies on the line. I began to feel the effects, over a lifetime, of these often-unconscious actions and reactions to my own experiences of racism and sexism.

Going deeper, I could see in the core of my very being a *mestiza* living in the southwest borderlands with the wound of colonization that goes back centuries, remaining open to the present day. When I was running for mayor, I had heard it said that I was "too Hispanic" in the eyes of some to lead our overwhelmingly "Hispanic" city. These words came back to me now, screaming "racism." They surfaced a reality that our people live with in this country: the pressure to leave as much of our brownness behind in order to rise up the ladder of success. Anyone—especially a Latina—who unapologetically and confidently celebrates and honors the gift of life just as it was given to her, with no desire for accommodation, is in for sanctions.

I was reminded of the time President Ronald Reagan came to visit San Antonio during a *Cinco de Mayo* celebration when I was on City Council. In advance of the visit, a call came in from his handlers, inviting professional Mexican-American women to stand behind the President on a public stage, wearing their colorful *tipico* Mexican dresses. They obliged. None of these same professional women were invited to the private meeting President Reagan had with Mexican-

American business leaders. As a member of the City Council, I received that invitation; I wore a business suit. I watched all this—and held it in. The sexism, the stereotyping, the being treated as colorful props. So much to hold in, centuries' worth.

Deeper still were shards of pain from a childhood wrought by poverty where children have to grow up fast. The worries of an observant young girl seeing need in her home and wanting desperately to alleviate it, having to wait so long to do it. Hidden fragments surfaced one at a time, each demanding to be addressed. It felt like a game of pick-up sticks, or *palitos*, as we called it as children. All the *palitos* were on the floor. Only by picking them up, one by one, very carefully, could I then put them aside.

At some point during this period in my life, the idea of the Dark Night of the Soul emerged. I had read about it earlier. A mystical idea described by St. John of the Cross, it is a time in life when one goes into the pain and darkness as a journey toward the spiritual maturity we are capable of possessing. Perhaps that was what I was experiencing, I thought. So when someone told me that Beth Landry, a woman I knew from her involvement in anti-domestic violence work, was a spiritual director at a local retreat center, I decided to call her. The fact that she was politically involved as well as a spiritual helper impressed me. After we met, I decided that she would become my spiritual director.

Beth was a devotee of St. John of the Cross and his writings on the Dark Night of the Soul. She helped me delve into the darkness, knowing it was a road that others had travelled before. In her careful way of listening, a well-placed word here and there, Beth helped me pick up the *palitos* and put them in place. With her, among other things, I was able to go back to the schoolyard and finally grieve the death of my little second-grade friend, Paquita.

During one of my talks with her, Beth asked if I wanted a massage. "I will give you an inexpensive one!" Beth told me she was completing her studies in massage therapy and needed to practice. She had gone into this study, Beth said, because of the powerful connections among body, mind, and spirit. I was very hesitant. Not only had I never had a massage before; I had never even thought of having one! For me it was *un lujo*—a luxury. No, no.

But it was Beth; I trusted her. I went. The experience was one of a powerful emotional release that unambiguously showed me how our bodies hold our emotional experiences, past and present. From that day, I incorporated massage as a ritual and key part of my healing. It was one of Beth's great gifts to me. Tragically, a few years later Beth died of cancer, but not before blessing a host of people with her holy life.

As I continued with this inner work, examining my own actions and reactions—my commissions and omissions—I yearned for the presence of God in my life. But the God I had been so certain of in my youth had become like gelatin—there somewhere, but not graspable. When had this happened? It was not just a matter of the changes between a child's and an adult's view of God; it went beyond that, linked I think to the keen disappointment I felt that the same institution that had taught me the principles of social justice was not with me when I started practicing them in a very public way. The institution was not there actively, forcefully, and publicly speaking out in accordance to its power on behalf of those who were hurting the most.

Again, grace intervened, this time in the form of women who stood side by side as we shared new ways to conceive of our spirituality *as* women, as Latinas. I had the privilege of participating in discussions with theologian Ada María Isasi-Díaz and Sister Yolanda Tarango, CCVI, and other women. They were creating a *mujerista* theology, giving voice to Latinas' ways of viewing faith and spirituality. They described a *mujerista* as a woman who works for her own liberation but also for the liberation of her community.

Ada María and Yolanda "did theology" from the perspective of the *mujeres* themselves. They honored our voices as we related to the Divine in *lo cotidiano*—the most ordinary, everyday actions of life that women have engaged in since time immemorial. For me that Divinity manifested itself in my relationship with my community and, as never before, in my relationship with Mother Earth.

Over time, I honed a language that had been unfolding in me as I discovered my own "spiritual heritage" as a woman. All our realities, social, spiritual, physical, sexual, and mental are unique. Our spirituality must be authentically woman centered. Another book that came as a guide at this time was *The Feminine Face of God* by Sherry Ruth Anderson and Patricia Hopkins. I was captivated by the words, "We are celebrating because you, a woman, have consented to accept full spiritual responsibility in your life. This is your initiation as one who will serve the planet."[4]

The idea that something as personal as our spirituality would prepare us for service to the planet seemed phenomenal to me. It would not be spaceships, or rockets, or nuclear bombs that would aid us; it was our woman spirit. That was our power. I was now taking responsibility for my life, leaving no stone unturned no matter how unpleasant. If I had been my own agent in the political and social arena, I certainly needed to claim that in my spirituality too. My connection to the Divine had to be through my own agency as a *mujer*, in whatever way I interpreted it.

Gloria Anzaldúa continued to accompany me in her writings about the *Coatlicue* state, which is that dark place that the *mestiza* enters to gain spiritual awareness. The journey into the dark womb-like place is where our "greatest disappointments and painful experiences—if we can make meaning out of them—can lead us forward becoming more of who we are. Or they can remain meaningless," Gloria wrote.[5] The *Coatlicue* state, she added, "can be a way station or it can be a way of life."[6] Gloria also wrote about *nepantla*, that in between space, where we rest and struggle before we are made whole again. These compelling images and insights served as powerful guides.

Very powerful also were a few key messages that resurfaced at this time from my childhood faith. A major one came from *La Virgen de Guadalupe* who, in her appearance to the Indian Juan Diego over 500 years ago told him, *"No te aflijas, Juan. No estoy yo aquí, que soy tu madre?"* ("Do not worry, Juan. Do you not know that I, who am your mother, am here?") Guadalupe had been a comfort in my youth; she was my comfort now.

Another light in the darkness, stemming from my childhood faith, came from a ritual that my family and I had performed each year. On Good Friday, our family made a sacred visit to Mary to *dar el pésame* on the death of her son. It was always stirring. This time, however, when I went to church to participate in the same ritual offering of condolences, something way more powerful happened. As I stood before Mary, I was filled with an understanding of love and mercy in a way that I had never understood it before. The image of the mother holding the body of her dead son was all about love. In the broken body of the son I saw someone who had loved deeply and been betrayed. In the broken-hearted mother I saw the broken hearts of all who hurt. I saw a love that transcends all differences, a love that crosses religious traditions, cultures, and geography. I saw a generative love that, if allowed to grow, can tear down walls of misunderstanding and hate—a love that is the only path to real peace.

At that moment, I was embraced by the Spirit that removes anger and forgives, that emboldens and sustains. I was embraced by the Mother/Father who loves us in our smallness and with all our imperfections. I was embraced by the Spirit that inspires the feeling, "It's all right. I will always be with you. Move on."

And I trusted.

NOTES
Chapter 9: Making Soul

1. Arthur David Waley, tr. and ed., *The Way and Its Power: Lao Tzu's Tao Te Ching and Its Place in Chinese Thought* (New York: Grove Press, 1958), Chapter 11.

2. Gloria Anzaldúa, *Making Face, Making Soul—Haciendo Caras: Creative and Critical Perspectives of Women of Color* (San Francisco: aunt lute foundation, 1990), xvi.

3. Gloria Anzaldúa, *Borderlands/La Frontera: The New Mestiza* (San Francisco: spinsters/aunt lute, 1987), 79.

4. Sherry Ruth Anderson and Patricia Hopkins, *The Feminine Face of God: The Unfolding of The Sacred in Women* (New York, Bantam Books, 1991), 3.

5. Anzaldúa, *Borderlands*, 46.

6. *Ibid.*

CHAPTER 10

Back in the Arena

After I closed my office at City Hall, I was offered space at the Center for Women in Church and Society at Our Lady of the Lake University (OLLU). It was a wonderful place. I used it not only for my personal work but also for directing the work of Hispanas Unidas, the women's network I founded with others in 1984. Over the years, Hispanas Unidas had continued to host biannual conferences for Latinas of all socio-economic backgrounds. The events focused on leadership, personal empowerment, history, health, employment, and a variety of topics of interest to our women. It remained an all-volunteer organization and I served as its principal volunteer.

One very successful program we launched was Conexión Latina, a mini-course for Latinas in San Antonio modeled after the National Hispana Leadership Institute program in Washington, D.C., on whose founding board I had served, acting as its board president for several terms.[1] Conexión Latina supported the leadership development of thirty young San Antonio women in a one-year program. Many of these outstanding women are now playing key leadership roles in our community.

At the OLLU Women's Center, I collaborated with and supported students and women in the community, alike, including many of the steady group of individuals who availed themselves of the Center's good programming. As I participated in public events in San Antonio or around the country, I would report back to the women who would gather there regularly. It was good to be part of that family of great women.

Women's Rights Are Human Rights

In the summer of 1994, I received an appointment from the Clinton Administration to serve as Principal U.S. Delegate to the Inter-American Commission on Women (CIM) of the Organization of American States (OAS). The appointment had been in process since April of 1993 and I had been serving as alternate delegate since that time.

The position provided me with a unique opportunity to engage with Latinas from throughout the Americas in the struggle for women's rights. CIM was the first inter-governmental agency established to ensure recognition of the human rights of women. Founded in 1928, CIM is made up of 33 representatives ("Principal Delegates"), one for each member state from Latin and Central America, the Caribbean, Mexico, Canada, and the United States. It has become the principal forum for debating and formulating policy on women's rights and gender equality in the Americas.[2]

During the years I served, from 1994 to 1997, my work focused on women's participation in sustainable development programs, their education and political participation, and on issues of violence against women, a global problem. In my last year, I was elected to serve the Commission as a member of its Executive Committee. At the time of my appointment in 1994, preparations were underway for the U.N. Fourth World Conference on Women that was to be held in Beijing, China, the following year. Input for the global "platform for action" to be adopted at Beijing was being gathered from women in their respective continents through several preparatory meetings.

I was chosen by the State Department to be a public member of the U.S. Delegation to the Preparatory Meeting for the Americas held in Mar del Plata, Argentina, in March 1995. I was delighted that Antonia Hernández, President of MALDEF at the time, was also a delegate. In Mar del Plata, women from throughout the Americas presented their concerns, raising issues impacting them that they felt should be included in the Beijing plan. My ability to speak Spanish quickly became an asset as I related to women from Latin American non-governmental organizations and indigenous communities, as well as the Spanish-speaking U.N. delegates themselves. The Earth is so small, our world so inter-related. Women from impoverished communities spoke against tree removal from their ancestral lands, carried out by mega-international corporations, many headquartered in the United States. I resonated with indigenous leaders from Peru who were calling attention to bilingual education. They wanted their people to learn Spanish but also to be able to maintain their native languages and culture. I understood the delegates from the Caribbean as they described their struggle for clean water.

My work in Mar del Plata earned me a place on the official U.S. Delegation to the Fourth World Conference on Women in Beijing in September 1995, led by First Lady Hillary Clinton. Prior to heading to Beijing, I had the opportunity in July to host the President of CIM, Ambassador Dilma Quesada-Martínez, in San Antonio. A Honduran woman of humble beginnings, we had become friends. San Antonio College President Ruth Burgos-Sasscer, Ph.D., a Latina who would be attending the gathering of non-governmental organizations (NGO's) in China, sponsored the special event. Open to the public, the forum was titled, "How Are We Connected to the U.N. Conference in Beijing?" I had also invited a few other dignitaries, including former U.S. Rep. Marjorie Margolies-Mezvinsky, who would be chairing the U.S. Delegation to Beijing, as well as the Honorable Bonnie Campbell from the Justice Department's Office of Violence Against Women and one of her counterparts in Mexico, Doctora Aixa Alvarado-Gurany, Coordinator of the Center for Victims of Crime in Monterrey, Nuevo León. To this day, Aixa continues to work closely with Patricia Castillo, San Antonio's most renowned anti-violence advocate, who also attended the NGO gathering in China in connection with the world conference. I was eager for women in San Antonio to learn about the Inter-American Commission on Women and to share ideas about the upcoming historic conference in Beijing. The event was attended by dozens of women, representing many San Antonio organizations and institutions.

As a member of the official U.S. delegation, my principal assignment was to serve as the delegation's liaison to the Latin American countries. This allowed me to collaborate in an official manner with delegates from Latin America and Central America, many of whom also served as their country's representative on the Inter-American Commission on Women. I also worked with indigenous and other women from the Americas who had come to the conference on their own to participate in the NGO gathering.

Because China feared having so many women in one place, the Non-Governmental Forum of the Conference was held 53 kilometers from Beijing, in Huairou. Each day before the Fourth World Conference started, members of our delegation boarded a bus to Huairou to find U.S. participants at the NGO Forum and support them in their efforts. During one of these forays, I met some Chicanas from California who were part of a farmworkers group, as well as women from a U.S. rural development organization. Because they held credentials for the conference, I was able to maintain my contact with them during the official event.

A magnificent moment occurred when these and other women from struggling rural communities in the United States met rural women "from the South"—the U.N.'s jargon for developing countries. Women from other countries were surprised to learn the extent of poverty in the United States. When I got back home, I wrote about how these women, after spending time sharing with each other, began to make the connections. A globalized economy not only creates poverty in the "South," I wrote, but also a "South *within* the North." That poverty and oppression exacerbates violence of every kind, especially against women. Key issues like disease, lack of basic necessities for families, and lack of education can be directly traced to who holds power, and who does not. Most women around the world, I wrote, "are still outside the loop of that power—no matter where they live."[3]

That women were able to make those connections was in itself the most powerful aspect of this conference. While the documents produced by the conference were good, they were not enforceable. What women were able to do with the information they gathered from each other and the networks they built, however, was incalculable.

During the conference, I was very attentive to what I was seeing and hearing in the informal gatherings, as women walked past me engaged in animated conversation. I heard the languages of the world spoken by women wearing burkas, color-coordinated African garments, indigenous dress, and lots of blue jeans! Amazingly, because many women spoke more than one language, we all found ways to communicate directly or through on-the-spot interpreters. It was surreal, as I thought about efforts back home to suppress the knowledge or use of other languages, pressing for "English only."

Towards the end of the conference, Hillary Clinton made her powerful speech where she reiterated the statement that women's rights are human rights, which, for the first time, was being written into an international declaration:

> If there is one message that echoes forth from this conference, it is that human rights are women's rights—and women's rights are human rights. Let us not forget that among those rights are the right to speak freely—and the right to be heard....
>
> As long as discrimination and inequities remain so commonplace around the world—as long as girls and women are valued less, fed less, fed last, overworked, underpaid, not schooled and subjected to violence in and out of their homes—that potential for the human family to create a peaceful, prosperous world will not be realized.[4]

During my stay, I visited the sights and was deeply moved by my walk on the Great Wall. I kept making connections to my Tejana reality, as the reflection I wrote in my journal after I got back to my room notes:

> The wall took hundreds of years to build, but it could not keep people out. The day after I climbed the Great Wall, I read Jesse

Helms wants to build a wall between the U.S. and Mexico. Man [and, yes, it's usually men doing these things] will never learn.

A country with thousands of years of history has many lessons for a young country like ours. But as far as any about building a wall to keep people out, they fell on deaf ears. We would soon spend billions of dollars to build one across our border with Mexico.

For months after I returned home, I responded to dozens of invitations to share my experience with large and small groups of women. I was particularly pleased to talk about the conference with young women. During my talks, I would show slides of the photographs I took, accompanied by music, bringing home the faces of the women of the world as a reminder that we are all connected. What indeed would happen, I would ask, if women held up half the sky, as the Chinese proverb goes?

Applewhite II

During the summer of 1994, when I began to turn my sights to international issues through the Inter-American Commission on Women, a local issue surfaced that grabbed my attention. The Applewhite groundwater reservoir project was resurrected in San Antonio. Even though then-candidate Nelson Wolff had promised during our mayoral run-off to abide by the mandate of the voters to abandon Applewhite, within two years as mayor, he was again proposing to build it.

In November 1993, Mayor Wolff appointed a 26-member citizens committee charged with making a recommendation regarding "the disposition of the city's investment in the Applewhite project."[5] The 2050 Water Resources Committee, as it was called, "represented a range of city powerbrokers," according to the authors of a book chronicling the environmental history of San Antonio.[6] "Notably absent were the opponents to the Applewhite reservoir and vocal supporters of aquifer recharge and spring augmentation."[7]

The thinking in City Hall was that people were worried about Applewhite because of its danger to our drinking water. If this objection were removed, they reasoned, the project would be acceptable to the voters. On May 12, 1994, the committee presented its 2050 Water Plan to the San Antonio City Council. Among other features, the plan called for making use of treated water "for industrial and irrigation purposes," which would thus "free the aquifer supply for purposes which actually require potable water quality."[8] As for where the treated water would be stored, the committee determined that "there is only one realistic solution to the problem of storing reuse water: Applewhite."⁹

After the 1991 election, when San Antonians voted against the Applewhite Reservoir through a ballot initiative forced by a 72,000-signature petition drive, the City Council had passed an ordinance providing that if the Applewhite project ever came up again, the issue would have to be brought before the voters. On May 19, one week after the committee presented its recommendation, a majority of the City Council followed Mayor Wolff's lead in voting for a citywide referendum on the issue, to be held on August 13, 1994.

I was approached by some activists who voiced concerns about the dangers posed to the water quality of the Edwards Aquifer by the 2050 Water Plan, and I began an intense period of research, examining the entire plan. A group of us met with Joe Aceves, head of the San Antonio Water System (SAWS), a supporter of the plan, who thoroughly explained it to us. I consulted professionals in geology, hydrology, and the law, who analyzed the details with me. After diligent study, I concluded that many of the features of the long-term water plan provided good solutions in areas such as conservation, reuse of non-potable water, drought management, and inter-local agreements that included all counties.¹⁰ Each of these recommendations could be acted upon without voter approval.

I also concluded, however, that the recommendation to complete Applewhite, with all its ancillary parts at an estimated cost of $321 million, was insupportable. The "new" Applewhite Reservoir project was little more than a convoluted rehash of the original, this time involving a diversion canal that would take discharged water to the Gulf Coast for petrochemical users, exchanged for water from the Guadalupe River pipelined down from Canyon Lake to a proposed water treatment plant in San Antonio. It was quickly dubbed "Applewhite II."

"No Means No!"

On July 13, 1994, after completing my study of the project, I called a press conference to cite my reasons for opposing Applewhite II and to help mobilize the "no" vote on the referendum. More than 100 people showed up to join me, most of them supporters of my previous campaigns. I chose to hold the press conference at the Arneson River Theater on the banks of the San Antonio River, just to remind everyone about what was at stake—our water. Although the 2050 Water Plan stated that Applewhite II would be constructed solely for industrial and other non-drinking uses, my research showed that the complex process proposed to move the treated water around posed a risk to our sole source of drinking water, the Edwards Aquifer.

To help myself, and then others, understand how this convoluted plan would work, I created a model of Applewhite II on our dining room table. A large water container served as the Edwards Aquifer with a pitcher representing the Applewhite II Reservoir. I placed a series of bowls as stand-ins for the various smaller reservoirs that would be involved in the project's complex water transfers. Straws and other small objects denoted the pipe system, showing how the treated water would move from one place to another. This model, made from items I pulled out of my kitchen, became a great educational tool to explain the dangers of Applewhite II to dozens of people I invited to my house before the referendum. Standing over my dining room table, I would read the words from the 2050 Water Plan and other materials from SAWS, pointing to the model to explain what they actually meant. A reporter found out about my model and wrote a story about it. More people wanted to see it.

During the next weeks, I poured all my energy into the grassroots campaign we called, "No Means No," working harder to defeat Applewhite II than I had against the first Applewhite project in 1991, when I was also busy running as a mayoral candidate. I focused on coordinating efforts across our city's diverse population, working with longtime Anglo water activist Kay Turner, who organized Protect Our Water (POW) and was working with the Homeowners-Taxpayers League, and Annalisa Peace with the Aquifer Guardians in Urban Spaces (AGUA); Representative Karen Conley who was organizing the largely African-American Eastside; and Rosa Rosales of LULAC who was very active and effective with Westside and Southside Mexican-American voters.

I also reached out to and coordinated efforts with a coalition of Catholic sisters representing different orders, led by Sister Jane Ann Slater, CDP, and Sister Margaret Ellen Gallatin, CDP, who had formed the Water Public Policy Task Force. The sisters prepared an article against Applewhite II for a Catholic publication that included their own water policy recommendations. I coordinated efforts with the Office of Social Concerns of the Archdiocese of San Antonio, working with its director, Fr. Michael DeGerolami, and Bob Comeaux, who issued position papers against Applewhite II. In cooperation with some parish priests, Sunday church bulletins carried the reasons why the Archdiocesan Peace and Justice Commission was recommending a "no" vote on Applewhite II. I also worked closely with Kirk and Carol Patterson,

Phil Ross, Hans Helland, and other environmentalists, who responded to questions and provided the technical information we needed for our educational efforts, and with Judith Sanders Castro, a MALDEF attorney, who was analyzing the legal ramifications of the referendum, addressing the Voting Rights Act.

Our "No Means No" campaign not only spoke against the negative impact of the 2050 Water Plan but also presented alternative solutions. A major recommendation, which we had argued for during the first Applewhite campaign, was to focus on spring augmentation and recharge dams. Recharge dams would not only maximize capture of rainwater into the ground, replenishing the aquifer, but also prevent the recurrent flooding that was wreaking havoc with our streets and then wasting into the city's sewage system.

The business elite of San Antonio was also mobilized—in support of Applewhite II. Along with Mayor Wolff and a majority of the City Council, the San Antonio establishment pushed for approval of the project. The Greater San Antonio Chamber of Commerce supported the project, as did the Hispanic Chamber[11] and other business organizations. The city's only daily newspaper, the *San Antonio Express-News*, twice editorialized in favor of Applewhite II.[12] And more than a dozen "Southside Elected Officials," as they dubbed themselves in a publicity piece, also supported the issue. Most of these officials were Latinos, so this was not a "Hispanic v. Anglo" issue. To help win public support, business interests poured hundreds of thousands of dollars into a pro-Applewhite advertising campaign.

Our grassroots campaign, on the other hand, had very little money to spend—but we maximized our efforts. I recorded short radio spots in Spanish that we aired on popular Spanish radio stations. Reporter Gene Rodríguez of *La Prensa*, San Antonio's Spanish-language newspaper, gave fair and equal coverage to both sides of the issue, including a debate I had in Spanish with businessman Victor Miramontes, who favored Applewhite II. Editor Gloria A. Ramírez of *La Voz de Esperanza* published an extensive article I wrote that provided eleven reasons for voting against Applewhite II. Serving as a spokesperson for the campaign, I participated in several public forums representing the opposition.

Handmade signs were posted all over town with the simple campaign slogan, "No Means No!" There were even poems and songs written by opponents, one to the tune of the Battle Hymn of the Republic: "Dirty, dirty, dirty water. Their greed is marching on."

On August 13, 1994, voters went to the polls. Despite the formidable forces arrayed in support of the project, the people, once again, defeated Applewhite—and by a wider margin than in 1991. Proponents had outspent opponents by nearly 10 to 1—"an estimated $900,000" compared to approximately $12,000; still, 55% of voters said "no" to Applewhite II.[13] The biggest gains were made in San Antonio's West, East, and Southside precincts, home to most of the city's people of color—the Southside being the site of the proposed Applewhite reservoir.

Applewhite II Post Mortem

Water activist Kay Turner appeared victorious the next day on the front page of the *Express-News*, whose banner headline read, "Voters: No means no."[14] Another front-page story bore the title, "Money fails to counter widespread distrust."[15] Media stories and news analysis focused on the voters' lack of trust in City Hall and their concern about patterns of growth over the Edwards Aquifer and the influence of big business and developers. What was really interesting was how some of the analysis harkened back decades to key issues that some of us had been raising for years. *San Antonio Express-News* political columnist Rick Casey wrote:

> What [the voters] don't trust is the way City Hall handles growth and development issues. A majority of San Antonians, including many of us who voted for Applewhite, believe that special interests—particularly the home-building industry—run the city's growth policy to benefit themselves at the expense of the taxpayers. Specifically, voters believed Applewhite to be a boondoggle that would benefit developers while failing to solve our water problems.[16]

Casey then reached back in time, reminding readers how, in the mid-1970s, "citizens overwhelmingly expressed their concerns regarding development over the aquifer recharge zone by voting to ban construction of a supermall."[17] This was the issue that provoked the start of my education about the Edwards Aquifer (see pp. 149-153). "Twenty years later," Casey concluded, "we have Fiesta Texas near that proposed supermall, and few city or state regulations designed to alleviate citizen concerns."[18]

Lynnell Burkett, then-Associate Editor of the Editorial Page at the *Express-News*, who, one week before the referendum, had endorsed Applewhite in her August 7 column, also looked to some of the major turning points in our city's lopsided growth to explain why different groups coalesced in opposition to Applewhite:

[C]itizens of the South and West sides who voted against Applewhite learned to distrust the establishment 25 years ago when their county hospital was moved far north, away from the people who needed it most. Those same people watched helplessly as long-desired University of Texas at San Antonio was placed nearer to Boerne than to them. Those wounds never have healed, leaving a deep distrust of the power structure. Now these lifelong San Antonians looked at Applewhite as something else dumped on the Southside, along with landfills and sewage treatment plants, while the goodies go north.[19]

Columnist Mike Greenberg focused on concerns about our water and uncontrolled growth:

The 2050 Plan ignored the concern of most San Antonians to maintain the purity of the Edwards Aquifer. Strict controls over growth in and above the recharge zone should have topped the agenda in any responsible, comprehensive plan. The 2050 Committee's failure to address that issue fed the widespread belief that the water plan was just a tool of self-interested developers and their golfing buddies....

Uncontrolled, unplanned growth has brought unremitting ugliness, congestion and inconvenience to suburbia while draining our inner city neighborhoods of commerce, jobs and middle-class role models....

Most people see, moreover, that economic growth and economic development are not the same, and given a choice they'd prefer development without growth to growth without development.[20]

The words of these columnists reflected what our community had been thinking for years about a host of interrelated issues—a host of issues that I had been arguing about during my entire time on City Council and had staked my mayoral campaign on. Applewhite II represented the perfect storm of issues that had been brewing in San Antonio for decades, coalescing into a single vote: First and foremost, it was a vote to protect our only source of drinking water—a vote reflecting the people's devotion to their water. It also was a vote against uncontrolled growth that both threatened our water and undermined the health and wellbeing of the inner city. Finally, it was a vote against a pattern of cronyism and decision-making in City Hall that placed the interests of the business elite ahead of the common good of the larger community.

For political scientists and the average person alike, Applewhite II offered a clear case study of the influence of power in San Antonio. It was the power of money on one side and the power of the people devoted to their water on the other. That day water won.

Soon after, term limits brought Nelson Wolff's service to an end and Councilman Bill Thornton was elected mayor in 1995. Another citizens water committee was named. Mayor Thornton asked me to serve on it. I accepted. Unlike the 2050 Water Committee, this one had a diverse make-up, representing the various competing interests in our community. We worked for more than a year on a plan, using outside facilitators, which helped make it possible for us to come up with a water plan we could agree on. We all made compromises; I put my name on the final report. One of the results, a few years later, was seeing SAWS enact stronger policies to protect our Edwards Aquifer. Even COPS celebrated with drinks of aquifer water at City Council; I watched with hope and delight on television. For a while the water wars subsided in our city, only to return again later.

Running Against Henry B.

In March of 1996, the St. Mary's Hispanic Law Alumni Association (HLAA) honored me with their Henry B. González Achievement Award. The recognition was significant for me because of its namesake, our congressional district's longtime and beloved Representative in Congress, and because of the group that had created it. Two young women who had recently graduated from the law school, Cindy Cano and Susana López, were instrumental in conceiving the award and engaging in activities through the HLAA that served both their alma mater and the community. I started supporting their efforts, getting to know them and their circle of friends.

One day, as we were talking about Rep. Henry B. González and the fact that he had recently announced he would not run for reelection in 1998, they both exclaimed, "María, *you* run!" As busy as my life had been since leaving public office, I was still in my self-imposed quiet time and felt rather happy with how my life was going. "We need somebody to represent the people. You will do it like Henry B. did," they said. "We know you can win and we will help you."

For years, people had been telling me that I should run for Congress after Henry B. retired. Now, after nearly four decades in office, he was stepping down.

As the young women lawyers talked, all I could see in my mind's eye was the work involved—raising the money, getting the volunteers, spending days and nights for months on end in a grueling campaign. Their enthusiastic and idealistic way of viewing the potential political race was not at all how I saw it! They were, well, *young*. But I listened and was touched by their youthful idealism—something age tempers but is never, one hopes, lost entirely. As they pressed the issue, I remembered all the times I had pressed young people, including them, to take risks and use the gifts God had given them in positive ways. After that conversation, I started to give serious consideration to running for the seat in Congress that Henry B. was vacating.

I thought I had an excellent chance of winning when I saw the list of individuals who had said they were throwing their hats in the ring. I had high name recognition and even if I couldn't outraise some of my competitors, I knew from my previous campaign experience and political activism that I could mobilize the grassroots. I decided to jump in.

Close to the filing deadline, Henry B.'s son, District Judge Charlie González, put the word out that he was running. It came as a surprise; it had not been common knowledge that Charlie might be interested. I knew right away that his entry into the campaign would change the whole dynamic, but decided to continue with my plans. It would be a bigger challenge.

My campaign started with a half-sheet invitation that I typed up myself. I made copies at Kinko's and sent it to family and friends, asking them to come to an announcement regarding my "plans for the 20th Congressional District race." On October 13, 1997, at our front porch on W. Russell Place and in the presence of about fifty family members and friends, I announced my candidacy for the congressional race. I asked those present "to join me on a journey of hope…a celebration of democracy." I reviewed some of the major issues to which I had lent my energies during the previous six years, since leaving public office:

> • At the local level, I had served as the very active Honorary Co-Chair of the successful effort to win passage of a critical $483 million bond issue for the San Antonio Independent School District and as a member of the Mayor's Citizens Water Committee where a consensus on water was achieved.

> • At the state level, I served as a member of the Border Region Citizens Committee that developed a consensus plan for a $2 billion higher education package that was adopted by the Texas Legislature, settling a lawsuit brought against the State of Texas by MALDEF for lack of educational funds for higher education in the entire border region of Texas. I also served as a member of the Texas Advisory Committee to the U.S. Civil Rights Commission and was a founding member of JUNTOS/Together, a San Antonio-based organization that fought the effects of the *Hopwood v. Texas* anti-affirmative action decision.

- At the national and international level, I had served as U.S. Delegate to the Inter-American Commission on Women of the OAS and as a member of the U.S. delegation to the U.N. Fourth World Conference on Women in Beijing.

I ran on the same issues I had always championed: education, job training, affordable housing, promoting home ownership, small business opportunities, protecting our natural resources, and strengthening our civil and human rights. In the face of political threats in Washington to cut back Medicare and Social Security, I added their protection to my platform. My campaign slogan was *"Investing in People! It's Good Business."*

Slowly, I started raising some funds and was able to rent a bright yellow Victorian house as our campaign headquarters at the edge of downtown. I remember the moment when the utilities had just been turned on; I was sitting on the floor with no furniture, no phone, no computer, no workers, and no volunteers. I thought to myself, "Wow, I start with nothing." But in time, my incredible campaign team started coming together.

My high school friend and long-time campaign treasurer, Mary Helen Alvarado, actually retired from her legal work to serve as full-time office manager for the duration of the campaign. Two young and promising political campaigners joined the staff—Kevin López as field director and Gabriel Salazar as phone bank coordinator. The rest were all incredibly talented and committed volunteers.

Dr. Henry Flores, political science professor at St. Mary's University, doubled as my campaign coordinator and data analyst; Elise D. García, an administrator at St. Mary's University School of Law, took a three-month leave of absence to serve as the campaign's media and communications director; Tomás Larralde, one of my students at Harvard, and Lilly Segovia, a community leader, were precinct organizers. Arabia Vargas, an attorney, and Olga Kauffman, a businesswoman, were in charge of fundraising with Arabia later helping to manage the campaign; Dean Barbara Bader Aldave of St. Mary's University School of Law served as senior legal advisor; Dr. Arturo Vega, on the faculty at UTSA, helped draft my issue papers; and a young woman, Adriana González, helped with special events.

We ran our campaign in a very cooperative and collaborative way, with people helping and filling in for each other when the need arose. It was a great team with many young people and a host of other volunteers doing an incredible amount of work.

I faced six opponents in the primary: Armando Falcón, a member of Congressman González's staff on the Banking Committee; Dr. Richard García, a medical doctor; Judge Charlie González; State Representative Christine Hernández; former State Representative and former City Councilman Walter Martínez; and Steve Walker, a Councilman in a local area municipality.

In that field of seven candidates, three had reported raising more than $100,000 one month prior to the March 10, 1998, primary election. According to the *Express-News*, Christine Hernández led the pack with $264,000, followed by Charlie González with $195,000 and Walter Martínez with $116,000.[21] The same story reported that the other four candidates had raised less than $50,000—altogether. That, of course, included me at this stage. When the Capitol Hill newspaper, *Roll Call*, featured a story about the candidates vying for Henry B. González's seat, the article noted that I did not even have enough money to make direct phone calls. The reporter had figured out I was using a phone card to save money.[22]

A national group that actively seeks out women's campaigns to fund—Emily's List—gave me a questionnaire to fill out. But I did not do well. They did not feel I was strong enough on the pro-choice issue. Although I answered, "yes," as to whether I was pro-choice, I added that I felt women also needed other things, like health care, education, good jobs, housing, and good quality of life. My answer was too broad, they said. So they would not support my campaign, contributing instead to Rep. Christine Hernández's.

There were two groups of women who gave the campaign their all—Latinas and Catholic nuns. A group of friends gathered the names of 100 women, mostly Latinas, who contributed to the campaign under the name, *Mil Marías*; their goal as to raise $100,000. Carol Coston, OP, a Dominican sister, organized *Sisters for María*, to help organize volunteer support in San Antonio and raise small contributions from women religious throughout the country who would support my broad social justice agenda.

A memorable fundraising event was held in the beautiful backyard of a supporter. Renowned writer and good friend Sandra Cisneros read from one of her novels and wonderful Texas singer/songwriter Tish Hinojosa serenaded the crowd.

What we lacked in funds, we made up for in energy, pouring our hearts into the campaign. Unfortunately, very little media attention was given to the congressional race—especially considering that the 20th Congressional District had not had a competitive race practically since the days Henry B. first ran in 1961! In an effort to attract media attention and center the race on issues rather than personalities, we drew from Franklin Roosevelt's Fireside Chats, organizing a series of "Riverside Chats." Over the course of several weeks, we went to different sites around the city and district to host a media event with various constituencies where I articulated my position on a particular issue, releasing a detailed policy paper on each. Topics included campaign finance reform, the economy, civil and human rights, the environment, culture and the arts, healthcare, families and children, education and gender issues.

We garnered no media coverage from these events. I held many candidate meetings on my own but there were very few forums where all the candidates could be seen together. With little money to spend, our campaign work focused on block walking, sending out mailers, and generating enthusiasm among new constituencies. I met members of the growing Latin American community in San Antonio, people from Colombia and Nicaragua, who helped me campaign in the colorful way they do in their countries with plenty of music and even street parades. A young musician, Daniel Zapata, wrote the *Corrido de Berriozábal,* recorded by the popular Grupo Division, made up of young Latin American musicians.

A nagging feeling about the direction the election was taking started coming to me as I did my extensive block walking. I would arrive at a house where I had previously gotten support and would now hear, "We're sorry but we are voting for Henry's son." Or, "Are you running against Henry B.?" At a senior citizens gathering, I went up to a woman I had known for many years. When I asked for her support, she said, "*Como es el padre, es el hijo. Voy a votar por González.*" The loyalty to Henry B. went deep; the son of a legend was running for his father's seat. And because Charlie's signs read simply, "GONZALEZ FOR CONGRESS," a number of people thought it was still Henry B. running for office.

We kept on campaigning with all our might and on March 10, 1998, the voters spoke:

Charlie González	43.94%
María Antonietta Berriozábal	22.28%
Christine Hernández	12.65%
Walter Martínez	9.77%
Armando Falcón	7.28%
Steve Walker	2.45%
Richard García	1.59%

To everyone's surprise, given the hugely lopsided fundraising figures, I came in second to Charlie González. He and I would be in a run-off election and it would be held on April 14—my fifty-seventh birthday!

With the campaign narrowed to two candidates, our fundraising efforts improved. We got a couple of large donations but most of our funds continued to come from small fundraising events, which doubled as get-out-the-vote efforts. I had the support of one union, the Teamsters, but the other unions went with Charlie. He also garnered strong financial support from lawyers and consolidated the support he had received earlier in the campaign from the big business community.

In community forums, as we sought to draw distinctions between our candidacies, Charlie brought out my opposition to city projects like the Alamodome, saying it was divisive. He cast himself as a consensus builder—a uniter not a divider. The biggest distinction I could draw was to contrast our records and accomplishments in public service. We took this too far, in my view. Passionate campaign workers put together a mailer that I approved. Comparing my list of accomplishments to Charlie's, it stated that he had done "Nothing…Zero…Nada" on "tough issues for San Antonio." In actuality, Charlie had been a judge; I was a community leader-activist who had served on the City Council. It was like comparing apples and oranges. In retrospect, I would have framed the contrast differently. But other than that, I am very proud of the campaign we conducted.

During the month-long run-off campaign, local media coverage continued to be very low profile, even though the campaign involved only two candidates. We had a couple of debates, one held at the local PBS station. Media exposure thus pretty much boiled down to what one could buy in the way of political advertising. What I kept hearing from the pundits—from the beginning—was that I just did not have enough money to be competitive. We could not afford any television media buys, as Charlie did, but we were able to run some radio spots. In the end, Charlie would outspend me almost three-to-one, raising $296, 888 to my $123,398.[23] But even if the spending playing field had been closer to level, I still probably could not have won that race.

On April 14, 1998, Charlie González won the seat his father had held for 37 years, with 62% of the vote. That evening, as I celebrated my birthday with family, friends, and supporters at a festive campaign party, I wished him well.

Coda

The last newspaper clipping I have in a four-inch binder containing all the materials of the campaign—policy papers, clippings, campaign materials, and photographs—is a story with the headline, "*Berriozábal's youth corps lost election, not idealism.*" It quotes two of my campaign workers, both former students at Harvard, Tomás Larralde and Sylvia Trujillo. Notwithstanding the loss, Tomás spoke about the importance of "getting young people involved" in politics. Sylvia, a young woman practicing law in California who had used her vacation time to come help me, said she felt she had "participated in something historic."[24]

Today, Sylvia Trujillo serves as Legislative Counsel and Senior Attorney for the American Medical Association's Government Advocacy Group. Tomás Larralde is Executive Director of the Hispanic Contractors Association of San Antonio. As for the other young people in my campaign, Kevin López went on to serve as a political consultant in many campaigns and is now chief of staff for San Antonio Councilman Diego Bernal. Gabriel Salazar manages his own successful political consulting firm. Adriana González Villafranca is Director of External Relations at City Year San Antonio. Cindy Cano is an employment attorney, managing her own firm, and Susana López Krulevitch is a full time mother and activist for education in California.

That clipping at the end of the book is the best ending I could have had for this political campaign—my last, which occurred over a decade ago. Our individual efforts are a part of building community; they are as good as what we leave behind. A prayer/poem* that has been attributed to Archbishop Oscar Romero, says it all for me:

> This is what we are about:
> We plant seeds that one day will grow.
> We water seeds already planted,
> knowing that they hold future promise.

Life Depends On It

After losing the congressional race, I returned with ease to my quieter life surrounded by family, friends, and community where, as always, I remained engaged. A little over a year later, Manny and I joined with

---

* For the entire text, go to: http://www.simonbarrow.net/reflect3.html

people around the world in the global celebration of a new century and millennium. I created some really blingy hats for Manny and me, as we quietly shared that momentous evening at home, listening to lovely music. We later joined friends (without the hats!) to watch the New Year's celebrations televised live from around the world, as Earth turned and yet another people greeted the new day. It inspired such a sense of hope.

The next time people from around the world joined together, just three years later, was in global peace demonstrations in the hope of stopping the Bush Administration's drumbeat to war against Iraq. I remember watching Secretary of State Colin Powell speak at the United Nations, spelling out the purported threat Saddam Hussein posed to the world and making the case for invading Iraq. Tears filled my eyes with the growing sense of futility that this could be stopped. Manny and I joined in publicly condemning the proposed war. Our names, Manuel P. Berriozábal and María Antonietta Berriozábal, were listed among hundreds of others in an issue ad appearing in our local paper, declaring, "NOT IN OUR NAME!" Despite the historic calls for peace issued by millions of people around the globe, the United States invaded a country with no involvement in the 9/11 terrorist attacks that had prompted the U.S. war against Afghanistan a year and a half earlier. War, violence, and more terrorism would dominate the decade that opened with such a sense of hope.

At home, early in the decade I would soon find myself embroiled in a different kind of battle—over water. Once again, this critical issue would divide our city. And once again, as with Applewhite I and II, the business elite in our city would join with our elected leaders in City Hall to do everything in their power to realize their desired project—this time, a "world class" golf course and luxury hotel and housing development—notwithstanding its impact on our water and the enormous public opposition rallied against it. The power elite won. But it took four years, from 2001 to 2005.

I mark this chapter in my city's history in two ways: It was one of the most painful and disappointing moments in our history, witnessing it as I did through the eyes of young people who earnestly and effectively engaged all the tools of democracy only to see them trumped by blatant power plays and collusion.

It also became a teachable moment when, three years later, several Latinas leading the effort, myself included, became subjects of a scholarly work that studied the entire issue from a theological perspective. In her master's thesis, "*Agua Es Vida*: Eco-*Mujerista* Theology in the Borderlands," Sister Elise D. García, OP, analyzed the struggle through the lens of social justice and the eyes of Latinas—of those of us who worked for the protection of our water as an act inseparable from justice-seeking for our people.[25] Building on the seminal work of Ada María Isasi-Díaz and Sister Yolanda Tarango, CCVI, Sister Elise coined the term "eco-*mujerista*" to describe a theology "rooted in ethical values, spiritual beliefs, and social-justice and ecological concerns," reflected in our efforts to protect our water and our people through this struggle, *la lucha*.[26]

Noting the reason for making the struggle against building a luxury golf course over the Edwards Aquifer the subject of her theological reflection, Sister Elise wrote, "I bring to this study urgent concern for our imperiled people and planet, as well as enduring respect for these brave and honorable women who dedicate themselves to community, as if all life depends on it."[27]

Not Over My Water! Not With My Money!

In late 2001, I received a request from Annalisa Peace, a water activist who now heads the Greater Edwards Aquifer Alliance (GEAA), to sign a letter addressed to neighborhood associations, urging them to oppose construction of a planned luxury golf course and resort hotel complex in northeast San Antonio, over the Edwards Aquifer. Built by Lumberman's Investments Corp.—the real estate arm of the multi-billion-dollar conglomerate Temple-Inland, Inc.—the resort's construction would be made possible through an unprecedented "special taxing district" that had been authorized by the Texas State Legislature exclusively for this project, "the bill having been drafted by one of Lumbermen's lawyers."[28]

It did not require much thought for me to decide whether or not to get involved and lend my name to this effort. First, granting a special taxing district was terrible public policy, removing new tax dollars from the city's coffers and granting them instead to a private entity. Secondly, the tax dollars would be granted to an entity that would place more impervious cover and toxic substances over the sensitive recharge zone of our aquifer, encouraging even further development over it. I decided I would not only join the fledgling group of activists opposing the development but also invite more people, especially communities of color, to engage in the issue.

The plan, a collaborative venture between Lumberman's and the Professional Golfers Association of America (PGA), was to develop a PGA "Village" that would include two golf courses and luxury hotel, as well as apartments, houses, condos, and commercial space on 2,856 acres over the recharge zone of the Edwards Aquifer. The taxing district would allow the entire PGA Village to operate like a small city with its own governing body that would collect property and other taxes, reimbursing the developer for building the roads and water infrastructure. In a nutshell, public funds would be used to construct a private development, draining resources away from poor inner-city neighborhoods and endangering everyone's sole source of water.

This on top of another reality: Just one year earlier, San Antonio voters had approved a measure to increase sales taxes by one-eighth of a cent in order to raise city funds earmarked to purchase land over the aquifer recharge zone in order to free it from development. We voted to tax ourselves more in order to protect our water! Now, our City Council was about to approve a plan that would give away millions of dollars in tax benefits to a developer for building over the same aquifer recharge zone that San Antonians had just voted, with their hard-earned dollars, to protect.

As usual, "economic growth and development" was the rubric used to headline and promote the development. As usual, this new growth generator would be situated on the city's Northside, just as the developments of the South Texas Medical Center, the University of Texas at San Antonio, and Fiesta Texas had been over the prior decades. Those massive development projects led to explosive growth in the northwestern areas of the city; this new development would end up promoting similar sprawling growth on the city's northeastern edges. Like the other growth generators, this exclusive private-resort project would be accomplished through local government action and tax dollars, not strictly private resources.

We soon developed a coalition of diverse organizations and individuals, called the Smart Growth Coalition, to oppose development of the PGA Village. I was asked to serve on its Executive Committee, along with environmentalist Chris Brown and Enrique Valdivia of the Esperanza Peace and Justice Center's Environmental Justice Project. The same scenario as in past water struggles repeated itself: Community groups, neighborhood associations, grassroots leaders, nonprofit organizations, and environmentalists stood on one side; developers with their lobbyists, the various chambers of commerce, and members of the business elite stood on the other, joined by civic leaders. Although initially hesitant, then-Mayor Ed Garza soon became a major advocate of the project, with four past mayors standing by his side.[29]

On March 21, 2002, at the first public hearing in City Hall where Lumberman's and their lobbyist were to explain the development project, more than 600 people, largely opponents, showed up. It was here that I first heard the developer's not-so-veiled threat: If the golf-course project were not approved, the owner would build thousands more houses on the site, which would be even worse for the recharge zone. Many people were swayed by this argument, thinking the resort would be the better of two evils. They did not realize that the golf resort itself would be the driver, the growth generator, stimulating construction of all kinds of additional housing and commercial development in the surrounding area.

Another realization that was not clear to the public until years later was that Lumberman's had quietly paved the way for this project through behind-the-scenes maneuverings a few years earlier. When an ordinance protecting the aquifer was enacted by City Council in 1995, calling in response to public pressure for more tempered and appropriate development over the recharge zone, representatives of Lumberman's skirted around a moratorium on filing development plans that had been established while the new rules went into effect. They were able to do so because Lumberman's engineer served as co-chair of the committee charged with writing the new environmental rules. By taking advantage of a loophole that he, as an insider, saw, he was able to "grandfather" (*i.e.*, exempt) twenty plans, including Lumberman's, covering 7,600 acres that would otherwise have been protected before the city caught its mistake.[30] Therefore, the new policies intended to protect sensitive recharge areas such as the one they owned did not apply to the Lumberman's proposed development.

Although another 300 people packed the chambers on April 4, 2002, when the City Council was scheduled to vote on the proposal— with most, again, speaking against it—the City Council voted nine to two to approve Lumberman's special taxing district before adjourning at 2:17 a.m.[31]

We were incensed.

The very next day, the Smart Growth Coalition in partnership with COPS/Metro Alliance started a petition drive, gathering signatures to force City Council either to repeal the special district or submit the development to a public referendum. Calling our effort, Save Our Aquifer, hundreds of us spent the next two months seeking signatures during a very hot and early Texas summer to obtain the 68,000 required to trigger a repeal or referendum. Few thought we could succeed.

Yet by the time the drive was over, we had gathered over 100,000 signatures. Although we often bemoan the absence of citizen participation, this level of engagement represented a great feat in democracy—Mayor Garza had won his mayoral seat the year before with 59,000 votes in what was considered to be a "landslide" victory![32] The extraordinary results of the petition drive and the ensuing political turmoil led to Lumberman's withdrawing the plan and the Council's rescinding it. A referendum was averted. But within just a couple of weeks, Mayor Garza announced another deal he had worked out with Lumberman's! Save Our Aquifer filed a lawsuit, "arguing that the right to petition for a referendum is meaningless if city officials can take an issue, put a new wrapper on it, change its name, and then claim it is un-related and not subject to a public vote."[33] A federal judge ruled that he would allow the city to continue its negotiations, withholding judgment until such time as the new development plan was adopted.

Two months later, on October 24, 2002, a new PGA Village pro-posal went before City Council. The controversial special taxing district was dropped, replaced with a fifteen-year non-annexation agreement. PGA Village II was approved unanimously by City Council.[34]

Adding to the sense of outrage we felt over this vote, the Save Our Aquifer coalition experienced a major blow. Our allies in the peti-tion drive, COPS/Metro Alliance, had negotiated a side deal with City Council, apart from the rest of the coalition. They secured a "last-minute wage concession," committing the developer to "a minimum salary of $8.75 per hour for all hotel workers and full-time PGA employees who don't receive tips." With that, COPS/Metro Alliance withdrew their opposition to the development.[35] This action by a credible community organization drove a wedge into the coalition, blunting the opposition effort and strengthening the position of supporters of the PGA Village agreement.

We waited until December 8, 2002, when the contract would be reviewed again by the City Council. The final document needed to be signed off on to ensure that all amendments and ancillary documents were in order and to approve some unfinished negotiations that had taken place subsequent to the October vote. The final version of the deal was accepted and signed by the Council. Three days later, the federal judge ruled against our petition and in favor of the city, upholding its new agreement.

After the splintering of the Save Our Aquifer coalition, we cre-ated a new group—Clean Water, Clean Democracy—and then set out on the task of meticulously going over every line of the PGA Village contract. Examining the documents were our lead pro-bono attorney Amy Kastely, professor of law at St. Mary's University; attorney En-rique Valdivia of the Esperanza Center's Environmental Justice Proj-ect; and Joleen García, a young Latina who had been involved in the Green Party when I invited her to join our efforts. I also reviewed the documents. We quietly examined the voluminous documents over the course of the next year, carefully comparing the plan adopted in October against the final version signed off on in December.

Fully one year and four months later, at the end of April 2004, we held a news conference and went public with our findings. "The PGA Village swindle is unauthorized and is illegal," attorney Amy Kastely announced, revealing the significant problems and flaws we found.[36] Among other things, new terms had been added to the PGA Village contract that had not been voted on by the City Council. Of major interest, given the action taken by COPS/Metro Alliance, an essential Exhibit was missing: the listing of employees who would earn the living wage secured by COPS/Metro Alliance. Further, according to Professor Kastely's statement at the news conference, there had been "a clear violation of the Open Meetings Act" in the process of closing the PGA deal.[37]

The revelations made headline news. And in their wake, Lumberman's and the PGA of America withdrew the project—for the second time.

For a while, it seemed that the hard work done by hundreds of people since the issue first came to light had paid off. Through a series of moves by Mayor Garza, however, mostly behind the scenes and aided by former mayor and now county judge, Nelson Wolff, a spinoff of PGA of America—PGA Tours—took up the project.

On January 6, 2005, at a hearing attended by 300 people, most opposing the deal, the City Council voted 10 to 1 in favor of the third PGA package, this one containing a new non-annexation agreement granted by the city. Newly elected Councilwoman Patti Radle cast the lone vote against the development.[38] A few months later, as if the deal were not sweet enough, elected officials went out of their way, operating below the radar of public scrutiny, to further sweeten it. The Texas State Legislature passed a bill allowing our county, under the jurisdiction of County Judge Nelson Wolff, to provide a special taxing district for the PGA Tour development.

The result: After four years of struggle and intense public opposition, our City Council voted 10 to 1 to approve the PGA project, granting the developers a non-annexation agreement. Our state legislators, working with County Judge Wolff and other PGA supporters, voted to allow our county to grant the developers a special taxing district so they could collect taxes. And all this public assistance was given to help developers build a massive PGA golf and hotel resort, now dubbed "Cibolo Canyon," over one of the most sensitive areas of our aquifer recharge zone.

Citing a news account that appeared later that year, Sister Elise paints this picture in her thesis:

At a posh hotel ballroom in December 2005, County Judge Wolff and "some of the city's biggest business interests were doing cartwheels about the official announcement of the PGA Tour's Cibolo Canyon development." Wolff entertained the group with his insider's view of the PGA story, as *Express-News* columnist Jaime Castillo wrote:

> Referring to the delicate tightrope the project's backers had to endure in the face of fierce public opposition, Wolff cavalierly talked about the behind-the-scenes machinations that were required to revive the hyper-controversial golf resort over the Edwards Aquifer recharge zone. Those dealings included secretly courting the PGA Tour after the pullout by the PGA Village, and quietly going to the Legislature to pass a bill that lets the development district levy taxes and issue bonds. "We tried our best not to let it get into the newspaper, and it worked for a while," Wolff said.... What Wolff was really saying—and the attendees by extension—is that the project's backers wanted to keep things like the taxing district a secret because a similar provision in the PGA Village deal emboldened 77,000 people to sign petitions opposing it.

City officials, business leaders, and developers alike clearly understood that, if put to the test, the people of San Antonio, a majority-minority and economically poor city, would choose a different path, a different future for their city."[39]

The so-called Cibolo Canyon development opened in January 2010, featuring a members-only PGA Tournament Players Club (TPC San Antonio), offering 36 holes of golf on 2,800 acres of land over the aquifer. Later that year, the JW Marriott San Antonio Hill Country Resort & Spa opened its doors, spread over 600 acres of the same sensitive area; rates range from $249 to $1,499 per night. Among other luxuries, the resort offers six acres of heated pools, waterfalls, and even a "Pedernales River," simulating a real river for tubing experiences. Hailed as a "world class" resort, the Cibolo Canyon complex also includes exclusive cul-de-sac neighborhoods with houses starting at $290,000 to over $1 million.

Our One Percent

Today, just as we had warned, an area of the city where growth should never have been encouraged is now dense with traffic from residents living in the additional surrounding housing complexes and frequenting new commercial establishments. This is true of all areas in the northern parts of the city, characterized by sprawl, congestion, and pollution brought on by unplanned and unsustainable development around mega "growth-generator" projects. Ironically and predictably, the very people who opposed this growth in the first place are now having to pay for it through expansion of highways and interchanges and the higher utility costs borne by all users of piping water to the uphill north.

Meanwhile, those of us living in and committed to the older areas of the city have to deal with the effects of continued lack of investment in our inner-city schools, infrastructure, housing, public recreation areas, and failure to address issues ranging from homelessness to toxins in our soils, and the violence brought on by poverty and scarcity.

From where I sit, there is a clear correlation between public decisions on mega projects like the PGA Village and public needs going unmet in working class and poor areas. When public resources—whether direct or indirect through tax benefits—are siphoned off and dedicated to constructing luxurious amenities for the rich, how do the poor benefit?

One of my friends who has a love-hate relationship with Catholicism, teases me when I complain about an injustice. "María, you actually believe what you were taught about social justice!" It's true. My analysis of public policy is centered on whether it serves the common good and how it affects the most vulnerable in our society—the "option for the poor," as it is known in Catholic social teachings. My view of the political world is from the underside of society. I believe that if we lift up the most vulnerable a few notches, everyone else will be lifted too—a trickle-up economics, you might say. It is through this lens that I view my city and the actions of our elected leaders on its behalf.

San Antonio is now the seventh largest city in the nation. Yet we still consider growth for growth's sake as "economic development." We have not stopped to analyze how this kind of growth—which typically provides material benefits to wealthier people and low-wage service jobs to working people, with indirect costs to all—impacts the overall health and wellbeing of our city. We have never assessed the long-term consequences of our unsustainable growth patterns. What has long been clear is that "we, the people" are not making these decisions. As is true in many other places in our country and around the world, we too have a ruling class—an establishment, movers and shakers, a power elite. But they are not our elected leaders.

I saw this clearly after an entire decade of observing how things worked at City Hall. A handful of people would come before us and, somehow, they always managed to garner the votes they needed for their projects. This was especially true when it came to the big votes—votes on energy, water, and growth where I was always on the other side. Votes on energy and water *were* votes on growth. What I did not see clearly was how these individuals worked together, until my mayoral race.

During that race, I saw how the city's major businessmen, who had supported incumbent Mayor Lila Cockrell, quickly consolidated themselves behind Nelson Wolff after he and I were left as the remaining candidates in the runoff. Their endorsements were big news in our newspapers. One day I made a list, drawing on my experiences in City Hall. I counted the big developers, bankers, realtors, construction magnates, media moguls, environmental engineers representing big businesses that wanted to locate over the aquifer, and other major business leaders. These were the individuals in town who wielded the power in City Hall to determine when, how, and where our city would invest major resources. That day I counted seventeen people—they all happened to be men and they all were white. So instead of using the terms "the establishment" or "the business elite," I started describing our establishment as "the seventeen white men" who run our city.

Over the past twenty years when I have used the term to drive home the point that "we, the people" are not determining our city's future, some have taken exception to the use of the term "white." But that is simply a fact, as much as is the fact that all are men. Most who hear me use the phrase want to know the names of the men, but that is irrelevant. One will leave and another one with the same interests and power to advance them will replace him.

What matters is that we are a city with a 70% majority-minority population, and more than half of us are women. We are a community that prides itself in our culture and our diversity but, as my father would say, *eso sale sobrando.* That falls by the wayside when we still lack the self-determination that goes with a democracy. Our voice is not present in shaping our city's key decisions about land use, urban planning, and economic policy. As the Occupy Wall Street people observe, we are the 99%.

La Lucha

Hope lives. It is in less visible but more far-reaching changes than the contours of a new luxury golf course. Marisol Cortez, a young woman activist who engaged with us in the struggle against the PGA, found the experience of going out every day to gather signatures for the petition drive to be profoundly moving and life changing.

> [T]here was such a big difference between the experience of attending marches and rallies and getting deeply involved in the concrete, hands on details of organizing a petition drive. This difference was not just about the kind of work I was doing either, but about the kinds of relationships created through the work. For the first time in my life, I experienced myself as part of a community, a group of people bonded together both in struggle and in love and friendship.[40]

After the PGA experience, Marisol returned to school to obtain a Ph.D. in Cultural Studies. She is now a scholar whose primary teaching and research interests are in the emerging field of environmental humanities. Marisol dedicates herself to exploring, as she writes, "the cultural and ideological dimensions of environmental problems, especially as they intersect with social injustices like racism, classism, sexism, and colonialism."[41]

Out of a struggle as prolonged as the PGA that ended in yet another loss for our aquifer and for a "landslide" number of people in San Antonio, this amazing seed was planted, sown, and grown. Young Latina women like Marisol have emerged out of this and other struggles with an ability to see, analyze, write, and teach—whether at universities or community centers—from an entirely new perspective. A perspective that emerges out of our daily relational experience, *lo cotidiano*, grounded in our social reality—and in our bodies, forged by the land of our indigenous ancestors.

Gloria Anzaldúa, the Tejana muse who opened doors of self-realization and understanding for *mestizas* like me, reminds us of the authentic roots that have the potential to provide sustenance. "*La madre naturaleza* succored me, allowed me to grow roots that anchored me to the earth."[42] Those roots anchor us too. Once again, my thoughts go back to the cold water I sipped as a child, drawn from the well by my Tío Blas. The urge to protect our water, our life, is profoundly visceral; like that memory, it will never go away.

In the end, I believe it is women anchored in deeply personal and daily relationships in communion with all life, who have the capacity to heal both planet and people.

NOTES

Chapter 10: Back in the Arena

1. Founded in 1987, the National Hispana Leadership Institute trains Hispanic women as national leaders with a focus on personal integrity and ethical leadership. See http://www.nhli.org/index.html (accessed September 11, 2011).

2. See http://www.oas.org/en/cim/ (accessed September 11, 2011).

3. María Antonietta Berriozábal, "La fuerza de mujeres," *La Voz de Esperanza,* December 95/January 96, 6.

4. Hillary Rodham Clinton, *Women's Rights are Human Rights,* Address at Plenary Session of U.N. Fourth World Conference on Women (Beijing, China: September 5, 1995).

5. Report of the 2050 Water Resources Committee (San Antonio, May 1994), 1.

6. John M. Donohue and Jon Q. Sanders, "Sitting Down at the Table: Mediation and Resolution of Water Conflicts" in *On the Border: An Environmental History of San Antonio*, ed. Char Miller (Pittsburgh: University of Pittsburgh Press, 2001), 187.

7. *Ibid.*

8. Report of 2050 Water Resources Committee (San Antonio, May 1994), 33.

9. *Ibid.*, 36.

10. See María Antonietta Berriozábal, "Applewhite: I will vote NO!" *La Voz de Esperanza,* July/August 1994, 6-9.

11. See "Hispanic Chamber supports Applewhite vote on Aug. 13," *La Prensa de San Antonio,* June 24, 1994.

12. See *San Antonio Express-News,* May 18, 1994, and August 13, 1994.

13. *San Antonio Express-News,* August 13, 1994. According to the *Express-News* (August 6, 1994), the anti-Applewhite groups spent $12, 216.70.

14. *Ibid.*, August 14, 1994.

15. *Ibid.*

16. *Ibid.*

17. *Ibid.*

18. *Ibid.*

19. *San Antonio Express-News,* August 21, 1994.

20. *Ibid.*

21. *San Antonio Express-News,* March 4, 1998.

22. *Roll Call,* March 5, 1998.

23. *San Antonio Express-News,* April 15, 1998.

24. *Ibid.*, April 19, 1998.

25. Elise D. García, OP, "*Agua Es Vida:* Eco-*Mujerista* Theology in the Borderlands.' Thesis Submitted to the Faculty of Oblate School of Theology, San Antonio, Texas, May 2009." The other subjects of the thesis are community activists Joleen García, Graciela Sánchez, Isabel Sánchez, and Leticia Vela. See http://www.sisterfarm.org/documents/Agua-es-Vida.pdf (accessed November 13, 2011). The thesis includes a 33-page historical chronicle of the PGA struggle constructed from several hundred citations of newspaper articles reporting on the construction of the golf course from 2001 to 2009.

26. *Ibid.*, 4.

27. *Ibid.*, 8.

28. *Ibid.*, 21.

29. Supporters of the PGA Village included former Mayors Henry Cisneros (1981-1989), Nelson Wolff (1991-1995), Bill Thornton (1995-1997), and Howard Peak (1997-2001).

30. García, *Agua Es Vida,* 87-88, citing Rebecca Rodríguez, "Golf course is a done deal," *San Antonio Express-News,* Jan. 7, 2005.

31. Councilmen Julián Castro and John Sanders were the two "no" votes. City Council minutes, April 4, 2002.

32. García, *Agua Es Vida,* 24, citing Jaime Castillo, "Signatures verified 'far' surpass threshold needed for election," *San Antonio Express-News,* July 11, 2002.

33. *Ibid.*, 25, citing Christopher Anderson, "New resort proposal is hauled into court," *San Antonio Express-News*, Aug. 16, 2002.

34. City Council minutes, October 24, 2002.

35. García, *Agua Es Vida*, 25.

36. Michael Cary, "The PGA vile-age swindle," *San Antonio Current*, May 13-19, 2004, 8.

37. *Ibid.*

38. City Council minutes, January 6, 2005.

39. García, *Agua Es Vida*, 28, citing Jaime Castillo, "Wolff's remarks illuminate secret backroom dealing on golf resort," *San Antonio Express-News*, Dec. 10, 2005. Note: Although, as noted earlier, we collected more than 100,000 signatures, 77,000 were officially certified.

40. Note to María Antonietta Berriozábal from Dr. Marisol Cortez, October 7, 2011.

41. Marisol Cortez received her degree in Cultural Studies from the University of California at Davis in 2009, served as Visiting Assistant Professor and New Faculty Fellow for the American Council of Learned Societies at the University of Kansas in Lawrence for 2010-2012. Because of her commitment to San Antonio, she is now a community scholar, teaching part-time in the Sociology Department of Texas A&M University in San Antonio, and works for the Esperanza Peace and Justice Center.

42. Gloria Anzaldúa, *Borderlands: La Frontera. The New Mestiza* (San Francisco: spinsters/aunt lute, 1987), xx.

CHAPTER 11

Acompañamiento

«¡Qué bueno que no ganaste! Ya deja eso. Ya has hecho mucho. Ahora descansa."

Those were my mother's words after I lost my congressional race. She was happy I had not won. She thought I had already done plenty and that now I should rest. She even said, *"Yo recé que perdieras."* She had prayed that I would lose. I did not believe her, but she made her point. My life, however, did not settle into some kind of quiet order, as my mother might have imagined. There was always some issue pulling—none more so than the PGA resort. By the time that struggle was underway, however, I was beginning another, much more personal one—caring for my aging parents.

My parents had turned 88 when I ended my race for Congress in 1998. Although suffering from chronic diseases they were in amazingly good health in mind, body, and spirit. With one or more of their children visiting every day, they were still able to manage pretty well on their own, living independently on W. Martin Street. Within two years, however, as they entered their 90s, Papá and Mamá started their slow but sure decline and diminishment. I remember the day it started. I still have that calendar on one of the walls at home with the date, June 21, 2001.

It was in the wee hours of the morning. The phone rang and my father, on the other end, said, *"Hijita, ven, me duele el pecho."* Daddy called to say he had pain in his chest. In less than ten minutes I was at their house. I checked him out and decided he needed to go to the emergency room. My sister Theresa came over to watch Mamá while I took Daddy to the hospital.

This, in and of itself, was not unusual. I had taken each of my parents to the emergency room numerous times over the years. We would get a diagnosis, a new protocol to follow or some new medication, and they went back to normal life. After each one of these bouts, Papá would say, *"Ganamos otro round."* It was not a knockout!

After that late-night run to the emergency room, my father did indeed win another round—but not before getting a pacemaker. "He is still in too good a shape," the cardiologist had said, making the recommendation. "We deal with how his body is not his chronological age."

What made this particular bout with the emergency room unusual was that my mother had also recently been there, having fallen and broken her wrist. It wasn't one or the other who was in need at this time, but both.

The time had come for me to process the inevitable questions that offspring of aging parents with growing needs face: How will I respond? How much can I do? To what extent am I willing or able to change my life to be there for them? These questions have no right or wrong answers. No one will answer them the same way, even within families. But I believe the questions must be asked. We owe it to those who brought us into this world and raised us, as well as to ourselves.

For me, the answer was clear. I had spent most of my adult years tending to the needs of others through my work. How could I not do likewise for my own parents when they needed me? I made a commitment that my parents' care would become my priority until their deaths—and began a journey of accompaniment. I had Manny's blessings. His parents had died long before; my parents had become his. They loved him very much and he had been a devoted and wonderful son-in-law. He wholeheartedly supported my decision, which was vital.

As it turned out, my parents' final journey toward eternity was long and slow. We would have most of the decade together and even with my caregiving responsibilities, I was still able to dedicate many hours to my work in the community. But in the summer of 2001, my priorities changed. From this point forward, everything was arranged around the needs of my immediate family—Manny, Mamá, and Papá.

A word here on the names I use for my parents: I am not sure when, but probably at some point after English became the language my siblings and I would speak with each other, even at home, we began to address our parents as "Mother" and "Daddy" interchangeably with "Mamá" and "Papá." As I write this chapter, chronicling their final years of life, both sets of terms come to my mind in ways they hadn't in previous chapters. I have decided to let whichever comes forth in this narrative have the day.

After making a decision about how I would respond to my parents' needs, I called a meeting of the family to discuss the matter. Our parents were still mobile and alert, happy, with a good quality of life. But they could no longer care for themselves on their own. I had prepared a packet for each of my siblings with details about our parents' healthcare and other needs, including care of their home, with a list of responsibilities. Although I would take primary responsibility for our parents' care, I could not do it alone; we would need to share in it.

All my siblings still had full time jobs. Nonetheless, our family's first decision was that we would keep our parents at home. Together, we would take care of their needs. We knew that eventually we would need outside help, but for the time being, with all of us living in San Antonio, we felt we could manage. We created a schedule and each of us pitched in, assuming different responsibilities. It didn't take long before we needed to make adjustments. By the beginning of the following year, 2002, someone needed to be with them 24/7. My father was losing his sight and my mother's glucose levels could fluctuate wildly. We adjusted our schedule to take turns so that someone would always be there, including overnight.

Another matter that can be very difficult for families to deal with are decisions around end of life measures like whether or not to resuscitate a parent under certain circumstances. Fortunately, we had already addressed these. My parents had each, instantly and separately, told me that they did not want to be kept alive with machines or be resuscitated should they stop breathing. I had brought up the subject during a conversation about surgeries or chronic illnesses when both were still doing well. All the siblings knew this. So anytime they needed hospitalization, we would sign the Do Not Resuscitate (DNR) document, which was kept with their charts.

For the elderly, life revolves around routines—and so it does for their caretakers. After winning his last bout against death, Papá resumed his vital interests in life. He used his exercise bike everyday, walked around the house, and kept up with world news and politics by reading his newspaper, watching television, and listening to talk radio. Mamá, ever the romantic, liked to read and watch her *novelas*. She also loved to recite poetry. I have a recording of her reading Amado Nervo's, *En Paz*, one of her favorites, giving special emphasis to the end of the poem: *Amé, fui amado, el sol acarició mi faz. ¡Vida, nada me debes! ¡Vida, estamos en paz!* "I loved, I was loved, the sun caressed my face. Life, you owe me nothing! Life, we are at peace!" Another favorite was Robert Frost's, S*topping By Woods on a Snowy Evening.* I do not know when she first heard the poem, but my sister-in-law Dolores copied it onto a plaque that Mamá hung in her dining room.

Doctor appointments made for good outings. I always made sure I carved out a chunk of the day, so we wouldn't feel rushed. Getting dressed, maneuvering in and out of the car, making it into the doctor's office—each of these steps could seem exasperatingly slow unless you counted on it. I knew an appointment would take at least a couple of hours and then there was always lunch out afterwards. These were special times for visits with my mother or father, while one of my siblings stayed with the other. Conscious of how precious each of these days was, I would say to myself as I headed over to pick one of them up, "I will take mental pictures of this day, so that when they are gone I will remember." One picture that endures as I look through my rear view mirror is seeing how they sank lower and lower into the car seat, as their bodies got smaller. I was fearful of what might happen if the safety bag exploded in the front seat, so I would have them ride in the back. Out of those diminishing bodies in the rear seat poured more and more stories! As they got older, their stories reached further into the past, ones I had never heard before. As soon as I got home, I wrote them down.

Our sleepovers with Mother and Daddy provided another type of routine. Whoever stayed with them slept on the sofa bed in the living room, which was adjacent to Mother's room. At some point, my parents each had his and her own bedroom, one right next to the other. Daddy was the first to need a hospital bed; Mother kept the luxury of her queen-sized bed, with lots of pillows!

They both woke really early. Mother would stay in her room, working hard not to make noise. She definitely was not successful! I covered my head to block out the sounds but still could hear the pitter-patter as she walked around. She would look for little things—her comb, safety pins, ribbons, and eyebrow pencil—in drawers, on top of her dresser or night table, making the most distracting little noises. She would tiptoe in and out of the bathroom getting ready for the day. Today, when I hear a tiny click-click or tat-tat, I feel her presence—profoundly in such a whisper of a memory.

The next movement in the morning ritual was Daddy walking into Mother's room, giving her a kiss, and then walking by me in the living room on his way to the kitchen to have his tea and cereal. Their daily greeting was as dependable as the rising sun. Papá would kiss her on the forehead and she would raise her hand to give him a blessing. Most of the time there were no words. As his sight began to fail she had to help guide him, taking his hand and putting it on her head so he would know where her face was to kiss. This started after Daddy pricked Rosie's eye accidentally with his fingernail while trying to give her a blessing; he felt terrible.

During these months and years, I saw them relish each day in the way two people who have known each other for a very long time can, relating to one another more in what is not said than what is said. Their love was expressed, not in sweet nothings—never; but it was tender in a tough kind of way. "*¡Déjanos solas, quiero hablar con mi'ja!*" Mamá would say, shooing him out, when she wanted a woman's privacy with her daughter. "*Pobre Mateo,*" he would respond, slowly walking out of the room, acting hurt. *"Mateo"* was his word for the suffering man who is outnumbered by strong women. The almost sly look as their faces softened was lovelier than the most passionate poem.

Apolinar and Sixta's home was never a somber place. There was always laughter. My brothers and sisters and I could always find something to make light of and Mother and Daddy gave us a good laugh at each other's expense. As serious as he was, Daddy had a dry sense of humor with perfect timing. A few days after we put mother in hospice, while he waited for the next person to come over to the house and take charge of things, he exclaimed with a twinkle in his eye, *"¡Gracias a Dios y los Estados Unidos de América que me están cuidando muy bien!"* "Thanks be to God—and the United States of America—for taking good care of me," he said, as if he were pledging allegiance to the flag.

Throughout these years, my parents' home continued to be the gathering place for all the family celebrations. Each of us went to their house to celebrate our birthdays. There was all the usual fuss—*la comida, los cakes y las velas para cumpleaños.* On their birthdays, Papá would always insist he wanted nothing. *"Hija, a mí no me traigan nada. No necesito nada."* Mamá, on the other hand, said, *"Yo sí. Yo quiero flores. ¡Las quiero cuando esté viva no cuando esté muerta!"* ("Bring me flowers. I want them when I am alive, not when I am dead!") She got plenty over the years. She also received the gift of song. Each year on *el día de las madres,* my sister Theresa would arrive with Mr. Jesus Zambrano and his mariachi band to serenade her for Mother's Day.

Mother and Daddy were model patients, which made their care so much easier. They followed instructions, took their medicines, adhered to the diets required for their ailments, especially my mother's diabetes. They were very accepting of *la voluntad de Dios.* The strong and deep foundation of unshakable faith that had carried them through their entire lives also held them on this last leg of the journey. My father had a special devotion to the Sacred Heart of Jesus and the Holy Name. He *never* uttered a swear word, not even the slightest hint of one. My mother was devoted to María in all her manifestations—Our Lady of Guadalupe, the Immaculate Conception. When my siblings or I had a chance to visit special Catholic sites, we would bring her back little statues, medals, rosaries, and prayer books. My mother displayed these gifts around her bedroom, making the entire room her altar. She read her prayer books there, prayed her rosary, and lit her candles, always praying for her family.

As time passed, Mamá's glucose sometimes would skyrocket. We responded with a regimen to keep it down, even if it meant five (yes, five!) insulin injections a day. Early in 2003, a heart stress test showed she had major blockages in one or more arteries. At the age of 93, she understood her cardiologist's recommendations to treat her conservatively with medications only; she would not have wanted surgery anyway.

By the time he reached 96, Papá had lost his sight completely to glaucoma. He never complained. "*Ya los tuve por muchos años,*" he would say, thanking God for all the years he did see—and thanking his ophthalmologists, who had extended his sighted years, treating his severe glaucoma. We made accommodations so he could eat in the kitchen, go to the restroom on his own, take his own medications, and even bathe himself with someone keeping watch outside the bathroom door. In his TV room, he sat in his easy chair with the walls full of maps, political and historical memorabilia, photographs of some of his heroes and heroines and family photographs.

Over the years, as each continued to diminish and we made yet another decision for them regarding their care, we all took one more step on the downward ladder. In their last years, my parents became the children I never had: Coaxing them to eat. Watching them with such peace in deep sleep. Bathing. The first time I helped my mother with her bath, tears fell as I cleaned her back, thinking this was how she had bathed me when I was a baby. The tender moment did not last! "*¡Ay, está muy caliente!*" she complained. Then, "*¡Está muy fría!*" The water was either too hot or too cold. When my father could no longer see, I would tell him what was on his plate, hoping he would like it. "*Ojalá que le guste, Daddy.*" He would reply with a smile. "*Lo que está mas bueno es el ingrediente.*" It was the "ingredient" that made the meal good, he said. That ingredient was love.

What became clear during these final years with my parents was the importance of simple gestures. Having someone to sit with, talk to, and listen to their stories. Tenderness shown in dressing or cleaning, patience as they forgot or lost things, a gentle touch on the shoulder or holding a hand. These were more healing than any pill. In time, nothing else matters to those in their final years as much as the person in front of them. The old know they are going to die; they need help with the little things that ease the journey.

Another thing that became clear was the shift in family dynamics. A family starts as one unit. As children mature they leave home, making their own lives. They return for visits, celebrations, and other significant events but different homes have been created over the years out of the one. When the time comes to attend to parents in need of care, the children return as adults, having had different life experiences, creating their own families, their own circles of friends, their own jobs and place in the world. This larger family with its differences must be understood in a new way because this will be the family that remains after the parents are gone. Coming together like this has challenges that can be very painful. It also, however, can bring siblings together as nothing else.

During all these care giving years, a few scary questions hung at the edge of my heart. They never quite penetrated, so I would not dwell on them. But they were always there: *When would the end come? How would it be? Would I be able to help them until the end?* By 2007, the questions moved right into my heart—and they answered themselves.

Beginning of the End

"Your mother's EKG changed overnight," the cardiologist said. "The next thing that will happen is that your mother will have a massive heart attack and she will die. At her age there is nothing we can do." The cardiologist had just finished examining my mother and asked us to go out into the hospital corridor. The day before, April 3, 2007, I had brought her to the emergency room, complaining of heart pains. While other family members remained with Mother, my brother Louis and I followed the doctor out into the hall where we heard the cold announcement.

In December 2006, Mamá had started having problems with dementia. Her anxiety, fear, and even hallucinations got to the point that we agreed to give her medication to alleviate the symptoms. That helped her continue a reasonably good quality of life until that Tuesday in April when I took her to the emergency room. Although her EKG turned out to be fine, they admitted her anyway. That night, I settled into Mamá's room. We never left our parents alone in a hospital. Hospitals are places that confuse even the healthiest elderly person. We served as our parents eyes and ears in the hospital world—and as their advocates. Hospital staff had always been accommodating in allowing one of us to be present for the duration of their hospital stays. We became part of the stabilization process, part of the healing.

As night fell, I put my chair next to her bed, held her hand, and we both fell asleep. She was secure and at peace, but contrary to outward signs, all was not well.

In the wee hours of the morning, the floor nurse came in and woke us up to tell us that Mamá had to be taken to ICU. Her heartbeat had slowed down and they could not take care of her on that floor.

The ICU became a place of isolation and terror for her. At this hospital, they would not let me in. I later found out that her assigned nurse did not even speak Spanish, adding to Mamá's feelings of isolation and terror. Theresa, Rosie, John, Felix, and Manny rushed over to be with me in the ICU waiting room. All of us tried to get permission for me to be by Mamá's side; they would not allow it. Hours passed. I was allowed in for a few minutes. Mamá was not doing well at all.

By morning, when I was allowed to see her again, Mamá had deteriorated horribly. I found her restrained in a jacket, with hand splints tied to the bed. She was hooked to a Foley catheter, which she had never experienced before. Her feet were hanging down over the edge of the bed, cold with no socks, her mouth was open, her speech slurry, her eyes closed. She was so confused, drugged with Ativan to reduce anxiety, she did not even recognize me. Never would we have had our mother in that condition—the indignity!

When she finally got back to her room, she was given another EKG and later in the day her cardiologist came to examine her and give us the report in the corridor. My mother's life was coming to an end.

"How long does she have?" I asked.

"It can happen in the next minute or in six months," he said, recommending that we put her in hospice care.

It does not matter how old our beloved is, when death comes—or word of its imminence—there is no getting around the pain. But I went into automatic pilot. The role of primary caregiver kicked in, overriding the message a daughter would have wanted to sit with for a while, and I began making all the necessary preparations. The following day, Holy Thursday of 2007, we took Mamá home to wait for the end. Hospice was waiting.

Mamá's Vigil

Mamá was happy to be back home after that ordeal and Papá even happier that she had returned. A vivid recollection I have is of her grabbing my hands as I was sitting by her bed, saying, *"Cuando yo estaba chiquita y me daba miedo me agarraba de mi mamá y se me quitaba el miedo y ahora me agarro de ti y se me quita el miedo."* She told me about how, when she was little and feeling afraid, she would grab her mother's hand and the fear would go away. Now, she said, I just hold on to your hand and my fear goes away.

This really scared me! It was so big. The realization of this inevitable, irretrievable turn in life.

That night I snuck in Mamá's bed, hugging her feet. It was so new—this idea of her dying within the next minute or six months; I had to get use to it. I thought she might stop breathing at any time. But presence is everything. I was there. She was safe. It was the start of a seventy-day vigil. A bittersweet time God granted us to say goodbye. Throughout it, Mamá would have a daughter by her side at every moment.

My sisters had already retired by this time. Rosie was with Mamá during the day, taking responsibility for meals, daily hygiene, medications, and attending to visitors. Early on, relatives and friends came to visit, which both Máma and Pápa enjoyed. Mamá's cordial and formal self returned as she welcomed and even chatted with her guests. But her hospitality had a limit. If she got tired, she would whisper to Rosie or whichever one of us was present, "*¿Cuándo se va?*" The guest, of course, usually heard the loud whisper and was soon saying goodbye.

Theresa and I alternated nights. I kept some day duties to help with Daddy and we also had a caregiver to assist us. My three brothers, still employed, took shifts in between, bringing meals and helping out in other ways. Miguel would help us at night with emergencies. He had come to stay and during the last few days of Mamá's life, helped lift her from the bed to a chair or the bathroom.

We maintained a medical journal so that everyone would be kept informed about medications, doctors' instructions, and other matters regarding our parents' care. It turned into an hour-by-hour and minute-by-minute account of what transpired, day and night. Mamá did not suffer much pain at the beginning but toward the end, she would say that her entire body hurt. Her main problem, which grew severe, was her restlessness, anxiety, and horrible insomnia. She hardly slept. Not during the day. Not at night. There were terrible sweats both day and night when all her clothing and hair would become soaked. Yet she was always cold and needed to be covered.

After weeks of lack of sleep, I would get very tired and frustrated, becoming impatient. I felt scared about being responsible for my mother's medical care, just looking at the morphine with all its instructions. Fortunately, she did not need it that much until the end. But she did need medication for her severe anxiety. My sisters and I felt like our mother's life was in our hands. Too much tranquilizer and she would conk out for the whole day. We made that error once. Too little and she would suffer agitation and restlessness.

Home was my respite. Manny and I would have a quiet meal and talk. I refreshed myself as much as I could, connecting with friends at night through the Internet. I started a journal, writing about all that was happening. It became a wonderful outlet for my extroverted self, to process what I was experiencing in this first time of caring for someone who was dying. It was a time of reaching out and then accepting the care and love of many people—a time of uniting in prayer with family, friends, and our loving community.

Even in her confusion, Mamá never lost her ability to pray. She recited long prayers she had committed to memory a lifetime ago, asking Mary not to deny her presence at the hour of death. *"Dulce María, mi querida, en aquella hora postrera no nos niegues tu semblante."* And for as long as she could, she welcomed Mrs. Rivera's regular visits to give her communion. Her dear friends—two priests named Larry—came to visit her. There would be no last anointing, as she had already been given this blessing many times in her final years and months. Papá was always there and he, too, received the blessings. They gave him immense sustenance as his Sixta continued to fail.

During this time, I saw my father express his love in many ways to my mother, usually with his simple presence. He was there for us, too, giving comfort and love, refusing our attentions. *"Déjenme, yo estoy bien,"* he would say.

On May 5, 2007, about six weeks before she died, Mamá told me God was calling her and she was going to die. *"Yo ya me voy a dormir y me voy a morir porque estoy muy cansada. Ya Dios me está llamando porque ya no puedo abrir los ojos."* I knelt in front of her and washed her feet, massaging them as I had done so many times before.

As her time to leave was drawing close, my mother seemed to go to another world even as she remained in this one. Her mind would travel far away from us, to some other place and time. With her eyes closed, she would fold her blanket, making it appear as if she was holding and caressing a baby—so tenderly. She would close her fingers, as if holding food, and feed the baby. Then the blanket would become a garment she was sewing. I saw her lick the end of the thread, insert it into a needle, and then start sewing. She would seem to hold an iron as she moved it back and forth over the blanket.

Her eyes remained closed as she engaged in tasks like these, often talking to people who had already crossed over. *"Ándale, Mague, ándale,"* she would call to her beloved younger sister, who had died many months earlier. Or *"¿Ya les dieron de comer a los niños?"* Where had she gone when she asked if we had fed the children? We tried to follow her. *"¿Dónde están los niños, Mamá?"* Where are the children? She would smile and say, *"Allí están."* Right there. I prodded further. *"¿Y qué están haciendo?"* What are they doing? *"Están jugando."* They're playing, she replied. Mamá went to a happy place and we went with her, as far as we could.

Close to the end, there were moments when the strong, self-assured woman, who had sustained a family for so very long, suddenly appeared. The most memorable time occurred one day when our family had gathered at the house. We were chattering away when Mamá suddenly straightened up on the couch and held her back very erect. Then, as if she were addressing a crowd of thousands, Mamá declared with great authority, *"¡A mí nadie me manda porque yo se que hacer!"* No one bosses me around because I know what to do, she declared.

Mamá always did know what to do. And she knew who she was. What a gift for a woman to give to her daughters—up until her last days.

Mamá's Goodbye

The last night I spent with my mother was completely different from all the sleepless ones that had preceded it for weeks. Perhaps her energy was all spent; the horrible restlessness that kept her fussing day and night was gone. Watching her rest calmly, I thought about how, during some of those episodes, she would go in and out of this world. I was overwhelmed by the feeling of being in the presence of a saint, ready to make her final journey home. I took Mamá's rosary, the one with seeds for beads, and knelt at her bedside. Fingering the first two beads, I called on Jesus and Guadalupe. Rolling my fingers over the next beads, I called on Melecio and Teresa, Sixta's parents, then on each of her siblings. As bead followed bead, on through the entire rosary, I prayed to all who had gone before her, asking them to come and be with her when her time came. I prayed that God give her peace.

That night she slept soundly and so did I. In the morning, I cleaned her, put on her pretty pink flowered dress, fixed her hair, and left for the day—a very busy one that included taking my father to the doctor's. When I returned in late afternoon, I learned that it had been a hard day for everyone; Mamá was back to the severe anxiety and restlessness. Rosie had tried to change her clothes but Mother would not let her.

When I sat next to her on the sofa, Mamá gently put her head on my shoulder. I was surprised not only because of how she had been all day but also because it was not the kind of thing my mother would do. Although our connection was powerful, this kind of intimacy was not common between us. It turned out to be my mother's last gift to me. I put my arm around her and just held her until she moved away. After a few minutes, she sat up again and the infernal restlessness resumed.

Felix and I fed her supper and then I left in such a hurry that I can't recall how I said goodbye. Theresa was taking over; I was anxious to get home and spend some time with Manny, having been gone the night before and all that day. Vaguely, I recall kissing her as I always did before leaving; I think I told her I was going home to see Manny. But I can't remember. I wish I could, but I can't remember my last goodbye to my mother.

The phone rang at 3:30 a.m. "Mamá is gone," Theresa said, simply. She had been sitting in the sofa chair just three feet away from Mamá, as each of us had been for the last couple of months, when my mother stopped breathing. Manny and I drove over right away, as did all my siblings. Daddy looked bereft. It broke my heart that his blind eyes would not permit him to see his beloved Sixta one last time.

While we waited for the funeral home to come take Mamá's body, Papá called Theresa, Rosie, and me to come over to the chair where he was sitting in front of Mamá's body. He wanted to talk to us. *"Vi como cuidaron a su mamá, se los agradesco mucho. Pero les pido que no hagan lo mismo para mí. Quiero que me pongan en un nursing home para que no batallen conmigo."* Papá told us that he had witnessed all the care we had given Mamá during her last days. He thanked us. Then he made a surprising request. He wanted us to promise that we would not do the same for him. "Put me in a nursing home," he said.

That was our dear father, even in pain trying to avert more pain. We listened respectfully but none of us said anything. I knew we would take care of him at home just as we had cared for our mother.

When all of us were there, we prayed together over our mother and sang a Spanish hymn of celebration as they took Mamá's body out of her beloved home. Sixta Arredondo Rodríguez, who crossed the Sierra Madre as a child to meet her destiny, died in her sleep on June 14, 2007, in San Antonio, Texas. She was 97.

Papá—Eight Months

After mother's death we continued to care for Papá at his home. He was suffering deep grief but, as always, kept most of his feelings to himself. Out of nowhere, a couple of weeks after Mamá had died, however, he asked me, *"¿A quién crees que eché menos mas cuando se murió, a mi mamá o a la tuya?"* He wanted me to guess who he missed more after she died, his mother or mine. With no hesitation, I replied, *la mía.* His feelings of loss were obvious those first couple of months. We all knew that my father adored his mother and mourned her deeply after she died. But I think even he was surprised at how much he missed his wife of almost seventy years.

After Mamá died, much changed. First of all, the quiet in the house; Mamá left a huge void. Our schedules changed considerably, adjusting to my father's needs. He had been in good health the whole time Mamá was sick; I thought he could live to be 100. We continued to have a caregiver come every weekday morning and Theresa was there weekday afternoons. Miguel was living at home with Papá, and watched over him at night. Others took in-between shifts on weekends. I continued to be responsible for getting the food, taking him to the doctor, and other such errands, spending the rest of my time at home catching up with repairs and even doing some long overdue remodeling.

My main day to be with him was on Sundays, when we spent long hours together. I would arrive between 6:30 and 7:00 a.m. with a loud, "Good morning, Daddy!" To which he always responded, "*¿Por qué vienes tan temprano? Yo estoy bien.*" He wanted to know why I got there so early—he was fine! He was up early and with nothing else to distract us, Sundays were a day full of story telling, which I loved. Papá seemed to want to get some things off his chest that he had long kept to himself. A professional had told me that he would probably die within six months after Mamá. That is how it goes with people who have been together for so long. Perhaps he knew he didn't have much time.

One Sunday he asked me, "*¿Sabes por qué yo nunca me hice ciudadano?*" Did I know why he never became a U.S. citizen? I responded with the story he had told us for years—that he had already given everything else in his life to this country and was holding on to that last piece of Mexico. But now he said something different. "*No. Fué por lo que nos hizo este país cuando regresamos de méjico. No nos dejaron pasar. Mis hermanitos se vinieron solos, trabajaron mucho y se enfermaron. Y se murieron.*" Papá had been holding on to a hurt towards the United States because of the way his family had been separated at the border when they tried to come back in 1932. He blamed this country for the illnesses and subsequent deaths of his three younger brothers after they crossed over alone in order to obtain employment, while the rest of the family was detained at the border.

This came as a surprise to me. First, that my father would hold on to a hurt and resentment towards this country for so many years, never talking about it. And second because he always spoke about how much he loved the United States, how grateful he was for all it had done for him and our family. He modeled this, raising us to honor our country and be respectful. But we could never persuade him to become a citizen, not even when I needed his vote. I had always wondered how he had been able to leave behind the pain of the horrible deaths of his father and brothers; perhaps this act of resistance somehow helped.

On the *diez y seis de septiembre*, three months after Mamá died, he started telling me a story out of nowhere, as I was getting him ready for his nap. *"Mira, hija, aquí está un detalle que nunca te he dicho. Mi abuela, María, no la llevó bien con mi mamá. Con su suegra, mi mamá tuvo un choque cultural. María era muy española; mamá, muy india."*

There was a detail about our family that he had never told me, he said. His grandmother, María Cervantes, did not get along well with her daughter-in-law, Sebastiana. His mother, Papá said, suffered a cultural shock because his grandmother María was very Spanish while she was very Indian.

This was news to me. But it helped explain why we hardly ever heard much about our great-grandmother María, even though she had died when Papá was already a young man and only three years before his own father, Félix, had died. Family secrets, held for so long. For some reason, on this day, celebrating Mexico's independence, my father wanted me to know about this family tension, rooted in colonialism.

We enjoyed one more Christmas with him. After a lifetime of family Christmas celebrations at W. Martin Street, this would be the last at my parents' house. When I went over to put up and decorate the Christmas tree and set up the nativity, as I did every year, my father said, *"Yo creí que ya no iban hacer la acostada."* He was surprised, thinking we would no longer have the ritual of putting the baby Jesus to bed now that Mamá was gone. It was a lovely Christmas. Most of the grandchildren and great grandchildren were able to be there for the *acostada*.

Vino el knockout

It was late February 2008 when Papá's caregiver called. "Your father wants to talk to you. He's scared," she said. At 98, Papá, a heart patient, had been doing so well that he would peddle his stationary bike for the entire hour he "watched" the Mass on TV each day. He stopped the routine short this day, explaining to me on the phone, *"No podía respirar bien, hija."* He could not breathe well. I called the home health people who had been watching him on and off, then went over to Papá's house.

Several hours later a respiratory therapist came. When the smiling man asked him how he was feeling, Papá said, "I am fine now. My daughter is here." After a quick test, he reported that Papa's oxygen intake was very low, probably caused by edema. His legs were swollen and he would need a diuretic. An oxygen machine was sent over, which Miguel and I installed, hooking it up in a way that allowed Papá to walk to the kitchen and bathroom.

Early the next day, Saturday, February 23, 2008, Papá's doctor, a gerontologist who had a great relationship with both my parents, responded to an email I had sent him. My father would need to be examined further before receiving diuretics; he encouraged us to take him to the emergency room. When I got to my father's house, I found him sound asleep on his chair with his baseball cap on. I will never forget how peaceful he looked, his hands lying gently on his tummy. I hated to tell him he had to go to the ER. As always, I explained the situation calmly and he accepted it. I gave him a clean shirt and pair of pants to put on and covered him with his thick robe. The caregiver helped me get him in the wheelchair and into my car. *"Es tu carro nuevo ¿verdad?"* He was pleased to ride in my new car.

Papá and I had made that six-minute drive to the emergency room so many times that even after going completely blind he knew exactly where we were as we drove downtown. Had we crossed Colorado? He felt the railroad tracks and knew we were close to the hospital. As we turned right, arriving, Papá was calm and trusting as ever; his *Cirineo* was taking care of him. But he would never return home.

After we got to the hospital I found out that Papá's doctor no longer made hospital rounds. Someone else would be taking care of him who did not know him or his medical history. Papá was hooked up to an IV with diuretics and taken to the ICU for monitoring. Hospitals are difficult for the elderly. Their sense of place is distorted, and Papá's blindness only exaggerated that—strangers speaking English too fast for him to understand, moving and poking him without his being able to see them. I spent the night with him in the ICU.

The next day my father's cardiologist came to check him out. He said Papá had developed congestive heart failure and would need to be watched for "four or five days." Papá was confused. I had to keep telling him over and over that we were in the hospital. At one point, out of nowhere, he said, *"¡Qué no ganen los Republicanos! ¡Qué gane Obama!"* He was rooting for Obama.

When Rosie and Miguel arrived to take over, I left for the day. Late that afternoon, I returned to find that Papá had gone ballistic with anxiety. He was still agitated, even under sedation. He had been pulling at his IV drip and the wires monitoring his heart so he was put on restraints. *"Hija, por favor ¡quítame estas cosas!"* He begged me to remove the restraints, which were making his hands red and scratched from his efforts to break free. It was terrifying and heartbreaking. I spent that night with him again in the ICU. Although he remained anxious and confused, his second night was better.

On the third day, a Monday, Papá was moved to a regular room. The hospital staff gave us instructions on how to care for him when we got home. Louis spent the night with him. Papá was restless and agitated all night. Rosie took over for Louis very early that morning so he could go to work.

By the time I got there, Papá complained of hurting in his "Foley area." I told the nurse and she adjusted the cords. After she left, I checked his leg, which he said was still hurting. I noticed it was swollen and hard. Eventually they examined it, finding a Baker's cyst, fluid filling behind his knee joint.

When the cardiologist came to see him, he reported "good news." He said Papá's blood pressure was good and the edema was responding to treatment. I asked him about the Baker's cyst and he said the hospitalist would take care of it. *"Señor Rodríguez, va estar bien,"* he told my father. *"El miércoles se puede ir a su casa."* Daddy was going to be fine; he would be able to go home in two days.

As the day progressed, my father's pain grew. I noticed bruises appearing behind his leg. Nighttime came and, still, there was no plan of action for treating the cyst—only another test prescribed for the next day.

My father's last night was horrible. Papá's anxiety and restlessness, combined with pain, were difficult for him to deal with. His characteristic patience and stoicism had left him. They started administering pain medication in addition to whatever else they were giving him for the edema. It was getting increasingly frustrating. We had to work with the hospitalist, a doctor who cares for hospitalized patients, who lacked compassion and was not giving me the information I needed to make good decisions. I had always been able to work with hospital staff, nurses, caregivers, home health personnel, and pharmacists. And I most certainly worked well with all my parents' doctors, whose numbers increased over the years.

This time, however, I felt impotent. During his fourth night at the hospital my father's pain got intense. The back of his leg was turning deeper shades of purple. The hospitalist was nowhere to be found. The night nurse was overwhelmed. The aides did not respond to my rings. My father had to go to the bathroom. Finally, an aide came, stuck a bedpan under him, and left. But Papá could not manage it. He kept moving and moving. He would extend his arm for me to help him sit up. I could only do so much. He was still very strong and his pulling hurt my hands. With my bad back, carpal tunnel, and arthritic thumbs I could not help him. Frustrated, I just stood there watching him struggle.

Papá ceased to be himself, starting to hallucinate. Around midnight two aides, a man and woman, finally came. To my surprise, they got him out of bed and sat him on the potty. He had been in bed, not allowed to get up, for four days. Was this all right? I stood behind my father as they sat him down, and he suddenly went limp. I thought he had died! My father had never fainted. They managed to get him back in bed and called the nurse, who checked his vital signs; they were okay. Papá "came back." The male aide even laughed. My father, however, had still not been able to have a bowel movement or urinate.

From this point on that night, Papá *se desvaneció*. He disappeared into another world, engaging in some strange movements—as if he had earphones, then moving his hands and arms as if he was working on something—moving further away from me. I got scared and called my brother Miguel. He came over right away. We both sat by his bed and just watched Papá as he went into this other world. When I felt better, I told Miguel to go back home; he had to go to work when day came. I kept watch the rest of the night as Papá continued his strange movements. Once in a while he would say something to me. A word, a comment; he could still talk.

At dawn some aides responded to my call for bathroom help. They put my father on the toilet and again he went limp. The nurse came in, said he was okay and just needed to sleep. When daylight came I brought him some coffee but he would not take any, nor any of the food I tried to feed him. He let me put in his eye drops and then tried to tell me something. His speech was slurred. The only words I could make out were *papa* and *Jesucristo*. I asked him if he meant *el papa*, the pope, and he nodded yes. His mother used to call an illness, *la cama de Jesucristo*. It was her way of making the suffering bearable. I had the feeling Papá was telling me he was lying on Jesus's bed, suffering like Jesus. My grandmother's *dicho* made sense to me, seeing what my father was experiencing.

The last things I did for my father were to try to feed him and put drops in his eyes. After that I just sat quietly with him. The nice day nurse came. "He is very tired. Let him sleep. Don't worry." When my sister Rosie came to take over for the day, I left the hospital to go home to sleep.

It was early afternoon when Rosie called. "Come over. Daddy is having trouble breathing." That February day was so beautiful and sunny. It felt like spring was almost with us. The cardiologist had said we could take him home; I was not worried. Still, I drove over right away. It took me fifteen minutes—door to door—to get to the hospital. By the time I got there, my father was dead.

It took me some time to get over the guilt I felt over not being able to help my father during his last night on Earth. If I had thought things through better, asked more questions, or if some medical professional had suggested it, we might have been able to have my father die at home without all those medications that made him crazy. The option was not even considered, much less available. As much as we have evolved in our medical care, we still do not have proper assistance for families dealing with end of life issues.

Eventually, I could see in my father's death a hand in helping me let go of feelings of responsibility and control. *"Vino el knockout y no pudiste hacer nada."* The knockout came and there was nothing you could do, I could hear him say. My father died quickly, as he desired. He did not want to linger and have us go through everything we went through with our mother. He left home, conscious and on his own two feet (with a little wheelchair assistance), dying four days later at the end of a very long life. He was a man who suffered a lot in his early years, but his golden years were truly golden.

Throughout his long lifetime, he never loosened his grip on the hand of his Creator. As I reflect on the last words he tried to share with me, I find comfort in thinking that Jesus—the image of the Sacred Heart of Jesus hung over Papá's bed his entire life—and his beloved Pope John Paul II came to take him at the end. Papá credited the Pope with his healing in 1987 when John Paul visited San Antonio. For months, at age 77, he had been suffering an undiagnosed malady that doctors could not pinpoint, affecting his quality of life tremendously. After John Paul's visit, all the symptoms mysteriously disappeared.

Apolinar Ramírez Rodríguez died on February 27, 2008, in San Antonio, Texas. He was 98.

CHAPTER 12

The Ordeal

I read somewhere that, "God gave us memory so that we could have roses in December." The author was obviously not a Texan, who sees roses all year round; but I still like the idea. Memories bless us when roses lose their bloom. In our many years of marriage, Manny and I have gathered precious memories, large and small, that we will cherish the rest of our lives.

After I left elected office, even during the caregiving years with my parents, I was finally able to do a lot of things with Manny that I had not been able to do before. For the decade I was on City Council, I had the opportunity to travel on city business to many places in the United States, Mexico, and to Switzerland once. But since Manny was always teaching, he could never join me. Conversely, when he was able to travel at the end of the summers, I was tied up with my Council work.

Once I was free, Manny and I could take off each year as soon as his teaching semester was over and another summer PREP program had concluded. I loved to join him at his annual mathematics professional meetings. Held in different locations around the country and a couple of times in Canada, those meetings gave Manny a chance to meet with peers who discussed math as if it were a work of art! I loved seeing that part of his life that he loves so much. Further, mathematics conferences are so different from political gatherings, I always found them fascinating and relaxing.

Each year we also took time to visit Manny's beloved role model, Arnold Ross, who had mentored him at Notre Dame. Dr. Ross was 94 when he stopped going to his office and teaching at a summer program he had created for high school youth at Ohio State University. In fact, Manny had modeled PREP after Dr. Ross's program.

In 1999, we enjoyed a wonderful excursion to Alaska. We marveled at Denali Park and Mt. McKinley, and were astonished when we took a little walk into a deserted area where we were surrounded by mountains of ice and all we felt was warmth.

In 2000, we celebrated our twenty-fifth wedding anniversary in grand form, traveling to Germany in search of Manny's maternal roots. In the little town of Kerzenheim, in the Rhineland southeast of Frankfurt, Manny sat conversing in German with the town clerk and found the birth records of his beloved grandfather, Phillip Wand. It was a precious time, seeing my Manny get all around Germany using his knowledge of the language. We toasted our marriage of 25 years over a memorable dinner for two at a little restaurant in the German wine country.

The following summer, in August of 2001, we went to Spain, searching for Manny's paternal roots. We found them in the tiny town of Elorrio in the Basque country between Bilbao and San Sebastian. We actually met a Berriozábal family. They hosted us with a Basque feast, complete with song and animated conversation—after all we were Berriozábals!

The best thing about these trips was that once we got off that plane, we were on our own free to explore. Manny drove and we tried to savor the local life, finding places and eateries where residents went. Our marriage felt rejuvenated and refreshed by these travels, driving long distances alone together.

In October of 2002, Manny and I went to Kansas City to celebrate his fiftieth class reunion at Rockhurst College. I had a chance to meet many of Manny's classmates and he was able to talk about his passions—mathematics and PREP—to his heart's content. His former classmates were very interested in his work, and for good reason. At this point, the PREP program he had started in San Antonio 24 years earlier was a nationally acclaimed success.

More than 10,000 students had been served by the San Antonio program alone. Through TexPREP, Manny had replicated the program in all of the major cities in the state and, in 1997, in collaboration with Dr. Gloria Zamora of the Hispanic Association of Colleges and Universities (HACU), the program went national. Funded by a grant from NASA, "Proyecto Access" became the vehicle through which Manny was able to replicate PREP in major U.S. cities in seven other states and in Puerto Rico. Over these years, Manny had raised more than $20 million in financial and in-kind support for TexPREP and Proyecto Access.

By 2002, Manny and PREP had been honored many times with local, state, and national awards and recognitions. PREP was highly effective in reaching children who would never have had the opportunity to obtain the educational preparation that PREP provided. Most were children from economically disadvantaged families qualified for the school lunch program and most were Latina/os. PREP prepared young people for success in college and in their chosen careers, not only in science and engineering but also in law, politics, and other professions.

Although Manny was making a major contribution to society, some in his profession criticized him for focusing his work on pre-college students. Manny was unperturbed, certain in his conviction that this was exactly where he wanted to place his professional energies, exerting pressure on mathematical associations to do likewise.

It was wonderful for me to see how Manny never seemed to tire in his work. Manny's students were like his children. His work gave him sheer joy. As the summers progressed, I would be amazed at his nonstop itinerary, as he visited all the sites throughout the country, during the eight weeks of programming, returning refreshed. "The students give me energy," he always said. At each site, he would give students the same admonition he gave San Antonio PREP students at their graduation each summer:

> Along the way to becoming a successful leader, it is important to realize that the acquisition of power should not be an end in itself but a means to responsible service to others. In your own conduct, I urge you to avoid mediocrity and strive for personal excellence.

It was Manny's philosophy of life. Little did we know, as Manny regaled his former classmates in Kansas City with stories about PREP that back home, that it was all about to unravel.

Manny's Ordeal

On November 7, 2002, a couple of weeks after we returned from Missouri, Manny came home with some shocking news. He recounted a meeting that had taken place at the University with UTSA police officer Thomas J. Calucci, concluding, "In the meeting, Officer Calucci read me my Miranda Rights."

Everything changed after that day in November. Those words—impossible to comprehend that they could in any way be associated with my Manny—marked the start of the most horrific time either of us have ever experienced in our lives. A great injustice would be done to Manny and, indirectly, to our community. It tore him apart, and me.

The UTSA campus police officer had advised Manny that due to allegations of wrongdoing by the San Antonio Education Foundation (SAEF), where Manny served on the board as its treasurer, he was part of an ongoing investigation.[1] The police told him they had conducted an investigation and would be sending their report to the district attorney and to the Alamo Community College District (ACCD), which oversaw the Foundation.

After reading Manny his Miranda Rights and informing him he was a suspect in the investigation, Officer Calucci advised him to get an attorney. Manny was not given any information on the procedures that

UTSA would follow on this matter and he was not allowed to ask any questions. His boss, Dr. Jude Valdez, then Vice President of External Affairs at UTSA, told him not to speak to anyone about the matter.

We were two people who had never been exposed to the criminal justice system. Of course we would respect the process—whatever it was! We were entering a quagmire of uncertainties and unchartered waters, with a terrifying word—"suspect"—put out there by Officer Calucci. But Manny had nothing to hide. He said he would cooperate fully.

Things soon got worse. Dr. Valdez imposed an administrative leave on Manny, effective November 29, 2002. This created an impossible dilemma. Manny was administering three PREP programs fulltime and teaching only one math course, pro bono. Although a tenured faculty member, his professional work at the University was now primarily administrative.

Dr. Valdez also banished Manny from his UTSA office for over a month. It was an excruciating time for Manny. For a man without an ounce of guile, highly respected for his honesty and integrity and lifelong service to community, this was incomprehensible. He went through a deep depression. He would not eat. He would not jog. He would not talk. A million-dollar NASA grant for Proyecto Access was due and, notwithstanding the administrative leave, there was no one else but him to write it. It broke my heart to see him in his office at home alone, pale, with no resources, surrounded by papers, writing a major government grant for a program he had been prohibited from administering.

Manny had a doctor's visit pending. Fortunately, he kept it because he was diagnosed with very early-stage prostate cancer. He underwent a biopsy. Because his immune system was weakened by his depression, he developed an infection soon after and had a horrific night of fevers. As he lay in bed shivering, his teeth chattering, I ran back and forth to the microwave to warm towels I could wrap around him to keep him warm. In all our years of marriage, I had never seen Manny so ill.

The first month's administrative leave was followed by another, and then another. Despite repeated requests, Manny was never told what policies or procedures the University was following in imposing the paid leave. By this time we had hired a pair of attorneys to advise us on the SAEF investigation. They did not understand the cause for the imposed leave either. According to information they obtained early on from the district attorney's office, Manny was not a *suspect* in the SAEF investigation, only a *witness.*

Manny meanwhile had learned that UTSA police had turned over evidence to the district attorney related to a PREP employee who had accused Manny—falsely—of coercing her into doing work for SAEF on University time. Our attorneys insisted that whatever concerns UTSA had over the PREP employee's allegations against Manny, these were not an issue of concern for the district attorney.

With these assurances, we thought Manny would soon be allowed to go back to work. But this was not the case; the forced leave would be imposed, unjustly, for the remainder of the academic year.

By January 2003, concerned about the University's continued imposition of leave on Manny, several members of UTSA's La Raza Faculty and Administrators Association met with Dr. Ricardo Romo, President of the University. The matter had implications for all faculty since it involved the University's process for administrative leave. During the meeting, Dr. Romo explained that Dr. Berriozábal was on administrative leave because University of Texas (UT) System regulations state that if an employee is criminally "charged" or "investigated," he or she cannot be running a state or federally funded program. This was not a UTSA issue, Dr. Romo said, expressing support and gratitude for all Manny had done. "TexPrep is fine," he concluded.[2]

We were greatly heartened by this news. Our attorneys had assured us that Manny was neither being charged nor investigated in the ACCD/SAEF case; he was only a witness. Dr. Romo's statement that the leave was not a UTSA issue and his expression of support for Manny and his work in PREP meant that once all this was made clear, everything would return to normal. Or so we thought.

The Unraveling

But Manny's leave from PREP continued to be extended. Although he resumed going to his office after the month-long banishment, Manny was still under strict orders from Dr. Valdez not to talk to PREP staff, who were located at an office in another building on the downtown campus. He was only permitted to continue coordinating Proyecto Access, the national PREP program whose individual programs were run in various cities off site, and to monitor and write reports on grants.

Even this work, however, was impeded. Dr. Valdez blocked Manny's email account. On February 13, 2003, he received 300 email messages, dated January 24 to February 12, after Dr. Valdez permitted them to be released. Two weeks later, on February 27, when he went to the UTSA post office to pick up his mail, it was withheld on orders of Dr. Valdez.

Increasingly distressed by this treatment of Manny, I contacted our State Representative, Mike Villarreal, and then the UT System's office to learn more about the regulation Dr. Romo cited mandating Manny's administrative leave. It turned out there was no such regulation!

As another summer of PREP programming loomed on the horizon, the University hired an interim director for San Antonio PREP and TexPREP. Another huge blow for Manny. It was PREP's 25th anniversary year and the program was being pulled out from under Manny, the very man responsible for its existence and extraordinary success.

The stress on both of us was enormous. The caregiving schedule with my parents had begun—both needed hospitalization at one time or another during these horrible months. I carried a nagging worry that my father, who still read the paper daily and watched news on television, would hear something about Manny's problems. In their condition, they did not need the heartache and anxiety it would produce. But the greatest stress I carried was the fear deep in my heart, given all the unimaginable things that were happening to Manny at UTSA, that something else more unimaginable might happen. When we first met with our attorneys and Manny had left the room for a moment, I asked, "What's the worse thing that can happen?" Their answer was, "The worst is that *anyone* can get indicted." The kind attorney went on to tell me, "If they do arrest him, we can see if they will not handcuff him."

One day, a knock on the door by an investigator and a sheriff's deputy totally unnerved me. They were delivering nothing more than a subpoena for Manny to attend a meeting—not even a court hearing! Manny was not at home. As the two men were standing at our doorstep, my heart pounded like a loud drum. What if they go over to UTSA and Manny is there? What if they arrest him? What will happen if he is taken out in handcuffs in front of all the students? A cold terror gripped me.

In April 2003, still on administrative leave, there was another blow. A communication from Dr. Valdez informed Manny that he was being relieved of all duties with Proyecto Access, the national PREP project. Then, in what can only be described as Kafkaesque, Manny received a very different communication from the University. The president of UTSA, Dr. Ricardo Romo, who to date had done nothing to end Manny's forced administrative leave and was permitting others to take over the education programs Manny had founded and directed for nearly 25 years, wrote to notify Manny that he had been selected to receive the "UTSA President's Distinguished Award for Excellence in University Service."

Public Outcry

Through much of this time, I had felt paralyzed—impotent out of fear that if I interfered it might cause Manny further harm. But as anger started to overwhelm fear in the face of the injustice that was being done to a man who had given his life in service to the community and the very institution that was harming him, I began to act. Doing what I would do if this was anyone else coming to me with a problem, I set up meetings with elected officials who knew of Manny's work and outstanding reputation. I wanted to let them know what was happening at our public University and enlist their help in resolving it.

On May 21, 2003, I received an email from the office of our State Senator Leticia Van de Putte.[3] After our meeting, Senator Van de Putte did some follow-up work, checking with the district attorney. Her office confirmed what our attorneys had been saying all along. "Manny was only a witness in the current investigation," the email stated. The next day, May 22, Clifford Herberg from the district attorney's office faxed a letter to UTSA attorney Elizabeth Mitchell, stating, "Regarding Dr. Berriozábal, he is a witness in the case and has offered his complete cooperation in the investigation."

Incredibly, the very next day, May 23, 2003, Manny received a letter from Dr. Valdez indicating that he "would proceed with an internal investigation in order to make an administrative decision regarding your employment at UTSA."

Around this time, a group of former PREP students and people in the community, outraged by what was happening, formed the PREP Support Committee to advocate for Manny's reinstatement as executive director. The PREP Support Committee created a website with information about the award-winning PREP program and its nationally acclaimed founder. They launched a petition drive and wrote letters, asking Dr. Ricardo Romo to meet with them; he declined.[4] They wrote opinion pieces and encouraged people to write letters to the editor; many did. There was an outpouring of support for Manny and deep concern expressed about the harm the University was doing both to him and the PREP program.

About a month later, on June 26, 2003, Dr. Valdez rescinded Manny's administrative leave. If the University's "internal investigation" actually took place, there was no report or statement of findings testifying to it or issuing from it. Instead, after a seven-month forced administrative leave—a step purportedly taken in compliance with a non-existing UT System regulation—the leave was rescinded, as arbitrarily as it was imposed.

The letter providing this long overdue news, however, carried yet another arbitrary and unjust decree: Manny's position as director of PREP was being revoked! With no explanation or cause cited, Manny was being demoted from his position as director of PREP. The letter from Dr. Valdez stated that Manny would assume the circumscribed role of "Development Director" for PREP, with no staff. His administrative responsibilities would be cut back to fifty percent of his time, working under the supervision of Dr. Valdez, with the other half of his time to be spent as a faculty member, teaching. There was no explanation justifying his removal.

With that action, approved by President Ricardo Romo, who one month earlier had awarded Manny with the President's Distinguished Award for Excellence in University Service, the University of Texas at San Antonio stripped Manny of all intellectual and academic responsibilities for the programs he had created and directed for 25 years.[5]

Facing demotion or no role at all in PREP, on July 1, 2003, Manny accepted the new position "under protest." As bad as things were for him personally, his major concern was PREP. Throughout the ordeal, Manny never spoke to funders about his situation or what was happening with PREP lest it hurt the program. In this role as development director, he would at least be able to help ensure the programs continued to obtain funding. He also continued to harbor the hope that he would prevail in his struggle for justice and would eventually resume his former role as founding director.

On July 25, 2003, San Antonio PREP graduated its twenty-fifth class. As always, the auditorium was packed with hundreds of jubilant young people who had attended that summer's PREP programs at various sites throughout the city, accompanied by proud parents, grandparents, siblings, and friends. Despite the occasion—the twenty-fifth anniversary of the program—its founder was not invited to participate in the proceedings! Manny still ended up on stage. But that was only because a friend asked that Manny present a scholarship she had donated to the University for a PREP graduate. The University would not refuse a donor's request. When Manny was introduced to make the presentation, he was greeted by a joyful standing ovation and thunderous applause.

One week later, on July 31, 2003, Dr. Ricardo Romo wrote a letter to Manny stating that if the issues between him and Dr. Valdez were not resolved, he would ask UTSA Attorney Elizabeth Mitchell to appoint a mediator. In the letter, Dr. Romo included a note of congratulations on the reception Manny had received at the PREP graduation. "I know that a standing ovation must make you proud, and it shows that 25 years of hard work and success has paid off," Dr. Romo wrote.

The tension and problems between Manny and Jude Valdez continued. But no mediator was ever appointed. Stories about Manny's situation had appeared in the local newspapers from the start of the SAEF investigation, which continued to follow its course, mostly away from public scrutiny. Manny had been interviewed a couple of times by the district attorney, responding to questions.

Finally, in May of 2004, the district attorney brought indictments against the former director of SAEF, Joan Drennan-Taylor, and her daughter, on three counts—theft, misapplication of funds by a fiduciary, and money laundering. A trial would be set. At last! The cloud hanging over Manny's head since the fall of 2002 would soon be lifted. At trial, he would be called as a witness, free at last to dispel rumors and misinformation that had made it to print—he could set the record straight.

A month or two later, when the academic year came to an end, Manny received a negative evaluation from Dr. Valdez. It was the first negative evaluation in Manny's entire career. Along with the negative evaluation, Dr. Valdez gave Manny further punishment—his involvement with PREP would be reduced to 25 percent of his time.

It was the last straw. From the start of his ordeal, Manny had been working under great duress; he could endure it no longer. Heavy hearted, at the end of July, Manny wrote to Dr. Valdez, outlining his reasons for resigning from the program he founded, his beloved PREP, effective August 31, 2004. He had hung on as long as he could.

Six months later, on February 14, 2005, former SAEF director Joan Drennan-Taylor pled guilty to misappropriating $919,000. She was sentenced to eight years in prison and restitution in the amount of $196,914.[6] Her plea agreement resulted in a dismissal of the charges against her daughter and in the case coming to an abrupt end, without a trial.

It also meant, however, that there would be no opportunity for Manny to tell his story. No chance to explain how he became tied to this dreadful case. Had he been able to testify, Manny would have revealed that Joan Drennan-Taylor had forged his name and that of other SAEF board members on a document she used to create a secret bank account, about which Manny and the other board members knew nothing.

Manny had discovered this two years earlier, in March 2003, at a meeting with district attorney staff. He never made the information public, appropriately, since it might have harmed the prosecution by providing evidence before the trial. At the end, it was he who was hurt. Notwithstanding his role as a witness in a criminal case, Dr. Jude Valdez, with Dr. Ricardo Romo's support, seized the opportunity—for reasons still unclear—to use the investigation against him to strip Manny of PREP.

In February 2005, concerned about the ramifications Manny's experience might have for any others at UTSA, the UTSA Faculty Senate convoked an Ad-Hoc Committee to investigate what happened. Conducted under the direction of Dr. Rudy Sandovál, six faculty members undertook a thorough investigation of the matter, issuing a unanimous report on August 15, 2005, that vindicated Manny.

In their report, the UTSA Faculty Senate Committee made several recommendations. One of these called for removing the UTSA PREP program from under the jurisdiction of Dr. Jude Valdez to be "relocated to the College of Engineering, an appropriate and logical placement for a pre-college preparation program for prospective engineering students." Another recommendation was that, "Dr. Manuel Berriozabál be named as Founding Director of PREP, complete with all authorities, benefits, and monies appropriate to that position."[7] The faculty report and its recommendations went nowhere. Dr. Guy Bailey, then-UTSA Provost, reportedly said he neither accepted nor agreed with it.

While the faculty investigation was underway, an incident occurred that further inflamed matters. On March 25, 2005, while Manny was walking down a UTSA Downtown Campus corridor to meet a colleague he and Dr. Valdez ran into each other. Dr. Valdez mumbled some words. Manny responded, "I do not want you to talk to me again." Dr. Valdez came towards him with his arms raised. Sensing a threat, Manny moved to protect himself, restraining Dr. Valdez. There were no witnesses to this exchange. Each man continued on his way.

A short while later, however, Dr. Valdez reported to UTSA police that Manny had struck him. The campus police filed the incident with the district attorney and several months later, the matter was brought before the Justice of the Peace—not a court of record. At the hearing, an employee of Dr. Valdez testified on his behalf that she had seen Manny following Dr. Valdez into his office. The jury found Manny guilty and gave him a fine.

Manny refused to accept the judgment; he had not attacked Dr. Valdez! Instead of paying the minor fine and being done with it, Manny insisted on having the case tried in a court of record. He risked having the incident go on his record if found guilty. But perhaps after all that time of being subjected to false accusations, he simply could not let one more false charge go unanswered. It took another four years for him to have his day in court. On April 6, 2009, in a county court, Manny was found not guilty. The ordeal that started seven years earlier, on November 7, 2002, came to an end that day.

PhD PREP

Manny was in his seventies when he went through the terrible ordeal at UTSA, including the allegation that he struck Jude Valdez. He is 80 now. Despite his mistreatment, Manny has never uttered a negative word against PREP or the individuals appointed to take his place. On the contrary, he continues to support PREP in whatever ways he can even though he is no longer associated with it, TexPREP, or the national program he founded, Proyecto Access. The latter continues but in diminished form. It is no longer associated with San Antonio PREP, operating now as PREP-USA in three cities—the Bronx, Jersey City, and Las Cruces.

Manny continues to teach his mathematics classes at UTSA, as a full-time member of the faculty, and continues to contribute his time and energies to the University. He currently serves on the UTSA Faculty Senate and on his college's Promotion and Tenure Committee. He sings in a community choir and serves on our church's financial committee. Notwithstanding his horrific experience with SAEF, Manny remains engaged in service to the community as a member of various boards, including the Board of Directors of Holy Cross High School, the Texas Higher Education Coordinating Board's San Antonio Pathways for Mathematics Committee, and the San Antonio Independent School District Academic Advisory Council.

In his Abrahamic years, when others are well into their second decade of retirement, Manny is actually giving birth to another long-held dream—creating a follow-up program to PREP he calls, "PhD PREP." Designed for academically achieving high school students who have already completed three years of San Antonio PREP, PhD PREP students enroll in one of Manny's upper division math courses at the University. The program aims to nurture the high school students' interest in pursuing doctoral studies in science, technology, engineering, and mathematics (STEM) and healthcare careers at UTSA. For the students, it is a wonderful experience that boosts confidence in their ability to succeed in pursuing doctoral ambitions. For Manny, it is a source of great pride to see young students, especially minorities and young women, master mathematics at the University level. His yet-to-be-achieved dream is to have UTSA provide these outstanding students with full academic scholarships for undergraduate study in STEM or healthcare and support their pursuit of graduate studies towards a Ph.D.

I do not know what the future holds for my beloved Manny and his dreams. Right now he is looking forward to his fourth summer of PhD PREP. All I know is that he has chosen to spend his life educating young people, doing all he can to give them, especially students of color, a chance to succeed in life. I honor him for that and will stand by his side to the end.

Out of the many things learned from Manny's "ordeal," as I came to call it, two key concerns emerged.

First, I believe that the violence done to Manny—who had an exemplary personal and professional reputation, winning more honors and awards than his office walls can accommodate—reflects not only a lack of respect for him but also for the very community UTSA was created to serve, which was and remains the focus of his work. It is still astonishing to me that even after so many people were told of the problems, people Manny had worked with closely for years—elected officials, business leaders, and many others in the community—no one could help him. How could this be? Further, if this could happen to a man of Manny's renown, how much more vulnerable to this kind of arbitrary violence are young faculty members and others less well known who also dedicate themselves to serving the community?

The second concern relates to an issue I posed in the form of two questions in a paper I wrote on September 16, 2003, about Manny's ordeal. Dedicated to my fellow Mexican-American/Chicana/o elders, and sent to members of our community, I asked in the paper: "When it is our own people who commit injustice, what do we call it? And more important, what is our response as a community?" No one ever responded. Our community has suffered greatly over the centuries from colonization and racism. Our social and political struggles historically have been around white vs. people of color issues, much of them institutional. But this painful issue was occurring within our own *comunidad*. What was left in my heart after Manny's ordeal was the sinking feeling that our struggles in the future will focus more and more within our own community—brown vs. brown increasingly—between those who have achieved power and those who have not. We will be divided by ideology, by divergent views on a host of issues affecting our community and our sense of commitment to that community. My hope is that we will have conversations about this and find ways to hold each other accountable. As our Latina/o population grows, a lot hinges on how we treat each other and how we use our newly acquired power.

On a very personal level, another key learning came from gaining a deeper understanding of how families cope with and survive shocking or tragic events in their lives. Huge parts of his life were taken from Manny that no one will ever return. I suffered greatly watching him suffer. But when it was finally over, one of the things that was clear was how we had hung in there together. Working our way through the painful days, day-by-day as best we could, we completed the journey together, surrounded by the love and support of our family, friends, and many community members.

Adversity can divide souls or bring them closer together. In our case, it was the latter. We love each other more than ever—the two of us, a family. It is now a time of *retoños*, new sprouts, for both of us.

NOTES

Chapter 12: The Ordeal

1. The San Antonio Education Foundation (SAEF) operated under the auspices of the Alamo Community College District (ACCD). It had already been made public that an investigation was underway of some irregularities with public monies at SAEF. Joan Drennan-Taylor served as director of both SAEF and the ACCD Center for Leadership in Science, Math and Technology. Drennan-Taylor worked under a small board of directors; Manny served as the board treasurer.

2. Notes taken at a meeting at our house, held on January 11, 2003, with professors who had participated in the meeting with Dr. Ricardo Romo, including Professors Rudy Rosales, Ellen Riojas Clark, Louis Mendoza, Roberto Milk, and George Negrete.

3. I had met with Senator Van de Putte and also with Representatives Mike Villarreal, Joaquín Castro, and José Menéndez to inform them of the issues Manny was facing and seek their support.

4. I too had written to Dr. Ricardo Romo, asking, as a community leader, to meet with him to discuss the matter. He declined, saying it was a personnel issue.

5. A June 27, 2003, memorandum exchanged between Dr. Valdez and Dr. Romo indicates the President of the University was aware of this action and agreed with it.

6. See http://www.theranger.org/2.13550/drennan-taylor-gets-eight-years-in-prison-1.1862174#.TrcDxWBQa5c (accessed November 6, 2011).

7. Final Report from the Faculty Senate Ad Hoc Case Review Committee, February 10, 2005 - August 15, 2005. Chaired by Dr. Rodolfo Sandovál, the Committee included Drs. Diane Abdo, Ronald Ayers, Steven R. Boyd, Sandy Norman, Chia Shih, and Armando Trujillo.

CHAPTER 13

Retoños

"We are called to be faithful, not effective." That's what my assistant and good friend Susan Klein would say when I was in the midst of some formidable struggle at City Hall, with no hope of prevailing. Her words always helped me move to a deeper place and sense of calm. Of course, I wanted to be effective! But in the face of votes where the issue basically boiled down to resources being spent to benefit the wealthy at the expense of those in the inner city, "being faithful" meant having the record show that voice was being given to another perspective in the debate—even though it had no chance of altering the outcome. At these times, I would hang a poster outside my office door with the labor movement words, *¡No. No. No nos moveran!* ("We shall not be moved!") And then I would do or say whatever I had to do or say.

I remain grateful for that reminder. There is definitely a price to pay for remaining faithful to one's values and principles. But I have found that as the decades pile up, a picture begins to form of all that happened in a lifetime, all the decisions made—for good and for ill. I am at that stage of life now. The picture of how I lived my life has taken shape; there is little I can do to alter it. I will live with this picture into my old age and take it to my grave. Being faithful, in the end, means being at peace with that picture—and maybe even feeling a sense of new life, of *retoños*.

My father called his grandchildren and great grandchildren—the joy of his life—his *retoños*, the new sprouts or shoots of his life. My parents died without leaving any kind of fortune, as the world sees it. But at the end, they judged their life by the family they raised. I know they took some regrets and sadness to their graves, but their later years were calm; they were at peace.

Now, as I take their place, an elder myself in my family and community, I count myself blessed with the gift of many *retoños*. The closest to my heart are my husband of 36 years and my growing extended family. My friends are also true blessings and sources of new life for me. The other *retoños* in my life arise from the community to which I am bound, heart and soul. These gifts grow out of the actions of hundreds of people who take their responsibility as citizens seriously, working towards a better future for our growing community.

The Gift of Leadership

Over time I have seen the evolution of leadership within our Latina/o community, with growing numbers of us attaining elected office, locally, regionally, and nationally. This is definitely a *retoño* of the hard work and sacrifice of generations past, especially the movement in the 1960s and 1970s led by Chicanas/os, who opened the doors of opportunity in our city and elsewhere in the United States. A source of hope for me, reflecting the progress of just one family, Mayor Julián Castro and Representative Joaquín Castro* are sons of La Raza Unida founder Rosie Castro, who continues her work in education.

The potential in our people is immense but so are the challenges that must be addressed to liberate and nurture that potential. Latina/o leaders in San Antonio today carry the heavy responsibility of addressing and solving a host of long-ignored problems in our city, with its low educational attainment levels, high rates of poverty, underemployment, and large environmental challenges as a growing urban center. The future of an entire generation is at stake in decisions that would change traditional patterns of economic development and growth in San Antonio, channeling investments that would allow more families to gain entry into the middle class, more to be lifted out of poverty, and ecological considerations to be given priority. These issues are integrally interrelated to each other and to the health and wellbeing of our city, its people, and the natural world on which it depends.

With majorities of Latinas/os now occupying the seats of elected leadership in San Antonio, our struggles, as noted earlier, will focus more and more on differences within our own community—on brown vs. brown. Divisions by class will become more acute. We are now choosing and will continue to choose potential Latina/o leaders who stand at all points on the political spectrum, holding divergent views on a host of issues affecting our community, as well as on their sense of commitment to the community.

As I write, in the fall of 2011, more than half (22 of 36) of the elected officials representing San Antonio area residents at City Hall, in Bexar County, the Texas State Legislature, and the U.S. Congress are Latinas/os.[1] This represents a sea change from over a generation ago. Of the 36 offices, however, only three (two in the State Senate and one on

---

* In 2012, Congressman Charlie Gonzalez decided not to seek re-election to the 20th Congressional District. Representative Joaquin Castro is the Democratic nominee for this seat in Congress in the general election of November 2012.

City Council) are held by Latinas, signaling an area where much more progress is needed. In the judiciary, fifteen Latinas/os serve on the 55 seats available on the bench, with Latinas holding eight and Latinos seven of those seats.[2] Most Latinas/os elected to office are Democrats, but there are also some Republicans.

As Latinas go, so goes our city.

When we consider that well over fifty percent of our city's population is Hispanic, with women representing more than half that number, it is clear that Latinas constitute the single largest group of people in San Antonio.

While still woefully underrepresented at City Hall, the State Legislature, and in the U.S. Congress, Latinas continue to lead at the grassroots level, promoting the basic human rights agenda of the Chicano Movement. In fact, they *are* the new Chicana Movement, founding and directing a host of community organizations that address key needs and issues in our city that continue to be neglected by those in power. Whether it is strengthening families through micro-lending for small business creation (Janie Barrera), struggling against environmental racism (Diana López and Yolanda Johnson), addressing the pandemic of domestic violence (Patricia Castillo), advocating for workers rights (Petra Mata and Viola Cásares), empowering girls and teens (Joleen García and Adela Flores), or protecting our cultural heritage (Graciela Sánchez, Gloria Ramírez, Patti Ortiz, and Malena González-Cid), Latinas are on the frontlines.

These and many other *mujeres* are working in the concrete reality of our daily lives but also in the intangible spaces within our hearts, imaginations, and souls—the only places where true change can occur. As I saw in my own family, with my grandmothers, aunts, and my own mother, it was their resilience, creativity, and moral strength that maintained the strong bonds of family and community during trying times. Latinas continue to do that today, with tenacity and courage. Healing broken relationships, nurturing health and wellbeing, prioritizing education, honoring the dignity of work, and feeding our souls with the beauty of culture. Artists and writers like Sandra Cisneros, Carmen Tafolla, Mary Agnes Rodríguez, Terry Ybáñez, Enedina Cásarez-Vásquez, Ruth Buentello, Deborah K. Vasquez, and many others use their words and images to heal. Latinas across the city are quietly at work building *comunidad* and "making soul," as Gloria Anzaldúa writes.

Retoños. What the *movimiento* of forty years ago did in my generation to crack open a system by raising consciousness about racial and economic injustice, promoting cultural awareness, and engaging in grassroots activism, these Latinas are taking to the next level today. As I journey with them, the women who truly inspire me are those who have chosen to engage the pivotal issues of our day at all levels, recognizing their interconnectedness. Remarkable women who connect the dots, identifying and analyzing social inequalities and injustices towards anyone deemed "different," and raising issues of environmental degradation that endanger all life on Earth.

Latinas in San Antonio are tending to all the "soft issues"—the very ones I was warned against in my early years as an elected official. As it turns out, these are among the toughest and most critical issues of our times. The organized efforts of courageous Latinas, dating back forty years and continuing to this day to create one organization after another, addressing needs in our community, is a litany of hope—full of *retoños* for the future.

A Litany of Hope

Founded and/or currently directed by Latinas, these organizations, including several established within San Antonio colleges and universities, continue to play a pivotal role in service to our community. Dozens of other Latinas in the city lead efforts to raise funds, mentor, and support these and other community activities and organizations. Our city would be immeasurably poorer, in every sense of the word, without the efforts of these extraordinary Latina leaders.

1972

Mexican American Business and Professional Women's Club: *Women's empowerment and mentoring.* Luz Escamilla, Founder; Francesca Guillen, President.

1973

AVANCE San Antonio: *Parenting and education.* Gloria Rodríguez, Ph.D., Founder; Rebecca Cervántez, Executive Director.

1977

Family Violence Prevention Services: *Shelter for battered women*. Martha Pelaez, President.

1982

Visitation House Ministries: *Transitional housing for women and their children, including parent education*. Sisters Yolanda Tarango, CCVI, and Neomi Hayes, CCVI, Co-Founders; Sister Cindy Stacy, CCVI, Executive Director.

1982

Center for Women in Church and Society (Our Lady of the Lake University): *Women's empowerment through education*. Co-Founded by Sisters María Carolina Flores, CDP, and Margit Nagy, CDP.

1983

Hispanas Unidas: *Education for girls and teen pregnancy prevention, and Latina empowerment*. Adela I. Flores, Executive Director.

1985

Hispanic Women's Network of Texas: *Latina working women's empowerment and leadership development*. Nora Silva, San Antonio Chapter Chair.

1987

Esperanza Peace and Justice Center: *Grassroots organizing, community venue, arts, culture, community education, ecological concerns, and GBLT issues*. Co-Founders Susan Guerra and Graciela Sánchez, Executive Director.

1987

Women's Center (San Antonio College): *Women's non-traditional educational opportunities*. Lina Silva, Ph.D., Founder; Helen Vera, Ph.D., Director.

1988

La Voz de Esperanza: News journal promoting social justice and peace, culture and arts. Gloria A. Ramírez, Founding Editor.

1990

Fuerza Unida: *Workers rights, family support, youth leadership, education, displaced workers/globalization issues.* Co-Founders Petra Mata, Executive Director, and Viola Cásares, Program Director.

1990

Committee for Environmental Justice Action (CEJA): *Environmental racism, struggle over toxic soil left after closure of military base.* Yolanda Johnson, Founder; Lupe Alvarado, President.

1993

Lo Bello de San Antonio Women's Club: *Women's empowerment and philanthropy.* Cristina González, President.

1994

Mujeres Unidas, Inc.: *HIV/AIDS education and support for women.* Dr. Yolanda Rodríguez-Escobar, Founder; A.R. (Tina) Grado-Signer, Executive Director.

1994

ACCION Texas–Louisiana: *Empowering families with small business creation through micro-lending.* Founding President and CEO, Janie Barrera.

1995

MujerARTES: *Culture, arts, original pottery creations by grassroots women's cooperative, a project of Esperanza Peace and Justice Center.* Verónica Castillo, *Maestra*.

1996

Center for Legal and Social Justice (St. Mary's University School of Law): *Providing pro-bono legal services through* *clinical programs.* Barbara Bader Aldave, J.D., Founder; Ana Novoa, J. D., Associate Dean for Clinical Education and Public Interest, Director.

1996

Chicana/Latina Studies: The Journal of Mujeres Activas en Letras y Cambio Social (MALCS): *Writings and critical analysis of and by Chicanas.* Tiffany Ann López, Ph.D., and Josephine Méndez Negrete, Ph.D., Editors.

1997

Southwest Workers Union Youth Leadership Organization: *Empowerment of Chicana/o youth, immigration, education.* Sandra García, Youth Organizer.

1999

San Antonio Birth Doulas: *Assisting women during pregnancy and labor.* Suzanne de León, Founder and Executive Director.

1999

Martínez Street Women's Center: *Empowerment of girls and women through health services and education.* Joleen García, Director.

2001

Mujeres Activas en Letras y Cambio Social (MALCS) of San Antonio: *Activism, advocacy, and networking of Chicana scholars and community leaders.* Antonia Castañeda, Ph.D., and Norma Cantú, Ph.D., Co-Founders, San Antonio Chapter.

2001

San Antonio Time Dollar Community Connections: *Neighborhood family support and community garden.* Silbia G. Esparza, Executive Director.

2001

Community Leadership Institute (CLI): *Grassroots leadership development.* Laura Calderon, Rosie Castro, Romelia Escamilla, and Carol Rodríguez, Founders; María Alejandro, Executive Director.

2001

American Sunrise: *Prospect Hill neighborhood family and student support.* Co-Founders Henry Cisneros and Mary Alice Cisneros, Executive Director.

2003

The P.E.A.C.E. Initiative: *Coalition of organizations addressing the crisis of domestic and relationship violence.* Patricia Castillo, L.M.S.W., Founding Director.

2007

Roots of Change Community Garden (Southwest Workers Union): *Workers rights, grassroots advocacy, neighborhood edible garden.* Diana López, Environmental Justice Organizer.

2009

Voz de Mujer: *Young working women's empowerment and networking.* Elizabeth Eguía and Dolores Zapata, Co-Founders.

2010

Trabajadoras del Hogar en Acción (Southwest Workers Union) *Domestic Workers of San Antonio, aligned with national groups in organizing domestic workers.* Araceli Herrera, Founder.

2010

Center for Mexican American Studies and Research (Our Lady of the Lake University): *Scholarly research, archives of Latina history, special events and student services.* Teresita Aguilar, Ph.D., Director.

2011

Corazón Para el Barrio: *Family support with immediate needs at grassroots level.* Martha Castilla, Founder.

In addition, a handful of community organizations founded by Latinos are now headed by Latinas, including Margaret Moran, National President of **LULAC** (1929); Linda Rivas, Executive Director of **SER Jobs for Progress** (1967); María "Cuca" Robledo Montecel, Ph.D., Exective Director of the **Intercultural Development Research Association** (1973); Lydia Camarillo, Vice President and Executive Director, **Southwest Voter Registration Education Project** (1974); Malena González-Cid, Executive Director, **Centro Cultural Aztlán** (1977); and Patty Ortiz, Executive Director of the **Guadalupe Cultural Arts Center** (1980).

⁂

The Gift of Voices in the Wilderness

The power of being a voice crying out in the wilderness comes from its very improbability. In the face of what appears to be a hopeless situation or formidable challenge, those who remain undaunted, using their voices to speak truth to power, are astonishing *retoños*, trusting democracy enough to use its levers for change. It is wonderful to see women and men in our community, especially young people, speak out, putting themselves on the line for what they think is right, no matter how seemingly hopeless or daunting the cause. I am proud to stand with them, as an elder now—and most recently in three key struggles.

1. Las Calles No Se Callan

The first of these began in 2007 in what might be called a prologue to the "Occupy" movement that began on Wall Street in September 2011 and then spread around the nation, including San Antonio, and the world. As I write, serious challenges have been made to the occupiers' right to free speech and peaceful assembly with a police-enforced dismantling of their protest sites. Four years ago, our city visited this very issue—with alarming results.

San Antonio has a long tradition of using public spaces to honor and celebrate special occasions. We use our streets to host the nation's largest Martin Luther King Day march every January; to remember an icon of the Latino movement at the annual Cesar Chávez march; and to celebrate Fiesta Week each spring with multiple parades. We also have a long tradition, as is our right, of using public spaces to protest, challenge, and hold our government accountable.

In the fall of 2007, however, this latter tradition appeared ready to be seriously curtailed, if not brought to an end, by City Council. Our city officials were proposing an ordinance that would impose high fees for "Parades, Runs, Walks, and Related Events." Its practical impact would be to take the "free" out of our right to free speech, with prohibitive fees that few grassroots organizations could afford.

The proposal came on the heels of two hugely successful pro-immigration marches, in 2006 and 2007, to protest the most draconian, anti-illegal immigration legislation ever proposed in the U.S. Congress. Millions of people throughout the country marched in the spring of 2006 against the legislation. In San Antonio, we gathered about 20,000 people in what was perhaps the largest march in our history. In May of 2007, we marched again, for comprehensive immigration reform.

When the city held hearings to discuss the proposed ordinance, I joined others in speaking out against it. I had been invited to do so by the organizers of our annual International Women's Day march. We had a special interest in this ordinance since we commemorate International Women's Day each year in March, with a large street march and rally. When our group and others took serious exception to the large sums of money being proposed for parades, runs, walks, and related events, the city decided to exempt certain groups, including the Martin Luther King and César Chávez marches, among a few others.

As we continued to press the issue, the city at one point offered to include the International Women's Day march among the "exempt" groups. But we refused the exemption. For us, the issue was way bigger than a single march. It was an infringement on our First Amendment rights to free speech. Organizing the Free Speech Coalition, we led the public opposition to the ordinance.[3]

Notwithstanding the many voices speaking against the ordinance, on November 29, 2007, by a vote of 8 to 2, the Mayor and City Council of San Antonio enacted one of the most stringent ordinances in the nation on use of public spaces.[4] It exempted a few groups; those, in essence, whose "speech" the city supports.

Our Coalition for Free Speech filed a lawsuit in U.S. Federal Court, challenging the constitutionality of the ordinance. The action galvanized the community. Under the slogan, "The Streets Will Not Be Silenced. *Las Calles No Se Callan,*" marches and rallies were held, and yard signs with this message were posted throughout the city.

When the case went before court, I was asked to testify. My testimony consisted of relating my experiences marching on San Antonio streets over the years and describing our city's long history of democratic transformation starting on the streets. The litigation took its course. We won some points but ultimately lost the case in federal court. We appealed to the Fifth Circuit Court in New Orleans, but lost there too on narrow grounds.

The Free Speech Coalition and the Esperanza Peace and Justice Center are now working to bring a broader challenge to this ordinance and others that restrict access to San Antonio's public space. I will again stand in solidarity with them. As the right to free speech is challenged around the country by government limiting assembly in public spaces with the Occupy movement, we see the makings of major constitutional confrontation. The voice of the people of San Antonio will be heard in this critical debate.

2. Energía Mía

On March 11, 2011, an 8.9 magnitude earthquake and subsequent tsunami hit Japan, devastating its Fukushima Daiichi nuclear plant. For days leading to weeks, the world's attention was riveted around the possible meltdown and release of deadly radioactivity. The dangers of nuclear energy were once again brought to center stage.

Ironically, in San Antonio, just a year and a half earlier, our municipally owned utility company, CPS Energy, had been arguing—with great success—to have San Antonio participate in the construction of two additional nuclear reactors at the STNP in Bay City, about 25 miles from the Gulf of Mexico. These would be the first new nuclear reactors to be built in the United States in 25 years—a message many of us did not want our city to be sending out to the rest of the country.

As I became involved in the opposition efforts, my thoughts were carried back three decades ago to my first days at City Hall and the debate over our continued involvement in the first two existing reactors at Bay City. The problems with nuclear energy today are the same as they were then, with questions about its safety, radioactive waste storage, enormous water consumption (in a drought-prone state), and huge taxpayer-subsidized costs.

There was, however, a big difference between the activists of thirty years ago and those who were galvanized to act in 2009. While the traditional environmental organizations were still involved in the issue, we now had Latina/o civil rights, social justice, and workers' organizations fully engaged.[5] I was especially touched by the involvement of young people who were not even alive thirty years ago, proud of their participation but saddened that another generation has to struggle against these same issues. Their creativity and energy in helping to organize rallies, marches, and other activities to educate our community was vital to efforts organized under the banner of *Energía Mía*, which ran from August 2009 to February 2010.[6]

Our opposition had the effect of extending and opening the decision-making process to more public scrutiny. It's what I call "spreading marbles"—activism that may not change the outcome but has the effect of slowing things down. We actually ended up winning because of it! Through the course of the added scrutiny, CPS stumbled over its own misstatement to the public about the costs of building the two new reactors. They were off by millions of dollars! The proposal that seemed all but sure to sail through City Hall in 2009 was withdrawn in 2010.

Plans for nuclear expansion are now on hold, especially in the wake of the near-catastrophic disaster at Fukushima. But as long as federal subsidies for nuclear energy remain a possibility, plans for new reactors could be resurrected at any time, requiring continued citizen vigilance. A cause for celebration now, thanks to many years of citizens pushing for renewable energy, is the news that CPS is a leader in wind energy sales.[7] CPS Energy recently announced that they are committed to generating 400 megawatts of solar energy. Welcome news, indeed. As for *Energía Mía*, we continue our vigilance.

3. Dreamers

In the fall of 2010, a group of UTSA students with whom I had worked on the nuclear energy and free speech issues asked me and other community members to help them lobby our U.S. Senators on behalf of the DREAM Act.[8] The proposed legislation would provide undocumented youth who entered the country as children with their parents—*i.e.*, as dependents, not as decision-making adults—a pathway to legalizing their status as residents and, under a rigorous six-year-long process, the possibility of citizenship. Similar legislation had been proposed and failed before; its passage now *highly* improbable. But the UTSA students were insistent. They were concerned about friends and classmates who had grown up just like them, as Americans, studying hard to realize dreams for their futures, yet living every day with the reality of a future that promised to bar them from employment and deport them away from the only home they knew.

On November 10, 2010, more than a dozen students began a teach-in and hunger strike at Sombrilla Plaza on UTSA's main campus, joining a national effort on college campuses to win passage of the legislation that the Senate Majority Leader promised to bring to a vote before the end of the year. Setting themselves up in front a bronze statue depicting a family crossing the border, the students handed out materials, urging others to join them in lobbying Senator Kay Bailey Hutchison (R-Tex.), who had previously supported the DREAM Act but now opposed it. Her vote was pivotal, becoming the focus of the students' efforts.

After fasting for four days, the students decided to march from campus to San Fernando Cathedral downtown—a fifteen-mile hike that took them seven hours to walk! I knew the march would bring them along a route two blocks from our home, so I went to the corner and prepared a little altar with a statute of Our Lady of Guadalupe and a candle, waiting for them to come by. A few friends and neighbors joined me. When we saw the small band of students, chanting and cheering, a couple looking frail from the fast, a blessing was not enough. We had to join them for the last few miles. It was dusk when we reached the plaza in front of historic San Fernando Cathedral, the nation's oldest continuously operating cathedral. Other students had already arrived and set up an altar lit with candles, ready for a vigil. By then, my commitment to stand in solidarity with the students for passage of the DREAM Act had gone from my head straight into my heart.

As the days passed, the students continued to lobby Senator Hutchison, asking to meet with her. She refused. A half dozen continued the fast, including the daughter of a friend and fellow activist, a young woman I had known since she was a child. In her early twenties, Yasmina Codina was very thin to begin with but was insistent on continuing to fast until the DREAM Act came to a vote. A few words in a news story captured our feelings about these students.

> On Day 1, dozens of DREAM activists at other Texas and U.S. universities were among the hunger strikers. On Day 8, the UTSA group appeared to be the only one still standing, and three more students had joined the cause.

Their elders, veterans of the civil rights movement, are watching in admiration but also with grave concern. Days-long fasting is an extreme form of nonviolent protest that can imperil the hunger striker's well-being. Many remember that labor leader Cesar Chavez's health problems late in life stemmed from the hunger strikes he staged to bring attention to the working conditions of farm workers.[9]

The students' hunger strike and their work on behalf of the DREAM Act continued, not only energizing other students but also educating an entire community through their use of social media and news-grabbing actions.

Shortly before Thanksgiving, I received an email from one of the Dreamers (as they came to be known). Increasingly frustrated because they could not get an appointment to see or talk to Senator Hutchison, they decided to go to her San Antonio office and wait all day until she agreed to speak with them. "There could be civil disobedience," the email said, if the Senator refused. The Dreamers invited the community to support them in the effort.

I knew I would support them, but the words "civil disobedience" took this to another level. I had never engaged in civil disobedience and I knew that arrest was possible. I vividly recall on Thanksgiving Day telling Manny that I would be joining the students in their sit-in and, depending on what happened, there was a chance I might be arrested. As usual, Manny supported me. I made the commitment—but confess that though I knew arrest was a theoretical possibility, I never really thought it would happen.

On the afternoon of November 29, 2010, I participated in the demonstration held at the entrance to the building where Senator Hutchison's San Antonio office was located. By the time I arrived, a few students accompanied by a Methodist pastor, Rev. Lorenza Andrade-Smith, had already been inside the Senator's office for hours. They had asked to speak to Senator Hutchison by phone and were just sitting inside, waiting for her to call, while the demonstration took place outdoors. When closing time came, the staff made clear that the Senator would not be calling and asked the students to leave. By this point, a number of us—my friend Antonia Castañeda, Ph.D. and myself included—had moved inside the building and were sitting in the hallway on the floor at the foot of the door to the Senator's offices.

The Senator did not call; the students inside refused to leave; the police were called. After another few hours that seemed intended to outwait the news cameras that were videotaping these events, the police moved in, arresting the students and those of us who were sitting at the Senator's door, also refusing to leave the building. Along with about nearly a dozen students, Rev. Andrade-Smith, two older men, and Antonia and I were arrested. Shackled with handcuffs, we were loaded into a paddy wagon and taken to the jail's detention center downtown. Charged with criminal trespassing, sixteen of us—ten women and six men—were held overnight.

It was a night I will never forget.

Being arrested and detained for the first time in my life, at nearly age 70, was memorable in itself. The women and men were separated. Most of us could not even think of sleeping. We talked into the night. In the cell, I spoke with some incredibly committed young women, who were deeply concerned about their fellow students, living in the shadows. They were willing to make huge sacrifices for the cause of winning justice for them, including starvation and arrest. It was the twentieth day of the hunger strike for Yasmina, one of the students arrested.

That night I also experienced the sexism and misogyny of the criminal justice system. It's true that we were incarcerated and in a city jail, but no woman should have to put up with the detestable verbal abuse and disrespect to which the detention officers subjected us. To make matters worse, the abusers were Latino. The men who were arrested along with us did not experience this. It gave me a real insight into what women in the criminal justice system go through—and it is a disgrace. The next morning we were released; the charges against us later dropped.

A week later, on December 7, the students experienced a victory in the House of Representatives—the DREAM Act passed! With a renewed sense of hope, and attention now fully focused on lobbying the Senate, I was invited to join a group of faith leaders in Washington, D.C., a few days before the anticipated vote. Ministers, rabbis, and a couple of priests were among the speakers at a news conference calling on Senators to vote for the legislation; I was asked to speak as a Catholic woman. Nearly 100 undocumented students from around the country also were part of the group, speaking out publicly. Together we marched to a park where the faith leaders formed a circle around the students. It was one of the coldest days of the year in the nation's capital. The students knelt as we prayed over them. Their faith was moving and their courage inspiring. Any one of them could have been arrested right then and there and sent back to their countries of origin.

Back in San Antonio, the night before the Senate was expected to vote, I joined the Dreamers for an overnight vigil at the Church of

Our Lady of Guadalupe on the Westside. The next day, huddled together in my living room, we watched the Senate proceedings. When the roll call was over, we witnessed the Senate's failure to pass *any* kind of immigration reform. It was the fortieth day of the hunger strike. Tears of disappointment and pain filled the eyes of my young friends as we watched Senator Hutchison, among others, cast her vote against the DREAM Act.

It was a heart-breaking end to a valiant struggle. And it would have been truly tragic if the struggle ended there, with so much hope dashed. But our young people are made of stronger stuff. Today, UTSA students continue to pursue similar legislation in Congress and young immigrants recently organized themselves as the San Antonio Immigration Youth Movement (SAIYM). They are working to stop deportations of immigrant youth and their families and addressing the growing issue of private detention centers where immigrants—children and adults alike—are being held in virtual prisons.

As our immigration policies continue to tear families and communities apart, I find great hope in these young people. Their willingness to put their lives on the line for something they believe in is a mark of character that our future can depend on.

◆•❖•◆

The Gift of Connecting the Dots

A Mexican *dicho* that I often heard growing up was, e*l diablo no sabe tanto por diablo si no por viejo.* The devil knows more because he is old than because he is the devil. Living long enough has its own rewards in coming to understandings or realizations that may have always been there but somehow remained elusive or unseen.

For years I used to call my work on behalf of social justice and on environmental issues "my two worlds." There was good reason for this. When individuals and groups would come together in San Antonio, galvanized to work on an issue, I knew that the room would be filled with either mostly people of color or mostly white people, depending on the issue. It felt like—and *was*—two worlds. I yearned to see them brought together. More deeply, I now understand, I also yearned to make these connections in my own soul. It was I who had to make the connection, to integrate all these issues in the core of my being and with my spirituality.

The connection was always there, of course. From the moment my mother taught me to love the vacant lot we called our *parquesito*; from the moment my Tío Blas first handed me the *dipa* with fresh cold water from the well; from the moment I would breathe in the air and, seeing into the distant open fields behind the silo at the *ranchito* in Lockhart, feel the presence of God. Anything that would diminish those experiences would diminish my spirit, no less than social oppression.

From its founding in 2002 until it closed in 2011, I served as President of the Board of a small nonprofit, Santuario Sisterfarm, that was dedicated to making these connections. A sanctuary on seven acres in the Texas Hill Country, less than an hour's drive from San Antonio, Santuario Sisterfarm's mission was to cultivate diversity—bio-diversity and cultural diversity—as a way of promoting peace in our world. It was the brainchild of Adrian Dominican Sisters Carol Coston, OP, and Elise García, OP, and became a collaboration between women religious and Latinas of the Borderlands.

Over nine years, I was part of this space where we created a model of sustainability for "living lightly on Earth," where principles of permaculture were practiced, and where both cultural and biological diversity were honored.[10] I had the privilege of time to replenish my spirit in quiet retreat, especially during the challenging years of caring for my parents—and for reflection on nature and our place in the community of life on Earth.

Memorable moments included early mornings when we would gather at the *nicho* my father built for us to shelter a clay statue of Our Lady of Guadalupe. It was his last work. We would serenade *la virgencita*, singing *Buenos Dias, Paloma Blanca*, an old and precious song dedicated to Mary—a favorite of my mother.

Another memory is of Elise leading a "cosmic walk" around the farm where each step represented a segment of time in the 13.7-billion-year story of our evolving universe, from the Big Bang to the present. The first time I experienced the walk, two things moved me. One was the humbling thought of the infinitesimally brief time we humans have inhabited the Earth. The other was Elise's reminder that we are the first generation of humans that has garnered the power to destroy the life that has evolved over billions of years.

Our work is not simply about "environmental protection." We are being called to a radical transformation in our whole way of thinking about ourselves as human beings—as one species in a larger interconnected web of life.

In this work, Carol would hold up the wisdom of nature as guidance, and all we could learn from her. Nature "doesn't create a forest or a meadow in straight lines and out of a single species the way agribusiness grows our food crops," she writes. "Nature loves a diversity of plants and animals and encourages useful connections between and among the plants and trees, the crawling creatures and the flying ones."[11] Earth Care; People Care; Fair Share. Those are the core values of permaculture that Carol emphasized over and again, values that connect how we humans treat each other with how we treat all other forms of life on Earth.

As I returned to my inner city neighborhood, reflecting on the many conversations we engaged in with people of all backgrounds at Santuario Sisterfarm, I realized more than ever the immense importance of personal integration. With the train blowing its horn a couple of streets away, the ambulances rushing in front of our house, and my own noise and that of friends organizing, meeting, and marching on the streets, it's easy to think in terms of dualities—social issues here, the environment there. But there was no division. The Creator makes no divisions. The dots were connected deep in my interior. We are one in our human diversity. We are one within the great diversity of life on Earth. All issues are interrelated—and they all reflect our spirituality.

Today, with the study and critical analysis of environmental racism, social and environmental issues have been joined. A great joy for me is seeing the deeper understanding that so many in my community possess, especially among the young, of the multiple layers linking these issues. During the first decade of the new millennium, Latina/o activists played critical roles in all the major struggles in our city and nation— the war in Iraq, PGA, free speech, nuclear energy, and immigration.

Among my young friends, I also see a beautiful spiritual dimension to their activism where, again, all is interconnected. I saw it in the Dreamers whose protests were always accompanied by rituals and whose fasting was sustained by deep spiritual roots and practice. Twenty-three year old Diana López, winner of a 2009 Brower Youth Award, offers another example.[12] Diana is the director of the Southwest Workers Union (SWU) "Roots of Change" garden, planted behind their headquarters. The union facilitates the planting of edible gardens on the Eastside in order to make fresh organic produce available in neighborhoods where there is none. The union is active in immigration, economic justice, and environmental justice issues. Diana describes their work this way:

> Our movement is rooted in the principle that "we speak for ourselves." SWU mobilizes community power for true participation and to achieve justice where we work, where we play, where we live and where we pray. I think care of the environment

goes further than just recycling and community gardens. It's about people being able to be part of the decision making table and knowing their story, the story of the land where they live and where they work. There is a strong disconnection between where we live, what we value and how we heal. The environment is not a part of this process as it should be at this point. But the reality is that people are part of the environment. We suffer because our environment suffers in the places where we live and work.[13]

An artful, handmade sign in the midst of the garden reflects profound understanding: "Many things grow in a garden that were never sown there."

The Gift of Family

La fruta nunca cae lejos del arbol.

The prevalence of a saying across cultures and languages must say something about its truth. "The fruit does not fall far from the tree." As I have become an elder in my family, observing our young, this *dicho* not only speaks truth but also holds deep meaning for me.

In my family, in the face of one child or another, I see the face of an ancestor—of the ones who taught me how to live. All but two members of my parent's generation are now gone. Tío Cosme is my father's last surviving sibling and Tía Betty, my mother's. Tía Betty recently lost her beloved husband, Emilio, a true pillar of our family.

Last year, my mother's sister, Tía María, died. A rosary was held in Lockhart, where she had lived all her life; it was led by her granddaughters. As they prayed, "Hail Mary, full of grace…" I saw their great-grandmother in them. I pictured Teresa as a young immigrant woman, after the long drive to Sunday Mass in Uhland, praying these same words, wrapped in her long black *rebozo*. I thought of how traditions and values are passed down from generation to generation. These young women raised in a very different time, facing entirely different challenges, had the same prayers move their lips as Welita Teresita.

Those traditional rituals do not, of course, hold the same power for all the young in our family. A number have found other ways to live in this complex modern world where faith takes many blessed forms, with the values they inherited and with great integrity.

Both the Arredondo and Rodríguez families continue to grow. We now number in the hundreds. A family composed of people named

Melecio, Sebastiana, Blas, and Fulgencio now embraces children named Ryder, Tyler, Marshal, and Krystal, their ethnic diversity reflecting the diversity of our world. Many of the Arredondo grandchildren and their families have remained in Texas, primarily around the Lockhart-Austin area. Most members of the Rodríguez family live in the San Antonio area, some having settled in other states and a few living and working abroad.

As we gather on happy occasions and sorrowful ones, our shared threads of memory continue to hold us together in the tapestry woven by our ancestors, even as we weave in new colors and textures. Our family crossed the U.S.-Mexico border in the early 1900s, but that, of course, is not when our history began. We hold ancient threads of memory that go back centuries on this continent. We are among the founders of communities in the Americas—and we are creating community still.

I saw this clearly at two recent family events—in July of 2010, when our Rodríguez family gathered to celebrate the centennial of our ancestors starting a new life here in the United States. And on November 6, 2010, 100 years to the day that my father came to this country as a baby, when I had the honor of celebrating the occasion with some 300 members of my family and larger community, reading stories from the early chapters of this book. On both occasions, it was clear how our family—like millions of other immigrant families—has enriched this nation. Among us we could count gifts given in many endeavors, including education, small business, medicine, law, finance, politics, science, the arts and others.

By the time my parents died, they had seen many *retoños* in their own immediate family.

- Felix married Veronica Arzola. They have three children, Alberto, Lupita, and Felix Gerardo.

- Louis married Leonor Lara. They have two daughters, Anna Laura (Petri) and Angela Cristina, as well as two granddaughters and two grandsons.

- Miguel was formerly married to Dolores Guajardo. They have two children, Cristina Marisol (Turowski) and Miguel Sergio, and four grandsons.

- Rosie married John Almaguer. They have two daughters, Rebecca Elisa (White) and Julie Ann, plus two grandsons and a granddaughter.

Theresa and Rosie are each retired after dedicated careers in elementary education. Felix retired from civil service and now works as a substitute teacher in inner-city schools. Miguel also works in education in a large inner-city district and Louis is employed with a major research institute. With the exception of one grandchild who is still in college, all the other grandchildren have graduated from colleges and universities throughout the country. Before they died, my parents had started celebrating the rituals of the next generation—their great-grandchildren— kindergarten graduations!

Our family's story mirrors that of millions of other immigrant families in another sense: In the miracle that people who came here with nothing, not even a formal education, built strong communities with the only thing they possessed—the values they carried in their hearts, souls, and minds.

A couple of weeks before she died, I asked my mother what advice she would give me for the rest of my life. Without hesitation, she responded, *"Que seas una buena persona."* Then, after pausing for a moment, she added, *"Y que le ayudes a la gente."*

One hundred years after Apolinar and Sixta Arredondo Rodríguez came to this country, their great-grandchildren are growing up quickly in a very different and fast-changing world. My mother's words, however, are as relevant as ever. I hold them in prayer for each new member of our family: May you be a good person—and may you help others.

The Gift of Peace

In south Texas, the season can change abruptly. One day it is summer and the next brings the chill of winter. This year winter is arriving more gently than usual.

Outside my window, as I sit at my computer, two plants accompany me as the days grow cooler. One is a lush, fuchsia bougainvillea; the other a young, three-foot Mexican agave or century plant—each planted in honor of my parents.

The bougainvillea is a transplant from a hanging basket I got for my mother when she was very ill. They were the last flowers she ever saw. After she died, I took the bougainvillea out of the basket and planted it in our backyard. The agave is a transplant from a tiny "sucker" I planted over 25 years ago from an agave my father had in his yard.

Overnight, from the moment we put my mother in hospice during Holy Week of 2007, that agave started growing its mast. It grew to be about twenty feet tall and then produced a gorgeous cluster of tiny yellow flowers that seemed to hang from the sky between the clouds. After its spectacular bloom, the plant withered and died, as agaves do. Now one of its offspring suckers has taken root, growing sturdily in its place.

This past summer of 2011, the U.S. recorded the hottest summer in history. In San Antonio, we had 59 days of over 100-degree weather. Because of the severe drought that accompanied the intense heat, I was only able to water my plants two or three times the entire summer. Most of our shrubs burned and my Bartlett pear tree dropped all its leaves, singed brown, in the middle of summer. Only the large trees with very deep roots survived, although even some of them suffered damage. The bougainvillea and the agave, however, not only withstood the heat and drought—a recent rain drew gorgeous blooms out of the bougainvillea.

These plants mirror for me the strength of the two individuals in whose honor I planted them—Apolinar and Sixta, who weathered life's struggles with faith and grace. They also mirror the great cycle of life on Earth. One life ends, another begins. *Retoños.* Nature transforms all. Our spirit simply is. In that wisdom, I find peace.

NOTES

Chapter 13: Retoños

1. U.S. House of Representatives: Representatives José Canseco, Henry Cuellar, and Charles González (3 of 4); Texas State Legislature: Senators Carlos Uresti, Leticia Van de Putte and Judith Zaffrini (3 of 4) and Representatives Joaquín Castro, Henry Farias, Roland Gutiérrez, Trey Martínez Fischer, John Garza, José Menéndez, and Mike Villarreal (7 of 12); Bexar County: Commissioners Paul Elizondo and Sergio "Chico" Rodríguez (2 of 5); City Council: Mayor Julián Castro and Councilors Diego Bernal, Ray López, Cris Medina, David Medina, Leticia Ozuna, and Ray Saldaña (7 of 11).

2. Serving in the judiciary in the fall of 2011: District Judges Antonia Arteaga, Richard García, Juanita A. Vásquez-Gardner, Charles Montemayor, Victor Negrón, Ron Rangel, Mary Roman, and Lori I. Valenzuela (8 of 34); County Court Judges Monica González, Irene Ríos, David Rodríguez, and Liza Rodríguez (4 of 15); and Justices of the Peace Monica Lisa Caballero, Rogelio López, and Edmundo Zaragoza, Jr. (3 of 6).

3. See the Esperanza Peace and Justice Center website http://esperanzacenter.org/freespeech/ (accessed October 28, 2011).

4. San Antonio City Council Minutes, November 29, 2007. Voting for the ordinance were Mayor Phil Hardberger and Councilmembers Diane Cibrian, John Clamp, Roland Gutiérrez, Delicia Herrera, Sheila McNeil, Justin Rodríguez, and Kevin Wolff. Councilwomen Mary Alice Cisneros and Lourdes Galvan cast the two votes against the ordinance.

5. The Esperanza Peace and Justice Center, Fuerza Unida, and Southwest Workers Union, as part of *Energía Mía,* were among the groups leading the effort along with Public Citizen, the SEED Coalition, and the Sierra Club.

6. See http://energiamia.org/. The group continues its vigilance through the efforts of long time anti-nuclear activist Cynthia Wheeler, supported by many individuals and groups.

7. In 2010, CPS Energy ranked among the top 10 utility companies in the U.S. Department of Energy's National Renewable Energy Laboratory's annual assessment of leading utility green power companies in the category of renewable energy sales—wind in the case of CPS. See http://www.nrel.gov/news/press/2011/1367.html (accessed November 21, 2011).

8. Under the rigorous provisions of the DREAM (Development, Relief and Education for Alien Minors) Act, qualifying undocumented youth who entered the country before the age of 16, would be eligible for a six-year-long conditional path to citizenship that requires completion of a college degree or two years of military service. See http://dreamact.info/ (accessed November 3, 2011).

9. See http://www.mysanantonio.com/news/education/article/Students-go-hungry-so-the-dream-won-t-die-819778.php#ixzz1eQzW8G8N (accessed November 22, 2011).

10. The Santuario Sisterfarm website is still available, providing virtual and interactive tours of the site, as well as information on Latinas in the Border-lands, Green Sisters, and books published by the organization's imprint, Sor Juana Press. See http://sisterfarm.org/

11. Carol Coston, OP, *Permaculture: Finding Our Own Vines and Fig Trees* (San Antonio: Sor Juana Press, 2003), 63.

12. Brower Youth Awards are North American awards given annually to honor "bold young environmental leaders." See http://www.broweryouthawards.org/.

13. Letter from Diana López to María Antonietta Berriozábal, November 2, 2011.

The Journey of Apolinar (Polo) Rodríguez and his family

Félix and Sebastiana Rodríguez at ages twenty-three and twenty-two, respectively, left La Hacienda Ibarilla with their nine-month old son Polo on a wagon to the nearby city of Leon, Guanajuato Mexico. There they took a train passing through Irapuato, Salamanca, Celaya and probably changed trains in Queretaro. During the next leg of their trip they traveled through Dolores Hidalgo, San Luis Potosi and Matehuala before arriving in Monterrey, Nuevo Leon. From Monterrey they again traveled by train to Laredo, Tamaulipas, Mexico. They were interviewed by U.S. authorities upon reaching Laredo and granted permanent residency, crossing the U.S. border on November 6, 1910.

In Laredo, Texas they boarded a U. S. train, passed through San Antonio and arrived in San Marcos, Texas. Family members picked them up in San Marcos for the final leg of their 800-mile journey and took them to their new home in Reedville, Texas. In time they would settle in Lockhart, Texas.

The Journey of Sixta Arredondo and her family

Melecio and Teresa Arredondo at ages twenty-nine and twenty-two, respectively, and their five children, including four-year old Sixta left La Hacienda de la Cardona Grande in Nuevo Leon, Mexico riding donkeys with some of the family members on foot. The first part of their journey took them through Mier y Noriega, Nuevo Leon and continued to Doctor Arroyo, Nuevo Leon. From there, still riding the burros and on foot, they took the crudely paved road towards Galeana, Nuevo Leon. That leg of their journey towards Linares, Nuevo, Leon took them through very steep and dangerous sierras.

They continued on the same road until they reached Monterrey, Nuevo Leon. There they stopped so Melecio could work a few days and also sell the donkeys and much of what they had carried so they could get enough money to buy passage on the train for the rest of their trip.

They arrived in Laredo, Tamaulipas, Mexico at the border with the U. S. and crossed on July 5, 1915. At the border, they were interviewed by U.S. authorities and granted permanent residency. There they boarded a U. S. train passing through San Antonio and ending their journey in San Marcos, Texas. They had traveled approximately 597-miles from the start of their trip in Mier y Noriega. Before they boarded the train in Monterrey, they had already traveled for 250-miles on burros and on foot. They arrived in San Marcos, Texas where family or friends picked them up and took them by wagon to their new home in Clearfork, Texas. Eventually, they too would settle in Lockhart, Texas.

REFLECTION

Relational Leadership in:
María, Daughter of Immigrants

Josie Méndez-Negrete, Ph.D.

Leadership is more than believing or speaking a certain way; it is acting out a philosophy that creates change to benefit the many over the individual. [For Chicana activist leaders], it is not enough to talk about change; leaders actively work to create it. Taking a stance and acting upon issues that have had a negative impact on others is part of their active involvement in creating and bringing about change. Moreover, key to their leadership is the ability to listen, to observe, and to keep an eye on the overall process, along with the flexibility to modify the process.

(Méndez-Negrete, 1999, 28)

A Legacy of Care and Commitment

Cultural memory and the stories she experienced and heard from her family unveil a legacy of care and commitment in the life of María Antonietta Berriozábal. The historical trauma she experienced because of poverty and a racialized gender identity as a child of immigrants, along with her keen eye for understanding the structural inequalities in which she and her loved ones experienced, have framed the leadership and activist actions in which María Antonietta Berriozábal became involved. This knowledge of self and others continues to inform the ways in which she negotiates day-to-day leadership and activist interactions. As a Chicana—a member of a racialized ethnic group—Berriozábal learned to relate inside socioeconomic experiences that presuppose multiple sites of subordination. Her story documents the gendered, raced, and classed experiences she navigated in her quest for social justice and social change—as a person as well as a public figure (Méndez-Negrete, 1995, Hardy-Fanta 1994). A woman of conscience who easily places herself in the subjective spaces she has had to resolve as a woman of color from a working class background, Berriozábal came to a consciousness of her own social positions by relying on deep self-knowledge and personal understanding of having negotiated cultural and social power inequalities in her day-to-day relationships, as she pursued, and continues to pursue, social justice issues, seeking to create social change.

Born María Antonietta Rodríguez, she had to negotiate matters of everyday life—from the playground to political arenas—in all she has engaged as an individual. In writing her personal story, Berriozábal bridges the early twentieth and twenty-first centuries. As the daughter of immigrants, she details her trajectory of involvement, documenting a path to political leadership and Chicana activism, instructing us along the way as to why she continues to pursue empowerment and change for her communities of interest—the working poor, spiritual and religious communities, environmental/ecological concerns, as well as the political arenas of everyday life at the local, regional, national, and global levels.

Inspired by the values of Apolinar (Polo) Rodríguez and Sixta Arredondo—her parents—in her leadership and activist interactions, Berriozábal starts from a position of strength. Her philosophy of social action began with a desire to create a better world for those who are adversely impacted by structures of inequality, and evolved into an ethic of responsibility that calls her to fight for equality, justice, and fairness for all—regardless of status and how they are socially positioned.

In *María: Daughter of Immigrants*, Berriozábal unearths memories of her family, narrating stories about her ancestors. She reflects on their legacy and the lessons that have shaped her life. Berriozábal produces a *testimonio*/autoethnograpy to confirm and document the ways in which the social and cultural forces of Mexico and the United States framed the lives of the Rodríguez and Arredondo families as citizens of a new nation. She speaks about early enactments of leadership in her household and community, which inspired Berriozábal to honor her roots and those of the people from whom she originates. For example, Polo, as her father was known, advised Berriozábal to judge herself by the accomplishments she reached, not so as to gloat about her achievements, but to recognize the potential in those who come from the bottom. He often reminded her that his family "empezó desde abajo," started at the bottom. Recognizing her contributions to the wellbeing of her community and her people, Polo delighted in Berriozábal's accomplishments, and he was quick to remind others that his daughter achieved them despite the limitations of originating among the working poor.

Her immediate family and communities were not the only ones that took pride in María Antonietta Berriozábal's achievements; scholars from various disciplines have written about her contributions. In their narratives, she proudly speaks of her origins. For example, she talks about the push of war, the movement of landless masses, and the struggles experienced by peasants who fled the Mexican Revolution in 1910. In an interview for an edited book by José Angel Gutiérrez, Michelle Meléndez, Sonia Adriana Noyola, *Chicanas in charge: Texas women in the public arena* (2007), Berriozábal discusses her ancestral migration/immigration story. She suggests that the Rodriguez and Arredondos' relocation was a consequence of volatile economic times that drove her paternal and maternal grandparents to leave their country.

Recalling the stories she heard, Berriozábal speaks of that time. In a code that is laced with Spanish, she recalls:

> Mother's family lived in a little town near Monterrey … [they were] *trabajadores de los hacendados* … my father's family in León, Guanajuato, Mexico … also campesinos … [that] worked … for rich people. When the Revolution came … *soldados and revolucionarios* … raided the hacienda for food supplies, they also violated the women. The rich landowners fled, leaving the *campesinos* to fare for themselves, [and] peasant families came to the United States, fleeing for their lives (Gutierrez, Melendez, and Noyola, 2007, 169).

In these days of anti-Mexican politics, Berriozábal continues to speak for the rights of workers, personalizing and humanizing the circumstances under which Mexicans continue to immigrate to the United States. Their stories are her legacy. She empathizes with their pain as she listens to the travails of unauthorized immigration stories, and to the plight of students who as children were brought here by their parents and who now seek the enactment of a DREAM Act. Her involvement and the imperative of her commitment led to her arrest for demonstrating her solidarity with undocumented youth fighting to achieve legal status—in a country they call home. Also, she fights for water rights, contesting political inequality and the lack of representations of Mexican Americans. In her philosophy of life, these issues are not disconnected from her past or the ethics of responsibility and accountability that inspire her to act for the greater good of others.

Carving her own legacy of social justice

Books about political leaders who are credited with creating a path for others to enter the political arena are appearing rapidly in the twenty-first century. For example, in Sharon A. Navarro's (2008) biography of Letitia Van de Putte, *Latina Legislator: Leticia Van de Putte and the Road to Leadership*, the author identifies nine Hispanic women who have served in the Texas State Legislature, and Berriozábal is credited with mentoring many of these women legislators. In *Políticas: Latina public officials in Texas* (2008), authors Sonia Rebecca García, Irasema Coronado, and Valerie Martinez-Ebers closely examine and document the contributions of political leaders like María Antonietta Berriozábal. However, more work needs to be done to analyze the everyday contributions of leaders and activists who do not fit conventional notions of political leadership. Berriozábal, in *María: Daughter of Immigrants*, provides us a view that has yet to be told by someone of her class and racialized ethnic background, as she provides a guide to everyday leadership among activists.

In an interview for the now dissolved Santuario Sisterfarm, Berriozábal addresses the issues she continues to engage. María *"of many firsts"* Berriozábal relies on the base that still supports her to advance social, political, and cultural change in San Antonio, Texas. Speaking in this interview, Berriozábal expresses:

> Most of my life I have been working on issues of social justice, issues of poverty, lack of education, housing, lack of economic opportunity, particularly for people of color and women. I have also worked on environmental issues, such as water, as our city of San Antonio has grown tremendously in the past several decades. [For] social justice, I work with communities of color. [For] issues of the environment, such as water, I work with white people, and, yet, I know that people of color have a long track record of working with the environment, such as César Chávez, and white people work for social justice, too. Santuario Sisterfarm[1] ... [is] the place where I can unite these two passions—my passion for social justice but also my deep concern for the planet, the devastation of the earth, [inside] a spiritual context.

A leadership of consciousness

Spiritual and religious faith drives Berriozábal to struggle for the rights of the dispossessed and most needy. From a very early age, she understood the meaning of helping others as a way to improve her community, and to make the life of others better. The stories and experiences she shared in common with her family provided many leadership lessons. A woman who is sensitive to the pain of others, from a young age Berriozábal was quick to console children who were picked on because of the color of their skin, having learned from her own experience how it felt to be so marked because of her own complexion. Also, she stood up for those who spoke the Spanish language, aware that Mexican Americans had been prohibited from speaking the only language they knew—her own parents were not involved in her schooling because they did not speak the language. Throughout her involvement, Berriozábal gained an affinity for language rights and was there for her constituents, confident in the knowledge she had gained from her parents who lauded her for being proficient in two languages—speaking Spanish of whatever type was not an issue of shame; it was something of which to be proud. In her relationships with her community and peers, Berriozábal quickly learned to fight for the rights of others, as well as her own, creating a way to understand change in a manner that gave her non-traditional and positive notions of difference.

Traditional thinking about leadership generally describes a person endowed with qualities, by birth and class, to lead others into action. Personal charisma and influence derived from position or authority are most often associated with traditional leadership. Standards and measurements that promote a model that is authority-informed are often used to determine the leadership qualities and abilities of those who purport to engage in social change. For these leaders, relationships with people in positions of power have been foundational to their formation. Although she possesses attributes that are generally assigned to male and traditional leaders, Berriozábal did not take on leadership positions to exercise influence over a flock of followers, although those with whom she interacted relied on these strategies as a means of serving their community (Méndez-Negrete, 1995). She created and nurtured a relational leadership approach based on mutual and reciprocal links to the greater good of her community, as she incorporated feedback given by constituents in her decision-making.

Sharon Navarro illustrates this point in her biography of Van de Putte. Navarro writes that Van de Putte perceived "María Antonietta as a broker who leverages the political anointment of future political figures in San Antonio or as 'the go-to person for endorsements of other Latinas who seek elected office'" (136). Clearly, her involvement in shaping leaders was not for personal gain, but rather it was to create a leadership pipeline that would ensure the continued representation of and advocacy for those in need. The cultural and political capital Berriozábal created and gained is a credit to her family and her community for having entrusted her with the responsibility to lead. Historically, María Antonietta Berriozábal has gone on record as having begun her leadership and activist trajectory in her own family. For example, when she was barely fourteen years old, she took on responsibilities that would make the education of her younger siblings possible. Rather than pursuing a college career path for herself, after high school graduation, Berriozábal worked in the private non-profit and public service sectors, which provided her with the first-hand knowledge to pursue a political and activist path. It was through such employment that she heard first-hand the concerns of citizens who relied on the support of the agencies and organizations whom she worked for and served in the community. A relational leader who cultivated her interactions with individuals interested in creating change, in her religious, work, and civic interactions, Berriozábal laid the foundation for entering politics, although by default (Méndez-Negrete, 1994).

Her trajectory as a leader and activist has been one of "firsts." According to Sharon Navarro, "In 1981, María Antonietta Berriozábal was the first Mexican American woman ... elected to city council (a position she held for ten years).... In 1991, Berriozábal was the first Chicana to run for mayor" (2008, 64). In her position as a city councilwoman, upon seeing the disparities that existed in the status and rights of women and girls, in 1983, she founded Hispanas Unidas[2] to focus on the advancement of Hispanic women, in San Antonio, Texas. In *Notable Hispanic American Women*, Diane Telgen and Jim Kamp (1993) document that María Antonietta Berriozábal was the "first Hispana to run for mayor in 1991, after spending ten years as a representative of District 1." Also, she "credits working class parents and worldview as the foundation for her political and activist involvement" (Issue 68, 56-7). In 1994, Berriozábal represented the United States at the Organization of American States (OAS) Inter-American Commission of Women for the OAS. In 1995, she was appointed to represent the United States as an official delegate for the United Nations Fourth World Conference on Women in Beijing, China. As the global citizen that she had become, she represented her nation and the interests of Latinos in the American continent.

Spiritual woman of faith and mentor of leaders

Berriozábal's spiritual community continues to nourish her leadership and activism. Her actions merge Catholic social values and her philosophy for social justice. She has said that it was Catholic and religious women who "gave me the language and the support to integrate my faith and my spirituality into politics, which is the only way I survived" (Espinosa, Elizondo and Miranda, 2005, 98). Her beliefs and cultural values allow her to integrate the political and Catholic world to connect the passions she has for social change. Reflecting on her activism for an examination of Filipina religious life, María Antonietta Berriozábal offered:

> As a woman of color, I have spent most of my life living in a society that does not understand my reality, the essential wedding of personal and community responsibility, of faith and community. But, like many sisters of color, I have not sat by, hoping that others would effect this integration for us. Each of us has sought in her own way to act on her reality. (De Jesús 2005, 63)

In her general view of the world and in her practical daily activism, María Antonietta Berriozábal fully integrates the lives of those who immigrate as a result of economic and political violence. As I have argued elsewhere for Chicanas like Berriozábal, power relations are a constant in the negotiations of leadership. This tension exists within external forces—outside the Chicano community's sphere of influence—as well as within internal structures, as activists enact leadership relationships within power struggles for change. On the other hand, gendered misperceptions held about Chicanas in leadership by dominant groups—male or female—complicates their struggles. The so-called private realm, while not as clearly demarcated for Chicanas because they have been part of the working class, still limits and shapes how they are perceived as leaders or activists. Thus gender, race, and class emerge in Chicana leadership involvement, forcing a self-reflexive engagement that must necessarily call for them to be aware of their subject position amid myriad structures of inequality.

For Chicanas, leadership is embedded in the everyday interactions of daily life. Their actions are not to promote themselves in positions of power or to obtain credit for their efforts in the struggle. For them, as is the case for Berriozábal, leadership and activism are tools for improving the lives of those who are most in need. Chicana leadership is a relational process, regardless of position or social location, where one's own self-gain or recognition are given up for the greater good. Self-promotion and getting the credit for results, in Chicana notions of leadership, are irrelevant—getting things done and improving conditions for the group are the driving forces for action (Méndez-Negrete, 1995, 311).

Throughout her life, Berriozábal has drawn the best from all with whom she interacts. Rather than being a leader who seeks special treatment or tenders favors to continue expanding the power that comes with leadership, María Antonietta Berriozábal mentors, supports, and opens doors for those who seek to improve the community in which we live. These beliefs are grounded in cultural knowledge, historical realities, material conditions, and ideological views. Her leadership and activism display a reflexive subjective consciousness she engages in the context of mutual exchange and reciprocity to carve out a path for social justice and social change. With a conscious use of self, a reflexive analysis of the situation, and data on the issues or the problems, for María Antonietta Berriozábal, listening for empowerment is at the core of her activist and leadership interactions, thus creating a place and space for change.

In her work, she starts by examining issues or problems from the perspectives of the very people who rely on her for support, thus creating a relational approach to making change, and thereby mentoring activists and leaders who will be ready to take her place. Her legacy, embedded in the lives of those who will become future leaders of our community, allows her to engage a future expectation for change. The legacy María Antonietta Berriozábal has given to San Antonio, Texas, and to the world, is in their hands.

NOTES and REFERENCES
Reflection by Josie Méndez-Negrete

1. Founded in 2002, Santurio Sisterfarm, was a non-profit organization founded by "Latinas of the Texas-Mexico Borderlands and Dominican Sisters;" it operated for the ten years until its dissolution on June 30, 2011. The organization's focus was on bio- and cultural diversity, created with the aim of "living in right relationship with the whole Earth community." Berriozábal served as its president until the dissolution of the organization. (Retrieved June 23, 2011, http://www.sisterfarm.org/).

2. The creation of this organization was feasible because of the social and cultural capital Berriozábal had amassed, as an unopposed candidate in her first re-election campaign. Her aim with the foundation of Hispanas Unidas was to share power with women and to build a leadership cadre that would reproduce and remain active.

Castañeda, Antonia, Armitage, Susan H., Hart, Patricia, and Weathermon, Karen (2007). *Gender on the Borderlands: the Frontiers Reader,* "Una historia de una de muchas Marías," 155-167, Lincoln: NE, University of Nebraska Press.

De Jesús, Melinda L. (2005). (Ed.) *Pinay Power: Peminist Critical Theory: Theorizing the Filipina/American Experience.* New York and London: Routledge Press.

Espinosa, Gastón, Elizondo, Virgilio, Miranda, Jesse. "María Antonietta Berriozábal, Latino religions and civic activism in the United States" (2005, 98, New York: Oxford University Press.

Gutiérrez, José Angel, Meléndez, Michelle, and Noyola, Sonia Adriana (2007). *Chicanas in charge: Texas women in the public arena.* Lanham, MD: AltaMira Press.

Méndez-Negrete, Josephine (1999). "Awareness, Consciousness, and Resistance: Raced, Classed, and Gendered Leadership Interactions in Milagro County, California." *Frontiers: A Journal of Women Studies,* Vol. 20, No. 1, Latina/Chicana Leadership, 25-44.

_____. (1995). "*¡No es lo que haces!*": A Sociohistorical analysis of relational leadership in a Chicana/Latino community. Dissertation for PhD in sociology. University of California, Santa Cruz.

_____. (1994). "We remember César Chávez: A catalyst for change." *San José Journal Studies*, 20(2), 71-83.

Navarro, Sharron Ann. (2008). *Latina legislators: Leticia Van de Putte and the road to leadership.* College Station: Texas A&M University Press.

REFLECTION

Speaking Truth to Power: María Antonietta Berriozábal's *María, Daughter of Immigrants*

Antonia I. Castañeda, Ph.D.

When María Antonietta (María) called to tell me the title of her book, *María: Daughter of Immigrants,* I demurred, commenting, "María, your family migrated to a historically Tejano landscape. We are migrants, not immigrants. We belong here. We are of this land María, claim historical presence."

"Yes Antonia, I know what you are saying," she replied, then continued. "Certainly our family's history does not begin when my grandparents crossed the U.S. Mexico border in the early 1900s. We hold ancient threads of memory that go back centuries on this continent. Indeed, we are among the founders of communities in the Americas—and we are creating communities still. But my family's story in the United States, my story in San Antonio, does begin with that epic crossing from one country to another, and the lives they made here. There is no better way to thank and to honor my immigrant parents and grandparents for their love and sacrifice than to write them into the history of the country to which they gave so much, for it is a history from which we are still absent! And in the present, viciously anti-immigrant political climate in the U.S., especially against Mexican immigrants, this is precisely the time to tell it."

Beginning at the beginning, with her paternal and maternal grandparents' immigration from Mexico to the Lockhart area of Texas in 1910, *María, Daughter of Immigrants* traces the arc of Maria Antonietta Berriozábal's life, from her birth on the eve of the U.S. entry into World War II to the end of the first decade of the 21st century. In this beautifully detailed narrative, Maria Antonietta recounts not only her own and her family's story, but also the story of working class Mexican/Mexican American life and culture in San Antonio---the people, relationships, institutions, and values that shaped her life, and framed her course in public service and social justice activism. Woven throughout are the gendered, racial and class-based relationships of power in the city named after the patron saint of lost belongings, including histories lost or silenced in the narrative of the City's official story. Thus, this is a story of re-membering San Antonio's history, of placing gender as a category of historical, political, social and cultural analysis at the center of the story; and of its telling in the inimitable voice of María Antonietta Berrozábal, a pivotal historical and political figure of the latter 20th century.

Experience and history authorize María Antonietta, the first Mexican American woman elected to the City Council in San Antonio's then 136 year history as a U.S. city, to render a finely-honed analysis and critique of politics, of the architects and architecture of power in the "Alamo" city. Her struggle against the politics of inequality and injustice, the warp and woof of Texas and San Antonio's political, economic, educational, social, cultural, and institutional fabric, as well as the resistance to those forces among the communities with whom she worked, are here powerfully rendered.

Just as her parents' sacrifices and struggles sowed the ground for their children and grandchildren, their retoños, to grow and thrive; so María Antonietta and her spouse, Manuel Berriozábal, who stood firm against assaults and attacks that would have undone most of us, and were vindicated in their resistance, have seeded a more just political and educational landscape for generations of San Antonians.

Centered in the ethos of María Antonietta's working class family and community, *María, Daughter of Immigrants* unfolds an uncommon life as well as the extraordinary dimensions of the work and struggle of common, everyday people. In its composition and narrative, this remarkable book crosses and blurs multiple genres: memoir, autobiography, and *testimonio*.

In the vein of a traditional memoir, which has historically dealt with public matters, María Antonietta relates her history-making, unprecedented campaigns for public office: City Council, Mayor, and Congress. She recounts her decade-long tenure in City Council, and the pivotal debates and decisions related to the economic development policies that expanded San Antonio ever farther Northward and that define city politics to this day. Central to her narrative are her principled, prophetic, and consistent "no" votes opposing the business elite's direction of the economy and politics of the city which were not in the best interests of the people of San Antonio, and particularly of her own council district: energy; water; and sports. To describe, analyze, and interpret public matters, María draws on numerous sources: her lived experience as an elected official and the extensive, meticulous primary research she conducts in the documentary record—minutes of City Council meetings, video recordings of the meetings, print and other media coverage, the documents of various organizations—and in her own archives.

If memoir's focus is on the public arena, autobiography generally addresses the personal and encompasses the writer's entire life span. In eight of thirteen chapters, *María, Daughter of Immigrants* narrates María Antonietta's familial and personal history, from birth to age seventy, and inscribes her values, ethics, culture, political and social philosophy in every remembrance, story, observation, and comment. Her compass always, for her private and public life, is her father's admonition to judge herself in terms of where she started: ". . .de donde empezamos. . .y empezamos de abajo." She identified with the underdog, with those persons who are characterized in Spanish as 'los de abajo.," her family and her community. Her core values center on faith, family, hard work, community, love of the natural world, laughter, and play. As she confronts, grapples with, and surpasses untold public and private trials, María's emotional, psychological and spiritual life is sustained and transformed by these values.

Across a lifetime of employment, public office, and social justice activism that took her from el Kress in downtown San Antonio to Beijing, China, as a U.S. representative to the UN Fourth World Conference on Women—where she joined the women of the world in writing the conference's Platform for Action and where the word went out that women's rights are human rights—María Antonietta has unwaveringly held to the values of "los de abajo." Her hard work as she moved up the employment ranks, her education, as well as marriage to a university professor changed her economic and social status. She has crossed multiple borders, boundaries, and demarcation lines, including those posting "no trespassing" signs—both figurative and literal—but her being and actions in the world remain rooted in the class and community to which she was born, in which she was raised, and which continues to sustain her. This is the community who elected her, whom she helped empower to speak for themselves in their own voices about the issues that concerned them: employment, housing, public services, energy, water, education, police brutality, discrimination.

María, Daughter of Immigrants is a *testimonio*, a narrative of bearing witness to a lifetime of trespassing boundaries, whether explicit or implicit, which women, in particular women of color, immigrants, workers, and poor people were not to cross. As a narrative of bearing witness, *testimonio* attests to what the author has experienced in society; it exposes and interprets historical, political, and social injustices, as well as ethical issues the official apparatus of Church, State, Military, and the Press ignore, erase, or cover up. *Testimonio* contests and belies the official story. What testimonio reveals may be considered, in Martin Buber's words when referring to the Holocaust, "this wound in the order of being;" what Gloria Anzaldúa calls, in reference to the grating of the U.S. and Mexico against the barbed wire now electrified digital fence the United States erected on its border with Mexico, "the wound that does not heal."[1]

Within the U.S. context, Chicana *testimonio* is rooted in oppositional consciousness and resistance to racial, gender, sexual, and other forms of institutionalized violence that permeate the fabric of life in the United States.[2] Critic Norma Klahn, who maps the "literary production of Chicanos/Mexicanos in the U.S., and particularly the self-writing practices by Chicanas" argues that Chicana autobiography/*testimonios* "mark both a commitment to and continuity of the decolonizing practices emerging with the civil rights movements and a rupture and discontinuity that insists on the inscription of gender and sexuality as the missing elements of the initial male nationalist propositions." Thus, continues Klahn, "Chicanas not only exert rights within the struggle for democracy and social justice," they "also have the added burden of necessarily engaging the discourses of a racist Anglo society and the patriarchal structures in both Anglo and Chicano cultures. . .to voice their experiences 'outside the laws of the fathers'."[3] Even still, within the frame of Euro American women's feminism, the working class realities of Chicanas, their struggles for democracy and social justice which centered on the intersecting issues of race and class as well as gender and sexuality, often put them in conflict with the middle class women's liberation movement, generally referred to as second wave feminism.

Chicanas, in whose communities women had been subject to coercive sterilization and who were acutely aware of the racial politics of reproduction, the issue of reproductive rights in U.S. society had meaning different than it did for middle class white feminists. Chicanas not only draw on multiple traditions of feminism but also, from lived experience, define their own; what historian Deena González and others call "Living Chicana Theory."[4]

In their Introduction to the anthology *Telling to Live: Latina Feminist Testimonios*, the authors, a collective of Latina feminists, avow, "We arrived at the importance of testimonio as a crucial means of bearing witness and inscribing into history those lived realities that would otherwise succumb to the alchemy of erasure."[5]

María Antonietta refuses to succumb. Quite the contrary; she writes an incomparable work of memoir, autobiography and *testimonio*, a critically important manuscript, the first single authored book by a publically elected Chicana official.[6] As historic as her election to the San Antonio City Council, *María, Daughter of Immigrants* is also an historic document, a primary source that historians, political scientists, literary and other scholars will mine, as well as a book the general public will avidly read.

When elected in 1980, María Antonietta was one of two Mexican American women to run for, and win, City Council seats in Texas. Anita Martínez of Dallas (Republican, West Dallas) served two terms, 1969-1973.[7] While the number of Mexican American women who have run and won election to City, County, and State government as well as to the Texas judiciary has increased, their numbers are still very small. The few who published *testiminios* that exist of their experience are in important anthologies and collections of interviews and oral histories.[8] María Antonietta's is included in these and other collections. Among the latter is theologians Ada María Isasi-Díaz and Yolanda Tarrango's *Hispanic Women, Prophetic Voice in the Church: Toward a Hispanic Women's Liberation Theology*, to which we will subsequently return.[9] Among past and present políticas in Texas, *María, Daughter of Immigrants* stands alone as the only single authored volume to date. In California, Linda and Loretta Sánchez, the sisters who are Congresswomen, co-authored their memoir, *Dream in Color: How the Sánchez Sisters Are Making History in Congress*, with Richard Buskin.[10]

Turning to briefly examine various issues Maria raises, and those that Chicana/o political scientists identified in their interviews with a wide range of Latina elected officials, who in Texas were almost exclusively Mexican American, one is struck by a host of patterns and trends that cut across time, space, geography and public office. Interestingly, the three major studies of Latinas, gender, and politics in Texas, and published in the first decade of the 21st century, and that contextualize the historical and political terrain within which Latinas were elected to public office from the 1970s -1990s, arrive at fundamentally the same conclusions.[11]

Focusing their study on the topic of political leadership, and on Latina's development and deployment of this political art, the authors of *Políticas* argue that precisely because Latinas are underrepresented, the first Latinas in public office, "already paid a price on crossing the barriers to their entry into politics; pressure is increased when she is the first one, or the only one, because of society's tendency to stereotype her...."[12] Accordingly, society stereotypes Latinas, and all women more generally, along the intersecting axis of gender, race, class, and sexuality. In Texas, a Jim Crow state with a history of tripartite apartheid whose legacy we still live, Mexican American women seeking public office confronted not only barriers of gender inequality, but also of racial, class and sexual inequality, and the corollary stereotypes that sustained systemic inequality throughout the state, including San Antonio.

Breaking through visible and invisible barriers alike, María Antonietta and her "firsts and onlys" colleagues created themselves as historical and political subjects. They did the unthinkable, and what many thought the undoable for Mexican American women at the time, they occupied elected public office and public space. They broke hard pack ground; upset and challenged the political status quo; became the role models for others when they had none in the public sphere, spoke the unspoken and the unspeakable in public forums, and created public space for others, including "los de abajo," to occupy. Addressing the political significance of María Antonietta's generation of Mexican American/Chicana elected officials, political scientist Rodolfo Rosales states "... they brought an agenda that, at its core, is radically opposed to how politics is played out. . .they were able and willing to provide a different paradigm."[13] Accordingly, the new paradigm is rooted in a particular point of departure, or standpoint: a personal and collective history and experience arising out of political reality of exclusion and injustice, which they sought to redress.[14] While certainly differences exist within this first generation of Mexican American women public officials, scholars point to similar core elements, experiences, frameworks, and approaches, all of which María Antonietta fully manifests and details in her book. I draw on the studies of political scientists Sonia García, Valerie Martínez-Ebers, Irasema Coronado, and Sharon Navarro to cite, due to limited space, only the most salient examples:[15]

> **Historical grounding:** Their experience challenges the notion that Latinas in Texas are political novices. While Latinas may not have been elected to public office until the latter third of the 20th century, they drew upon a long history of Latina political actors and agency within and without their communities as leaders of organizations that included, among others, mutualista/mutual aid societies; church organizations and sodalities; and labor unions. In some cases, Latinas who ran for office had founded and led organizations comprised of professional and/or businesswomen. Moreover, the experience of historical disenfranchisement of Mexican Americans from the political process was itself a searing political education for generations of Americans of Mexican descent.

> **Political socialization:** Political socialization varied, but as women of color, all were exposed to the discriminatory and unequal politics

of gender, race, class and sexuality, writ large and small, in daily life in American society and politics.

Decision making process to run for public office: Latinas were not socialized to consider running for public office, and the traditional recruiting institutions, meaning political parties, were largely absent. Like María, Latinas were asked by their community, including colleagues, friends, and supporters to consider running for office. On the contrary, in many cases, they ran against the person anointed by the party, with few exceptions, the opponents were male and sometimes were also Mexican American. Also like María, most of the support upon which the women drew, was the grass root support centered in community relationships and connections, especially with women. With few exceptions, they all ran grass roots campaigns.

Leadership and gender differences: Of critical import, studies conclude, are the gender differences in Latina leadership/leadership styles from those of men, irrespective of the latter's racial-ethnic background. Accordingly, Latinas have a propensity for building consensus, inviting participation, and empowering others; for collectivism, interdependence, and no emphasis on hierarchy. In particular, most were committed to the notion of bringing new people and communities into political engagement and processes. Culture, particularly manifested by a strong connection to family and community, was central to leadership style and was also reflected in terms of personal values. That is, a strong cultural identity, especially the importance of language, of religion, and of having faith was consistently present. These interconnected traits shaped the attitudes and perspectives that Latina elected officials brought to bear in their political life.

Genealogies of power: Women of action, whether mothers, grandmothers, or other women in the community in myriad leadership roles and whether visible beyond the immediate community or not, were pivotal sources of authority for Latinas who ultimately ran for public office. They, and the community who implored the woman to run for office and who supported her, were the power base to whom the candidate/public official was accountable.

It is this larger frame that takes history, gender, race, class, sexuality, and culture into account when relating her experience in public office, that María Antonietta makes a singularly important contribution to our understanding of American politics in general, and San Antonio politics in particular. Working from the historical, political, and related experience discussed above with respect to Latina public officials, María changed the course of San Antonio's political history. The hallmark of

María's political history is that she was not beholden to the business interests that dominated the economic and political life of San Antonio. Moreover, while the majority of publicly elected officials were invested in the existing structures of political power, based as they were on the historical exclusion of women, people of color and working class persons, María was not. Thus, her approach to most issues, whether economic, political, social, cultural, etc., differed from what was generally considered the norm. The "norm" in San Antonio with respect to electoral politics and occupation of public space was: gendered male; racially white, meaning Euro American; middle class in socio-economic status; and heterosexual. María Antonietta, whose very body and presence represented the diametric opposite in all but one aspect, greatly disrupted that norm.

Moreover, precisely because she consistently challenged the ideological norm, political pundits, including university professors and some male politicians, cast her in disparaging terms, characterized her as anti-business and anti-economic development, as focused on the "soft issues", as if the economy, energy, and water were not women's issues. At the core was María Antonietta's vision of economic development, which focused on investment in human capital, especially education, and thus markedly differed from that of the profit motive and expansionist policies of the ruling business elite. In all the major issues, energy, water, and sports, María was ultimately proven right.

In the political realm, María represented what particular groups of Catholic and other women religious did in the institutional Christian church. They placed gender and women at the center of their inquiry of the theological underpinnings of the Church, and challenged fundamental concepts and precepts of a theology from which women and women's religious understanding and practices are excluded; from which women, specifically Latinas, as a source of theology are also excluded.[16] Similarly, Women's Studies and most specifically feminist studies as well as gay and lesbian studies, posed major challenges not only for academia in general, but also for the newer interdisciplinary fields of ethnic studies which Norma Klan describes as being centered in "male nationalist propositions."[17] In these cases too, the work to place gender and women as well as sexuality at the center of historical, religious, political, social and cultural development of American society, at the center of research, publishing and teaching, were met with derision and ridicule, with efforts to silence, to delegitimize, to ban from the academy. Here too, struggles to change reigning paradigms and to challenge patriarchal, gender, racial, class and heterosexual norms, not unlike those María Antonietta experienced were also fiercely waged.

The struggle María Antonietta and women of all racial ethnic backgrounds of her generation engaged in every field and institution, changed American society. Beginning with her election/s and physical occupation of public space; to her intellect—the world of the mind and ideas; to the issues she raised; the issues in which she was sometimes the lone dissenting voice; to those she championed, Maria Antonietta expanded the idea, concept and practice of democracy. She put theory into practice, created space, opened doors, and brought new constituencies into civic life and the democratic process. She did it standing on the ground her immigrant grandparents and parents earned for her with their labor, and which their faith in themselves, their God, and this country, made flourish. We, San Antonio, owe much to María Antonietta Berriozábal; she has left us a great legacy upon which to stand, grow, and thrive as a city and a people.

At this juncture of María Antonietta's life, and in that of the United States, the issue of Mexican immigration looms large still again. Always centered in her family's history of immigration to the United State, with all the pain and triumphs in that story María, who has consistently served immigrant communities, has further intensified her advocacy for social justice and immigrant rights. Most recently, she has been engaged in working for passage of the DREAM Act with immigrant youth, specifically with the college and university "Dreamers," whose parents brought them to the U.S. without documentation while very young. Fearlessly advocating for an issue that is right and just, María Antonietta put her body on the line. In November of 2010, while the Dream Act was about to be voted on in Congress, she engaged in an act of civil disobedience with the Dreamers; was arrested with them; and spent the night in the city jail.

Observing María Antonietta in her unwavering, immensely courageous advocacy for immigrant youth, it was clear that she knew and understood the Dreamers' reality at a fundamental level, and that she identified with them. In each of the Dreamers, especially the young women, Mariá sees herself, her siblings, and her immigrant family's struggle. Like her, they are from working class immigrant families who work for their daily bread, in many cases at two and three jobs. I thought of the little girl, growing up on Picoso and Martin streets in the highly segregated city of San Antonio in the 1940s and 1950s and remembered that her family had been in Texas, in Lockhart since 1910. I wondered if her relatives were among Lockhart residents celebrating the nation's independence on July 4, 1941, in the section of the street blocked off for the public celebration when, in the middle of the activities, Anglo authorities announced from the bandstand that all "Spanish people" had to leave immediately because "Since this is an American celebration, it is for white people only." The crowd again broke out in cheers."[18] The "Spanish people" were Tejanos, Mexican Americans and Mexican immigrants who, like María Antonietta's maternal and paternal families, worked the land as tenant farmers, sharecropper and farm laborers in Lockhart and its environs.

A precocious child of myriad sensibilities, María understood early, as children do, the relations of power that defined her family's life as Mexican immigrant workers in San Antonio. Even as she delighted in the love, care, and tending her parents provided, she witnessed, understood, and internalized the arduousness of their lives, the physical, psychic and emotional stresses of poverty, of institutionalized racism, and discrimination, and was acutely aware of the toll they took on the body, heart, mind, and soul of her parents; her father suffered a serious injury at his workplace and did not receive the insurance coverage to which he should have been entitled; her mother, who had no respite, ironing, cooking and cleaning, making ends meet and making a home in the unremitting blistering South Texas heat. Neither poverty nor other socio-economic difficulties diminished her parents' love of nature, of beauty, of music, which they created, and taught their daughter, to see and appreciate beauty.

Translating for her mother and other people in the community, she quickly comprehended the disdain, disrespect, and dismissal to which poor, working class immigrants are subject to whether in the educational, political, commercial, government or other institutions of the society. The relations of power were ever clear.

As a child translator, she learned and took on the weight of adult issues she was asked to translate: someone's serious illness; educational issues; family business dealings with the city or utilities; handling important papers and addressing other necessities. Studies reveal that working class children all too often must take on the burden of adult responsibilities and in general, do not have a childhood. Maria, who took on those responsibilities as a very young child, vowed to change her family's economic situation. And so she did.

The education her parents struggled mightily to provide served her well in the business world, and she worked steadily to provide for her family, and to ensure her siblings graduated from high school and could pursue post-secondary education. And so they did. Once they all graduated with a university education, María Antonietta, now married to Manuel Berriozábal, continued her own post-secondary education, and graduated with a BA in Political Science.

It is the trajectory of her own life, the struggles of her grandparents and parents, the striving for education, and the contributions she, Manny, and all of the people who struggled for educational equity have made to our society that María sees when she looks at the Dreamers. She sees the first generation Mexican American child that she was, with the dreams and promise that she held and accomplished. She struggles with and for them, that they may thrive, grow, and contribute their knowledge, skills, talents, and advocacy of social justice to their communities and to this country. As a student at UTSA, María Antonietta Berriozábal "fell in love with Democracy" and since then, has put theory into practice in her ongoing struggle for the rights, privileges, and responsibilities of a Democracy that lives up to its ideals and principles. *María, Daughter of Immigrants* powerfully documents her story of that struggle.

NOTES and REFERENCES
Reflection by Antonia I. Castañeda

1. Alan L. Berger, "Bearing Witness: Second Generation Literature of the Shoah." *Modern Judaism* (Oxford and New York: Oxford University Press, 1990): 43.

Gloria Anzaldúa, *Borderlands/La Frontera: The New Mestiza* (San Francisco: Aunt Lute Press, 1987).

2. Chela Sandoval, *Methodology of the Oppressed* (Minneapolis and London: Minnesota University Press, 2000).

3. Norma Klan, "Literary [Re]Mappings: Autobiographical [Dis]Placements by Chicana Writers," in Gabriela Arredondo, Aida Hurtado, Norma Klan, Olga Nájera Ramírez, and Patricia Zavella, Eds., *Chicana Feminisms: A Critical Reader* (Durham and London: Duke University Press, 2003): 115; 117-118.

4. Elena R. Gutiérrez, *Fertile Matters: The Politics of Mexican-Origin Women's Reproduction* (Austin: University of Texas Press, Chicana Matters Series, 2008).

Deena J. González, *Speaking Secrets: Living Chicana Theory, in Carla Trujillo, Ed., Living Chicana Theory* (Berkeley: Third Woman Press, 1997).

5. Latina Feminist Group, "Introduction, " in *Latina Feminist Group, Telling to Live: Latina Feminist Testimonios* (Durham and London: Duke University Press, 2001): 17.

6. Linda and Loretta Sánchez have co-authored an autobiography with Richard Buskin. See Linda Sánchez and Loretta Sánchez, and Richard Buskin, *Dream in Color: How the Sánchez Sisters are Making History in Congress* (Grand Central Publishing, 2002).

7. Sonia García, Valerie Martínez-Ebers, Irasema Coronado, and Sharon Navarro, Eds., *Políticas: Latina Public Officials in Texas* (Austin: University of Texas Press, 2008): 123.

8. Sonia García, et. al., Políticas: Latina Public Officials in Texas (Austin: University of Texas Press, 2008).

Sharon Navarro, *Latina Legislator: Leticia Van de Putte and the Road to Leadership* (College Station: Texas A&M University Press, 2008).

José Angel Gutiérrez, Michelle Meléndez, and Sonia Adriana Noyola, *Chicanas in Charge: Texas Women in the Public Arena* (Lanham, New York, Toronto, Plymouth, UK: Altamira Press, 2007).

See also a political science study that is not based solely on interviews, but María Antonietta is interviewed for this study. Rodolfo Rosales, *The Illusion of Inclusion: The Political Story of San Antonio, Texas* (Austin: University of Texas Press, Center for Mexican American Studies, 2000).

9. Ada María Isasi-Díaz and Yolanda Tarrango, Eds., *Hispanic Women, Prophetic Voice in the Church: Toward a Hispanic Women's Liberation Theology* (New York: Harper Collins, 1988).
Ada María Isdasi-Díaz, *Mujerista Theology: A Theology for the Twenty-First Century* (New York: Orbis Books, 1996).

10. Sánchez, Sánchez, and Ruskin, *Dream in Color: How the Sánchez Sisters are Making History in Congress* (2002).

11. Luis Ricardo Fraga, Valerie Martínez-Ebers, Linda López, and Ricardo Ramírez, "Representing Gender and Ethnicity: Strategic Intersectionality," in Beth Reingold, Ed., *Legislative Women Getting Elected, Getting Ahead* (Boulder, Colorado: Lynne Reiner Publishers, 2008): 157-174.
García, Martínez-Ebers, Coronado, and Navarro, Eds., *Políticas: Latina Public Officials in Texas* (2008).
Navarro, *Latina Legislator: Leticia Van de Putte and the Road to Leadership* (2008).
Gutiérrez, Meléndez, and Noyola, *Chicanas in Charge: Texas Women in the Public Arena* (2007).

12. García, Martínez-Ebers, Coronado, and Navarro, Eds., *Políticas: Latina Public Officials in Texas* (2008): 3.

13. Rosales, *The Illusion of Inclusion* (2000): 159-160.

14. *Ibid.*, 160

15. García, Martínez-Ebers, Coronado, and Navarro, Eds., Políticas: Latina Public Officials in Texas (2008).

16. Isasi-Díaz and Tarrango, Eds., *Hispanic Women, Prophetic Voice in the Church: Toward a Hispanic Women's Lilberation Theology* (2000): 1.

17. Klan, "Literary [Re]Mappings: Autobiographical [Dis]Placements by Chicana Writers," in Arredondo, Hurtado, Klan, Nájera Ramírez, and Zavella, Eds., *Chicana Feminisms: A Critical Reader* (2003): 115.

18. As quoted in Lorena Orozpeza, Raza *Si! Guerra No!: Chicano Protest and Patriotism During the Vietnam War Era* (Berkeley: University of California Press, 2005):13-14.

Contributor Notes

Antonia I. Castañeda was born in Texas and grew up in Washington. She received her BA from Western Washington State College, MA from the University of Washington, and Ph.D. from Stanford University, where she studied the "gendering of colonization in early California via the bodies of indigenous women." She was one of the very first Chicana Ph.D.s in the United States. Castañeda has held teaching appointments at the University of California, Santa Barbara, the University of Texas at Austin, and at St. Mary's University. Castaneda is co-editor of the Chicana Matters Series (University of Texas Press) and is on the board of the Recovering the U.S. Hispanic Literary Heritage Project (Arte Público Press). Dr. Castañeda is currently an independent scholar.

She is the author of numerous articles, including the prizing winning "Women of Color and the Re-Writing of Western History." Her most recent work is the co-edited anthology, *Gender on the Borderlands: The Frontiers Reader* (University of Nebraska Press, 2007).

A founding member of Mujeres Activas en Letras y Cambio Social (MALCS), Dr. Castañeda received the NACCS Scholar of the Year award in 2007. NACCS offers an annual award named after Dr. Castañeda in recognition of scholarly work on "the intersection of class, race, gender, and sexuality as related to Chicana/Latina and/ Native/ Indigenous women."

Josie Méndez-Negrete was born in Zacatecas, Mexico. When she was eleven, the family moved *al norte* and settled in the Santa Clara Valley in California. She received her Ph.D. from the University of California at Santa Cruz. In 1988, she began writing what would become *Las hijas de Juan: Daughters Betrayed* (Duke University Press, 2006), a powerful memoir of childhood sexual abuse, called by Norma L. Cardenas "story of courage and resistance to patriarchy too frightening to be imagined and too hurtful to be forgotten." Dr. Méndez-Negrete is a lead editor for the MALCS journal, *Chicana/Latina Studies*. Dr. Méndez-Negrete is an associate professor in Mexican American studies at the University of Texas at San Antonio.

Acknowledgments

Many people helped to make this book a reality. I want to honor and thank all the people whose stories I have shared. My gratitude goes to my great grandmother, María Cervantes Rodríguez, my grandparents, all my Arredondo and Rodríguez aunts, uncles, and cousins from several generations for your lives to share. Thank you to my amigas, friends, fellow workers, and community companions for your inspiration.

To my students at the Institute of Politics at Harvard University: thank you for planting the seed of this book in my heart with your listening, prodding, and encouragement.

To my friends, Antonia Castañeda and Josephine Méndez-Negrete, thank you for your insistence over many years that I write this story. Thank you for sharing your reflections, which appear in this book, and for your assistance during my writing journey.

Thank you to Marisol Cortez, Claudia Guerra, Amy Kastely and Theresa Torres for being excellent sounding boards on particular issues. To Kamala Platt deep gratitude for the tedious work of indexing so much information! To Allen Buck and Eduardo Dueñez for your help with Macaria, my computer! To Donna Guerra for helping me master the City of San Antonio's online archives.

My deepest appreciation to gifted artist and friend Enedina Cásarez-Vásquez for your gift of the cover art for the book and to photographer, Cynthia Edwards, for photographing it. Thank you to Roberta Barnes for my most up-to-date photograph and to Santuario Sisterfarm Board Members Janie Barrera, Sisters Carol Coston, OP and Pat Sieman, OP, Olga Garza Kauffman, and Beth Blissman for helping to birth the book through Sor Juana Press.

To Elise D. García, OP for being my book's midwife and my listening ear. This book would not have been written had it not been for your insistence that I write it because you would edit it and Sor Juana Press would publish it. Even after our decision to close the press, you continued to assist me with your incredible editing. Thank you!

Muchas gracias to Bryce Milligan of Wings Press for your trust and for making it possible for this story to be told.

I thank my siblings Felix, Louis, Theresa, Miguel and Rosie for journeying with me and helping me to remember and refine the memories of our lives together. I appreciate more than you know your encouragement, support, and love during my writing of this book. I am profoundly grateful that you cheered me on as I wrote your story, too. To Dolores, Leonor, Veronica, and John—you are a special part of our story.

Thank you to Mamá y Papá for teaching me the value of storytelling by sharing your lives in story.

Most of all, my love and deepest gratitude goes to my beloved Manny for your support, patience, reassurance, and love. This was our journey.

¡Gracias a Dios!

María Antonietta Berriozábal
San Antonio, Texas
2012

Index

Note: Persons and topics included in photographs are cited by the number of the photograph (not the page number) in **bold** type.

Colophon

This first edition of *María: Daughter of Immigrants*, by María Antonietta Berriozábal, has been printed on 55 pound "natural" EB paper containing a percentage of recycled fiber. Titles have been set in Papyrus type, the text in Adobe Caslon type. All Wings Press books are designed and produced by Bryce Milligan.

On-line catalogue and ordering available at
www.wingspress.com

Wings Press titles are distributed
to the trade by the
Independent Publishers Group
www.ipgbook.com
and in Europe by
www.gazellebookservices.co.uk

Also available as an ebook.

Notes

Notes

Notes

Notes